Illustrator 9
f/x & Design

Sherry London

President, CEO
Keith Weiskamp

Publisher
Steve Sayre

Acquisitions Editor
Beth Kohler

Marketing Specialist
Patti Davenport

Project Editor
Don Eamon

Technical Reviewer
David Xenakis

Production Coordinator
Meg E. Turecek

Cover Designer
Jody Winkler

Layout Designer
April Nielsen

CD-ROM Developer
Michelle McConnell

The Coriolis Group, LLC
14455 N. Hayden Road
Suite 220
Scottsdale, Arizona 85260

(480)483-0192
FAX (480)483-0193
www.coriolis.com

Library of Congress Cataloging-In-Publication Data
London, Sherry
     Illustrator 9 f/x and design / by Sherry London.
          p. cm
     ISBN 1-57610-750-7
     1. Computer graphics. 2. Adobe Illustrator (Computer file) I. Title.
T385.L6482   2000
006.6'869--DC21
                                                                                                00-060219
                                                                                                CIP

Printed in the United States of America
10 9 8 7 6 5 4 3 2 1

Other Titles for the Creative Professional

Paint Shop Pro™ 6 Visual Insight
By Ramona Pruitt and Joshua Pruitt

QuarkXpress™ 4 In Depth
By William Harrel and Elaine Betts

Adobe PageMill® 3 f/x and Design
By Daniel Gray

Painter® 6 f/x and Design
By Sherry London and Rhoda Grossman

Photoshop® 5 In Depth
By David Xenakis and Sherry London

Adobe InDesign™ f/x and Design
By Elaine Betts

Looking Good In Print, 4E
By Roger Parker

Adobe® LiveMotion™ f/x and Design
By Dan Gray

To Friendship:
I want to dedicate this book to Don Eamon, my tireless Project Editor,
and David Xenakis, tech editor and all-round graphics guru.
—Sherry

≈

About the Author

Sherry London is a principal of London Computing, a full-service graphics and design studio. She is author of numerous books on Photoshop and other graphics and Web programs. Sherry is also a fiber artist whose work has been displayed in many group shows. She has taught Photoshop, pre-press, and QuarkXPress at a number of local colleges and has spoken at industry shows, such as the Thunder Lizard conference and the Professional Photographers of America. Sherry offers Photoshop courses online through **www.ed2go.com**.

Acknowledgments

I would like to thank the vendors who have contributed to this project:

- Direct Imagination

- Ultimate Symbol

- Virtual Mirror

- Adobe

I also want to thank the staff at Coriolis. Beth Kohler acquired this book. I cannot possibly do an adequate enough job of thanking my project editor, Don Eamon, for his work on this book. He has been infinitely patient and always accessible and his caring attitude is intensely appreciated. Melissa Olson, who stepped in when things got really hectic, was a huge help to all of us. Thanks also to the following Coriolis crew: Meg Turecek, our Production Coordinator; April Nielsen, Designer; Patti Davenport, Marketing Specialist; and Chuck Hutchinson, who copyedited the book.

David Xenakis, the technical editor, has also done work "above and beyond…" David, your encouragement and your perfectionism have been valued beyond anything that I can possibly say. I also need to thank David for both the Trapping Appendix and for writing Chapter 9, the Text effects chapter. It's awesome!

I want to thank Michael Perani, of Virtual Mirror, for writing the tutorials on Vector Studio for Chapter 3. I also want to thank Eric Floch, Brenda Sutherland, and Karen Tanner at Adobe for writing assistance and for explaining some of the new features.

I need to thank the entire Adobe Illustrator team for creating this powerful upgrade. I cannot recall being this entranced with an upgrade since Adobe first added layers to Photoshop. Ted Alspach and the other Adobe project managers did a superb job of shepherding this program to market.

My husband, Norm, as always, has borne the brunt of my long hours, frequent temper tirades, and total lack of cooking without complaint.

Contents at a Glance

Table of Contents

Foreword

Sometime in 1995, in the process of purchasing every third-party book on Photoshop I could find, I acquired a treasure titled *Photoshop 3.0 Special Effects How-To* (Waite Group Press) by Sherry London, an author whom I hadn't previously encountered. For several weeks, I read through this book as if it were a novel, learning so much that I had not suspected that Photoshop could do. In those days—when Layers and Blend modes were still new—special effects in Photoshop were usually manual activities. They required a significant amount of planning and an extraordinary knowledge of the deepest workings of the program. I was aware of some of those workings, but I was bowled over by how many things I realized I had missed. I learned so much! *Photoshop 3 Special Effects* became my favorite Photoshop book and, to this day, it remains one of my favorites.

Later that same year, I attended an annual trade show in North Philadelphia that my company organizes and presents. One of the vendors at the show, knowing my interest in Photoshop, informed me that she had a friend who had recently written a Photoshop book. Her friend, she said, intended to come to the show and she promised to introduce us. During the confusion of one very busy day, a tiny woman introduced herself as the Photoshop author mentioned by my friend. We chatted for a few minutes before I had the sense to ask the name of her book. To this day, I have never dared to ask Sherry if I looked as much a moron as I felt when I discovered that I was speaking to the author of that incredible *Special Effects* book. Certainly, a woman of Sherry's gracious charm would never suspect that the man before her had become suddenly clumsy and as shy as if conversing with a rock star. (Even geeks have heroes, you know!)

Fortunately, Sherry is one of those people with extraordinary abilities and with virtually no ego. She simply does what she does, enjoying it all the while, and never suspecting that what she can do is far from ordinary. I finally relaxed, we became friends, and as time passes, I have come to admire her as much as a person as a writer—and my admiration for her as a writer is boundless.

To Sherry, I owe my own introduction into the world of computer graphics books. Shortly after the release of Photoshop 4, Sherry called me, asking if I would consider co-authoring, with her, a large-scale Photoshop book aimed at Intermediate and Advanced users. Would I *consider* it? Walking barefooted through fire and broken glass couldn't have stopped me! Not only did I have the opportunity of writing in my own area of specialty, but I also had the opportunity of collaborating with one of my favorite people. To say that the experience was wonderful is an understatement. As always, whenever I have been fortunate enough to work with her or speak with her, I come away having learned so much more than I suspected there was to be learned. She is one of the most masterful teachers I have ever known. I learn from her, but more important, she sets off sparks in my mind, sparks that suggest wonderful possibilities and explorations.

I suppose that I have made Sherry seem a little academic, a little formidable; she is not. As you glance through these pages, you will see in her work a sense of exuberant fun and fancy. As you work through the projects that she has devised here to teach you some wonderful Illustrator 9 effects, you will probably discover, as I so often have, that she sets off sparks in your mind too. You will learn wonderful things, but you will also learn how an inventive—and playful—mind approaches the tasks of high-level illustration. This is the kind of book a woman such as Sherry London cannot help but write. This book has the same quality of being a treasure as that first book I discovered. After all, a book that teaches you technique has merely a price; a book that teaches you the joy of using your developing skills is beyond price.

—*David Xenakis*
September, 2000
Sioux Falls, South Dakota

Introduction

I'm so glad that you're reading this page. Whether you've just purchased this book or you're thinking about it, I want to tell you why I've written *Illustrator 9 f/x and Design* and what you can expect from it. You'll find many Illustrator books on the market, and each one does something slightly different—or does it in a different way. Almost all of these books are good; so, how do you begin to select which one or ones to buy?

Illustrator books seem to fall into several categories. There are the "manual replacements." This category of books are usually of mid-length and repeat the commands in the manual, restating them, in case you couldn't understand Adobe's directions. These books are for total beginners or for infrequent users of Illustrator who need reminders of how to perform a specific task.

Then there are exhaustive reference volumes such as Ted Alspach's *Illustrator Bible* and Deke McClelland's *Real World Illustrator*. These wonderful books belong on everyone's shelf. You can learn something new from either of these books each time you look at them. Due to the all-embracing nature of these volumes, they are not true competitors of this book.

Finally, there are books that showcase the design tricks of a variety of artists. These books are like wonderful eye candy, and just looking at them can inspire you. They are all excellent sources of creative ideas. You can learn something different from each one of them.

About This Book

So, what approach does this book take? Actually, *Illustrator 9 f/x and Design* takes a bit of every category and a lot of "none of the above." In your hands, you hold a book written by an opinionated artist (and some friends). I picked a wide (but by no means exhaustive) range of techniques, and I am giving you a tutorial to follow. Although this book is not really written for the rank beginner—I assume that you already know the basics of Illustrator—I go to extreme lengths to ensure that you can follow the instructions for the projects. Every step is clearly stated, so even if you're not an expert when you start this book, you'll be much closer to that status when you finish it. If you work your way through it at the computer (it isn't a novel—you really need a computer sitting in front of you as you read), you'll find that you learn things about Illustrator that you never knew. I tried to give you a range of start-to-finish projects that go from basic idea to completed artwork.

I've also tried hard to find a balance in the amount of work you'll need to complete each project. Sometimes, you start from a blank document; at other times, we give you the critical pieces. To make working through each chapter easier, I've included a companion CD-ROM with the book. For each project, you'll find at least two figure areas on the CD-ROM. One area contains all the images that you need to start and build the project. The other folder contains the finished projects so that you can learn by looking at the completed work and see what objects were defined and how. Illustrator is much better than Photoshop in this regard. Many things that you do in Illustrator leave "tracks" so that it's easier to reconstruct the way that the project was worked. In Illustrator, for example, if I applied a gradient to an object on this book's companion CD-ROM, you will see by clicking on the object exactly what gradient was applied (and if you like it, you can reuse it in your own images). In Photoshop, there is no reasonable way to figure out the colors in a gradient. The raster format of Photoshop simply applies and moves on.

You also get the full benefit of multiple authors in this book. Although I wrote most of the book, I did have help from David Xenakis, technical editor and Illustrator expert extraordinaire, and from Brenda Sutherland, Karen Tanner, and Eric Floch at Adobe Systems. It's always good to get multiple opinions—and in this book, you do. You can never have too many teachers.

Teacher. This is what I've been for many years, and this is what I consider myself to be as I write this book. *Teacher. Guide. Friend.* The best part of this work is seeing the "student" surpass the teacher. Many of you will—and that makes this book worth writing (for me) and worth reading (for you). Enjoy! I had a great time writing this book, and I hope that you enjoy it.

Keep in touch. My email address is **sherry_london@yahoo.com**. I have a Web site (under construction as I write this book) at **www.sherrylondon.com**.

—Sherry London
August 23, 2000

Chapter 1

What's New in Illustrator 9?

Illustrator 9 has so many new features that you might ask, "What hasn't changed?" This upgrade is comparable to the change between Photoshop 2.5 and 3, when Layers were introduced. This chapter looks at some of the many changes to Illustrator 9.

By Sherry London

Illustrator 9 brings many new changes—big changes in features and capabilities, and changes to the interface. The good news: Everything you know and love about Illustrator is still there—smooth integration between Illustrator and the rest of the family of Adobe products, a familiar, easy-to-use interface, and the same great performance across computer platforms that is gaining even more importance in today's computer graphics world.

Some very new concepts and capabilities are present in this version of Illustrator. Perhaps the biggest change is the combination of raster and vector editing that is now possible—and the newly added capability to use multiple strokes and fills on a single object. A lot of what you've seen used in raster-based image editors like Adobe Photoshop is now possible in Illustrator (and some features that you might have longed for in Photoshop are available *only* in Illustrator). You can also apply many of Photoshop's raster-based effects (filters, transparency, and layer blending modes) to Illustrator's vector-based objects and elements.

Illustrator 9's new approach to illustration blends the concepts of vector and raster objects into a more unified, more versatile, more comprehensive toolbox of solutions, offering you incredible creativity solutions and capabilities.

Workflow Changes

Will you notice the changes right away? Yes—as soon as you start to work with a new image, you'll realize that Adobe has made significant changes. In the past, you could mix RGB and CMYK objects in a single image. That capability is gone (and will not be missed by service bureaus throughout the world). Now, you need to decide whether to work in RGB until you need to convert to CMYK for printing, use a completely CMYK workflow, or work from start to finish in RGB. Every new document created must have a color mode assigned.

Your decisions aren't final. You can convert between CMYK and RGB as often as you want (though I would advise doing it as little as possible). Illustrator now offers the same color management capabilities as Photoshop, and you can embed International Color Consortium (ICC) profiles or simply use an ICC profile as your working space. If you're not a fan of color management, you can also tell Illustrator to ignore it and forget that color management capabilities exist.

The Illustrator file format has also changed. Illustrator always understood the PDF format, but now the native Illustrator format writes a version of PDF (as well as "real" EPS and "real" PDF). The new file format is somewhat "forward-compatible," so older versions of Illustrator can open Illustrator 9 files—though not always correctly. If you need to use earlier versions of Illustrator along with Illustrator 9, and you make use of many of the new features of 9, such as transparency and blend modes, you probably should put the blocking plug-in into your earlier versions so that they cannot accidentally open files in Illustrator 9 format.

Most of the workflow changes are beyond the scope of this book, which is, of course, an *f/x and Design* book. My mandate is to show you interesting creative techniques with Illustrator—not production-related techniques. David Xenakis, the technical editor for this book and one of the leading prepress authorities, has written an appendix on trapping that covers in detail this most necessary piece of Illustrator production work. One of the major changes that Illustrator 9 includes is the capability to preview your trapping directly on screen in Illustrator. (However, Adobe has decreed that objects containing even one percent of common color don't need trapping, so this feature might not be as useful as it could be because you need at least 20 to 30 percent common color to be able to avoid the need to trap.)

Why a "What's New" Chapter?

My purpose in writing a chapter about the new Illustrator features is not to convince you that Illustrator is a great program. It is, but you probably already know that. I want to provide the background that you need in using the new features so that you're comfortable working through the examples in the book.

Because this book is for intermediate-to-advanced Illustrator users, I assume that you know how to use the basic features of Illustrator: the pen tools, the geometric creation tools, and the fill and stroke indicators. I assume that you know how to create and edit basic objects and find your way around the program. However, because so much has changed, I want to introduce you to some of the basics again: setting strokes and fills, using the Layers palette, and selecting objects. You'll then have a good basis for understanding the new Illustrator features of transparency and blend modes.

Back to Basics

The most basic item in Illustrator is the object. An Illustrator *object* is a path or a shape. The path or shape can be stroked and/or filled. A closed path becomes a shape. In previous versions of Illustrator, this most simple of all elements could contain one stroke and one fill. You had no other options. An object had a stroke and/or a fill—simple, complete, no room for negotiation. If you wanted to create an element such as an outlined stroke to indicate a street on a map, you created a path with a wide black stroke and, aligned on top of it, a duplicate path with a narrower white stroke.

A New Object Model

Illustrator 9 allows you to create multiple strokes and fills per object. This means that you could create the street indicator that I mentioned previously by using a single path. The path could contain two strokes. One stroke could be black and wide, and on top of it could be a white, narrow stroke. The path that contains both strokes, however, is a single object, and its points can be edited as such.

You can create neon effects, for example, by layering strokes along a single path. That seems like a useful feature. Why, though, would you want to create multiple fills? If you were using Illustrator 8, multiple fills would be useless because one fill would cover up the other. However, Illustrator 9 permits you to use transparency, so you can easily create, for example, a blue, 50 percent transparent fill on top of a red-to-green gradient.

If you're going to create transparent objects, you need to be able to manage the transparency of the object: set it, change it, or remove it entirely. For that, you need a new palette, and Illustrator has introduced a new Transparency palette (you'll meet it in a minute). You also need to know how many strokes and fills an object has. You add, delete, and edit the strokes and fills in the new Appearance palette. Finally, to help you keep track of the individual objects in the image, Illustrator 9 has introduced a new Layers palette.

These three new palettes (Transparency, Appearance, and Layers) work together to give you unprecedented control over your objects. They are the Control Center of all the creation work that you'll do in Illustrator. The new object model of multiple strokes and fills would not be feasible without them. Let's take a look at these three palettes next.

I don't usually share my writing problems with my readers, but I spent three hours trying to decide which palette to write about first. The problem is that all three palettes are related and need to be used together. I'm going to talk about the Transparency palette first because it's the easiest to explain (if I ignore its capability to create opacity masks). Then, I'll talk about the Layers palette, and finally, I'll discuss the Appearance palette. Please bear with me because they won't completely make sense until I'm done. You'll also see these palettes again in more detail in Chapter 2. Brenda Sutherland of Adobe Systems has done an excellent job of explaining how the three palettes work together to enable you to create repeatable styles.

Transparency

One of the most requested and long-awaited features in past versions of Adobe Illustrator was the capability to define objects with transparency. Illustrator 9 allows you to specify any percentage (from 0 to 100) of object opacity. That sounds easy enough, but Adobe has added some interesting twists to this tale.

Transparency Palette

Let's take a look at the Transparency palette and see how it works. Figure 1.1 shows two objects. The selected object (the one on top) is black and has a 50-percent opacity in the Transparency palette. You can "see through it" to the object below. Figure 1.2 shows the Transparency palette as it looks with the top object in Figure 1.1 selected.

Figure 1.1
You can make one object transparent so that the lower object is partially visible.

Setting the opacity of an object is a simple matter of typing a number into the Opacity field on the Transparency palette or clicking on the arrow next to the field to drop down a slider. You cannot simply type a number on your keyboard as you can in Photoshop, however. You need to actually select the field or drag the slider.

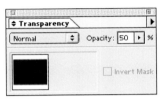

Figure 1.2
The Transparency palette shows that the object is dark but has a 50-percent opacity applied to it.

So, where's the catch? The catch (though it's actually a fantastic new capability) is that you can apply transparency to elements other than plain objects. You can apply changes in opacity to individual strokes and fills, to groups, and to an entire layer. The Transparency palette allows you to set the transparency of the *targeted* element (another new term that I'll explain momentarily), but it doesn't tell you what's been targeted. You need the Layers palette and the Appearance palette for that (stay tuned!).

Before I leave the topic of the Transparency palette, however, I want to briefly identify its other functions. The Transparency palette also enables you to change the blend mode of the target and to add an opacity mask.

Blend Modes

Blend modes define how an element interacts with the elements that it touches. If you're familiar with Photoshop, you'll immediately understand the concept. If you're not, you need to do some serious exploring. Figure 1.3 shows the Mode menu drop-down on the Transparency palette.

Figure 1.3
You can change the blend modes on the Transparency palette.

The default blend mode is Normal. This means that the element does not react at all to whatever is under it. At most, Normal mode shows only a simple transparency effect when it has less than 100 percent opacity applied to it. There's no point to trying to show blend modes in black and white; however, the Color Studio section gives you a better idea of the result of each mode. The best way to learn to use them is simply to try out each mode in turn and decide empirically which one is best in each situation. Chapter 3 shows you how to use transparency and blend modes to create changes in color.

One difference that I need to point out if you know Photoshop is that Illustrator's *canvas* doesn't react to the blend modes at all. An element that isn't over another Illustrator element and that has a blend mode defined looks as if it's in Normal mode. In Photoshop, objects on layers that have had blend modes defined react to the white background layer if they aren't on top of anything else.

You can apply blend modes to objects, strokes, fills, groups, or layers. Like transparency, the results differ depending on which elements are targeted.

Opacity Masking

Another trick that you can perform with the Transparency palette: creating opacity masks. What's an *opacity mask*? An opacity mask is similar to a clipping mask, but it allows for soft edges and changes in opacity.

You can use a clipping mask to show a number of Illustrator elements so that they appear to be inside a single, unstroked, unfilled shape. An opacity mask allows you to use one or more Illustrator objects (both vector and/or raster) to show or hide portions of an element (stroke, fill, object, group, or layer) based on the values in the mask. You'll use opacity masking extensively in Chapter 6.

Opacity masking in Photoshop is done through layer masking or alpha channels. In Illustrator, as in Photoshop, where the opacity mask is black, you hide the masked element. Where the opacity mask is white, you reveal it. Shades of gray in the mask partially obscure the masked element, depending on how close the gray is to black.

Creating an Opacity Mask

Try this short example to see how to construct a simple opacity mask:

1. In Illustrator, create a new document (by choosing File|New). Accept whatever default size is offered and make this an RGB document.

2. Choose the Rectangle tool. Select red as your fill color and create a rectangle that is filled but not stroked. The size is not critical.

3. In the Transparency palette, choose Make Opacity Mask from the side drop-down menu. Figure 1.4 shows what happens to the Transparency palette display when you add an opacity mask (the thumbnail gains another preview image for the mask).

4. In Figure 1.4, the object thumbnail is selected. When you select the object in the Transparency palette, all changes you make to the image affect the main image. To create the opacity mask, you need to first click on the empty opacity mask thumbnail to select it. After you select the opacity mask thumbnail (as shown in Figure 1.5), you can create as many objects and effects as you want, and they are used only in the mask that you are building.

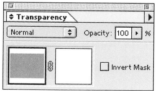

Figure 1.4

Adding an opacity mask also adds a mask thumbnail to the Transparency palette.

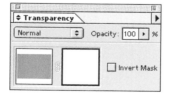

Figure 1.5

You need to select the opacity mask thumbnail to be able to create an opacity mask.

5. Figure 1.6 shows the Layers palette with the opacity mask active. Although you haven't seen the "regular" Layers palette yet (remember I told you that everything was interrelated), notice that the Layers palette makes it perfectly clear what's being edited. When you see the opacity mask listed in the Layers palette, it's your invitation to construct the objects that you want to use for the opacity mask. To start, draw a rectangle that's on top of the red rectangle that is your to-be-masked object, but make it smaller than the red rectangle. Give it a black fill and no stroke. Figure 1.7 shows the Transparency palette, and Figure 1.8 shows the image. Your red square has a hole cut out of it (the black rectangle hides the corresponding area of the masked object from view).

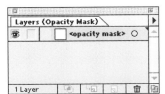

Figure 1.6
(Left) The Layers palette tells you when you're working in the Opacity Mask layer view.

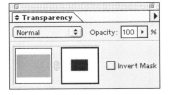

Figure 1.7
(Right) The Transparency palette shows the masked object and opacity mask.

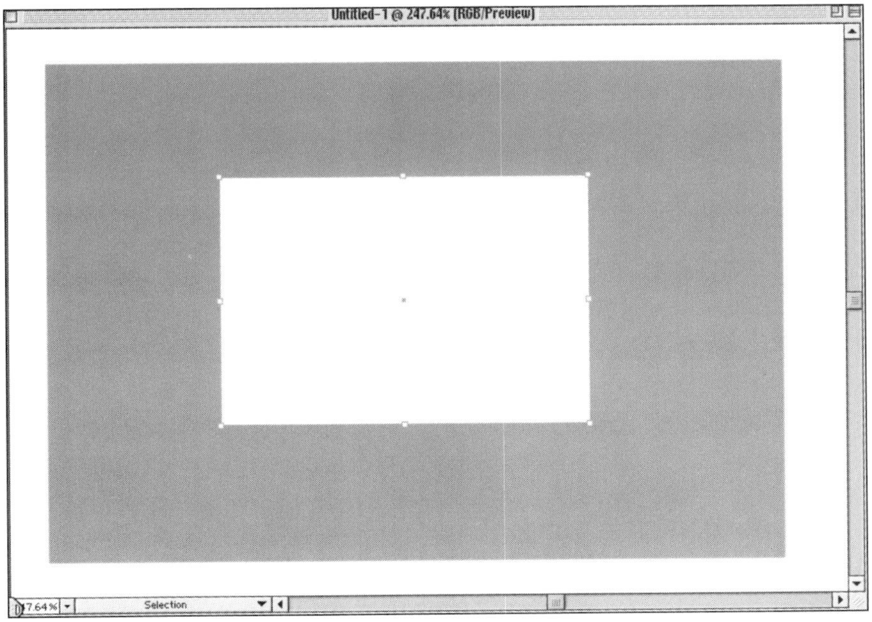

Figure 1.8
The black shape in the opacity mask cuts a "virtual" hole out of the object.

6. You can easily reverse the colors so that you invert the mask. Click on the Invert Mask checkbox on the Transparency palette. Figure 1.9 shows that you can now see only the red (or gray—as it appears here) rectangle through the area that is selected. It's the same area that was selected in Figure 1.8. The only change between images is the selection of the Invert Mask checkbox.

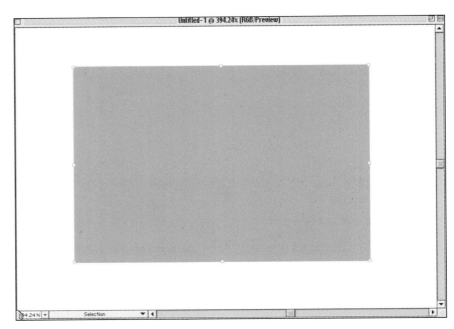

Figure 1.9
Checking the Invert Mask checkbox reverses the mask and reveals the area inside the masking object.

Can You Use a White Masking Rectangle?

What would happen if you created a white rectangle instead of a black one when you first set up the mask? Would you then not have needed to invert the mask? It seems logical, but your mask would not have masked anything at all, unfortunately. Remember that only *objects* participate in the mask. A white rectangle, therefore, masks nothing. When you invert the mask, however, Illustrator creates a "virtual" rectangle out to the bounding box of the element.

Clipping Mask

Clipping *paths* have become clipping *masks* in Illustrator 9. You can create a clipping mask exactly as you did in Illustrator 8, but you can also create a layer-based clipping mask. The main difference is in what you need to select to be able to create the clipping mask. To make a standard clipping mask, you need to select all the participating objects. To use the new layer clipping mask feature, you only need to target the layer and then choose Make Clipping Mask from the Layers palette menu, as shown in Figure 1.10. The results are exactly as you've seen them in Illustrator's previous versions, but captive to the layer where the mask resides. The top object in the layer becomes the layer clipping mask and loses both fill and stroke. You can still apply certain distortion and path effects to it. However, effects that need to rasterize, such as Feather, have no effect on a clipping mask. You can also create a layer clipping mask by clicking on the Make/Release Layer Clipping Mask icon in the Layers palette (it's the first icon on the bottom left of the palette, as shown in Figure 1.11).

Figure 1.10
(Left) Applying a clipping mask to elements in a layer is as easy as choosing Make/Release Clipping Mask in the Layers palette.

Figure 1.11
(Right) You can click on the first icon (Make/Release) to create or release a layer clipping mask.

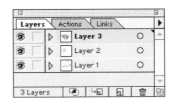

You can locate all the masks in your image by choosing Edit|Select|Masks. This command finds and selects every mask in your document. You can then use either the Layers palette to view your *clipping set* (another new AI9 term) or the Group Selection tool to locate the other participating objects. You can tell that you're looking at a clipping set in the Layers palette because the lines between the participating objects are dotted, as you can see in Figure 1.12.

You can have multiple clipping masks in a layer if each one is in a different sublayer. If you click on Make/Release Clipping Mask while the layer is targeted, the top object in the layer, even if it's a sublayer, is designated as a clipping mask. Making a sublayer into a clipping mask is not usually useful (in most cases, your entire layer becomes invisible), so you need to remain aware of what you're doing. Chapter 2 provides much more information about proper targeting.

What's a Clipping Mask?

A clipping mask is a hard-edged path. Enabling a clipping mask creates a "cropping" window through which you can see any elements that fall within the boundaries of the mask object. Disabling the clipping layer makes visible again all the elements of the sublayers below it. The mask object is always the object on top. You cannot create a feathered or partially transparent clipping mask. If you want to achieve a softer look, you need to create an opacity mask.

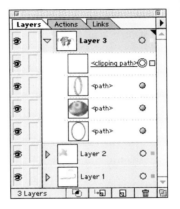

Figure 1.12
A clipping set is identified by the dotted lines between the participating objects.

A New Layers Palette

Illustrator 9 has gone "hierarchical." The new Layers palette enables you to "nest" layers in a document. Nesting layers allows you to manage your layers better by organizing them in a hierarchical system of sublayers and sub-sublayers. When you view the Layers palette, you can reveal the individual objects on each layer. Using the Layers palette as "Control Central," you can organize your layers, order and reorder them, and select individual objects—a huge time-saver if you have one object stuck under another one. You can also hide or lock individual elements on a layer and just as easily show and unlock them.

What's on a Layer?

You can think of layers as invisible sheets of clear acetate into which you can place elements of an illustration. Now, imagine that each of these layers can be rearranged, reordered, and even replaced in the hierarchy of layers in your illustration with click-and-drag simplicity. The layer is not the object itself. The layer is a *container* for the objects that "sit" on it. Each layer can, in turn, have sublayers.

Anatomy of the Layers Palette

At first glance, the Layers palette looks much the same as it did in Illustrator 8. However, a closer look reveals many new features. Figure 1.13 shows the many new parts of the Layers palette. As you can see, you can lock and hide layers directly in the Layers palette, and you can reveal or conceal the detail in each layer. The pen icon that Illustrator 8 used to indicate the current layer is replaced by a small triangle. Let's take a closer look at some of these new additions to the Layers palette.

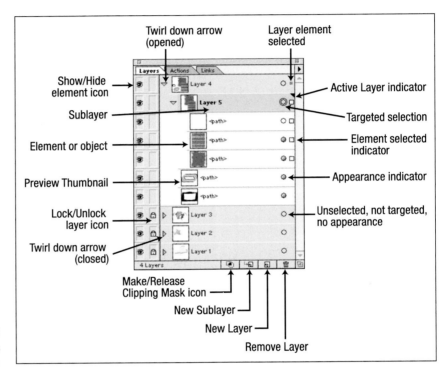

Figure 1.13

The Layers palette definitely sports a new "look" in Illustrator 9.

Twirl Down Arrows

Each layer, sublayer, or group contains an arrow icon at the left of the entry that can be twirled down to reveal the details of the layer. It is also called the *disclosure triangle* (Adobe LiveMotion calls it the *twisty*). When you twirl down the disclosure triangle, you see the entire layer hierarchy.

Active Layer

An active (current) layer in Illustrator 9 has a tiny black triangle to the right of the layer name entry. It indicates that the layer is currently active and able to be edited. It also indicates that any new object that is created or pasted into the document will appear on the layer and sublayer that "contains" the current object in the hierarchy. If you have one element of a group active when you create a new object, your new object automatically becomes a member of that group.

Create New Layer/Sublayer

You can create either a new layer or a new sublayer by using the icons at the bottom of the Layers palette. That sounds simple enough. However, there's a catch—of course. If you have a subelement selected or active when you click on the New Layer icon, you create a new *sublayer*—not a new layer—regardless of which icon you click on. I don't agree with Adobe's logic, but the Adobe engineers do have a reason. They felt that, if you were working within a layer, any new element you would want to create should be in the same layer. Therefore, if you really want a new, independent layer, you need to make a top-level layer active before you choose the New Layer function.

Show/Hide Layer or Sublayer

A layer or group of layers can be made visible or invisible with a few simple mouse clicks. To toggle the visibility of any layer, just click on the "eye" icon to the left of the layer name in the Layers palette. The eye icons all appear in the same column in the Layers palette; it's known as the "visibility" column.

Lock Layer or Sublayer

You also can "lock" a layer or sublayer in the artwork. When a layer is locked, it's still visible in your document window, but you can't edit or change it until it's unlocked.

You know that a layer is locked if you see a small padlock icon in the Layers palette to the left of the layer name. You can select a locked layer. You can even move a locked layer in the layer hierarchy, but you can't make changes to that layer. If you select a locked layer and try to make changes to its contents, the familiar "can't write" cursor becomes visible.

Rename Layers

You can change the name of any layer, sublayer, group, or element by double-clicking on the element entry in the Layers palette. You then see a dialog box, as shown in Figure 1.14, that enables you to enter a more descriptive name for a top-level layer. Figure 1.15 shows a slightly different dialog box that enables you to change an object name.

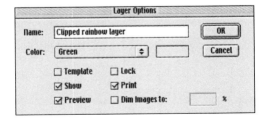

Figure 1.14

You can rename a layer or change layer options by using the Layer Options dialog box.

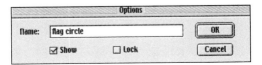

Figure 1.15

You can change the name of an object, but you have fewer options available at the same time.

Drag to Re-Order Layer

You can drag layers to change their stacking order or their position in the hierarchy. In Illustrator 8, you could drag a layer above or below another one. In Illustrator 9, you can also drag a layer *onto* another one. If you drag Layer 2 onto Layer 1, Layer 2 becomes a sublayer of Layer 1. You need to try dragging to understand this principle.

PROJECT 1.2 Ordering Your Layers Around

In this short project, you'll open an existing Illustrator 9 file and rearrange the layers that it contains.

1. Open the file PRACTICE.AI from the enclosed CD-ROM. Figure 1.16 shows the Layers palette with all the disclosure triangles closed.

2. Twirl down the disclosure triangle on Layer 1. Layer 1 contains only one object, as you can see in Figure 1.17. Double-click on the <path> entry and change the name to "Yellow Rectangle".

3. Place your cursor on Layer 3 and drag it between Layers 1 and 2, as shown in Figure 1.18. Notice that a double line with arrowheads appears between layers as you drag.

Figure 1.16
(Left) PRACTICE.AI contains four visible layers with the disclosure triangles closed.

Figure 1.17
(Center) Layer 1 contains only one object.

Figure 1.18
(Right) When you see the double line with four tiny arrowheads, you know that you are dragging between layers or elements.

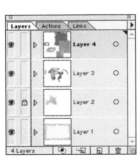
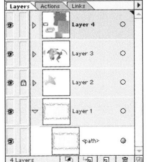
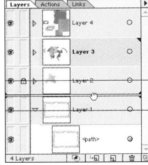

4. Expand Layer 2 and Layer 4 by turning down their disclosure triangles.

5. Drag the path named Flag Circle until it is on top of Layer 4 and then release the mouse button. As you can see in Figure 1.19, you can tell that you are on top of a layer when you see a large arrowhead at each end of the layer entry. At that point, release the mouse button. The Flag Circle object is now the top object in Layer 4.

6. You can also move the Flag Circle object onto the <group> entry. If you drag the object onto the group or you drag it so that it is under the group hierarchy, the Flag Circle object immediately becomes an integral part of that group.

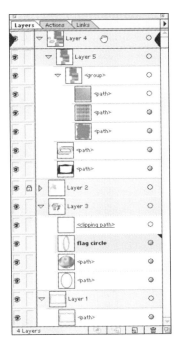

Figure 1.19

When you drag an entry onto a layer, sublayer, or group, you see a large arrowhead at each end of the entry where your element is located.

Layers 2 and 3 also contain clipping masks. Try rearranging layers and dragging elements between other elements and onto other layers. See how the image changes as you do. You'll get more practice in Chapter 2.

The Layers palette menu contains many new commands. Figure 1.20 shows the various layers options available to you. At various points throughout the book, I'll talk about almost all of them.

The Appearance Palette: A New "Info Central"

The third new palette is the Appearance palette. Think of the Appearance palette as kind of a central information panel for each element in your illustration. The Appearance palette is the place where you add additional strokes and fills and where you place Live Effects. You can tell that an element has something extra applied to it in the Appearance palette because a shaded circle appears at the right of the entry in the Layers palette. The design team at Adobe affectionately calls this icon the "meatball."

Figure 1.21 shows the Appearance palette as it looks with the purple <path> entry selected in Layer 5. This object uses the Purple Puddle style, contains a 1-pt stroke, and uses the Offset Path and Roughen effects. You'll learn how to use the Appearance palette to apply effects and create additional strokes and fills in Chapter 2.

The Appearance palette also contains a number of other commands. You can apply them by using the menu found when you click on the arrowhead in the upper-right corner of the palette. Figure 1.22 shows the side drop-down menu.

Figure 1.20

The Layers palette options.

Figure 1.21

(Left) The Appearance palette
consolidates information about
each object.

Figure 1.22

(Right) You can use the side drop-
down menu in the Appearance
palette to add additional strokes
and fill and get more control over
an element's appearance.

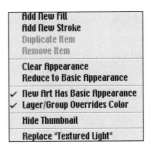

Figure 1.23

The Effect menu shows the
categories of dynamic effects
that you can apply to shapes,
fills, strokes, groups, or layers.

Live Effects

One major change that Adobe has made in Illustrator 9 is to enable Illustrator
to create Live Effects. In many cases, the effects are filters that have been in
Illustrator in previous versions. The astounding change is that when you apply the Effect version (from the new Effect menu shown in Figure 1.23), the
filter stays "live." You can change the settings any time you want. An even
more exciting benefit is that you can modify the shape itself, and the effect
immediately calculates a new result.

In previous versions of Illustrator, if you wanted to apply a filter such as
Gaussian blur, Illustrator had to first rasterize the object. When the vector object was changed to a raster object, it was that way forever. Live Effects allows
you to keep your object in vector format but preview the effect as if the object
were a raster object. If you need to print the document at a variety of sizes, the
effect rasterizes at print time from the *printing* size of the document. Thus, you
maintain the highest possible image quality even as you apply effects that
can be printed using only rasterized objects. As you'll see shortly, you also
have control over how much of your image is rasterized before it's sent to the
rip (raster image processor) to be imaged.

You'll have a chance to apply Live Effects in Chapter 2 as well as in many chapters throughout this book. One of the most amazing aspects of Live Effects is that
you can apply pathfinder filters and transform commands dynamically. The
caterpillar-like creature in Figure 1.24 might not look terribly impressive, but it
consists of a single circle. The rest is merely smoke and mirrors! To the single
circle, I've added a second fill and several effects, as you can see in Figure 1.25.

It's an RGB (or CMYK) World

In early releases of Illustrator, images were all in CMYK mode (with some
grayscale or spot color permitted). Illustrator was used only as a print application—Adobe assumed that anything you created in Illustrator was destined
for print. Several recent developments have rendered that assumption invalid.

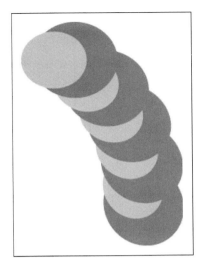

Figure 1.24
(Left) Gus the caterpillar is really just a single circular object with an altered appearance.

Figure 1.25
(Right) The Appearance palette shows the effects used to change a circle into a wiggly creature.

Inkjet print technology is one factor that has caused Adobe to re-evaluate the exclusive use of CMYK in Illustrator. As inkjet printers have gotten cheaper and better, many Illustrator users need to print to them rather than take their files to a service bureau. Many Inkjet printers use RGB images directly rather than demanding that CMYK color separations are created.

The other major development is the World Wide Web. Vector graphics make wonderful, tiny Web elements. They can be used as the basis for Flash animations. The World Wide Web Consortium (W3C) has recently approved a new vector image format called Scalable Vector Graphics (SVG). The Web can be viewed only on RGB devices such as computer monitors, pagers, and cell phones (if it uses light, it's RGB). Therefore, to better help users create Web graphics, Illustrator needs to be able to create images in RGB color mode.

Although previous versions of Illustrator could create RGB *objects*, Illustrator 9 insists that you select a color space for an entire *document*. This change really benefits the users even if it seems at first glance to be an inconvenience.

The Document Color Mode—Pick One

Now, you can establish a color mode for an entire document without having to worry about whether any of the elements in the document have been assigned attributes outside the color mode you've chosen for your document. In addition, you aren't captive to the color mode you establish at the start of the project. You can always change your color space at any point in the process. However, the important point to remember is that the document supports only *one* color model at a time.

Although this support for only one color model might seem like a pain in some instances, it's really a safety feature to help you avoid unexpected output results.

You can design and work in whatever color space your work will be seen and adjust your work to fit your designated production or publishing method: CMYK, RGB, or both.

You can easily establish a color space prior to creating a new document, and you can convert the color space of an existing or already opened document by choosing File|Document Color Mode|RGB or File|Document Color Mode|CMYK.

Color Management

If you've ever cursed at Illustrator or Photoshop when you open an Illustrator document and discover no relationship between the colors as they look in Photoshop and the way they looked in Illustrator, you should be happy with the Color Management system that is now compatible with the one in Photoshop. You can use the same profiles (or ignore everything, if you prefer), and your colors should look the same in both programs.

Web Enhancements

Adobe has added several features to Illustrator to enable you to more easily design for the Web. One enhancement, of course, is the RGB Document Color Mode. You can also view your image as pixels as you work. Additionally, Illustrator provides support for the new SVG standard and for creating Flash animations. As a final "goodie," Illustrator 9 has added the Save For Web dialog box found in Photoshop and ImageReady.

Previewing Pixels

You can now preview your work in actual pixels at the size you're planning to output. Pixel Preview accomplishes two very important tasks. First, it allows you a realtime, real-world look at how your project will appear when output. That's a very handy time-saver when you're exporting your work for use on the Web or in raster-based media. Second, the preview allows you to easily determine which objects in your work have transparent fills. You can turn on Pixel Preview in the View menu. You'll get a chance to work with Pixel Preview in Chapter 12.

Flash and SVG Output

Among the hottest new features in Illustrator 9 are some new output options. Illustrator 9 now enables you to save your work in Flash and SVG formats. If you're creating art for the Web or any other kind of interactive format, this new capability is going to be one of the most exciting new features in this release of Illustrator.

Macromedia Flash is possibly one of the most talked about software products at the moment. It uses the .swf format (ShockWave Flash). You can export layers as sequential animations, as an individual Flash file, or as a single file per layer. One exciting possibility is to create a blend in Illustrator, release the blend elements to individual layers, and export each layer as a new frame in an animation.

Although few browsers support SVG today, Illustrator is ready for the time when this format will be readily accepted. You might not want to use SVG right now, but check back in a year and see what has happened to it.

Rasters Aboard!

Illustrator gives you some extremely complex options when you output images. The new blend modes and transparency options create a major printing challenge for Illustrator. PostScript doesn't like transparent objects, so Illustrator needs to trick *something* when you create a transparent object. Either you only *think* that you're seeing transparency, or the printer thinks it *isn't* seeing transparency. In either case, Illustrator is doing some fancy footwork.

To accomplish this smoke-and-mirrors magic, Illustrator gives you five options when you set up your file for printing.

The Document Setup Dialog Box

In the Document Setup dialog box, you establish the way Illustrator treats your image at print time. You can find the Document Setup command under the File menu. Figure 1.26 shows this dialog box with the transparency options visible.

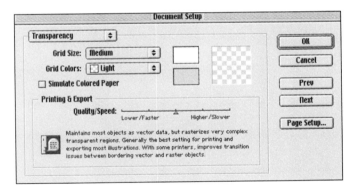

Figure 1.26
You can change your transparency settings in this dialog box.

The Transparency Settings

With all the cool new features in Illustrator 9, you now have a much broader set of choices to make when saving, exporting, and even rendering your work. One new choice is in determining how Illustrator 9 rasterizes your artwork when sending it to production. This means that you can now specify the degree to which your flattened artwork will be rasterized on final output. You do so by adjusting the Quality/Speed slider in the Document Setup dialog box that appears when you choose File|Document Setup.

Understanding how each of the following settings affects the processing of your final output can help you decide which setting works best for your configuration. As with all output decisions, you'll find it helpful to consult with your output services provider or service bureau for their recommendations and preferences when you submit files.

Illustrator gives you these five settings, which go from faster but less quality to slower and high quality:

- *The entire illustration will be rasterized.* When you use this setting, Illustrator rasterizes your entire image using the settings that you've left in a variety of dialog boxes scattered throughout the program. The effect of this setting is the same as choosing Object|Rasterize with the entire image selected. Your best use for this setting is if you have a complex image that you want to output at a fairly small size. Outputting a large, complex file at prepress resolution takes a lot of time and RAM and results in a huge output file.

- *Maintain simpler vector objects, but rasterize more complex areas involving transparency.* This is another decent option for a system that has fairly low RAM. It's also a good choice when you have only a few transparent objects. You don't get good transitions between the vector objects and the objects that are rasterized, so you might not be happy with this setting.

- *Maintain most objects as vector data, but rasterize very complex transparent regions.* This is Illustrator's default setting. Most documents can use this setting fairly well. Some *stitching* might still occur where the region being rasterized overlaps the vector areas. (Stitching means that you can see the areas where the rasterized image blends—or doesn't blend—into the vectors.)

- *Maintain most of the illustration as vector data, and rasterize only extremely complex areas.* This setting provides a high degree of resolution-independence but can be time- and RAM-consuming.

- *Maintain vector data to the greatest extent possible.* This is the highest quality setting possible but is the most time-consuming and RAM-intensive option. Illustrator doesn't rasterize any area unless it has absolutely no other choice.

Keep in mind that with all major new capabilities and software features, there are bound to be some fairly serious caveats to be considered when making these production and output decisions. Again, it's a good idea to communicate closely and thoroughly with your service bureau to find out what its rip and rendering device configurations are best able to handle.

The Printing and Export Settings

The Document Setup dialog box also enables you to determine how you want to export your image (see Figure 1.27). You can set your output resolution, decide whether you want to split long paths, and determine the output ppi for gradients and gradient mesh objects.

When you determine the optimum settings for objects that contain gradient mesh objects, you also need to look at the Raster Effects Settings dialog box found under the Effect menu.

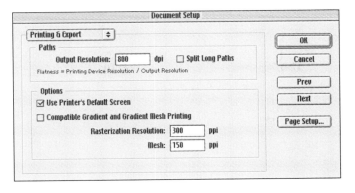

Figure 1.27
The Printing & Export settings page of the Document Setup dialog box.

The Raster Effects Settings Dialog Box

Some effects need to rasterize the object that they are applied to when you export or print the file. The Effect|Rasterize|Rasterize Settings menu option opens the Raster Effects Settings dialog box, which enables you to set a global resolution for any object to which an effect needing to be rasterized is applied (see Figure 1.28). The setting applies to all objects in the document.

As you can see in Figure 1.28, you can choose from a number of different options when Illustrator needs to rasterize an object. I find the placement of this command to be a bit peculiar. It's really a type of preference and isn't specific to just the Rasterize effect. It takes effect when you apply a drop shadow or a Gaussian blur, or any other effect that is output as a raster object.

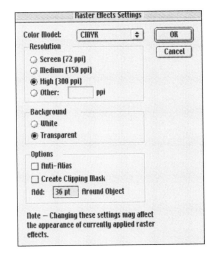

Figure 1.28
The Raster Effects Settings dialog box.

Overprinting

Illustrator 9 hasn't forgotten its core audience—the print designers of the world. The new blend mode and transparency features also enable Illustrator to grant the wishes of millions of designers who want to be able to preview their traps or to see the effect of their overprint settings *before* they put ink on paper.

Trapping is the way that the print world compensates for potential shifting and stretching of paper that can cause adjacent ink colors to not align properly when printing. You can trap by specifying certain areas in your artwork to print a little larger (or smaller), with part of the area overprinting an adjacent colored area. When you trap an image, you add a visible flaw to the image in the hope of preventing a worse occurrence (seeing white paper) at print time. You can now preview your overprint settings in Illustrator 9. With this powerful new feature, you can see on screen how spot-color objects, chokes, spreads, and overlays will overprint in your illustrations. (However, be aware of the odd choices that Adobe has made about which objects will show trapping.)

Moving On

In this chapter, you learned about several new features in Illustrator. I didn't mention all the new features or the usability enhancements because the list is actually too long. Because this is an *f/x and Design* book, I touched lightly on some features (such as overprinting and output considerations) and ignored other non-design type features (such as the new capability to create custom keystroke shortcut commands).

You learned about the three key new or revised palettes: Layers, Transparency, and Appearance. You also learned about the major new Web features such as RGB document color space, Pixel Preview, Save For Web, Release to Layers, and Flash or SVG output.

Finally, you learned about color management, Live Effects, and styles. In Chapter 2, Brenda Sutherland will show you how to use the Layers, Appearance, and Transparency palettes and create styles that you can apply to other objects with a click of the mouse.

Chapter 2

Styles and Appearance

With the introduction of the Appearance palette and the innovations made in the Layers palette, not only are the changes in what you can create in Illustrator revolutionary, so are the ways you can create them!

By Brenda Sutherland

Three Palettes—Working Together

As you have already seen in Chapter 1, you can now select, delete, and change the stacking order of objects, groups, and layers within the Layers palette. In this chapter, you will also learn that you can target any of these items as well and then use the Appearance palette to modify the selection in more ways than possible before.

Even the most experienced Illustrator users will be amazed at the advances in their workflow as they use the Appearance and Layers palettes together to apply color, effects, and transformations to objects. Add the Transparency palette to the mix, and you can see just how powerful this triumvirate is.

The Appearance palette makes it possible not only to change the fill and stroke of a path, but also to add additional fills and strokes to a single path. You can also select any of these fills or strokes and apply effects to them individually or to the object as a whole. The same is also true when it comes to applying transparency or blend modes. Later in the chapter, you'll look at some *styles* (saved appearances that are stored in the Styles palette and can be applied later, like swatches) to see how innovative these new features are.

The Layers Palette

Before getting into the nuts and bolts of the Appearance palette, take another look at the Layers palette to make sure you understand targeting.

Targeting within the Layers Palette

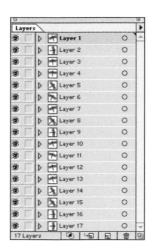

Figure 2.1
Each layer has a Targeting icon on it.

Every item in the Layers palette has a small circle to the right of its name, as you can see in Figure 2.1 This Targeting icon can be used not only to target items, but also to move and delete appearances and styles and offer visual feedback. When the Targeting icon is a hollow circle, the item does not have any appearance attributes (effects, brush strokes, or transparency at the object level, or any of these attributes as well as fill and stroke at the layer or group level). When the icon is a gray, filled circle (as shown in Figure 2.2), some type of attribute has been applied to the item. When an item is targeted, as it is in Figure 2.3, a ring circles it in either its hollow or gray, filled state.

In many ways, targeting is similar to selecting. When a group or layer is targeted, all the objects within that group or layer become selected. The significant difference is that because all appearance attributes are applied at a container level (that is, the group or layer entry on the Layers palette), any object later added to that container automatically receives the same attributes. By the same token, any item moved out of the container no longer has the attributes.

For example, if you have a layer with three objects and apply an effect, such as a drop shadow, to the layer, all three objects then display a drop shadow. If you then add a new object to the layer, the new object automatically has a drop shadow applied. If you then move any of these objects to another layer, the drop shadow is removed.

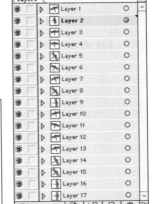

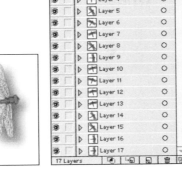

Figure 2.2
The Targeting icon looks like a "meatball" when the layer or object contains an effect or appearance.

You need to be aware of whether a selection is targeted or merely selected for another important reason. Effects are applied differently, depending on whether they are applied at the object level or container (layer or group) level. To go back to the preceding example with the three objects, if any of the objects are overlapping and you apply a drop shadow at the layer level, the drop shadow is applied only to the outline of the three objects together. In other words, if one object overlaps another, it does not cast a shadow on the object beneath it (that is part of the same layer). Sometimes, this is exactly the effect you want, so you want to be sure that the effect is applied by targeting the group or layer and applying it at the container level. If you want the drop shadow to be applied to each object individually instead, you need to select everything on the layer (click to the right of the targeting icon on the layer or group to select all objects within the container without targeting them) and apply the effect. As you can see, targeting and selecting are different. You can target something without selecting the underlying objects, and you can select the underlying objects without targeting the container.

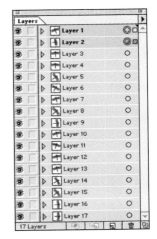

Figure 2.3
The layer Targeting icons look like this when they are targeted.

You also can move appearance attributes from one item to another by clicking on the Targeting icon and dragging it to another item in the Layers palette. Similarly, you can copy appearances by Option/Alt+dragging in the Layers palette and delete them by dragging to the trash can icon on the Layers palette.

The Appearance Palette

Now that you know how to target, it's time to see how the Appearance palette fits into this new workflow. After you have mastered this exciting new palette, you will soon wonder how you ever worked without it.

The Appearance and Layers palettes work in harmony, much like the Color and Swatches palettes do. While one palette shows the status of a selection, the other reveals the details. When a single object is targeted or selected, the Appearance palette displays the attributes of the object. When a group or layer is targeted, it displays the attributes assigned specifically to that group or layer.

These attributes include strokes, fills, effects, and transparency. If strokes and fills have not been assigned at the group or layer level, the palette displays fills and strokes of None. If a selected object is part of a layer or group with a fill or stroke applied, the Appearance palette displays a small fill and stroke icon (like the icons used in the Tool and Color palettes) at the top with either the word *Layer* or *Group,* as you can see in Figure 2.4. This icon symbolizes that the object has a fill or stroke applied at either the layer or group level. When you click on this icon, you target the layer or group from the Appearance palette.

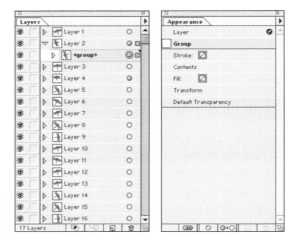

Figure 2.4

The Appearance palette can target a group.

The Appearance palette does not exist merely to offer feedback on an object's attributes. It is a powerful tool in and of itself that can be used to add additional strokes and fills to objects. It can also be used to apply effects and transparency to as much as an entire layer or to as little as a single stroke or fill of an individual object.

To add a new stroke or fill, first select an object. The Appearance palette shows that an object is selected and displays the current attributes. If the object was created from default, the palette displays a white fill, a black 1 pt stroke, and object opacity of 100%. To add a new fill or stroke, access the pop-out menu from the Appearance palette and choose Add New Stroke. The new stroke appears at the top of the painting order in the Appearance palette. To reorder it, select the stroke in the Appearance palette and drag it beneath the fill or stroke you want it to appear behind. New fills are added the same way. You can modify fills and strokes by first selecting them in the Appearance palette and then changing their attributes. When an individual fill or stroke is selected, not only can its paint style and stroke weight be changed, but also its opacity. You can even apply effects such as Roughen or Free Distort to a single fill or stroke. Figure 2.5 shows an object with a variety of strokes, fills, and effects applied.

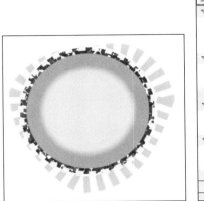

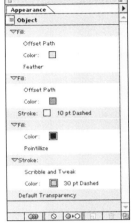

Figure 2.5

The Appearance palette reports the status of all the fills, strokes, and effects in this object.

To apply a Live Effect to an entire object (or layer or group, if that's what you have targeted), either have nothing selected in the Appearance palette (click in the gray area at the bottom of the palette) or select the object/group/layer next to the thumbnail in the Appearance palette. Next, choose an effect from the Effect menu and apply it. You are limited to the number of effects you can apply by the amount of memory on your system.

Illustrator's new effects have several advantages over the traditional static filters they are based on. The biggest advantage is that they are *live*. This means that when an effect is applied to an object, the object retains its original shape. So, if you apply an effect such as ZigZag to a line drawing you created of a holly sprig and then later decide to remove or lengthen the leaves, you can still modify the original path by using the Pencil tool. The ZigZag effect is reapplied automatically after you make the modifications. It's also possible to modify the effect itself at any time. Simply double-click on the effect name in the Appearance palette and make whatever changes necessary in the effect's dialog. The effect is reapplied with the new settings.

Because effects are live, they can be moved and deleted as well without destroying the remaining artwork. Click on an effect to drag it to a new position in the Appearance palette, including to or from an individual stroke or fill. Option/Alt+dragging can also be used to duplicate the effect. Simply drag the effect to the trashcan to delete it.

Keep in mind that effects are applied in the order they appear in the Appearance palette. The higher up the effect, the earlier in the painting order. So, if you want your holly sprig with ZigZag applied to have a drop shadow, the drop shadow should appear beneath ZigZag in the Appearance palette. Otherwise, the drop shadow is smooth, like the original drawing, and not bristly like the path with the effect applied. Figure 2.6 shows the holly sprig both ways.

How I Lightened the Leaves in Figure 2.6

I used the holly sprig in the Flower brushes library, but I wanted to lighten the green of the leaves for better contrast in the printing process (although you can't see the color here). I used a very cool trick suggested by artist Eric Reinfeld. It's been around since version 5, but not very many people know of it. If you hold Shift as you move one color slider on the Color palette, all the sliders move at the same time.

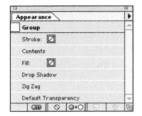

Figure 2.6

The holly sprig with the drop shadow on top (left) is bristly; where the drop shadow is the first effect applied (right), the shadow shows the original shape of the leaves.

Figure 2.7

You can see the "live FX" symbol beside both the Layer and the Group notation here.

Because effects can be applied at the group and layer levels as well as the object level, an icon is also used to indicate when a selection has an effect applied at the group or layer level. The effect icon (small black circle with a stylized letter *f* for *FX* through it) appears at the top of the Appearance palette with either the word *Layer* or *Group,* as you can see in Figure 2.7.

The Transparency Palette

The third palette in this new tri-part working method is the Transparency palette. Transparency and blend modes will be covered in depth in Chapter 3. This section will focus on how to apply and manage opacity in conjunction with the Layers and Appearance palettes.

You have probably already noticed that when anything is selected or targeted, the Appearance palette displays its opacity. The term *default transparency* means 100 percent opaque and Normal mode.

To change the opacity of the currently targeted selection, click on the Default Transparency line at the bottom of the Appearance palette to select it. Now, any changes made in the Transparency palette are applied to the selection currently targeted in the Layers palette and displayed in the Appearance palette. Next, change the opacity in the Transparency palette to 70%. Notice in Figure 2.8 that the Appearance palette now displays Layer Opacity 70%, and the Targeting icon in the Layers palette has changed from hollow to gray. The same is true when a blending mode other than Normal is chosen. The Appearance palette displays the blending mode next to the object's opacity.

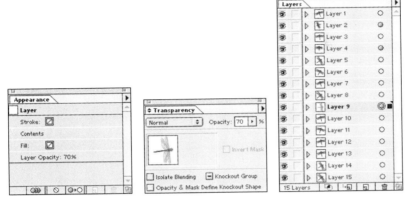

Figure 2.8

The Layers palette reflects the change made to the opacity of a layer of objects.

Opacity and blend modes, like effects, are not limited to object level. By targeting a group or layer, you can apply them at the container level, and the same rules apply. If you target a layer and set the opacity to 50% or the blend mode to Color Burn, any object created on or moved to that layer has 50% opacity and a blend mode of Color Burn. If that object is selected, the Appearance palette, as you can see in Figure 2.9, displays a transparency grid (checkerboard) at the top next to either the word *Layer* or *Group* to show that this object has transparency applied at either the layer or group level. If you click on this icon, you target the layer or group from the Appearance palette, and all changes you make will be at the container level.

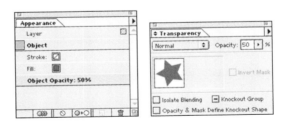

Figure 2.9

Notice the Transparency grid icon next to the Layer entry on the Appearance palette.

Anatomy of a Style

Now, you have an idea of how much potential the Appearance palette has to offer. With multiple strokes, fills, Live Effects, and transparency, you can create some fantastic and highly complex artwork within the Appearance palette. It would be a shame if you had to re-create these effects from scratch every time, wouldn't it? Well, thanks to the Styles palette, you can save these custom appearances as *styles* and then apply them as easily as swatches. You also can choose from many predefined styles installed with Illustrator. You can use them straight out of the box (so to speak) or modify them to give them a customized look. You can also examine them for inspiration.

Meet the Styles

Start by taking a look at the default styles. When you open a new document, the Styles palette loads styles based on the CMYK and RGB startup files. Open a new CMYK document and look at the Styles palette (choose Window|Show Styles if the palette isn't visible). Each style in the default palette was chosen to demonstrate a different effect attainable through styles. Create a large star and select each of the default styles in turn to see how they use strokes, fills, opacity and blend modes, Live Effects, and brushes.

The Standard CMYK Styles

The standard CMYK styles are as follows:

- *Bizzaro*—The fill is plain with no effects, but the two strokes are different widths and each has Roughen applied at different settings (see Figure 2.10).

- *Black Red Dashes*—Dashed lines can be used very effectively, especially with multiple strokes (see Figure 2.11).

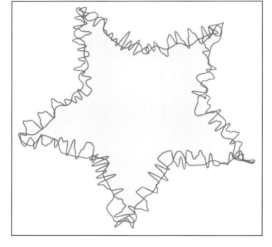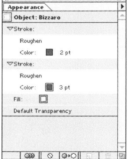

Figure 2.10
An example of Bizzaro's plain fill with no effects.

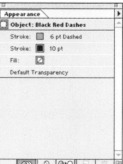

Figure 2.11
Here, you see how dashed lines can be used effectively, as in Black Red Dashes.

- *Fantasmic*—This vaporous style uses blend modes to achieve its surrealistic feel (see Figure 2.12).

- *Purple Puddle*—Using an offset path on a fill only can make the object's fill smaller than the object. This style adds a Roughen effect for a liquid appearance (see Figure 2.13).

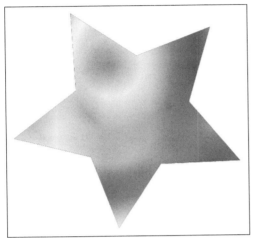 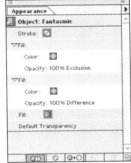

Figure 2.12
Fantasmic's style uses blend modes to achieve a surrealistic feel.

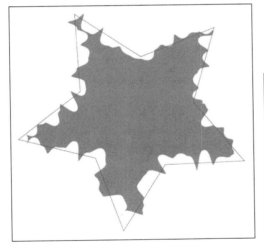 

Figure 2.13
Purple Puddle uses the offset path only on a fill to make the object's fill smaller than the object and adds a Roughen effect.

- *Patriotic Ribbon*—Brushes are a natural for styles. Figure 2.14 shows three Calligraphic brushes combined for a Ribbon. Try changing the colors to three tints of the same hue for a satin ribbon.

- *Rainbow Plaid*—Even old standards, like the rainbow gradient, are given new life when combined with opacity (see Figure 2.15).

- *Rounded Edges*—Dashed lines with rounded caps and joins can look like beads or petals. Adjust the weight of the stroke and size of the dashes to see how much this can vary (see Figure 2.16).

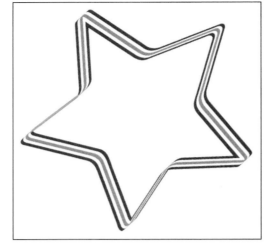

Figure 2.14
Patriotic Ribbon uses three
Calligraphic brushes combined
into a Ribbon.

Figure 2.15
In Rainbow Plaid, old standards
such as the rainbow gradient are
given new life.

Figure 2.16
Rounded Edges features dashed
lines with rounded caps and joins.

- *Scribbly*—Dramatic effects can be applied to both stroke and fill (see Figure 2.17).

- *Soft Red Highlight*—This style provides a smooth, 3D-modeled look. Using it is also an easy way to do buttons for Web pages (see Figure 2.18).

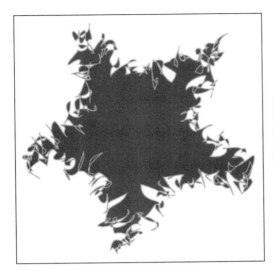

Figure 2.17
Scribbly shows dramatic effects applied to both stroke and fill.

Figure 2.18
Soft Red Highlight's smooth, 3D-modeled look.

- *Rustic Pen*—When Outline Stroke is applied as a Live Effect and Roughen is applied on top of it, the effect is applied slightly differently to the inside and outside of the stroke, creating a beautiful, uneven, and weathered appearance (see Figure 2.19).

- *Textured Light*—Patterns, gradients, and opacity combine for a futuristic, industrial style (see Figure 2.20).

- *Sketchy*—Multiple strokes with a loose scribble and tweak setting create a free-form, loose sketch look (see Figure 2.21).

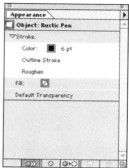

Figure 2.19
A result of the Rustic Pen style, when Outline Stroke is applied as a Live Effect and Roughen is applied on top of it.

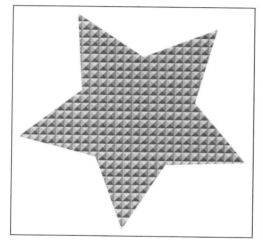

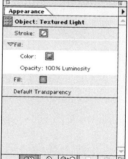

Figure 2.20
Textured Light features patterns, gradients, and opacity that combine for an interesting style.

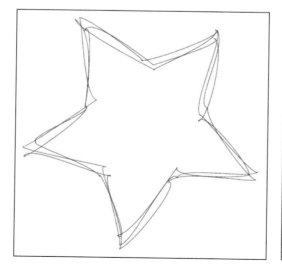

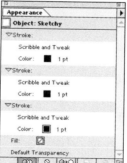

Figure 2.21
Sketchy uses multiple strokes with a loose scribble and tweak setting to create an unusual sketch look.

- *Cast Shadow*—This style provides a dramatic back-lit shadow by using the Free Distort effect. It also works well with text (see Figure 2.22).

- *Ice Pot*—At last, Illustrator now provides a way to preserve your gradient angles! You no longer have to apply linear gradients with the same vertical angle and adjust them later with the Gradient Vector tool. Now, you can adjust your gradient angles as you like and save and reapply them as styles (see Figure 2.23).

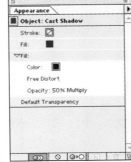

Figure 2.22
Cast Shadow provides a dramatic back-lit shadow, courtesy of Free Distort.

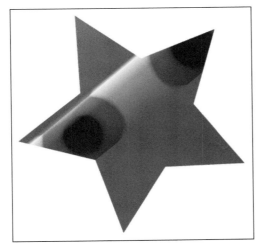

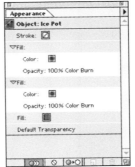

Figure 2.23
Ice Pot uses blend modes on gradients.

- *Acidic*—This style provides another example of gradients, patterns, opacity, and blend modes combined for interesting effects (see Figure 2.24).

- *Engraving Plate*—The smooth, 3-D border around this reflective copper image is a result of multiple strokes (see Figure 2.25).

- *Bristly*—This style uses ZigZag applied at both the fill and stroke level for an organic feel (see Figure 2.26).

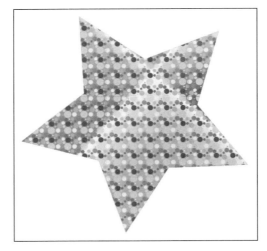

Figure 2.24
Acidic provides another example of gradients, patterns, opacity, and blend modes combined.

Figure 2.25
A smooth, 3-D border around the reflective copper image in Engraving Plate is a result of multiple strokes.

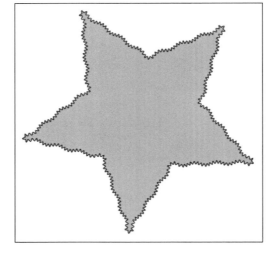

Figure 2.26
Bristly uses the ZigZag effect at both the fill and stroke level for an organic look.

Additional RGB Standard Styles

The styles for the RGB documents are mostly the same as the CMYK versions. However, Illustrator also contains three RGB styles that make use of Photoshop filters (which work only on RGB images). Take a look at these styles as well so that you can see the range of possibilities in the Styles palette:

- *Rough Steel*—The Grain filter is used on two different gradient fills along with a change of blend mode (see Figure 2.27).

- *Froth*—Crystallize and Ocean Ripple are used on a pattern fill (see Figure 2.28).

- *Endorific*—This style uses a Free Distort effect to shrink and change the shape (see Figure 2.29).

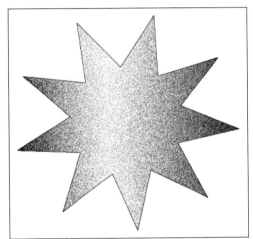

Figure 2.27
Rough Steel features the Grain filter used on two different gradient fills and a change of blend mode.

Figure 2.28
Froth uses Crystallize and Ocean Ripple on a pattern fill.

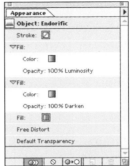

Figure 2.29
Endorfic uses a Free Distort effect to shrink and change the shape.

Deconstructing a Style

Your first step in learning how to create a style is to analyze the styles that are already created for you. (That's one of the reasons that I included all these screen shots of the standard styles.) When you click on a style (even with nothing selected), the style's appearance is reported in the Appearance palette. You can then see exactly how the style is constructed.

Now, take an in-depth look at how a few of the standard styles were created. Figure 2.30 shows the toucan from the Ultimate Symbol Nature's Icons collection. Figure 2.31 shows the same image with the Sketchy style applied. How would you know to create a style like that to produce a sketch-like result? If you don't know, you can easily find out by looking at the Appearance palette (refer to Figure 2.21).

Figure 2.30
The "plain" toucan from the Ultimate Symbol Nature's Icons collection.

Figure 2.31
You can convert the toucan to a sketch with one mouse click on the Sketchy style.

Sketchy (refer to Figure 2.21), has three 1-pt strokes, no fill, and uses default transparency. Each stroke uses the Scribble and Tweak effect. The Appearance palette gives you the basic information, but then you need to explore a bit further to really figure out what makes the style tick.

2.1 Exploring the Sketchy Style

Take a closer look at how a style is put together:

1. Create a new RGB document.

2. Draw a simple star shape and apply the Sketchy style to it.

3. In the Appearance palette, click on the Scribble and Tweak entry under the first stroke. Figure 2.32 shows the Scribble and Tweak effect dialog box. Both controls are set to 5%. Click on Cancel to close the dialog box.

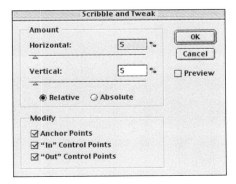

Figure 2.32
You can see the actual settings for any applied effects by double-clicking on the effect name in the Appearance palette.

4. Repeat Step 3 for the other two instances of the Scribble and Tweak effect. Notice that they have the same settings as the first Scribble and Tweak effect.

5. If you want to see what happens if you alter the settings, first unlink the object from the style (from the Styles palette menu, select Break Link to Style). Now, you can experiment and not change the original version of the style.

6. Try clicking on the top Scribble and Tweak entry in the Appearance palette and changing the amounts to 12%. Then, click on the Stroke Color entry directly underneath and change the Stroke color to green.

7. To see what happens to your style when you change the object, choose Object|Path|Add Anchor Points. This command (which doesn't have an Effects version) adds a point in between every two points on the path. The resulting star looks even more complex.

Effects Vs. Filters

Just in case you're curious, most effects also have filter versions. However, the items on the dialog boxes for effects and filters often differ from one another because of the need to keep the effect "live."

Deconstructing that style was easy. It had no fills, and the stroke was a solid line. Now, look at one that's a bit more complex. Figure 2.33 shows the Crusty style (it's in the Strokes and Fills [RGB] Styles palette that you need to load via the Window|Style Libraries command).

Figure 2.33
The Crusty style contains a combination of effects with some applied to the stroke and others to the entire object.

Notice the Appearance palette shown in Figure 2.33. The 6-pt stroke entry is gray, but the three entries directly under it are white. This arrangement indicates that the three entries "belong" to the stroke. The color and the 6 pt stroke amount are clearly properties of the stroke. However, the drop shadow and the Pointillize effect are also properties of the stroke. They don't affect the fill at all.

The fill has no effects applied to it. You can tell because the items that follow it are separated by a thin white line and appear in gray. Therefore, the Dry Brush effect is applied to the entire object after all the other effects. The Dry Brush really shows up on the stroke area only because few filters and effects other than Grain or Pointillize make any changes on a solid area of color (if you're a Photoshop user, you can safely translate what you know about Photoshop filters to filter effects in Illustrator).

The Pointillize effect applied to the stroke, however, is applied *after* the drop shadow (it comes below it in the Appearance palette). Therefore, the drop shadow itself is pointillized. The Pointillize effect causes the irregularity on the drop shadow, and the final Dry Brush filter accentuates it.

Altering Styles

Altering a style is just a matter of selecting a style and making changes to it in the Appearance palette. Say you want a style similar to Soft Red Highlight. You could modify the style or create a new one very quickly. First, select the style you want to alter. If you want to keep the original (always a good idea), choose Duplicate from the Styles pop-out menu and work on the copy. You might want to start by filling an object with the style so that you can have a larger preview of the modified style than the thumbnail in the Appearance palette.

Altering a Style

In this project, you'll apply the Soft Red Highlight style to an object and then change some of the items that create the style.

1. Open a new document in Illustrator. The default page size is fine.

2. Click on the Soft Red Highlight style and choose Duplicate Style from the side menu in the Styles palette. The duplicate is named Soft Red Highlight 1.

3. Create a star shape or any other filled shape. Leave the shape selected.

4. Click on the Soft Red Highlight 1 style to apply it.

5. Highlight the item in the Appearance palette that you want to change. For this example, click on the gradient fill Color entry to highlight it, as shown in Figure 2.34. The Gradient palette displays the selected gradient.

6. Click on the red stop in the Gradient palette, as shown in Figure 2.35, and then change the color of the stop to green by adjusting the sliders in the Color palette.

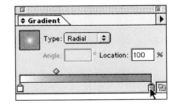

Figure 2.34
(Left) Click on the entry in the Appearance palette that you want to change.

Figure 2.35
(Right) You need to first select the color stop before you can change the color in a gradient.

7. Select the Gradient tool from the Tool palette and drag across the shape to reposition the gradient angle.

8. Choose Add New Fill from the side menu of the Appearance palette. Fill with the Blue Tablecloth pattern and change the blend mode (on the Opacity palette) to Saturation.

9. Target the Object entry in the Appearance palette and choose Effect| Texture|Texturizer. Figure 2.36 shows the settings to use.

10. Add a glass effect (Effect|Distort|Glass). Set the Distortion to 20 and the Smoothness to 3. Choose the Tiny Lens. Leave the Scaling at 100%.

11. You don't need to leave an effect where you applied it. The Glass effect also colors the drop shadow, which, in this case, is not an improvement. Click on the Glass effect and drag it on top of the gray Fill entry for the gradient fill. Don't release the mouse button yet. As you begin to

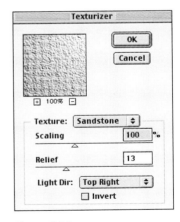

Figure 2.36
Use these settings to apply the Texturizer effect to your shape.

drag the Glass effect entry downward, a double line appears under each item as you slowly drag past it. Release the mouse button when the double line appears below the gradient's Color entry.

12. Double-click on the Drop Shadow effect entry and change the X and Y offsets to 27 pts. Figure 2.37 shows the Appearance palette as it should now look. Figure 2.38 shows the finished effect.

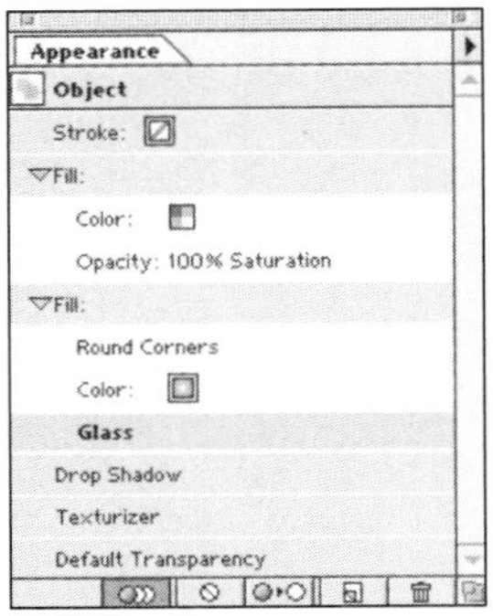

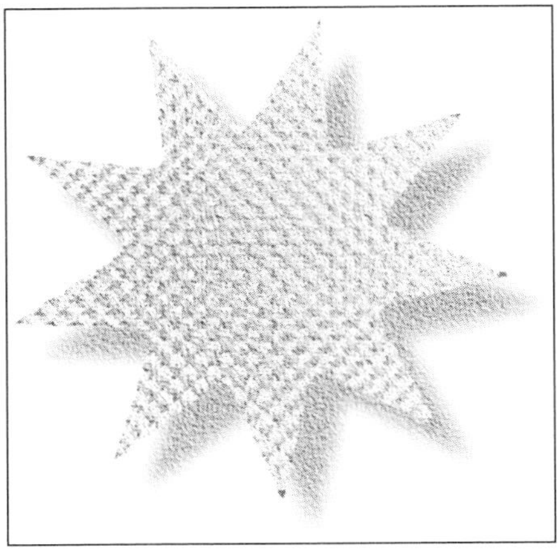

Figure 2.37

(Left) The Appearance palette reflects the changes that you made to the copied style.

Figure 2.38

(Right) The Texturizer and Glass effects make a huge difference to the look of the object.

When you've changed your style to the point where you want to save it, you have two choices. You can replace the style you started with by choosing Replace "Soft Red Highlight" (or whatever style it was) from the Appearance palette pop-out menu, or you can create a new style for the Appearance by choosing New Style from the Styles palette pop-out. If you have any objects that use the original style in your document and you choose Replace, they are updated to the new style. If you choose New Style, they retain the original style.

Styles can be deleted and duplicated within the palette, just as swatches and brushes can from their respective palettes. To delete a swatch, drag it to the trashcan icon. To duplicate it, select it and click on the new swatch icon. To rename it, double-click on it to open the Style options dialog box and enter a new name.

Styles are global, like spot and global colors and patterns. This means that if you have several objects that use a style and the style is later modified, the objects are updated to the new style. If you would rather not update your object, the best thing to do is to disassociate a style from the object. Do so by selecting the object and then clicking the Break Link to Style button in the Styles palette.

Note: Any time a named style is modified while an object using that style is selected, the link is automatically broken.

Style Libraries

Styles can be saved, stored, opened, and applied as libraries, just as swatches and brushes can. Illustrator 9 contains several Style libraries, along with default libraries (CMYK and RGB). When you do an Easy installation or a Custom installation and choose to install additional Style libraries, several libraries are installed into the Style Libraries folder in the Illustrator application folder. You can access these libraries by choosing Window|Style Libraries and selecting the desired library from the pop-out menu.

Just like the swatch and brush libraries, Style libraries can be created simply by saving an Illustrator document that contains the styles you want to save. You also can open these libraries by selecting Window|Style Library. If you want your custom Style libraries to appear in the pop-out list, place the AI9 files into the Style Libraries folder. Or, you can open any Illustrator 9 file and retrieve its styles by choosing Other from the pop-out list and navigating to the location of the file.

You can't add, delete, or edit any open Style library. You can, of course, go back and alter the original document. The only Style library you can edit is the current library that is in your Styles palette. That library is saved with your document. The Styles palette is directly linked to a document. If you have no open document, then you have nothing in the Styles palette. If you save a style, it's saved only in the Styles palette for that document, and you don't see it when you create a new document. You can reuse it only by opening the document as a Style library.

RGB Vs. CMYK

Illustrator has supported both the CMYK and RGB color modes since version 7. Version 9 is the first version to force you to choose a specific color mode (CMYK if the document is intended for print, RGB if the document is intended for Web or dynamic media). Some effects (based on Photoshop bitmap filters) can be used only in RGB mode. For this reason, some of the Style libraries distinguish between RGB and CMYK styles.

Using Styles and Appearances

You've read a lot of abstract material about creating styles and using the new palettes in Illustrator. Now, you can try out the new features.

PROJECT 2.3 Updating a High School Logo

With this project, you'll learn how to use the Appearance palette to apply additional strokes, fills, and effects to an object. You'll also apply bitmap effects in RGB mode.

1. Open the file HALEYHIGH.AI from the CD-ROM enclosed with this book. Think of it as your teenager's high school logo (if you don't have a teenager, imagine that you do!), and someone on the PTA, knowing of your advanced graphic skills, has volunteered you to update it. As you can see in Figure 2.39, the logo is a very plain two-color design (three colors if you count white), designed long before affordable color printers and Web pages raised the bar on what is expected in even a simple school logo.

Can I Add a Style So it Is Always Available?

If you really like a style, you can make it one of the standard styles by adding it to the Illustrator startup document. In the Illustrator application folder, you'll find a document for CMYK startup and another one for RGB startup. Open the startup file in Illustrator (it's a regular Adobe Illustrator document). If you place your styled object into the open startup file and then choose File|Save, you can make a permanent addition to the startup file. Close Illustrator and relaunch. Your new style appears whenever you create a new document of the same color type. (Colors, Gradients, and so on attached to startup files also become available as defaults.)

Figure 2.39
The original Haley High logo is
somewhat plain and boring.

2. First, you need to get used to using the Layers palette to target and select. Click on the disclosure triangle to expand the contents of the Two Color Logo layer in the Layers palette. The items in this layer are all named with the default names (within the <> marks) that Illustrator gives them at the time of creation.

3. Rename the items in the Layers palette to make them easier to identify. The first item is a <group>. If you click on the disclosure triangle for this group, you see that it consists of compound paths. These compounds were created from the original type objects used for Haley High School Comets with the outline type filter. Double-click on <groups> in the Layers palette to open the Options dialog box and rename this to "Text". Do the same thing to rename the <path> items below Text. Rename the top path "Comet". Rename the path beneath it "Tail" and the last item "Background". Figure 2.40 shows the renamed layers in the Layers palette.

Figure 2.40
Rename the items in the Layers palette for clarity.

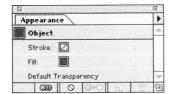

Figure 2.41
If your Appearance palette looks like this, you've correctly targeted the Background layer.

4. Target the background by clicking on the selection icon next to Background in the Layers palette. (At the object level, there is really no difference between targeting and selecting; however, to minimize confusion and to get you used to this new functionality, I will use the term *target* for these exercises.) Notice that the rectangle is now selected, and the Appearance palette displays *Object* to indicate the current selection is targeted at the object level. The Appearance palette, as you can see in Figure 2.41, also displays a blue fill and stroke of None.

5. Highlight the stroke in the Appearance palette by clicking on it. Change it to black. In the Stroke palette, make it 10 pts.

6. Now, you're going to add an additional stroke to give the border more definition. Choose Add New Stroke from the pop-out menu of the Appearance palette. Change its color to white and its weight to 4 pts.

7. The border already looks better, but if you add a simple effect, it will stand out even more. With the white stroke highlighted, choose Effect| Path|Offset Path. Enter –5 pts and click on OK. Observe in Figure 2.42 how the second stroke now sits neatly inside the first.

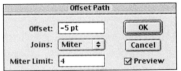

Figure 2.42
The Offset Path effect moves the white stroke to the inner edge of the black stroke.

8. Highlight the blue fill in the Appearance palette. Bring the Gradient palette to the front and click on the default black-and-white gradient to change the fill to a gradient.

9. Modify the gradient by changing it to Radial in the Gradient palette. (Double-click on the Gradient palette tab to see the options.) Select the black color stop by clicking on it and change the color to a dark blue (either pick a new color in the Color palette, after changing it to CMYK, or drag the original blue swatch from the Swatches palette on top of the stop in the Gradient palette). Adjust the angle of the gradient by selecting the Gradient tool, clicking in the center of the comet, and then dragging to the lower-left corner of the rectangle. The gradient is now evenly dispersed in the rectangle. To make the gradient denser away from the comet, grab the blue color stop in the Gradient palette and drag it to the middle.

10. To now give the background even more depth, add another gradient stop by clicking on the far right of the gradient (where the blue stop was) to add an additional blue stop. Click on this stop to highlight it, and in the Color palette, click+drag the black slider (K) all the way to the right to increase its black percentage. This action gives you a smoother looking gradient than changing the stop to pure black (without the blue). If you want to see the difference, change the stop to black by clicking on the black swatch in the Color palette and then undoing if you don't like the result. Figure 2.43 shows the Gradient palette with the radial gradient defined.

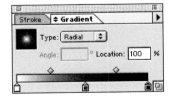

Figure 2.43
Create a tri-color gradient for the background.

11. Now, you're going to jazz up the comet in a similar way. Begin by targeting the comet in the Layers palette.

12. Click on the gradient in the Gradient palette to paint the comet. Although it is now painted with the same dark blue gradient used in the background, you can quickly change this color. First, drag the middle blue gradient stop off the palette to delete it. Next, drag the gold swatch from the Swatches palette on top of the black stop to replace it. Then, select this stop and enter "85" into the Location field.

13. Use the Gradient tool to adjust the gradient angle. Click on the upper left of the comet close to the edge (about 11 o'clock) and drag across at a diagonal (to about 5 o'clock).

14. You'll use this gradient later, so save it by dragging the thumbnail from the Color palette to the Swatches palette.

15. This logo is already starting to look great, except that the comet is blending in too much with its tail. To define it better, choose Effects| Stylize|InnerGlow. With mode set to Screen, Opacity to 100%, and Blur at 5 pts, as shown in Figure 2.44, click on OK to apply the effect.

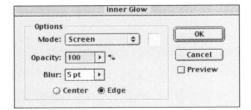

Figure 2.44
Add the Inner Glow effect to the comet.

16. To make the comet's tail really come to life, you can add some additional strokes. Target the tail in the Layers palette. Select the stroke in the Appearance palette and set the color to white and the weight to 1 pt.

17. With the stroke still selected, choose Effect|Distort & Transform|Roughen and set the size to 2%, detail to 5, and Points to Smooth (see Figure 2.45). See how the stroke now appears to be a separate path from the fill, with the Roughen effect applied only to it?

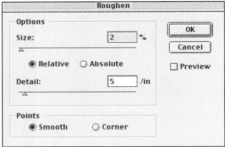

Figure 2.45
The Roughen dialog box, showing your changes.

18. Add an additional stroke. Leave it white, but change the weight to 2 pts. Now, select Roughen in the Appearance palette and Option/Alt+drag it from the first stroke to the new stroke. This action copies the effect, settings and all, and applies it to the second stroke.

19. Add one more stroke. Change the weight to 3 pts and the color to the same gold used in the fill. Once again, drag+copy the Roughen effect to the new stroke.

20. To apply transparency to the entire object, highlight the Default Transparency line at the bottom of the list in the Appearance palette and set Transparency to 50% in the Transparency palette.

21. Next, you'll add a new fill to give the tail a little more "flare." After you add the new fill, drag it beneath the strokes but above the original fill. With the new fill still selected, choose Effects|Offset Path and set it for –3 pts.

22. You won't see the effect of the Offset Path effect until you change the fill and the blend mode. Change the fill to a gradient. The last gradient you used was the white-to-gold, which should still be in the Gradient palette. If it's not, select it from the Swatches palette.

23. When you have the white-to-gold gradient, use the Gradient tool to reset the gradient vector. Click in the center of the comet and drag to the end of the comet's tail.

24. Change the blend mode by highlighting the new fill in the Appearance palette and changing the blend mode to Hard Light in the Transparency palette. (You'll get a chance to experiment more with blend modes in Chapter 3.) Figure 2.46 shows the Appearance palette at this stage.

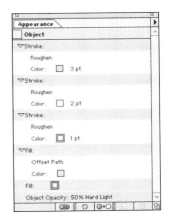

Figure 2.46

The Appearance palette shows the changes that you've made to the comet's tail.

25. With transparency applied to the comet's tail, there is no reason to keep it above the letters. You can scale it and move it so that it overlaps the text and do it as a Live Effect. Because you want to apply the same transformations to both the comet and its tail, select both objects and press Command/Ctrl+G to group them. Notice the change in the hierarchy in the Layers palette?

26. Target the group. The Appearance palette now shows "Group" above the black line to show at which level the current selection is targeted. Note that the fill and strokes are set to None because no fills or strokes appear at this level. The default transparency of 100 percent for the group is used for the same reason.

27. Choose Effects|Distort & Transform|Transform. Turn on Preview and change the scale to 130% for Horizontal and Vertical, and Move to –20 pts horizontal and –35 pts vertical, as shown in Figure 2.47.

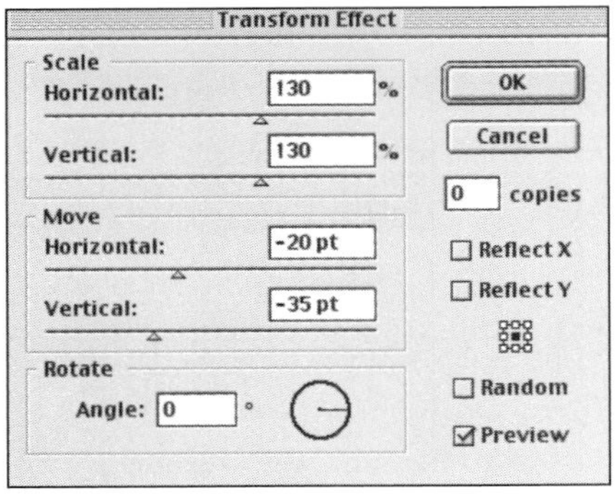

Figure 2.47

Use these settings to add a live transformation to the comet and its tail.

28. The comet's tail now has transparency, but it's not interacting with the text. To change this, select the <group> in the Layers palette and drag it above the Text to reorder the objects. You'll know it's in the right place when you see a thin double line appear above the text layer as you drag the group. If you see, instead, a set of large arrowheads pointing inward on the text layer, don't release the mouse button. You'll *add* the group to the text layer if you release the mouse button at that point.

29. The only thing left to update now are the letters. Target the Text group in the Layers palette. When you have the text targeted, choose Effects|Stylize|Drop Shadow. Set the Opacity to 100%, the X and Y Offset to 7 pts, and the Blur to 7 pts. Also, click on Color and set the color to black. If black does not come up automatically when you turn on color, click on the color proxy to open the Color Picker and change the color to black within the picker. Figure 2.48 shows the finished logo.

Figure 2.48

The logo, updated and current.

That's it! You have now brought the old high school logo into the new millennium! Save the file as HALEYHIGH FINAL.AI.

Next, take a quick look at how you can further update the logo with raster effects in RGB mode—something you might want to do if you plan to use it for a Web page.

1. Open the file HALEYHIGH FINAL.AI that you just saved.

2. Because the file is in CMYK mode, the bitmap effects are disabled. To change the file to RGB, choose File|Document Color Mode|RGB.

3. Styles are easy to save, open, and use as libraries. To see a few examples of what you can do with bitmap effects, import the Style library for this file from the CD-ROM. Choose Window|Style Libraries|Other and select the file RGBBACKGROUNDS.AI. A new palette with four new styles opens.

4. Target the background in the Layers palette, and one by one, click on the different styles in the RGBBACKGROUNDS palette. Observe that the effects are applied only to the fill so that the strokes remain clean and sharp. Also, notice that the order in which the effects are applied makes a difference. Try switching some of them around to see how this changes the look.

5. Do some experimenting. The bitmap effects are all located in the Effect menu. Apply them to the object's fill. All four of these sample styles were created with the same blue-to-white gradient originally used in the logo. Try experimenting with different fills, including patterns. Figure 2.49 shows a possible RGB image.

> **Caution When Working with Raster Effects**
>
> These effects use a lot of memory! You might want to change the status bar to show how much free memory you have left (the pop-out next to the zoom level in the bottom of your document window) and keep an eye on it. If you notice a slowdown in performance, you are probably getting low on memory and should save your file. The larger the object that you are applying the raster effect to, the quicker the memory will go down. If the memory gets too low, you get a message that says the system doesn't have enough memory to process an appearance. When this occurs, part or all of your artwork may then appear in Outline mode. Saving and closing your file purges the undos, which will free more memory. You can then reopen the file and change it back to Preview mode. If this trick doesn't work, try quitting and relaunching Illustrator.

Figure 2.49
This background style has Pointillize, Gaussian Blur, and Sprayed Strokes.

6. When you finish, save the file as HALEYHIGHRGB.AI. You'll learn about exporting to various Web formats in Chapter 12.

PROJECT 2.4 Creating a Flyer

With this project, you'll continue to work with multiple strokes, fills, and effects. You'll also add brushes into the mix and learn how to target and work with text, which can be just a little tricky. The project is to make a flyer with a country-crafts feel to it for a Garden and Crafts Faire. You'll be amazed at how easy it is to use effects to achieve a more "handmade" style.

Creating a Background Object

In this part of the project, you'll create a simple rectangle and change it into a complex and exciting background:

1. Open the file FLYER.AI from the CD-ROM. It's a very simple file—just five circles together like a bunch of grapes. And, that's what you're going to do with it—make it into a scatter brush to create a hand-stamped or stenciled look of a grapevine. (You'll learn more about creating brushes in Chapter 4.)

2. First, you need to duplicate the Grape Leaf brush so that you can quickly create a new brush with the same settings. Select the Grape Leaf brush in the Brushes palette and drag it to the New Brush icon at the bottom of the palette. This action creates an identical brush. Next, press Command/Ctrl+A to select all the purple circles and then Option/Alt+drag them onto the new Grape Leaf brush you created. When the Brush Options dialog box opens, you will see that all the scatter settings are the same as the Leaf Brush. Rename this brush "Grapes".

3. With the Grapes brush created, you don't need the objects in the document, so select all again and delete.

4. Create a rectangle 400 pts x 200 pts.

5. Target the rectangle in the Appearance palette. Highlight the stroke and change the fill to brown. (An easy way to get brown is to pick the orange swatch in the Swatches palette and then drag the K slider to the right to add black to it. You can then adjust the other sliders to tweak the hue.) Change the stroke weight to 7 pts.

6. Add a new stroke. Keep the color and the stroke weight. Choose Effects|Path|Offset Path and set it to 30 pts.

7. Add another new stroke. The color doesn't matter, but change the weight to 1 pt. Then, with this stroke highlighted, select the Grape Leaf brush.

8. Do the same thing again (add a new stroke) and this time select the Grapes brush. Even though the brushes have the same setting, notice how they are still applied randomly to each stroke? The grapes seem a little small compared to their leaves, so change the stroke weight to 1.5 pts.

9. Now that you've built the border, it's time to work on the fill. You want to give the image a more textured background. How about a lace or brocade look? Highlight the fill and change the color to the lightest of the gray swatches in the Swatches palette (20% black).

10. Add a new fill and select the Azure Rings pattern. See how quickly you achieved the country look (see Figure 2.50)? But, the art still looks computer generated. Now, you can add some transparency and effects to give it the craftsy style you're aiming for. Figure 2.51 shows the Appearance palette.

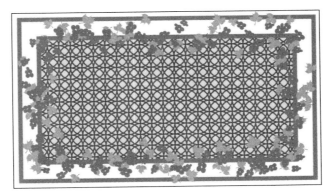

Figure 2.50
A few fast effects produce the start of the flyer.

11. Highlight the Azure Rings fill and set the Opacity to 50%. The image still looks a bit overpowering, so change the blend mode to Overlay. Now, it looks like lace or white lattice.

12. Highlight the Grape Leaf stroke and choose Effects|Stylize|Inner Glow. Set the mode to Screen, Opacity to 75%, and Blur to 5 pts. Then, turn on Edge.

13. Option/Alt+drag the Inner Glow effect from the Grape Leaf stroke to the Grapes stroke to copy it. When this stroke is applied, these settings seem to soften up the grapes a little too much. Double-click on the effect under the Grapes stroke and change the Blur to 3 pts.

14. The grapevine looks great, but now you need to give the brown strokes a more rustic look to match. Highlight either of the two brown strokes and choose Effect|Path|Outline Stroke. When this effect is applied, all effects applied to the same stroke are applied separately to each side of the stroke.

15. With the stroke still highlighted, choose Effects|Distort & Transform| Roughen. Set the size to 1 pt and the detail to 4. After you apply this effect, you need to move it so that it is directly beneath the Outline Stroke effect. This way, the Outline Stroke effect is applied first.

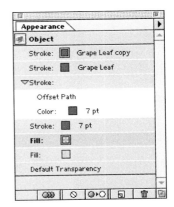

Figure 2.51
The Appearance palette shows the various additional strokes and fills.

16. To soften the stroke, choose Effects|Stylize|Feather. Set the radius to 3 pts. Again, make sure that feather is positioned beneath Outline Stroke and Roughen.

17. To apply these same effects to the other brown stroke, simply Option/Alt+drag to copy them. Be sure to get them in the right order.

18. Option/Alt+drag the Feather effect one more time to the pattern fill to soften it up and make it retreat a little more into the background. Figure 2.52 shows the finished background. Figure 2.53 shows the Appearance palette.

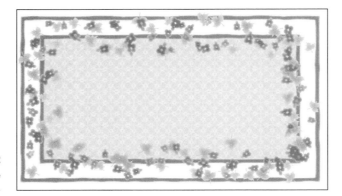

Figure 2.52
The finished grape leaf background.

Figure 2.53
Look at all those fills, strokes, and effects!

19. Now, you're done with the background of the flyer. Choose New Style from the Styles palette pop-out menu to save the style. Name it "Grapes & Lace".

Adding Text

Now that you have made the background, it's time to add some text to it. Anything you can do with styles (multiple fills, strokes, and effects) can be applied to type objects. This means that you can do things with type in Illustrator 9 that were not possible in previous versions. For example, you can now apply brush strokes to type or give type gradient fills without having to convert it to outlines first. This means the type remains fully editable!

Setting Type

In this section, you'll set the type that you need by doing the following:

1. Create a new layer for the text by clicking on the New Layer button in the Layers palette. This way, you can apply effects at the layer level that affect only the type. Also, you can change the view mode independently for each layer.

2. Make sure the new layer is highlighted in the palette and drag a rectangle inside the art you have already created. Create it so that it fits inside the grapevines. This rectangle will be your type container. Select

Command/Ctrl+A and use the Align palette to center the two objects together by clicking on the Horizontal Align Center button.

3. Select the Area Type tool (click on the Type tool in the Tool palette and hold down long enough to see all the type tools; then drag over to the right to select the one with the letter *T* inside the box). Click it anywhere on the edge of the new rectangle. Make sure the rectangle is selected before you do this. Now, the type cursor is inside the box.

4. Type the following, with carriage returns:

    "Garden & Crafts Faire"

    "Saturday, May 12, 10 a.m. to 4 p.m."

    Notice that the type is created with default black and whatever font and character attributes you worked with previously—or the default font and character attributes.

5. Look at the Layers palette in Figure 2.54. Notice that the first few words of the type appear as the name of the object. Also, notice that the text appears in the Layers palette as a single object. It doesn't have a disclosure triangle like a group does. Target the text in the Layers palette and take a look at what shows up in the Appearance palette. Although the black fill of the selected text is visible in the Tool and Color palettes, the Appearance palette shows a fill and stroke of None. It also shows a line for "text." Above the line, it shows that a "type object" has been targeted. This indicates that the text has a fill assigned to it at the text level, but the type object does not have a fill or stroke.

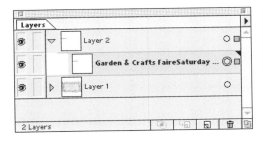 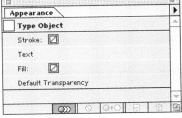

Figure 2.54
The Layers and Appearance palettes show the type characteristics.

Think of "text" as individual characters, or what can be selected by drag+ highlighting, whereas the "type object" is what is selected when you click on the type baseline with the Selection tool. Sometimes you need to give an individual character a different color fill or stroke than the rest of the text, and in this case, you highlight the character(s) and assign a new fill or stroke at the text level. However, because you'll be giving all the text the same Fill and Stroke colors, it is much simpler to work at the type object level to paint.

Styling the Type

You will be working at the text level to assign different point sizes to the text, but because character attributes such as font, point size, leading, and so on are not recorded in the Appearance palette, this will not make a difference or trigger the Mixed Selection mode.

1. If it's not open already, press Command/Ctrl+M to open the Character and Paragraph palettes. With the type object selected, click on the center button in the Paragraph palette.

2. In the Character palette, choose a new font. Use any font that you feel is appropriate, preferably a bold or heavy typeface. I used ITC Esprit, which is included on the Illustrator CD.

3. Remembering the difference between working with "text" (highlighting individual characters) and working with "type objects" (targeting or selecting by baseline), drag+highlight the first line "Garden & Crafts Faire" to change the point size. I know the difference between "text" and "type object" is confusing, but after you work with it for a while, it will become clearer. Change the point size of the first line until it causes a line break after the ampersand (for me, this broke nicely at 48 pts). Drag+highlight the second line and adjust the point size so that it fits neatly under the first. I set this at 18 pts.

4. Because point size will be the only nonuniversal attribute for the type object, you can work from now on by targeting the type object. Selecting the text by the baseline automatically targets the type object, or you can target the type object by clicking on the Targeting icon in the Layers palette.

5. Applying effects can really alter the look of a font. Try out a few for fun. With the type object targeted, choose Effects|Distort & Transform|Scribble and Tweak. With Preview on, adjust the settings lower. I found that setting Horizontal to 4% and Vertical to 6% with Relative on worked well with my font. When you find a setting you like, apply it. Try some of the other vector effects, such as ZigZag and even Punk & Bloat. You will probably want to keep the settings low when working with type, but don't be afraid to experiment. Remember that these effects can all be used in conjunction with each other, and that they work differently depending on the order they are applied. When you are happy with the look you have achieved, move on to the next step.

6. To continue with the hand-crafted look, choose Effects|Stylize|Inner Glow and set the blur to 3 pts. Doing so makes the type look like the ink is still wet. Turn on the preview for Layer 1 to see how this looks with the background.

A Fast Way to Change View Modes

You will find working on the type much faster if the background layer is in Outline mode. To change the view mode, Command/Ctrl+click on the Eye icon of Layer 1. Now, you won't have to wait for the background to redraw as you adjust the type, and you can still view the type in Preview mode.

7. This result may seem a little too soft for you. If it does, sharpen it up by making the stroke (remember you are targeting the type object) black and 1 pt. Now, drag your effects to the fill, positioning them after the color.

8. The black works well to give the type an antiquated printing press look. Change the color of the fill to create a watercolor look. Purple, green, and brown work for harmony. Yellow, orange, or peach work for contrast. With the Type object targeted, save the style and then save your file. Figure 2.55 shows the finished file.

Figure 2.55
The finished crafts flyer.

Now that you've finished the second project, I would like you to see how the Grapes & Lace style you created can be applied to type (and for that matter, any compound path). Go ahead and save the file you just finished as FLYER FINAL.AI, but don't close it. Instead, do a Save As and name it FLYER LETTER.AI so that you have a new file with the style to play with.

1. Select all and delete. Make sure you are working in the new file, not the file you just put so much work into!

2. Type one letter. Choose a letter that will create a compound path, such as capital *R* or *B*. Use a bold typeface. Drag the letter out by its bounding box so that it's very large, at least a quarter of the page.

3. With the letter targeted, select the Grapes & Lace style you created. Figure 2.56 shows the style applied to the letter *G* from the Adobe Garamond Bold font.

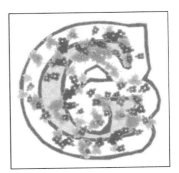

Figure 2.56
A medieval manuscript illuminator would have killed for this feature!

4. If the grapevines seem too big or busy to you, you can easily change their size in the Appearance palette by selecting the stroke and adjusting the stroke weight. You can also make other adjustments to fit the font and size of your type object better, such as changing the offset path setting for the third stroke so that it's closer to the fill.

Moving On

You learned a tremendous amount in this chapter, thanks to the talents of Brenda Sutherland of Adobe Systems. You learned how to use the new Layers, Appearance, and Transparency palettes and how to target items and apply effects, new strokes, and new fills. You also learned how to create styles and save them for future use, and you learned how to create area text and apply effects to it while keeping the text live. Finally, you learned how to apply a decorative style to text.

In Chapter 3, you'll learn about the transparency and the new blend modes, and you'll also learn how to apply some vintage Illustrator color tricks.

Chapter 3

Color Effects

The most exciting new Illustrator 9 feature is the arrival of transparency—long anticipated by Adobe enthusiasts who envied the ability of CorelDRAW and Freehand users to create areas of varying opacities. However, Adobe added even more features, including Photoshop-style blend modes, to make the program more exciting.

By Sherry London

Illustrator and Color

What facilities has Adobe given you for color manipulation in Illustrator? Many of the third-party color filters are gone. You can use some native color filters and the Mix Hard and Mix Soft commands on the Pathfinder palette. However, the major advance in color manipulation is the addition of transparency and blend modes—and what a major advance it is! Let's look first at the "old" color commands and filters and then examine how some of Illustrator's new filters affect image colors.

Before Illustrator 8, several third-party vendors offered filters that could make interesting color changes to objects. Few of these filters are compatible with the current version of Illustrator. Notable exceptions that remain on the market are Virtual Mirror Corporation's Vector Studio, which includes filters called Color Factory, Gradient Factory, and Gradient Textures, and KPT Vector Effects 1.5 (now owned by Corel Corporation), which contains a filter called Color Tweak.

The Colors Filters

Figure 3.1 shows the Colors Filters menu options. You can adjust the components of the CMYK colors in an object; you can blend colors front to back, horizontally, or vertically; you can change colors to CMYK, RGB, or grayscale; and you can invert and saturate colors. However, you can't randomize colors as you can with the Corel KPT Vector Effects Color Tweak filter or Virtual Mirror's Color Factory, nor can you fade them, as you can in Photoshop. The Color filters are also interesting because they are almost the only filter set that cannot also be applied as an effect.

Figure 3.1
The Colors filters available in Illustrator 9.

The blending options on the Colors Filter menu are somewhat intriguing and merit a closer look.

Blend Horizontal

You can use the Blend Horizontal color filter to simulate a two-color gradient if your shapes don't contain any compound paths. Although I haven't found anything that I can't also do with a gradient, the Blend Horizontal filter keeps each shape in a single color—which isn't always the case with the Gradient tool. Project 3.1 introduces you to the Blend Horizontal color filter.

PROJECT 3.1 Around and About

This project shows you how to apply the Blend Horizontal filter to outlined text objects. Because outlined text consists of compound paths, you need to release the compound paths first, then apply the filter, and finally, re-create the compound paths again. This process is tedious enough that you should do it with only a small amount of text. In this project, you'll just apply the Blend Horizontal filter. However, a bit later in the chapter, you'll learn how I created the starting heart image.

1. Open the file HEARTSTART.AI from this book's companion CD-ROM.

2. Choose the Text-On-A-Path tool. Click on the Text Outline Path layer to target it in the Layers palette. Click on the path itself about halfway between the bottom point of the heart and the top of the left side of the heart to start typing.

3. I used Copal Solid, 48 points, but you can use any font installed on your system. The technique shows up best if you use a fairly wide font (Hiroshige, Bees Knees, and most black weights are good choices).

4. Enter "Hearts Around The World". I used all caps in Copal. After you enter the text, switch to the Selection tool. Figure 3.2 shows the position of the text as I first entered it.

Another Way to Handle Text Counters

If you have a letter with a counter, you can click with the Pen tool outside the letter, click again inside the counter, and use the Slice command. Then, if you release the Compound Path, the appearance of the letters won't change. This is also time consuming, but you only need to do it once. However, because the theory is more complex, I've taken the longer route in the main part of this project's directions.

Can't Find a Suitable Font?

If you don't like your selection of fonts, you can use the already-created type path in the HEARTSTART.AI document. Simply click on the Eye icon to make the Text layer visible and hide the Type Outline Path layer. Then, go on to Step 7 in the project.

Figure 3.2
The text is not placed correctly around the heart.

5. If you cannot see the Baseline Shift option in the Character palette, choose Show Options from the side drop-down menu in the Character palette. Change the baseline so that the text is all inside the heart (I used a baseline shift of –38). Next, grab the I-beam and drag the text down so that it moves around the heart. Figure 3.3 shows the desired position of the text.

Figure 3.3
Moving the I-beam with the Selection tool changes the starting position for Text-On-A-Path.

6. Choose Text|Create Outlines. Choose Object|Ungroup. While all the text is selected, choose Object|Compound Paths|Release. Figure 3.4 shows the text with the compound paths released (all the counters in the letters are filled in).

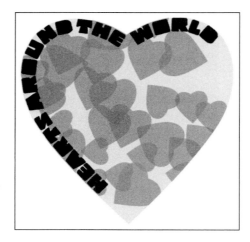

Figure 3.4
When you release the compound paths, all the counters in the letters are filled in.

7. Drag a marquee around the text on the left half of the heart. Change the Fill to a strong red (Red M=100, Y=100).

8. Drag a marquee around the remaining text on the right side of the heart. Change the Fill to blue (Blue C=100, M=50).

9. Select the entire image (Command/Ctrl+A).

10. Choose Filter|Colors|Blend Horizontally. The colors blend across the letters from orange to cyan.

11. Deselect all the text. Now, you need to put back the compound paths. Unfortunately, you can't create the compound path in one step the way you released it. If you try, you'll create one large compound path of all the letters that contains only one color. Instead, use the new Lasso tool to drag a tiny marquee around the first letter that needs to be fixed (the *a* in *Heart*). Press Command/Ctrl+8. The compound path appears good as new. Repeat this procedure for any letter that's missing its counter.

12. Click on the radio button next to the Text Outline Path layer so that you can see the double circle around the radio button. The Appearance palette should show Layer as its top object, as you can see in Figure 3.5.

13. In the Transparency palette, change the mode to Multiply.

14. From the side drop-down menu in the Layers palette, select Duplicate Text Outline Layer (or the Text Layer if that is what you've been using). The Multiply mode is also copied, and the text becomes a bit darker and stands out a bit more. However, you can still see the text interact with the heart shape that is under it.

Figure 3.5
The Appearance palette shows that the entire layer is targeted.

The Blend Horizontal color filter takes the color in the shape that is farthest to the left and blends it into the Fill color that is farthest to the right. The filter blends only the Fill color; it doesn't affect the Stroke color at all.

The Blend Horizontal filter also gives you a fast way to generate a palette of blended colors if you don't want to bother creating a gradient and then expanding it in steps. You could create a small rectangle and duplicate it a number of times, dragging each new copy to the right (say you wanted 10 steps between red and green). To do so, fill the leftmost box with red and the rightmost box with green. Then, use Blend Horizontal. Click on each box in turn and drag the color swatch onto the Swatches palette for permanent storage. If you save the document to the Swatches folder of your Illustrator installation, you can open the Swatches document any time you choose.

The Blend Top To Bottom filter is similar to the Blend Horizontal filter. It blends from the object closest to the top of the document to the object closest to the bottom.

Blend Front To Back

The Blend Front To Back filter is similar to the Blend Horizontal filter. In this one, the color blends from the object that is the highest in the stacking order to the object that is at the bottom. You can easily exert control on this filter even if you do not remember the stacking order of your objects. You just need to send one object to the back and one to the front.

In Project 3.2, I created a random composition. I'll show you one way to use the result. I frequently like to use luck or controlled randomness in my designs. I like the spontaneity and freshness of the unplanned work, and it can lead me down unexpected paths, especially when I'm freely creating or just playing. I hope that you'll also find the technique useful.

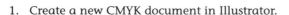

PROJECT 3.2 Fish on the Move

You're going to create a fish and add seemingly random color to multiple copies of the fish. You'll use the results of this project in several other projects in this chapter.

1. Create a new CMYK document in Illustrator.

2. Choose the Pencil tool and draw a very simple fish shape (even if you have no drawing ability, you should be able to draw this shape). Fill the fish with yellow. Figure 3.6 shows the fish shape that I used. Remember, you can refine the shape just by drawing near the selected shape.

3. Draw a small circle for the eye (color it dark green) and a wiggly, closed shape for a piece of seaweed. Make the seaweed a lighter green. Figure 3.7 shows my interpretation.

Figure 3.6
A simple fish shape is easy to draw.

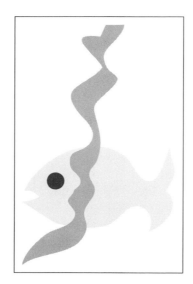

Figure 3.7
Now, the fish has an eye and a long strand of seaweed.

4. Select the entire image (Command/Ctrl+A). Drag the selected shapes (that is, the fish, its eye, and the seaweed) onto the Brushes palette. When the dialog box pops up, asking which type of brush you want to create, choose Scatter Brush. Figure 3.8 shows the suggested settings for the new brush (although your size percentage depends on the size of your original). You'll learn much more about brushes and brush types in Chapter 4.

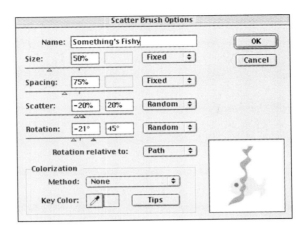

Figure 3.8
Use these settings for your fish brush.

5. Group the original fish (Command/Ctrl+G) and cut it (Command/Ctrl+X). Create a new document and paste (Command/Ctrl+V) the fish into it—just in case you need it again. Save the image. You can close the image containing the original fish now if you want. However, you need to leave open the image in which you defined the fish brush. You need to work in this document.

6. Select the Paintbrush tool. Set the Fill to None and the Stroke color to black (although the Stroke color doesn't matter in this instance). Draw random paths covering the image area of the document (see Figure 3.9).

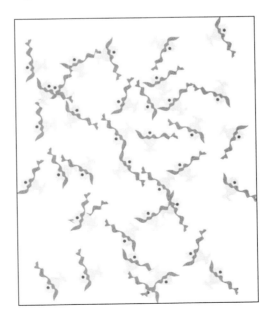

Figure 3.9
Use the fish brush to draw multiple paths in the image.

7. Select the entire image (Command/Ctrl+A). Choose Object|Expand Appearance. As you can see in Figure 3.10, the Layers palette shows many groups.

Figure 3.10
Expanding the appearance of the objects changes each path into a group.

8. Select the entire image (Command/Ctrl+A). Ungroup (Shift+Command/ Ctrl+G) two times to remove all the groupings in the file.

9. Each former stroke now contains a fish, an eye, a piece of seaweed, and the original unfilled, unstroked stroke. You need to remove all the invisible strokes from the image. Select one of the strokes. Figure 3.11 shows what this image looks like. Choose Edit|Select|Same Fill Color. Figure 3.12 shows that only the invisible strokes are selected. This trick is an easy way to find them all. Press Delete or Backspace to remove all the selected strokes.

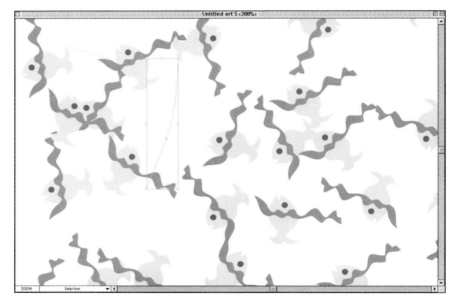

Figure 3.11
One selected invisible stroke.

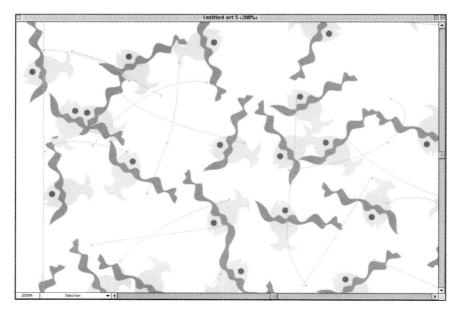

Figure 3.12
Edit|Select|Same Fill Color chooses only the invisible strokes that originally formed the spines of the scatter brush strokes.

10. Select the entire image. Select Object|Transform|Transform Each. Figure 3.13 shows the settings that I used in the Transform Each dialog box. Make sure that you select the Random checkbox and then click on Copy. Repeat the transformation five more times (Command/Ctrl+D). Figure 3.14 shows the result.

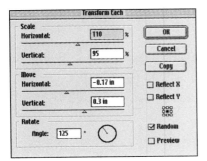

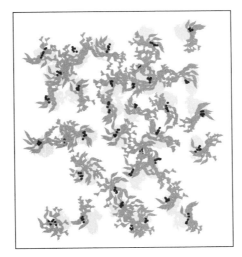

Figure 3.13
(Left) The Transform Each command allows you to randomize the transformation of each object in an image.

Figure 3.14
(Right) The result is an impressionistic "stamping" of the original design.

11. Now, the project gets interesting. It's time to select colors. Select a fish shape and give it a bright yellow fill. Send it to the back (Object|Arrange|Send To Back). Select another shape and fill it with CMYK: 64, 84, 5, 0. Bring it to the front (Object|Arrange|Bring To Front).

12. Select the entire image. Choose Filter|Colors|Blend Front To Back.

13. Now, you need to rearrange the shapes. Leave the entire image selected. Click on the Horizontal Align Center command and then on the Vertical Align Center command in the Align palette. You now have a clump of fish, fish eyes, and seaweed in the center of the image.

14. Randomly select objects, and then drag them to all the areas of the image. Figure 3.15 shows the slight scattering that is needed.

15. Select the entire image. Click on the Vertical Distribute Center command and then on the Horizontal Distribute Center command in the Align palette. Choosing these commands will probably create clumps of shapes similar to those shown in Figure 3.16.

16. You need to rearrange the fish into a less regular pattern. I do so by selecting random fish and moving them and then selecting only some of the areas of the image. If you then click on one or more of the Align or Distribute commands, you can move the shapes over different areas.

An Easy Way to Select the Invisible Stroke

The easiest way to select an invisible stroke is to select it in the new Layers palette. All the filled shapes have a preview. If you click on the unfilled meatball to the right of any path that has nothing in its thumbnail, you select a spine path. Because all the "real" objects are filled, when you ask Illustrator to select all objects with a Fill of None (the fill of the selected spine), you select only the spine paths that you want to delete.

64 Chapter 3

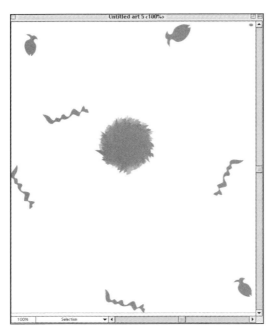

Figure 3.15

(Left) After the objects are centrally aligned, drag some of them at random to far-flung corners of your image.

Figure 3.16

(Right) The Distribute commands move the fish into regular clumps.

This iterative process can continue for a while (until you like the result). I move shapes and select areas and use the Align and/or Distribute commands repeatedly. Figure 3.17 shows a result that is more visually pleasing than the one shown in Figure 3.16. It took an additional 50 to 75 steps to get the image to this point. (One request for Illustrator 10 is that Adobe create a Random command that is more effective than Transform Each—which really doesn't work to randomly arrange this image).

Figure 3.17

You can create a more random arrangement by repeatedly moving and selecting areas and by using the Align and Distribute commands.

17. As a final "arranging" step, choose Object|Transform|Transform Each and use the settings in Figure 3.18 (or your own). Do not click on Copy. Figure 3.19 shows the result. Notice that the fish "eyes" have now been transformed into confetti.

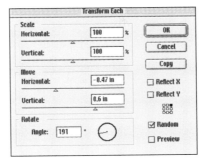

Figure 3.18
Use the Transform Each command for a last touch of randomness.

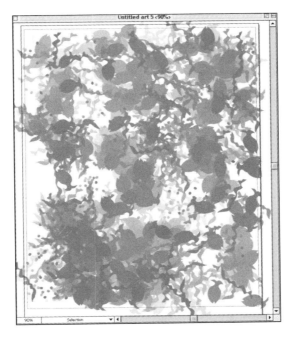

Figure 3.19
The fish are scatted randomly—and the fish eyes have become confetti.

18. Select the shapes that lie outside the printable areas of the document and drag them back into the image.

19. Select the entire image. Click on Stroke and change the Stroke color to black. Set the width of the stroke to 1 pt. Figure 3.20 shows the result.

20. Create a new layer and drag it to the bottom of the image. Lock Layer 1.

21. Choose the Rectangle tool and create a rectangle the size of the image. Set the Stroke to None. Click on the Gradient palette and drag the purple to the start color of the gradient. Drag black to the end color. Choose a Linear gradient with an Angle of 0.

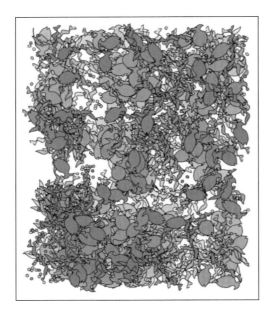

Figure 3.20
Stroking the shapes in the image
helps to define them more clearly.

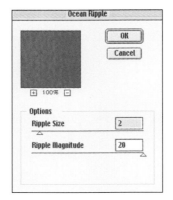

Figure 3.21
Use these settings for the Ocean
Ripples filter.

22. Choose File|Document Color Mode|Convert to RGB to apply RGB-only effects. Apply the Ocean Ripple effect (Effect|Distort|Ocean Ripples) with a Ripple Size of 2 and a Ripple Magnitude of 20, as shown in Figure 3.21.

23. Hmmm. Purple on purple is a bit dull. Perhaps the colors need to be rearranged so that the yellow objects are closer to the top. Although it would be lovely to have a command to invert the stacking order of the objects, I haven't found one. However, you can reapply the Blend Front To Back filter. First, lock Layer 2 (the background layer) and then un-lock Layer 1.

24. Select a yellow fish and bring it to the front. Select the darkest purple fish (or apply the dark purple to the fish) and send it to the back. Now, select the entire image. Choose Filter|Colors|Blend Front To Back. Now, the yellow fish are closer to the surface.

25. Save the image at this point. Figure 3.22 shows the fish in grayscale. Save a copy of your fish as FISHY.AI in Illustrator 9 format.

Now that you've created this random image, two questions remain: How can you vary the effect, and what can you do with it? Let's tackle each question in turn.

Fish Variations

In the fish that you just created, the fish eyes turned into confetti. If you prefer fish eyes, the easiest way to keep them in place is to create a compound path when you first create the fish. The steps are simple: Create the fish, create the eye, and choose Object|Compound Paths|Make. The eye is knocked out of the

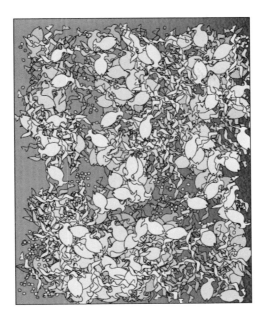

Figure 3.22
The fish image is complete.

fish. You can then proceed as you did in Project 3.2, but all the fish retain their eyes (of course, you get no sprinkles—unless you also create a tiny circle or two to live near the seaweed). The only problem with this variation is that none of the Blend commands work on compound paths (as you discovered in Project 3.1). Therefore, you can do it, but you have to release the compound paths before you apply the color filter and then individually re-create each compound path. If you have the patience, you can make this change, but I'm not sure that it's worth the effort.

Another variation is to use different ranges of color for the fish, the seaweed, and the confetti. This change is fairly easy to make. Before you apply the Blend Front To Back color filter, select a fish, change its fill, and send it to the back. Select another fish, change its Fill color, and bring it to the front. Select one of the remaining fish. Choose Edit|Select|Same Fill Color. Then, all the remaining fish are selected. With Shift pressed, add the top and bottom fish to the selection, and then choose Filter|Colors|Blend Front To Back. Do the same thing with the seaweed.

To distribute the colors more randomly in levels, you can apply the color filters to the untransformed objects (prior to Step 10 of Project 3.2). When you then execute Step 10, your colors are already blended, and you get multiple levels of color blend. Figure 3.23 shows another fish image created using combinations of all the variations. You can also see it in the Illustrator 9 Studio.

You'll use FISHY.AI a bit later in the chapter—after you learn about transparency and blend modes. First, I want to show you the Hard Mix and Soft Mix commands.

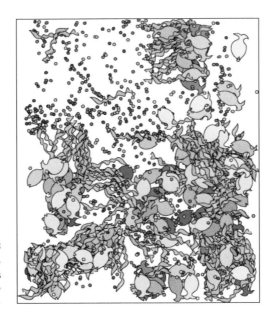

Figure 3.23
The fish and the seaweed are colored separately, and the colors are applied before the objects are transformed and copied.

Mixing a Logo

The Pathfinder palette contains two commands that are useful for creating color effects. Although they are "legacy" pathfinder commands, you might still find them useful. To see them, however, you need to select Show Options from the Pathfinder palette menu bar. The Hard Mix and Soft Mix commands are then available.

You can use the Hard Mix and Soft Mix commands to approximate transparency (which is why I call them "legacy" commands, as you can do real transparency in Illustrator 9). These commands don't work on compound paths, nor do they work on gradient fills or gradient mesh objects. If you can tolerate the limitations, they are a good addition to your arsenal of tools.

The Mix Hard command keeps the highest percentage of each color component. For example, if you mix an object that contains CMYK: 100, 0, 0, 0 (cyan) with an object that contains CMYK: 0, 0, 100, 0 (yellow), you get CMYK: 100, 0, 100, 0 (green). You have no options on the Hard Mix command.

The Soft Mix command allows you to select the percentage of mix. Using the previous example with a 50 percent mixture of the colors, you would get CMYK: 33.33, 0, 66.67, 0. The math is not intuitive, but the color is a soft green, which is about what you would expect to see.

One advantage of using either command is that you can create a harmonious range of colors, regardless of the original colors in the image. Project 3.3 shows the use of these commands in a technique that I frequently use when I am asked to develop an abstract logo design for a company. The technique is very simple, but the effectiveness comes from the design principle of repeating elements and shapes. The unity of the colors comes from the use of the Hard Mix or the Soft Mix command.

Steven's Study Skills

3.3 You're going to develop a simple logo for a company called Steven's Study Skills.

1. Create a new RGB document (Command/Ctrl+N) in Illustrator.

2. Using the Ellipse tool, draw an oval shape that resembles a head (see Figure 3.24).

3. With the same tool, draw an elongated body, as shown in Figure 3.25.

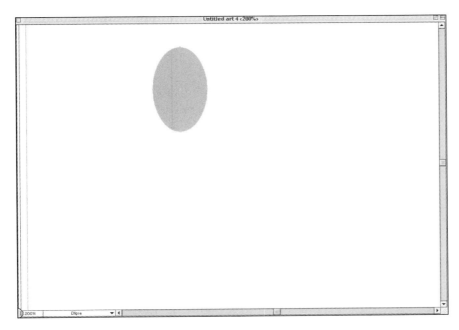

Figure 3.24
A vaguely head-shaped object is the start of a logo.

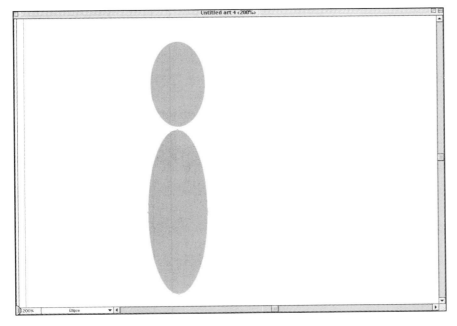

Figure 3.25
An elongated oval can suggest a body.

4. Draw another oval to resemble an arm and then use the Rectangle tool to draw two shapes that look like books. Figure 3.26 shows this stage completed.

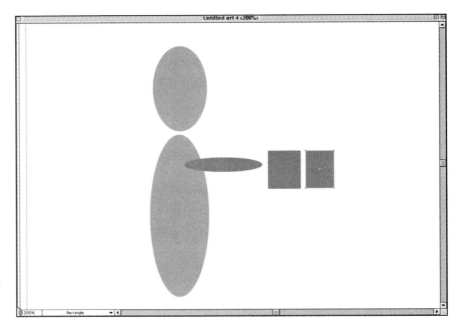

Figure 3.26
With simple shapes, you can create a very abstract student.

5. Change the Fill color for the shapes to whatever you want them to be. I used a different color for each shape and chose them randomly.

6. Select the entire image (Command/Ctrl+A). Choose Object|Transform|Transform Each. Figure 3.27 shows the settings that I used. Select the Random checkbox but don't click on Copy. Repeat the transformation (Command/Ctrl+D) at least four times (or more) until you're happy with the result. The shapes should then take on a more abstract look.

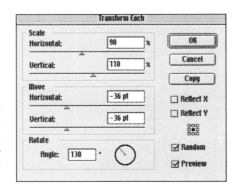

Figure 3.27
After you specify parameters in the Transform Each dialog box, you can choose to have Illustrator apply them randomly to each object.

7. Rearrange the altered shapes so that they are vaguely in their starting positions. You can rotate them as you feel necessary. Figure 3.28 shows my arrangement.

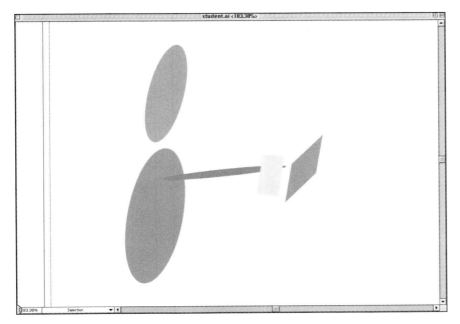

Figure 3.28
After you transform the shapes, you can rearrange them as you like.

8. Select the Rectangle tool. Set your Fill color to a bright red. Drag a rectangle so that it extends fairly far out on the left but doesn't quite cover the original shapes on the top, bottom, or right side. Figure 3.29 shows the position of the rectangle.

Figure 3.29
The rectangle should not quite cover the entire set of underlying shapes.

9. Click on Mix Soft in the Pathfinder palette. Choose 50% for the mix rate. Figure 3.30 shows the selected mixed item. Illustrator creates the illusion of a blended, transparent shape by merging the individual shapes into one grouped object that might also contain compound paths.

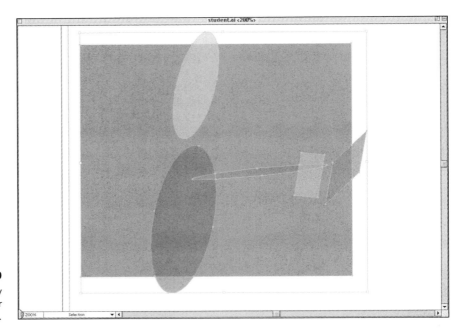

Figure 3.30
Illustrator creates a mix by grouping the objects together into one.

10. Ungroup (Shift+Command/Ctrl+G). Select the red rectangle and move it slightly to the left. With the Rotate tool, rotate the shape about four degrees. Figure 3.31 shows the final spacing I used.

Figure 3.31
By rotating and moving the background shape, you create an attractive negative shape in the logo.

11. Add the logo text "Steven's Study Skills". I used FFJustlefthand Caps at 72 points with 64-point leading. Any handwriting font should work as well. If you like the logo text, I have included an outline version of this text as LOGOTYPE.AI on this book's companion CD-ROM. Figure 3.32 shows the logo with type added.

Figure 3.32
Lettering added to the logo completes the design.

The design principle behind this exercise is that you create a negative shape that mimics the positive one formed by the original objects. Rotating this shape adds interest to the design but isn't necessary. You can vary this technique in many ways. One way is to take the completed logo into Photoshop. Figure 3.33 shows my additions to the logo in Photoshop. I created three layers in Illustrator. The bottom layer contains the red background shape, the top layer contains the text, and the middle layer holds all the other objects. I exported the image as a layered Photoshop 5 file. In Photoshop, I added 200 pixels to the canvas size in each dimension and created a white Background layer. I applied the KPT Texture Explorer filter to the red background shape, using Procedural + "Glue" in the Filter dialog box. I then used Fade Filter (Shift+Command/Ctrl+F) to change the blend mode to Multiply and the Opacity to 25% so that it has a much gentler mix of the original and KPT filters. I used the Inner Bevel filter in the Eye Candy 3 filter set to create the bevels on the student shape. I then cut Opacity of the red layer to 91% to slightly soften the color. The altered image looks more impressive, but I also like the stark colors and flat texture of the original.

Figure 3.33
You can use Photoshop to
enhance your logo design.

Blending Some New Colors

Adobe has given Illustrator users their heart's desire in full measure in this release. The new transparency and blend mode options change the whole way in which Illustrator files are constructed. You've already learned the power of styles and seen how to use the Appearance palette in Chapter 2. Now, let's see how blend modes can simplify your color choices. You'll create a shadowed and shaded coffee cup still life from a starting image that contains only two basic colors. You'll add only one pattern plus red as additional colors.

PROJECT 3.4 Coffee Blends

Starting from an image that has all the needed shapes already created, you'll add shading by changing blend modes and opacity and by applying effects.

Setting the Table

The first step in adding shading to your morning is to set the table:

1. Open the image COFFEECUP.AI from the companion CD-ROM. The image contains a light blue, a yellow background, and a black stroke.

2. Build the tablecloth first. All the layers should be locked except for the Table layer. Twirl down the Table layer arrow on the Layers palette and click on the path radio button to select the path.

3. Choose New Fill from the Appearance palette side drop-down menu. Drag the new fill below the stroke in the Appearance palette. In the Swatches palette, click on the Azure Rings pattern to apply it to the new fill that you created.

4. Change the tablecloth to a blue and red. To do so, you first need to add a red fill. Make sure that the pattern fill is targeted in the Appearance palette. Then, choose New Fill from the Appearance palette side drop-down menu. Click on the Red swatch in the Swatches palette. Leave the red fill targeted. In the Transparency palette, change the blend mode to Color Burn. Leave the Opacity at 100%.

5. The tablecloth is still too dark (it needs to be able to show shadows). One way to reduce the colors is to add a white fill and then reduce the opacity of the fill. To do so, choose New Fill from the side drop-down menu in the Appearance palette. If you had the red fill targeted when you selected the New Fill, then the new fill appears correctly above the red fill. Change the blend mode to Screen. Then, reduce the Opacity to 60%. Your Appearance palette should look like the one in Figure 3.34.

6. Lock the Table layer in the Layers palette.

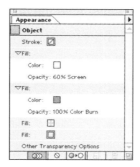

Figure 3.34
The Appearance palette shows four fills applied to the table object.

Painting the Coffee Cup

In this section of the project, you'll change the blend modes on the various areas of the coffee cup and add a few gradients as well.

Deconstructing the Cup

Before you begin, however, take a good look at the construction of the Coffee Cup layer. You can deconstruct the layer like this:

1. Click on the Eye icon next to the Coffee Cup Copy layer and hide the layer. You'll notice no change in your image because that layer is underneath the Coffee Cup layer.

2. Press Command/Ctrl and click on the Eye icon next to the Coffee Cup layer. The modifier key allows you to change the view mode of the layer from Preview to Outline (and back again). Figure 3.35 shows the image with the Coffee Cup layer in Outline mode.

3. The Coffee Cup layer contains five sublayers. The cup body sublayer was the first shape that I created. I then added a bottom and a handle for the cup, an area inside the cup body to show the inside of the cup, and a shadow sublayer to somewhat hide the bottom of the cup. Command/Ctrl+click on the Coffee Cup layer Eye icon again to turn on Preview mode. Then, click on the radio button next to each layer to select the layer contents. Look at how each sublayer relates to the whole cup.

Figure 3.35
You can view a single layer in Outline mode.

4. When you understand the construction of the cup, go on to the next section.

Brewing a Cup

Finally, you can add the shading via blend modes and gradients.

1. Twirl down the arrow on the Cup Inside sublayer so that you can see the path in the Layers palette. Click on the path sublayer radio button to select the path. Notice that this object is directly on top of the top portion of the cup body object. It's not obvious because the objects are both the same color.

2. In the "old days" (Illustrator 8), you would have had to add black to this object to create the illusion of a shadow inside the cup. No longer. Using the same color over itself in Multiply mode does even better and is much easier to remember. The only trick is that you need to check very carefully to make sure that you are targeting the correct area of the Appearance palette.

   If you have selected the path object (not the sublayer), the Appearance palette shows Object at the top and the correct fill and stroke for the object. As you can see in Figure 3.36, the object has a fill and no stroke. Click on the fill entry in the Appearance palette to target it. Now, your changes affect only that fill.

3. In the Transparency palette, change the mode to Multiply. Figure 3.37 shows the Appearance palette now.

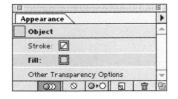

Figure 3.36
The Appearance palette shows a fill and no stroke for the inside of the coffee cup.

4. The darkness helps, but so would some additional shading. Because your fill is already in Multiply mode, you can change the solid fill into a gradient fill without changing the blend mode. You'll learn how to construct and work with gradients in Chapter 8, so I've already made the base gradients for you to make this project a bit easier to manage. With the Cup Inside object still selected (and the solid fill targeted), click on the Cup Inside Gradient swatch in the Swatches palette. The inside of the cup changes to the gradient. I set the angle of the gradient with the Gradient tool when I first created the image, so I already know the correct angle. Therefore, type the number "–164.16" in the Angle field in the Gradient palette, as shown in Figure 3.38.

5. The body of the cup could also use some shading. Although you'll apply a "simple" gradient, you need to do some fiddling to get it to be the correct angle and length. Twirl down the arrow next to the Cup Body sublayer in the Layers palette. Click on the radio button next to the path (not the sublayer) to select it. You should see the object in the Appearance palette.

6. Click on the Cup Gradient in the Swatches palette. Although this applies the gradient, it stretches too long across the object. Because Illustrator doesn't provide an automated way to set it correctly, you need to choose the Gradient tool to specify the range.

7. Make the Info palette active. Place your cursor on the point that's circled in Figure 3.39. Press Shift and drag the Gradient tool cursor approximately 40 points to the right (use the W: field in the Info palette to calculate the distance). After you set the Gradient so that the light area occupies only a small portion on the left side of the cup, enter "6.01" in the Angle field on the Gradient palette.

8. Place a shadow over the bottom of the cup so that it looks as though the cup body is casting it. To make this shadow, twirl down the arrow next to the bottom shadow sublayer. Click on the path radio button in the Layers palette to select the bottom shadow object. Make sure that you can see Object at the top of the Appearance palette. Click on the word "Object" to target it.

9. In the Transparency palette, change the mode to Multiply and the Opacity to 56%. Press Return/Enter to make the opacity change "stick." You get a nice shadow effect, but it's a bit too harsh.

10. You can make the shadow softer by adding a Gaussian Blur effect to it. To add the effect, choose Effect|Blur|Gaussian Blur and choose a radius

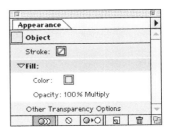

Figure 3.37
The Appearance palette records a blend mode change for the fill.

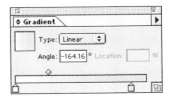

Figure 3.38
A gradient angle of –164.16 shades the inside of the cup from left to right.

Figure 3.39
Start dragging the Gradient cursor at the circled point.

Figure 3.40
The Appearance palette for the highlight object on the cup handle looks like this.

of 5.6. Click on OK to exit the Effect dialog box. Now, you'll see a lovely soft cast shadow. Notice that the color of the shadow is the same as the color of the cup. The Multiply mode gives the shadow its color—and its color effect.

11. Now, add some shading to the cup handle. Twirl down the Cup Handle sublayer. This time, you'll see two paths. Click on the radio button next to the <path>Hilight object (it's the top object in the sublayer). Make sure that you can see Object at the top of the Appearance palette.

12. The object has a 4-point stroke and no fill. Target the stroke by clicking on it. Change the mode to Screen. Leave the Opacity at 100%. This action creates a highlight on the edge of the cup handle. However, the stroke in Screen mode is too harsh. Choose Effect|Blur|Gaussian Blur with a radius of 2. Then, choose Effect|Stylize|Feather. Choose a feather of 2. The blur softens the edge and feather adds additional softening. Figure 3.40 shows the Appearance palette with all the effects added.

13. The final location to shade in this part of the project is the cup rim. That's the stroke on the Cup Inside sublayer. Click on the radio button next to the cup inside path to select it. Now, you can see why you needed to be so careful to target the fill when you made your previous changes. The Appearance palette should still be the same as it was in Figure 3.37. Click on the Stroke entry in the Appearance palette to target it. Change the stroke to 3 points in the Stroke palette.

14. Make the Stroke the active swatch in the Toolbox. Click on the same blue as the cup (New Color Swatch 2) in the Swatches palette to change the Stroke color of the Cup Inside object. Again, check that the stroke is targeted in the Appearance palette. Change the mode in the Transparency palette to Color Dodge and set the opacity to 48%.

15. To soften the rim of the cup, choose Effect|Stylize|Feather and enter a feather amount of 1. Then, choose Effect|Blur|Gaussian Blur and enter a radius of 1.8. Again, the combination of effect and blend mode creates the color change—the actual Stroke color is no different from the color of the coffee cup.

Decorating the Cup

The original coffee cup photograph (which you can still see in the image if you hide all the other layers) shows a cup with some indented designs on it. You'll create your own version next.

1. Lock all the layers except the Pattern layer.

2. Twirl down the Pattern layer arrow to show the path that it contains. Click on the radio button next to the path to select the stroke. The Appearance palette shown in Figure 3.41 shows that the path contains a stroke of the same color as the cup and no fill.

3. Make the Brushes palette visible. With the path selected, click on the Leaf brush in the Swatches palette—it's the last brush in the palette. You can't see much of the result because the brush, like almost every other element in the image, uses the same blue as the cup.

4. The inset look needs to use the leaf pattern with the original cup color, but you need to also create a shadow to make the pattern look indented. Therefore, you need to make a second copy of the stroke within the same object. To do that, target the Stroke in the Appearance palette and choose Duplicate Item from the side drop-down menu in the Appearance palette. As you can see in Figure 3.42, the Appearance palette now has two of the same stroke entries.

5. Target the lower copy of the stroke. Change the blend mode to Multiply in the Transparency palette. Although you can't see the color change now because the top stroke obscures it, you'll be able to see the changes as soon as you apply a blur to the stroke.

6. Choose Effect|Blur|Gaussian Blur and set a radius of 5.6.

7. Save your work.

How to Create a Leaf

If you were wondering how I created the leaf shape, wonder no more. I drew a simple oval, selected the oval with the Direct Selection tool and then chose the Pen tool. With Option/Alt pressed, I clicked on the top point in the oval. The curve changed to a sharp crease. I then did the same thing with the bottom point.

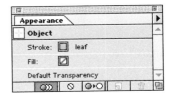

Figure 3.41
The stroke for the pattern has already been created for you.

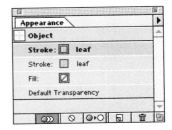

Figure 3.42
Duplicate the stroke in the Appearance palette.

Why Not Copy and Paste in Front?

Copy and Paste in Front, which was the standard way of working in Illustrator 8, still works. However, the advantage of using a multiple stroke on the object comes if you need to adjust the shape of the path for any reason. If you have two separate shapes, making identical adjustments to both shapes can be tricky. With one shape and two strokes, as soon as you edit the path, the changes apply everywhere.

You've finished all the decorations and shading needed on the cup itself unless you want to try to add more shadow detail using the cup photo as your guide. I wanted to create only the minimum amount for you to do so that you could get the general idea. In the next section, you'll use the Transform effect to create some intriguing shadows.

Transforming Your Colors

In this section, you'll learn how to use the Transform effect to create multiple copies of a single object. This method has the same benefit as does using multiple strokes and fills: All changes only need to be made to one object, and the effect can be altered or removed at any time.

Shadows on the Table

In the presence of multiple light sources (three lights and the sun, for example), an object casts multiple, overlapping shadows. You can make the cup cast a shadow like this:

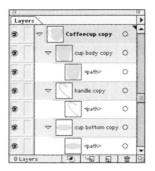

Figure 3.43
The Layers palette shows all the items on the Coffee Cup Copy layer.

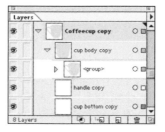

Figure 3.44
After you group the three objects, two of the sublayers are empty.

1. Unlock the Coffee Cup Copy layer. Twirl down the arrow next to it on the Layers palette and the arrows on the sublayers so that you can view the actual paths on the layer. Notice that the layer contains fewer elements than does the actual coffee cup. I removed the Cup Inside sublayer because you don't need it here. I also removed the highlight stroke for the cup handle for the same reason. Figure 3.43 shows the Layers palette for the Coffee Cup Copy layer. All the objects are simple; notice the absence of "meatballs" on the Layers palette.

2. You need to transform the objects on the Coffee Cup Copy layer as though they were one object. To do so, you need to group the objects. The Coffee Cup Copy layer should be the only unlocked layer. Choose Edit|Select All (Command/Ctrl+A) to select all the objects on the layer.

3. Choose Object|Group (Command/Ctrl+G). Figure 3.44 shows the Layers palette after you've grouped the objects.

4. Click on the group sublayer to highlight it and then keep the mouse button pressed as you drag the sublayer toward the Coffee Cup Copy layer. As you pass the Coffee Cup Body sublayer, a large black arrowhead appears at the left of the sublayer. Keep moving the Group sublayer up until you see a tiny arrowhead with a line, as shown in Figure 3.45. This line means that the sublayer will be moved directly under the Coffee Cup Copy sublayer on the same level as the Coffee Cup Body sublayer (and not as a sub-sublayer). When you see the line, you can release the mouse button.

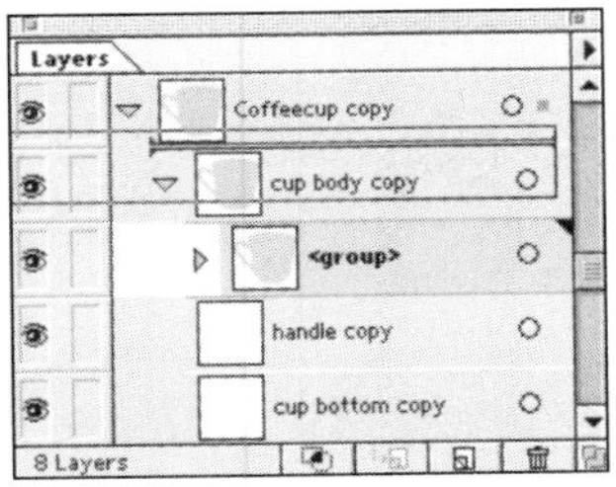

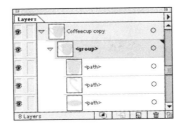

Figure 3.45
(Left) Learn to read the Layers palette symbols when you move a layer.

Figure 3.46
(Right) The coffee cup group now occupies its own sublayer on the Layers palette.

5. Delete the three empty layers by dragging each one to the trashcan icon on the Layers palette. Figure 3.46 shows the way the Layers palette should look with the empty layers removed.

6. Select All again (Command/Ctrl+A). (Remember, only the Coffee Cup Copy layer is unlocked.) Look at the Appearance palette (see Figure 3.47). It shows several possibilities for targeting (the objects or the group). Click on Group in the Appearance palette. You'll add your effects to the group. The Appearance palette immediately changes to show the view in Figure 3.48.

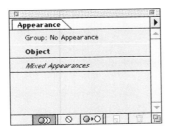
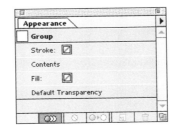

Figure 3.47
(Left) The Appearance palette isn't targeting anything specific on the layer.

Figure 3.48
(Right) Now, the Appearance palette shows that the group is targeted.

7. You could combine the group into a single object using the Unite Pathfinder command. However, just to show you that you can do it, you'll use the Pathfinder effect instead. To do so, choose Effect|Pathfinder|Unite. The Appearance palette now shows that an effect has been applied to the group, as you can see in Figure 3.49. Now, the objects in the group will transform as if they were a single object (not three individual objects).

8. Now, you make the "magic" happen. Target the group again in the Layers palette. Choose Effect|Distort and Transform|Transform. Figure 3.50 shows the settings to use. You need to change the Horizontal and Vertical scale, change the Rotate Angle, make three copies, click on the Reflect Y checkbox, and click on the bottom point in the tiny icon on the right that shows the origin of the transformation.

9. You still don't see shadows because the three copies are solid. In the Appearance palette, target the group again. In the Transparency palette, change the mode to Multiply and the Opacity to 50%. Figure 3.51 shows the Appearance palette.

How to Target from the Layers Palette

The new activity of targeting seems strange at first. Especially if you're used to choosing Select All to select the objects on a layer, you'll find that the Appearance palette doesn't reflect the place that you want to add effects or make color changes. You can get the Appearance palette to always target the correct area if you change your methods a bit. If you want to target the group, all that you need to do is click on the <group> sublayer in the Layers palette to highlight it and then click on its radio button to select it. This action immediately makes the <group> the target in the Appearance palette.

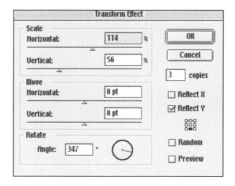

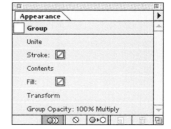

Figure 3.49

(Left) The *f* inside the black circle next to the group shows that an effect has been added to the group.

Figure 3.50

(Center) These settings produce multiple objects from a single one.

Figure 3.51

(Right) The Appearance palette shows the effects, blend modes, and opacity applied to the targeted object.

How Do I Find the Fude Brush?

The Fude brush is in the Brushes palette. You can let the tooltips cursor show the name, or you can select the View By Name option in the side drop-down menu on the Brushes palette.

Steam Heat

In the final section of this project, you'll use the Transform effect several times to create steam coming from the top of the coffee cup.

1. Lock all the layers except for the Steam layer.

2. Twirl down the arrow next to the Steam layer and click on the radio button next to the path to select it. You then see the path object in the Appearance palette.

3. Click on the Fude brush in the Brushes palette to apply it to the stroke. The Stroke width should be set to 1 point. If it isn't, change it. Then, change the Opacity for the object to 67%.

4. Target the stroke in the Appearance palette. Change the blend mode to Multiply and the Opacity to 34%. (Yes, you can have different opacities for the object and its stroke or fill.)

5. With the stroke still targeted, choose Effect|Blur|Gaussian Blur. Set a radius of 7 pixels. That's fairly weak steam! Let's add some more.

6. With the stroke still targeted, choose Effect|Distort and Transform|Transform. Set a Horizontal scale of 112% and a Vertical Scale of 94%, move the steam horizontally 15 points, and rotate it 10 degrees. Change the number of copies to three and click on the bottom, center box in the origin point icon, as shown in Figure 3.52.

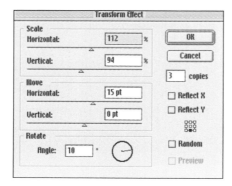

Figure 3.52

Use these Transform effect settings to create the first part of the steam.

7. The steam could still use a little more punch, so you need to add a new stroke to the object. To add the stroke, choose Add New Stroke from the side drop-down menu on the Appearance palette. Change the stroke to the Fude brush, the mode to Multiply, and the Opacity of the stroke to 10%.

8. Make more copies of this stroke as well. Choose Effect|Distort and Transform|Transform. Change the Horizontal Scale to 132% and the Vertical scale to 94%, move the object 15 points, and change the angle of rotation to 7%. Make three copies and leave the origin point icon set in the center. Figure 3.53 shows these settings. Figure 3.54 shows the Appearance palette, and Figure 3.55 shows the final image.

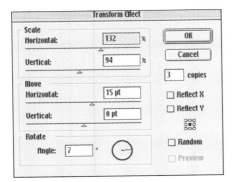

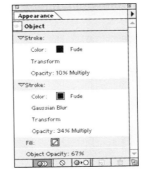

Figure 3.53
(Left) These settings create the second layer of steam.

Figure 3.54
(Right) The Appearance palette shows the two strokes and their effects.

Figure 3.55
The coffee cup image has achieved a large degree of realism by using blend modes and effects.

One of the most interesting aspects about using the Transform effect on the steam is that you can edit a single stroke at any time to rearrange the shape of the steam, and all your copies are immediately updated.

Rasterizing for Color Changes

When you rasterize Illustrator imagery, you can add more effects to it, and you can use it in either Photoshop or Illustrator. The advantage of rasterizing in Illustrator versus leaving huge numbers of objects as vector images is that you can conserve memory by making Illustrator do less juggling of images. You get an increase in performance speed. You also significantly increase your image size and lose the ability to easily resize the image. However, you can find trade-offs in almost anything, and this is just another example.

Using the Multi-Fish Image in Photoshop

You can take the fish that you've color-blended and embed them in a raster image in Photoshop (or you can finish the image in Illustrator). I'll show you both ways, but the ideal way, which involves no rasterizing, is not practical. Even with 150MB RAM devoted all to Illustrator, I get out-of-memory errors because the file becomes too large and complex. Let's look at finishing the image in Photoshop first.

 ### Fishing in Photoshop

You can use a raster version of FISHY.AI to create an image composite in Photoshop with blend modes and color changes.

1. Open the image SHARKREEF.PSD in Photoshop. This image is cobbled together from two of my photos. I also included an alpha channel in the image.

2. Also in Photoshop, open either your version of FISHY.PSD (rasterize your FISHY.AI image) or my version from the companion CD-ROM.

3. Load the Alpha 1 channel (Command/Ctrl+Option/Alt+4), which contains the outline of a fish. Using the Rectangle tool (not the Move tool), drag the selection outline into the FISHY.PSD image. This way, you move *only* the marquee and none of the shark. Position the marquee where it encloses an attractive area of the fish image. Press Shift+Command/Ctrl+Option/Alt and drag the marquee (this time with the fish inside it) back into the SHARKREEF.PSD image. It should appear exactly over the marquee area in your image. The drag-and-drop operation creates Layer 1. Figure 3.56 shows the image covered with a fishy shark.

4. Make the Background layer active. Load the Alpha 1 channel again. Create a New Layer Via Copy from the selection (Command/Ctrl+J) to create Layer 2. Drag the thumbnail for Layer 2 above the thumbnail for Layer 1 in the Layers palette.

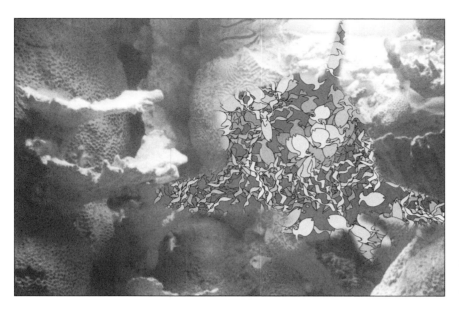

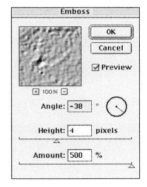

Figure 3.56
The marquee-surrounded shape is now filled with part of your fishy image.

5. Apply the Emboss filter (Filter|Stylize|Emboss) with the settings shown in Figure 3.57. Desaturate the image (Shift+Command/Shift+Ctrl+U). Change the Apply mode to Hard Light.

6. Make a new layer (click on the New Layer icon at the bottom of the Layers palette)—Layer 3. Drag Layer 3 so that it is between Layer 1 and the Background layer in the Layers palette. Fill the layer (Option+Delete/ Alt+Backspace) with a purple selected from your FISHY image. I used RGB: 114, 70, 120. Change the Apply mode to Color.

7. Make the Background layer active. Double-click on the thumbnail for the Background layer to bring up the Make Layer dialog box (see Figure 3.58). Accept the default name of Layer 0 and set the Opacity to 48%. Click on OK.

Figure 3.57
The Emboss filter adds texture to the fish-covered shark.

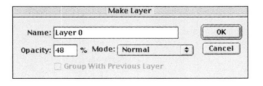

Figure 3.58
By changing the Background layer to Layer 0, you can adjust its opacity.

8. Create a new Background layer (Layer|New|Background). Figure 3.59 shows the Layers palette at this point.

9. Drag the thumbnail for Layer 0 to the New Layer icon in the Layers palette to create a Layer 0 copy. Choose Filter|Stylize|Emboss and use the settings shown in Figure 3.60 (the same angle and pixel height but a different Emboss amount from Step 5). Change the Apply mode to Hard Light. Leave the layer Opacity at 48%. Figure 3.61 shows the image at this point.

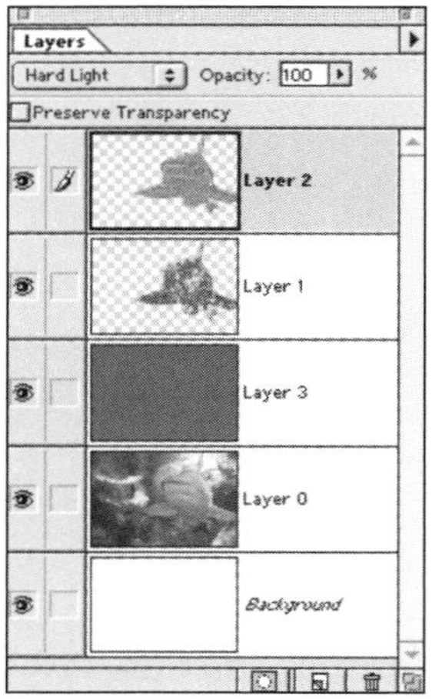

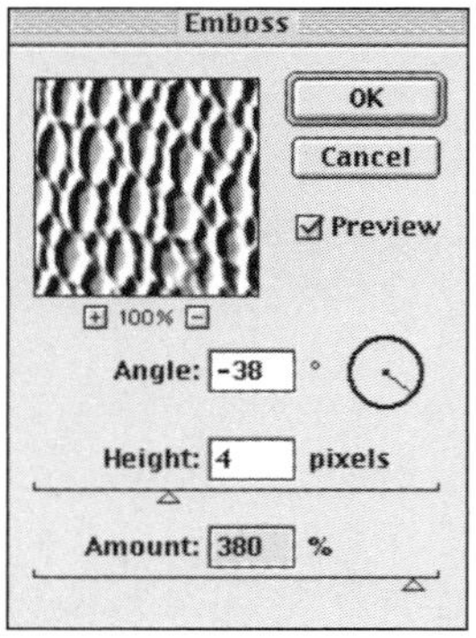

Figure 3.59

(Left) The Layers palette after you have added a new Background layer.

Figure 3.60

(Right) These Emboss filter settings add texture to the entire base image.

Figure 3.61

The image looks as if it is starting to become a unified piece of work.

10. Make Layer 0 the active layer. Press Option/Alt and click on the Eye icon next to Layer 0 to hide all the layers but Layer 0. Select the Lasso tool and trace around the eye of the shark. Press Option/Alt and click to reveal all the layers again. Create a New Layer Via Copy from the selection (Command/Ctrl+J)—Layer 4. Drag its thumbnail to the top of the Layer stack and change the layer Opacity to 100%.

11. Make the FISHY.PSD image active. Using the Move tool, drag the FISHY.PSD image and drop it into your working image. Position it so that the bottom left of the FISHY.PSD image is in the bottom left of the working image.

12. Use the Free Transform command (Command/Ctrl+T) and drag the control handle of the bounding box on the right over to the right edge of the image. This action scales Layer 5 disproportionately, but the distortion isn't obvious. It also manages to make the layer the same size as your working image. Figure 3.62 shows Layer 5 being transformed.

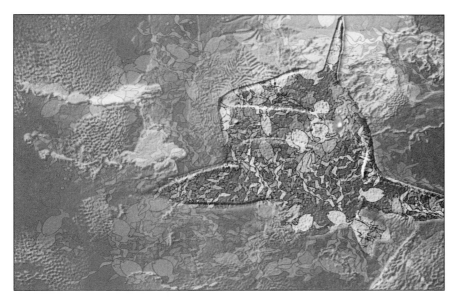

Figure 3.62
The Free Transform command scales the FISHY image so that it covers the entire working image.

13. Drag the thumbnail for Layer 5 until it is above the Background layer but below Layer 0 in your image. Change the layer Opacity to 70%. Now, you should see fish swimming in the coral background. Figure 3.63 shows the current image.

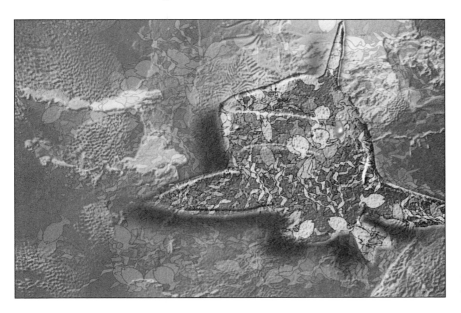

Figure 3.63
The shark still looks a bit flat.

14. Finally, you need to add shadow to give the shark more depth. Make Layer 1 the active layer. Drag the thumbnail for Layer 1 to the New Layer icon at the bottom of the Layers palette to make a copy of the layer. Drag the thumbnail for the Layer 1 copy *below* that of Layer 1 in the Layer stack.

15. Your foreground color swatch in the Toolbox should still contain the color you used as a fill for Layer 3. Make the Color palette visible if it is not and change the slider to CMYK. Even though you are working in RGB color, by using the CMYK slider, you can easily darken the color in your foreground color swatch. Add a little black to the purple foreground color to darken it.

16. Fill the Layer 1 copy with the foreground color with Preserve Transparency On (Shift+Option/Alt+Delete/Backspace). Change the Apply mode to Multiply and the Opacity to 78%.

17. Use the Move tool to move the shadow substantially to the left and down. Apply a Gaussian Blur filter (Filter|Blur|Gaussian) with an amount of 18.0 (see Figure 3.64).

18. Finally, make Layer 1 active. Change the Opacity to 87%. Figure 3.65 shows the finished image in grayscale. You can see it in color in the Illustrator 9 Studio section.

Figure 3.64
These settings are used in the Gaussian Blur filter to make a shadow.

Figure 3.65
The finished image.

Using the Multi-Fish Image in Illustrator

You're probably going to hate me for this one. You can composite the FISHY image in Illustrator, but you should be prepared for Illustrator to misbehave or squawk about memory. If you have no patience with waiting for slow redraws, you might prefer to open the finished image (FISHYDONE.AI) from the Chapter 3 ENDS folder on the book's CD-ROM. You can poke around to see what is in each layer and what effects are applied. I created the image with 150MB RAM devoted to Illustrator and, even with rasterizing at 72 ppi, got error messages telling me that Illustrator could not show the error message because it was out of RAM. When these messages appeared, all my tools and palettes disappeared. However, Illustrator didn't crash. It allowed me to save my work, and I was able to individually go back and show each of the palettes that I wanted (I just selected them from the Window menu).

With these warnings firmly in place, I'll show you how to create a menacing shark that eats the fish you've created.

PROJECT 3.6 Fishing in Illustrator

In this project, you'll learn how to rasterize portions of your image, apply shadows and glows for color change, and create effects that emphasize the lines in your image. The one procedure you won't learn is how to emboss the fish details as you did in the Photoshop-based project. The Emboss filter is not one of the filters that Adobe has certified for use with Illustrator. Because applying an embossed copy of an image in Hard Light or Overlay mode is a technique I use quite often, I really feel its lack. You could, of course, emboss the shark in Photoshop and place it in Illustrator, but by then, you might just as well keep it all in Photoshop.

Before you start this project, look at the finished image in the Illustrator 9 Studio. You'll find it useful to know where you're trying to go with this image.

Building the Background

This project is long enough that I decided to split it into several parts. In this first segment, you'll create the background for the image.

1. Open the file FISHY.AI that you created or use mine from the book's CD-ROM.

2. Change the orientation of the image to Landscape by changing it in the Page Setup dialog box (File|Page Setup). Changing the orientation there also changes it in the Document Setup dialog box.

3. Unlock all the layers and choose Edit|Select All. In the Transform palette, change the Angle of Rotation to 90 degrees. Lock the bottom layer again.

Rasterize and Rasterize Effects Settings

You could also rasterize the layer by using the Rasterize effect. However, I felt that the image was too complex for that. You have the option in the Effect|Rasterize|Rasterize Settings of setting global options for any effect that rasterizes the image. The default is 72 ppi and I recommend that, for now, you leave it that way.

4. You need two copies of the Fish layer. Target the Fish layer to highlight it and choose Duplicate Layer 1 from the side drop-down menu on the Layers palette. Lock the copy layer that is on top. Hide it by clicking on its Eye icon in the Layers palette.

5. Click on the radio button next to Layer 1 (which should be the center Fish layer in the image right now) to select the layer. Choose Object|Rasterize. Figure 3.66 shows the correct dialog box settings. Set the resolution to 72 ppi. Although this setting isn't sufficient for printing, for practice it's fine. Use RGB mode. Anti-alias the image but don't create a clipping mask. Make the background transparent.

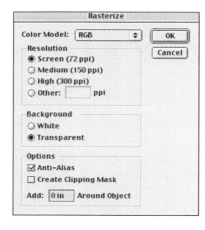

Figure 3.66
In the Rasterize dialog box, you can set the parameters for the object to be rasterized.

6. Lock all the layers in your image. Click on Layer 1 to select it and then click on the New Layer icon on the Layers palette. The new layer is created directly above Layer 1.

7. Choose File|Place and select the SHARKREEF.PSD image from the enclosed CD-ROM. Embed rather than link the image. Drag the image so that it is in the upper-left corner of the printable area of the page and overlaps the upper-left corner of the other layers. Press Shift and drag the lower-right bounding box control handle until the image reaches the right page margin. You reduce the resolution of the image by enlarging it, but you don't change the number of pixels in the image.

Can You Explain Resizing a Raster Image a Bit More?

Chapter 11 discusses resizing and setting image resolution when placing Photoshop imagery in Illustrator.

8. After you size the image, lock the layer that it's on. Unlock the bottom two layers (the background and the rasterized fish). Select the unlocked layers (Command/Ctrl+A). Drag the control handle on the center-bottom edge toward the top until the two layers are the same size as the placed image. Lock the layers again.

9. Unlock the SHARKREEF image layer. Select the image by clicking on it in the Layers palette to highlight it and then clicking on the radio button next to the <image> layer to select it. In the Transparency palette, set the Opacity to 70%. Don't change the mode from Normal. Lock the layer again. Click on the top layer but don't unlock it.

10. Click on the New Layer icon at the bottom of the Layers palette to add another layer. It should become the new top layer.

11. Choose the Rectangle tool and create a rectangle that covers the entire image (and is the same size as the other image elements). Choose RGB: 114, 70, 120 as your Fill color. Give the Rectangle no stroke. With the object still selected, change the blend mode on the Transparency palette to Color and change the Opacity to 70%. These settings color the image a uniform shade of purple to make everything suitably murky. Lock the layer. Figure 3.67 shows the way that your Layers palette should look at this point (I've named the layers for clarity—you can use my layer names or not, as you prefer.)

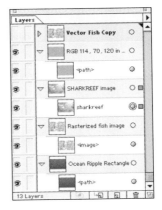

Figure 3.67
Your Layers palette should look like this at the end of Step 11.

The Fish-Eating Shark

In this section of the project, you'll add a freestanding shark to your image and use the shark-shape to mask the vector fish inside it. You'll rasterize the fish-eating shark and then create some different effects to add contrast to the shark.

1. Target the RGB: 114,70,120 layer. Click on the New Layer icon at the bottom of the Layers palette to add a new layer. You can name this layer "Vector Shark".

2. Choose File|Open and open SHARK.AI from the companion CD-ROM. Select the entire image and copy it to the clipboard. You can then close the image. Make sure that the Vector Shark layer is highlighted and paste the shark in from the clipboard. Drag it into position over the shark embedded in the SHARKREEF image. Although it should be approximately the correct size, you can adjust it if you want.

3. The Vector Shark layer should be between the RGB: 114 layer and the Vector Fish layer. This copy of the shark will be the background for the shark image. The Vector Fish layer provides the content. Choose Duplicate Layer from the side drop-down menu in the Layers palette. Hide the original Vector Shark layer by clicking on the Eye icon in the Layers palette. Drag the copy layer to the top of the layer stack.

4. Make the Vector Fish layer the active layer. Show the layer by clicking on its Eye icon on the Layers palette.

Would other Blend Modes Work?

Try the other blend modes. I usually try each one in turn to evaluate them all. The advantage is that you don't need to remember the theory behind each one (although I usually have a general idea of what to expect from each mode). However, even when you know, for example, that Overlay mode affects neither the darks nor the lights in an image, the results still can surprise you. In this project, Overlay mode, Color Burn, and Difference mode have possibilities. Some other modes look wonderful at this stage, but they will not provide enough contrast in the finished image.

5. Twirl down the arrow next to the top layer (the shark copy), target the path, and click on the shark path's radio button to select the path. In the Transparency palette, change the Opacity to about 15%. Now, you can see through the shark to the fish below. Drag the shark around in the image until you like the positioning of the fish underneath the shark. Change the Opacity back to 100%, choose Edit|Copy to copy the shark to the clipboard in its current position, and lock the layer.

6. Select the Lasso tool. Make the Vector Fish layer active and unlock the layer. Make a loose selection around the areas not covered by the shark (as shown in Figure 3.68) and then delete the selected fish. This step helps to make your file size smaller. Hide the Vector Shark copy layer.

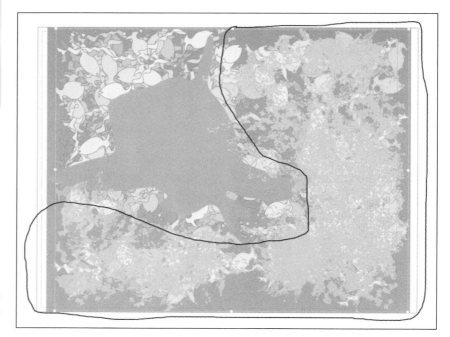

Figure 3.68
Select and delete the unneeded fish.

7. Target the Vector Fish layer so that Layer is the object in the Appearance palette. Choose Edit|Paste in Front. The shark should be pasted into the same position as it is on the hidden layer above. Again, make sure that the Layer is targeted and selected and appears in the Appearance palette. Choose Object|Clipping Mask|Make.

8. Select the entire layer and choose Object|Rasterize. Use the same Rasterize settings as before. Drag the rasterized Vector Fish into the desired position on top of the Vector Shark layer (which you need to show again).

9. Choose Duplicate Layer from the side drop-down menu in the Layers palette. Make sure that the copy layer is on top. You can name this layer "Shark Effects". Guess what you're going to do to it!

10. Twirl down the arrow next to the Shark Effects layer, target the image, and click on the image's radio button to select the image. The Appearance palette should show Image at the top. Choose Filter|Color|Saturate and drag the slider to –50. Then, choose Effect|Stylize|Glowing Edges (use the Stylize command in the bottom section of the Effect drop-down menu). Use the settings shown in Figure 3.69. These settings convert the raster image into a black-and-white version.

11. Leave the object selected. Choose Effects|Blur|Gaussian Blur. Create a blur of 1.2 pixels. The Gaussian Blur effect should be listed below the Glowing Edges effect in the Appearance palette. Change the Opacity of the selected object to 54%.

12. Open the file DETAILS.AI. This document contains the top four layers for the shark. Select the entire image (Command/Crtl+A). Choose Paste Remembers Layers from the Layers palette side drop-down menu. Copy the selected objects to the clipboard. Then, close the DETAILS.AI image.

13. Unlock the layers in the Layers palette of the half-finished sharkreef image (it's now the only open image). You shouldn't need to, but I got an error message when I tried to paste into the locked image. Choose Edit|Paste. You can't see the objects that you pasted because they are at the bottom of the Layers palette (they remembered that they were at the bottom of the Layers palette in their original location). Drag the layers to the top of the Layers palette so that the order of the four new layers from top to bottom becomes Nostrils, Eye, Face Details, and Shark Head. Figure 3.70 shows the top-level order of all the layers at this point.

14. You need to add a Gaussian Blur to the Nostrils layer. Click on the radio button to select the entire layer. You should see Layer at the top of the Appearance palette. Choose Effect|Blur|Gaussian Blur and set a radius of 3 pixels. Make sure that your Effects|Rasterize Settings allow at least .5 inch around the object.

15. You need to create a more menacing set of colors for the shark. Target and select the Vector Fish layer. Choose Duplicate Vector Fish layer from the Layers palette side drop-down menu. Drag the copied layer above the Shark Effects layer. Lock all the other layers in the document. Leave the copied layer unlocked. Name this layer "Gradient Shark". Next, you'll create a gradient color fill.

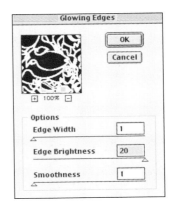

Figure 3.69

These settings change the image to grayscale.

Why Glowing Edges?

I tried in vain to discover some filter that would "trick" Illustrator into creating an embossing effect similar to the one produced by Photoshop's Filter|Stylize|Emboss command. The Glowing Edges filter had possibilities because I could coax it into a black-and-white range and get edge detail. However, that was as close as I could get to duplicating the effect that I wanted. I liked the look of the Glowing Edges filter, so I kept it. Thus are some design decisions made.

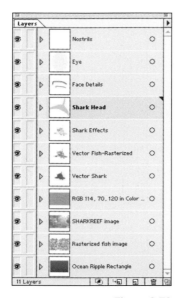

Figure 3.70
The Layers palette list gets even longer when you add four more new layers.

16. Select the shark object. Target the fill in the Appearance palette. Click on the gradient palette. Set the Type to Linear. Click on the color stop at the left edge of the gradient bar and set it to RGB: 220, 210,154. Click on the right color stop and set it to RGB: 127, 217, 230. Drag the Location diamond to 63%. Change the gradient angle to –75 degrees. Change the Object Opacity to 65% Color mode. If you don't like the way the gradient falls on the shark, use the Gradient tool to change it. Lock the Gradient Shark layer.

17. Finally, give the shark some shadows and eerie glows. First, select the Vector Shark layer. Unlock the layer and twirl down the arrow next to the layer. Click on the path radio button to select the object in the Appearance palette. Choose Effect|Stylize|Outer Glow. The mode should be set to Screen. Choose RGB: 250, 250, 190 for the glow color. Set the Opacity to 75% and the Blur to 1.17 inches. Click on OK.

18. Next, select Effect|Stylize|Drop Shadow. Use the settings shown in Figure 3.71. For Color, select RGB: 0, 73, 137. Click on OK. Notice the lovely blue haze that seems to seep out of your image and onto the surrounding pasteboard. It is the "afterglow" from the effect, and it needs to be removed from the layer.

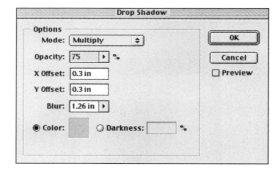

Figure 3.71
Use these Drop Shadow settings.

What's in the DETAILS.AI File?

The DETAILS.AI file contains four layers: Nostrils, Eye, Face Details, and Shark Head. The Shark Head layer was created from a copy of the shark. I used the Scissors tool on the shark and removed the lower portion of its body. I then used the Pen tool to reconnect the endpoints and to make a new bottom subpath for the object. The purpose of the Shark Head layer is to shade the top of the shark to add detail to his body. The Shark Head path is a 100 percent Opacity Color layer.

The Face Details layer contains four open paths. One set of paths forms the mouth, and the other set forms the line along the snout. The paths are stroked and given a Gaussian Blur effect. In addition, the dark gray stroke in each pair is in Multiply mode, and the light gray stroke is in Screen mode. The blur makes the mode and color changes look natural.

The Eye layer is simply a circle with a white fill and an aqua 4-point stroke. The stroke was dragged *below* the fill on the Appearance palette so that it appears behind the fill. The Gaussian Blur effect with a radius of 1 pixel softens the eye a bit.

The Nostrils layer is another layer added to help create detail in the image. It consists of two white, partially transparent ovals to which a Gaussian Blur effect needs to be added.

And the Rasterize Effects Settings Are...

When you apply effects to an object, the object is generally rasterized on the fly to accommodate the effect. You've seen that when you've rasterized objects permanently by using the Object|Rasterize command, you have the option of setting an extra amount of "canvas" around an object. You need to set this for your effects as well. If you don't allow for extra canvas around an effect, such as the Gaussian Blur, the effect is cut off where it runs beyond the bounding box of the object; the result looks awful. Start with a setting of .5 inch and increase if needed.

19. With the Vector Shark layer still targeted, use the Rectangle tool to create a no-fill, no-stroke rectangle the size of the actual image (that is, the same size as the content of the Ocean Ripple layer). Target the layer (so that Layer appears in the top of the Appearance palette) and click on the radio button to select the layer. Choose Object|Clipping Mask|Make. The blue haze should disappear from the areas outside the image.

20. Adjust any settings in the image so that the shark looks as if he is swimming in murky waters. Remember, my monitor colors can differ quite a bit from yours. Save your work. Figure 3.72 shows the finished image.

Don't Use the Place Command for Multiple Layers

Don't use the Place command on the DETAILS.AI file. When you place a file with multiple layers, Illustrator reduces the objects to a single layer. In addition, if the layers contain Appearance items, as these layers do, the Place command flattens the appearance of the objects and removes the effects. Therefore, the layers don't react in the needed manner when they're placed in the image. In this instance, Copy and Paste work best. However, you must turn on Paste Remembers Layers.

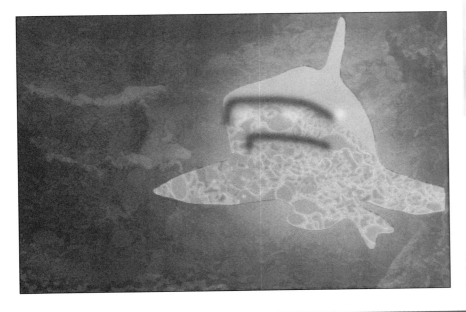

Figure 3.72
You wouldn't want to be scuba diving here!

Need To Know More about Embossing?

After I finished the shark instructions (and decided that I liked the image), I accidentally discovered how to create the embossed effect I was looking for. It's an old Photoshop "trick" explained by Kai Krause, but it works within Illustrator. Make two copies of the background image. Choose Filters|Color|Invert on the top layer and change the Layer opacity to 50%. Move the image slightly to the right and down, and the embossing appears as if by magic. Of course, because Illustrator has no equivalent to Photoshop's Merge Down command, you have two huge image files besides the weight of the rest of the image.

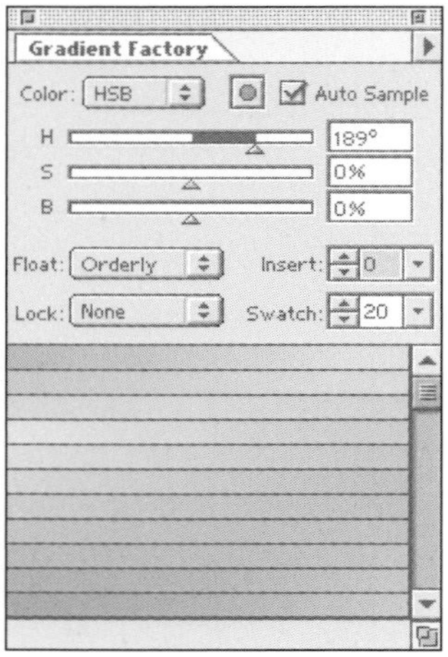

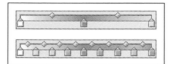

Figure 3.73
Virtual Mirror Gradient
Factory palette.

Figure 3.74
The original multi-stop gradient,
and one created automatically by
Gradient Factory.

Stoke Up the Gradient Factory

Virtual Mirror Corporation has cooked up an ideal tool for automatically creating families of gradients based on one you've created by hand. You supply the rules for how to vary the gradient, and Gradient Factory displays a palette of gradients you can apply with a single mouse click. Virtual Mirror has also created the Gradient Textures tool that lets you make textures that resemble water, fabric, and stone based on Illustrator gradients.

To use Gradient Factory (see Figure 3.73) or Gradient Textures you need to install the demo version of Vector Studio included on this book's companion CD-ROM. Vector Studio includes Gradient Factory, Gradient Textures, and five other plug-ins: Envelope Mesh, Morph Brushes, Selection Hat, Gradient Textures, GlassWorks, and Color Factory.

PROJECT 3.7 Creating a Family of Gradients

In this project, you'll learn how to change all the color stops in a gradient (see Figure 3.74) in one fell swoop:

1. Open the Gradient Factory palette by going to the Window menu and selecting Vector Studio|Gradient Factory.

2. Draw an oval and fill it with a gradient from the swatches palette.

3. Select the oval.

4. Press the green circle at the top of the Gradient Factory palette. This "Sample" button will pull the gradient of the current selection into the palette.

5. Adjust the Inserts to 20. This gives you a larger number of gradients to choose from.

6. Choose a color space in which to perform color shifting of the stops in your original gradient: CMYK, RGB, or HSB. For now, choose HSB.

7. Adjust the H slider to 30. You should now see that each of the gradients in the palette is slightly different.

8. Click on a gradient in the palette to apply it to the selected object.

PROJECT 3.8 Drawing with Textures

In this project, you learn how to create organic-looking fills based on the colors in a gradient. You can make textures (see Figure 3.75) that look like watercolors, satin, wood, marble, fire, and even mood rings (see Figure 3.76)!

1. Open the Gradient Factory palette by going to the Window menu and selecting Vector Studio|Gradient Factory.

2. Draw an oval and then select it.

3. Click on a swatch in the Gradient Texture palette.

4. Leave the oval selected for the next four steps.

5. Change the texture's look by adjusting the band and detail controls.

6. Go back to the Gradient Factory palette and click on the green Sample button.

7. Use the Gradient Factory controls to dial up a new family of gradients.

8. Click on a gradient swatch—see how the gradient texture automatically updates.

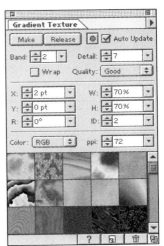

Figure 3.75
Virtual Mirror Gradient Texture palette.

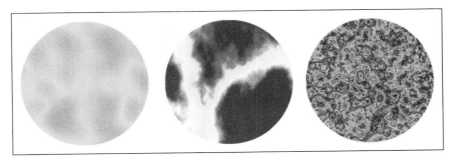

Figure 3.76
Some Gradient Textures, from left to right, watercolor, fire, and marble.

Moving On

In this chapter, you explored some of the many color effects now possible in Illustrator 9. You learned to use the Blend Horizontal and Blend Vertical filters in various ways. You also explored the Saturate and Adjust Colors filters. You used the Mix Hard and Mix Soft commands and learned how to use transparency, blend modes, and effects. Finally, you learned about the new Vector Studio effects.

In Chapter 4, you'll learn how to create objects that use Illustrator's special brushes. Just think what brushes you can make by applying transparency, blend modes, and effects to them!

Chapter 4

Different Strokes

Illustrator sports some unique brush tricks that allow you to create calligraphic strokes, paint with an object or scatter the object along a path, make pattern brushes, and use brushes to create additional brushes or pattern fills.

By Sherry London

In the last Illustrator release (version 8), Adobe introduced a bevy of brush types that added new meaning to the "Different Strokes" of this chapter title. The Art brush, for example, allows you to use an object as a stroke. The object follows the shape of the stroke, which allows you to create left- and right-facing leaves or shapes that undulate and curl.

Brush Up Your Brush Skills

No new brush types or features have been added to this release. However, because of the newly added capability to use transparency and blend modes, you have an infinite new way to alter brush strokes. You can also make patterns out for brush strokes without having to expand them. In addition, Adobe has added a Release To Layers command that is intended to help you manage brush strokes that you expand to objects. You'll actually work more with the Release To Layers command in Chapter 12, where Web effects are discussed.

You'll explore a variety of brush types in this chapter. Let's start by comparing the four types of brushes.

A Quartet of Brush Types

When you select the Paintbrush tool in the Toolbox, you can apply any of the four types of brushes found in the Brushes palette. Figure 4.1 shows Brush libraries that are included with Illustrator 9. However, only the Default Brushes palette contains all four of the brush types. Figure 4.2 shows a closer look at the Default Brushes palette. As you can see, it's divided into four sections.

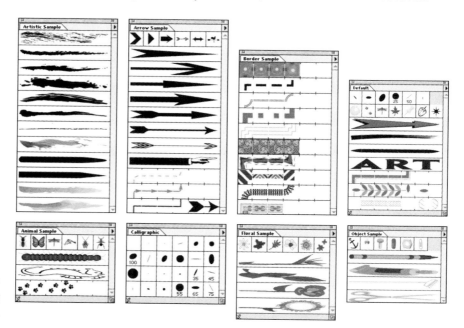

Figure 4.1
Illustrator contains a variety of existing brushes that you can use.

The Calligraphic brushes are at the top. They are easily identified because they all are some variation of a black circle—round, oval, squished, and/or rotated. You can't create your own calligraphic shapes from scratch, but you can modify a circle into the nib shape of choice. Calligraphic brushes allow you to achieve thick and thin strokes. This brush type is excellent for lettering or for creating oriental brushwork. You can add more control to the calligraphic brush stroke with a pressure-sensitive drawing tablet (such as a Wacom tablet) as you work. Figure 4.3 shows an example of an image that was stroked with a variety of Calligraphic brushes. The Calligraphic brush adds thick-and-thin areas to an individual stroke, something that the older Calligraphic pen (pre-version 8), couldn't do because it created filled shapes instead of strokes.

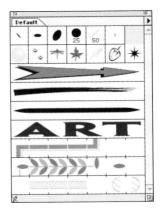

Figure 4.2
The Default Brushes palette contains four types of brushes: Calligraphic, Scatter, Art, and Pattern.

Figure 4.3
Calligraphic brushes are excellent for lettering or creating oriental brushwork.

The Scatter brushes are next in the Brushes palette. You can recognize them because each brush fits into a small square. Scatter brushes take a single design element (actually, whatever object you drag to the Brushes palette) and repeat it along a path. Unlike the Pattern brushes, however, you can have these elements disperse themselves about in an orderly or random fashion. Figure 4.4 shows an example using Scatter brushes.

The Art brushes stretch objects along a path. Each Art brush occupies one entire row of the Brushes palette and makes up the third set of brushes in the palette. The Art brushes look best when they use a shape that can logically be stretched, such as a combined, decorative stroke like the one you'll see in the coupon example in Chapter 5, or an element—such as a dachshund—that is long and stretchy anyway. You can stack individual instances of an Art brush in sequence to create animations. Figure 4.5 shows some examples using Art brushes.

Figure 4.4

Scatter brushes place image elements along a path in either random or orderly fashion.

Figure 4.5

Art brushes stretch elements along a path.

A Pattern brush repeats an element along a path. The Pattern brush, first introduced in Illustrator 8, replaces the older Path Patterns and is even easier to use. You can create a pattern for the straight areas of a stroke and special tiles for inner and outer corners and for the starting and ending tiles of a stroke. You therefore can create excellent borders as well as apply patterns along a path. Figure 4.6 shows some examples of Pattern brushes on hand-drawn text and a border.

Penmanship

Although the Brushes palette has four types of brushes, the Calligraphic brush is not quite in the same category as the others: It's the only brush type that doesn't permit dragging an object in the palette to create a new brush. To make a new Calligraphic brush, you need to click on the New Brush icon near the bottom right of the Brushes palette or choose New Brush from the sidebar menu on the Brushes palette.

Figure 4.6
The Pattern brush repeats the element along the path.

In concept, the Calligraphic brush is very easy to use. (It's even easy to use in practice; it's just a bit harder to get decent results.) Figure 4.7 shows the process of designing a new Calligraphic brush. After you click on New Brush and choose a Calligraphic brush, you simply fill in the parameters that you want your brush to have. You can set the angle interactively just by dragging the arrow on the picture of the brush. You can also set the roundness of the brush interactively, but it is not obvious how you do it. If you look carefully at the brush diagram, you'll see two small dots at the perimeter of the brush across the center. By moving those dots closer together or farther apart, you can set the roundness of your nib. You can also set a diameter for the brush and specify whether it produces a fixed stroke, a random stroke, or a pressure-controlled stroke (if you have a pressure-sensitive tablet). Your best results with the brush are from pressure-controlled settings, as long as you intend to draw your strokes individually.

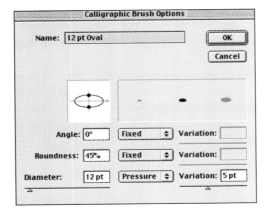

Figure 4.7
In the Calligraphic Brush Options dialog box, you can set the performance of the brush.

P R O J E C T 4.1 **The Write Stuff**

You can try out the brushes in this project combining the use of text and clip art with the Calligraphic brush. Along the way, you'll learn some of the pitfalls and techniques for working with Calligraphic brushes. Project 4.1 creates a "hang tag" for a line of children's clothes. This first section shows you how to modify a clip art file and add calligraphic strokes.

Building a Sun

1. Open the image SUN.EPS. It's an image from Ultimate Symbol's Design Elements sampler (though it is in the Chapter 4 Start folder on your CD-ROM). Figure 4.8 shows the original image.

2. Turn on the Rulers (Command/Ctrl+R). Drag the zero point of the rulers to the upper-left corner of your image. Set the Units preference to "inches" if it isn't set up that way now. Drag a vertical guide from the left margin to the 4 1/8-inch tick mark on the horizontal ruler. Drag a horizontal guide from the top ruler to the 5 1/2-inch tick mark on the vertical ruler to mark the center of the image. Lock the guides (View|Guides|Lock Guides).

3. Select the entire image (Command/Ctrl+A). In the Transform palette, enter both a width and a height of 3 inches for the sun. Press Return/Enter to execute the transformation. Drag the sun image so that it's centered on the intersection of the two guides. (The easiest way is to drag it by eye near the center of the image and then, with the bounding box showing, use the arrow keys to nudge it until the center control handles on the bounding box are on the guide lines.)

4. Ungroup (Shift+Command/Ctrl+G).

5. Carefully select the sun's face (but none of the rays). Create a new layer and transfer the selection rectangle on the Layers palette to the new layer.

6. Lock all the layers except for the sun's face. Select the entire image. Choose the Rotate tool and rotate the sun face slightly to the right (approximately 6.3 degrees).

7. Turn off the Eye icon next to the new layer. The sun's features should disappear, as shown in Figure 4.9.

8. You're going to use the Calligraphic brush to redraw the sun's rays. Currently, the sun's rays are filled shapes. If you change them into outlines, the Calligraphic brush strokes only the edges. You need to

Figure 4.8
Sun image from the Ultimate Symbol Design Elements collection.

Ultimate Symbol Collection?

I want to "plug" the clip art produced by Ultimate Symbol. I don't work for them, and I don't own stock. Their icon-based clip art collections are the most useful clip art I've ever purchased. Every day, these products are the work-horses that I turn to time and time again. The images can be combined to form many different elements. They are generic and unobtrusive enough that they don't compete with me as the designer. They are clean and elegant, and the variety is immense.

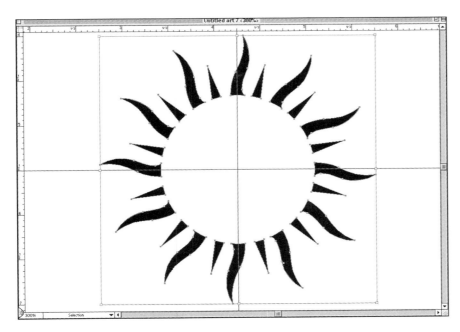

Figure 4.9
The sun's features disappear when you hide the layer to which you have moved them.

actually redraw each ray as a single stroke. To do so, you need to take some preparatory steps first. Change the fill color for the sun's rays to 50% black (use the Grayscale slider in the Color palette). Double-click on Layer 1 to open the Layer Options dialog box. Select the Template checkbox to make this layer both nonwriteable and nonprintable. Lock the template layer as well so that nothing can be accidentally selected.

9. Create a new layer. Select a Fill of None and a Stroke of black.

10. In the Brushes palette, choose New Brush from the sidebar menu. Accept the Calligraphic brush default brush type. Enter the settings shown in Figure 4.10 for the new brush.

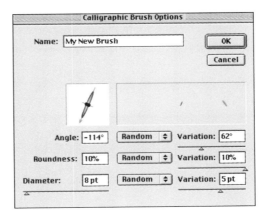

Figure 4.10
Settings for the Calligraphic brush that you will use to redraw the sun's rays.

11. Select the Paintbrush tool and the new brush. Carefully paint over all the sun's rays. Draw only one stroke per ray, from tip to just inside the empty circle (you can stroke from the circle out as well). A built-in randomness in the brush will give you results that differ somewhat from mine, (see Figure 4.11). The rays are selected in the image so that you can see their composition.

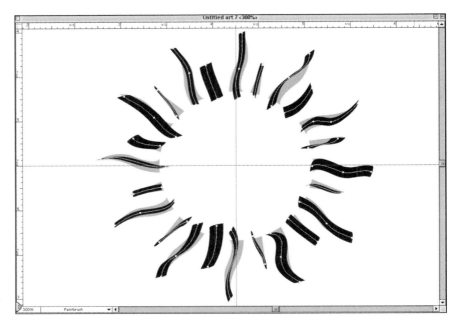

Figure 4.11
The sun's rays redrawn as single strokes.

12. Select the entire image (Command/Ctrl+A), although only the rays are selected (because only the rays are not locked). Try out several of the other Calligraphic brushes on the image (simply click on them to apply them to the strokes). If you like them better, leave them. If not, either click on the brush that you created (which will now generate a completely different set of strokes) or undo back to your original brush strokes.

Doing a Little Sun Ray Clean-Up

You now need to get rid of the points of the strokes showing in the center of the sun's face. You could build a clipping mask to hide them, or you could expand the strokes and use the Divide Pathfinder command to remove the points inside a circle. Because you might want to use the entire image as an opacity mask later in this project, I'm going to have you use the Divide command to prepare the image. However, the following section gives directions for building a clipping mask should you prefer to do that. (A clipping mask used inside an opacity mask is an added layer of complexity that almost guarantees problems.)

An Alternative Method: Creating a Compound Clipping Path

Before going on, here's another method you can use. You could create a clipping path to mask the edges of the sun's rays that extend into the face of the sun, as follows:

1. Select the rectangle tool. Draw a rectangle that encloses the sun's rays. The actual size is not critical as long as it's larger than the sun.

2. Select the Ellipse tool. Place your cursor at the intersection of the guides (that is, the center of the image). Press Option/Alt to draw the circle from the center. Press Shift as you start to draw to make a true circle. Draw a circle that's the same size as the circle around the sun's face (until the circle reaches the start of the gray sun's rays on the template layer).

3. Select both the circle and the rectangle. In the top row of the Pathfinder palette, click on Minus Front to punch a hole out of the rectangle and create the needed mask shape (you want the image to show the sun's rays).

4. Select the entire image (Command/Ctrl+A). Make a mask (Object|Masks|Make; Command/Ctrl+7). Figure 4.12 shows the ends removed from the new sun-ray strokes.

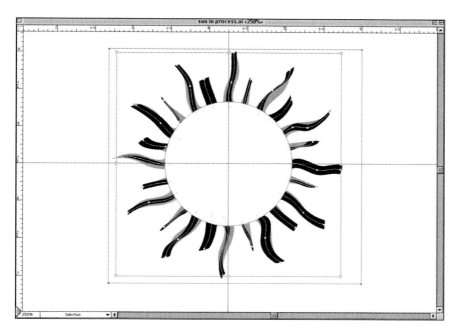

Figure 4.12
A mask makes the edges of the strokes look clean and sharp and shows the original circle.

Now, let's go back to actually start cleaning up the sun rays:

1. Select all the sun's rays (click on their radio buttons in the Layers palette with the Shift key held down). Choose Object|Expand Appearance.

2. Twirl down the layer in the Layers palette to show all the paths stored in it. You'll notice that you now have a group for each path instead of a simple path. Twirl down the first group on the layer. If you wait for the screen redraw, you'll see two paths in the subgroup. One of them shows up in black in the thumbnail, and the other doesn't show up in the thumbnail at all. Click on the radio button next to the blank thumbnail to select that path. In the Appearance palette, you'll see a path with no stroke and no fill. This path had originally contained the calligraphic stroke before you expanded the object. Let this path remain selected.

3. Choose Select|Same Fill & Stroke. All the single unstroked paths are selected. Press Delete/Backspace to remove them from the image.

4. Unfortunately, you now have a bunch of groups with only one path in each group. Target the layer and click the radio button to select the entire layer. Choose Object|Ungroup. Now, you should see all paths in the Layers palette.

5. Make a new layer. Layer 4 should appear just above Layer 3.

6. Select the Ellipse tool. Place your cursor at the intersection of the guides (that is, the center of the image). Press Option/Alt to draw the circle from the center. Press Shift as you start to draw to make a true circle. Draw a circle that's the same size as the circle around the sun's face (until the circle reaches the start of the gray sun's rays on the template layer).

7. Select all (Command/Ctrl+A). In the Pathfinder palette, click on Divide. The sun's rays and the circle become one group.

8. Choose the Direct Selection tool. Carefully click on the inner tip of each sun ray to select it. Press Shift to select additional rays. Keep the Shift key pressed as you click between the rays to select the invisible circle. Figure 4.13 shows the selected objects. Press Delete/Backspace to get rid of them.

For Trouble Selecting...

If you have trouble selecting the tiny shapes or the circle, press Command/Ctrl+Y to view the outlines only.

Figure 4.13
These objects need to be deleted from the divided group.

Figure 4.14
The sun now sports calligraphic rays.

9. Hide the Template layer and reveal Layer 2 (the sun's face). Figure 4.14 shows the sun image with calligraphic rays.

Adding a Flourish

In this part of the project, you'll prepare a circular border for the sun:

1. Make a new layer and drag it to the top of the Layer stack. Open the image FLOURISH2.AI. This image is a copy of a clip art image from Ultimate Symbol's Design Elements collection. I redrew it using the Pen tool so that instead of filled shapes, the printer's ornament is a single stroke.

2. Select the entire flourish. Then, either copy it to the clipboard and paste it into the sun image, or drag and drop it into the image. In either case, when you're finished with this step, the sun image should be active, and a copy of the flourish should be in the sun image.

3. Drag the flourish so that the center-top control handle on its bounding box is at the exact center of your image (you need to show the Template layer again because your guides are located there). When the flourish is in position, choose Object|Transform|Move. Enter a vertical distance of 2.5 inches and a horizontal distance of 0. Click on OK. Figure 4.15 shows the result.

4. Choose the Rotate tool. Press Option/Alt and click at the exact center of the image. Enter a rotation amount of 30 degrees in the dialog box and click on Copy. Transform Again (Command/Ctrl+D) 10 times, so that you have 12 copies of the flourish, as shown in Figure 4.16.

5. Drag the Flat 6 Pt brush from the upper left of the Default Brushes palette to the New Brush icon at the bottom of the Brushes palette to duplicate the brush (or choose Duplicate Brush from the side drop-down menu in the Brushes palette). Double-click on the copy and change its angle to 78 degrees and the diameter to 2 points.

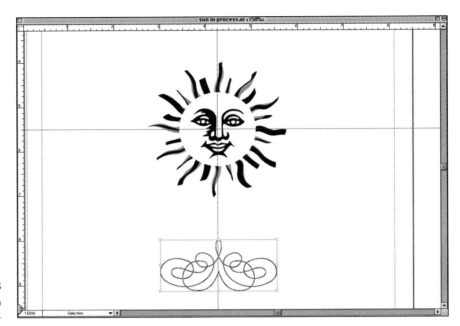

Figure 4.15
Move the flourish 2.5 inches down from the center of the image.

Figure 4.16
(Left) Twelve copies of the printer's flourish frame the sun face.

Figure 4.17
(Right) The tiny calligraphic brush leaves thick and thin strokes.

6. Lock Layers 2, 3, and 4. Select the entire image (Command/Ctrl+A). Click on the newly copied brush to apply it to the circle of flourishes. Figure 4.17 shows the brush's calligraphic effect.

Creating Sundae Text

Next, you're going to create some text on a circle and then re-create the letterforms calligraphically.

1. Lock all the layers. Create a new layer (Layer 6). Select the Ellipse tool. Place your cursor on the center of your image at the intersection of the guides. Press Option/Alt and click. Enter 3.5 inches as both the width and the height in the dialog box that appears. This circle is the basis for the text that you'll create.

2. Select the Path Type tool. Click on the circle. Using Adobe Garamond Bold (if you have it or another serif font if you don't), enter "Put On Your" at 48 points. Choose the Selection tool and leave the type circle selected.

3. Double-click on the Scale tool. Choose a Uniform Scale of 100% and click on Copy. With the Path Type tool, edit this new text so that it reads "Sundae Clothes". Choose the Selection tool.

4. Grab the large I-beam in front of the words "Sundae Clothes" and drag the text to the bottom of the circle. As you drag, flip the words so that they read properly. If the Baseline setting on the Character palette is not visible, select Show Options from the sidebar menu in the Character palette. Set the Baseline Shift to –33 pt (or the amount needed to make your font move from the inside to the outside of the circle). Drag the text "Put On Your" and center it at the top of the circle. Figure 4.18 shows the image with the added text.

Figure 4.18
Text has been added and the sun face given a new direction.

5. Lock all the layers except Layer 6. Select the entire image. Change the Fill color to 50% gray. Double-click on the Layer entry in the Layers palette and designate Layer 6 (the Text layer) as a Template layer. Create a new layer (Layer 7).

6. Set the Fill to None and the Stroke to black. Select the Paintbrush tool. You may use any calligraphic brush (or brushes) that you want. You might need to create one or more new ones. They should be fairly tiny because the text is small. Draw over each letter that's on the Template layer to re-create the text as combinations of single strokes. The original 6-point Flat brush works quite well for this task. Figure 4.19 shows the finished image.

Figure 4.19

(Left) All the text has been redrawn.

Figure 4.20

(Right) A garment "hand tag" for "Put On Your Sundae Clothes."

What else can you do with this image when it is finished (besides use it in black and white)? Figure 4.20 shows this image in less-than-glorious grayscale.

In the first edition of this book (for Illustrator 8), I placed the image into Photoshop to create the garment tag. However, you can now complete the entire project in Illustrator. Because it's an interesting use of the new features, I'm including instructions for finishing the project.

SUNDAETAG.AI, in the CH05STARTS folder, contains all the layers that I used. I grouped each of the layers for the sun face individually and then grouped all four layers together. I then deleted the template and empty layers. I created a background by making a rectangle and changing it to a gradient mesh object (you'll learn how to create these objects in Chapter 8). I filled the intersections of the gradient mesh object with different colors and then applied the Pixellate|Pointillize effect to the object. Finally, I duplicated the pointillized rectangle and made it smaller but changed the Blend mode to Multiply with a 64 percent opacity to give the texture more punch.

Why Isn't this Process as Easy as I Thought It Would Be?

Hand-stroking text is really a pain—unless you love calligraphy anyway. Adobe hasn't made this task any less painful by its wonderful Pencil and Paintbrush tool editing behavior. When you draw near a selected shape, Illustrator assumes that you *want to change the shape of the selected object*. This editing behavior is wonderful when you *do* want to edit objects. However, it's less wonderful for freehand drawing. When you finish a stroke, the stroke stays selected. Therefore, if your next stroke is in the general vicinity, it will change your last stroke rather than create a new one. When you redrew the sun's rays, they weren't close enough to one another to make Illustrator enter Edit mode. However, unless you remember to press Command/Ctrl and deselect all objects before drawing the next stroke, you'll spend as much time cursing as you do drawing.

Drawing the strokes to re-create serif text is also time-consuming. Your strokes will look better if you don't try to draw each letterform in one pass. Each serif and each down stroke should be done as a different unit. To draw the *P* in *Put*, for example, uses three strokes: the serif at the foot of the *P*, the stem of the *P*, and bowl of the *P*. Take your time creating these strokes.

Making the Tag

All the layers in the image are ready for the next steps, which will create an embossed effect. Just follow these steps to finish:

1. Open the image SUNDAETAG.AI.

2. Hide the Background layer and the Black Shadow and White Highlight layers.

3. Lock the Mask layer and click on the Cut layer. Select the entire image (Command/Ctrl+A). Cut the selection to the clipboard (Command/Ctrl+X).

4. Unlock the Mask layer. Click on the Mask layer entry in the Layers palette to target it. Click on the radio button next to the Mask layer to select it. You should see the preview of the texture rectangles in the Transparency palette.

5. Choose Make Opacity Mask from the side menu in the Transparency palette.

6. Click on the Opacity Mask thumbnail in the Transparency palette to make it active. Choose Edit|Paste In Front. Check the Invert Mask button. You should see the entire sun face, text, and flourish in the texture with no background behind it. Click on the object thumbnail in the Transparency palette to return to the object editing mode.

7. Show the Background layer and the White Highlight layer by clicking to reveal their eye icons. Hide the Mask layer for the moment. Save your work—just for security.

8. Make sure that the Background is locked and remove the lock from the White Highlight layer. Notice that the White Highlight layer is black. You need to change that color.

9. Twirl down the White Highlight layer arrow to show the group and the four subgroups. Lock the last three of the four subgroups. (Everything in your image except for the top subgroup should be locked.)

10. Choose the Group arrow tool. Drag-select all the letters. In the Toolbox, you should see a black stroke. If you see No Stroke/No Fill or question marks, then you haven't selected the objects correctly.

11. Lock the first subgroup and unlock the second one. Drag-select the entire group and change the Stroke to white.

12. Lock the second subgroup, unlock the third one, and change the Fill to white.

13. Lock the third subgroup, unlock the fourth one, and change the Fill to white. Remove all the locks on the White Highlight layer and collapse the layer.

14. Show the Mask layer but leave it locked.

15. Click on the White Highlight layer to target it and then click on the radio button to select all the objects on the layer. Press the up-arrow key twice and the left-arrow key twice to move the white object up and to the left. Lock the layer.

16. Unlock and show the Black Shadow layer. Target and select it as you did the White Highlight layer. Press the right-arrow key two times and the down-arrow key two times. Lock the layer.

If you want to make the background layer fade out on the edges, you can target the layer and add an opacity mask. With the opacity mask inverted and active, create a rectangle that is a bit smaller than the image size and give it a Fill of black and a 90-pixel Stroke of medium gray. Add a Pixelate|Pointillize effect of about 16 pixels to the stroke.

Before I leave the topic of Calligraphic brushes completely, I need to discuss the Expand command (again). It is an extremely useful command to use with Calligraphic brushes. With the Calligraphic brush, you don't have a filled shape that you can edit. Although you can add points along the stroke, you cannot selectively alter the width of the calligraphic line. However, if you use the Expand command when you're done (and you *are sure* that you're done), you can tug on the shape of the line to make it anything you want. Figure 4.21 shows the Calligraphic brush-stroked letter on the left and the same letter expanded into filled shapes on the right. I edited the letter on the right to change the shape of the fill. You can't get the same letter shape using only strokes. Although I think the stroked letter is more elegant, sometimes you aren't going for this look.

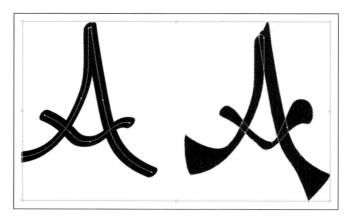

Figure 4.21

The stroked letterform is on the left, and the edited letter that has been expanded into a filled shape is on the right.

Seeing Stars

Now that we've thoroughly covered the Calligraphic brush, in Project 4.2, you'll turn your attention to the three remaining brush types: the Pattern brush, the Art brush, and the Scatter brush. You'll work a short example that shows you how the brushes differ from one another—even when defined with the same tile.

PROJECT 4.2 One Tile—Three Brush Types

In this Project, you'll use a star as the pattern element and create a tile that can seamlessly repeat. For this reason, you'll be given detailed instructions on dimensions, even though the specific dimensions aren't critical to the success of the project (it's also easier for you to duplicate my work if I give you specific measurements). I'm not enamored of using guides when I draw, but they make communicating the expected results much more predictable—which is why I teach with them more often than I use them in practice.

1. Create a new document in Illustrator.

2. Turn on the Rulers (Command/Ctrl+R). Drag a horizontal guide from the top ruler to the 8-inch mark on the vertical ruler. (I'm assuming the default arrangement of your page where Illustrator has numbered the vertical ruler from zero at the bottom.) Drag another guide down to the 7-inch mark on the vertical ruler. Drag a vertical guide from the side ruler to the 2-inch mark on the top, horizontal ruler. Magnify your screen to 800% so that you can see the area where the three guides intersect. Unlock the guides if you need to move them now that you have zoomed in so closely (you'll usually notice that the guides were not placed exactly). Drag a third horizontal guide to the tick mark on the vertical ruler that is three small ticks above the 7.5-inch mark (technically, it is at 7 35/64). Figure 4.22 shows the layout of your document.

3. Select the Star tool (it pops out of the same spot as the Ellipse tool). Choose a Stroke of None and a Fill of bright green. Place your cursor on the middle horizontal guide where it intersects the vertical guide. Press the mouse button and drag the cursor straight down to the bottom guide where it intersects the vertical guide. This action creates a star about 1-inch high that points directly down. Figure 4.23 shows an enlargement.

4. With the star selected, drag a vertical guide from the side ruler until it touches the control point marked with the arrow in Figure 4.24. (I've lightened the color of the star so that you can see the guides and control points better.)

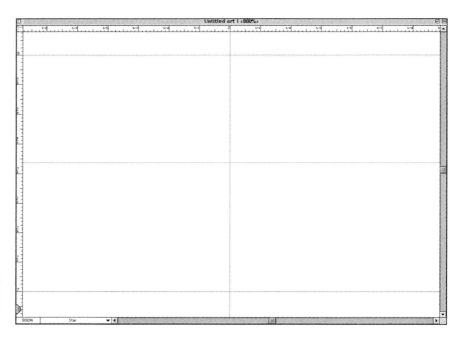

Figure 4.22
Preparing your image with three horizontal guides and one vertical one.

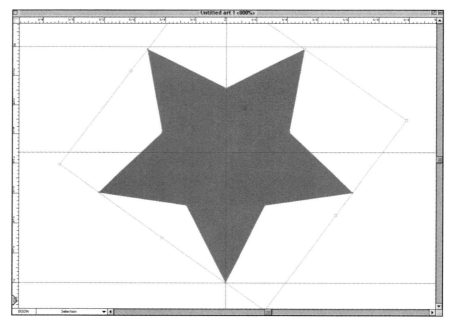

Figure 4.23
You've created a downward-pointing star.

5. Choose the Selection tool. Press Option/Alt and drag a copy of the star to the right until its leftmost point touches the new guide that you placed in Step 4. Press Shift after you start to drag the star to constrain motion to the horizontal. Leave the new star selected. Fill the star with cyan. Figure 4.25 shows the result.

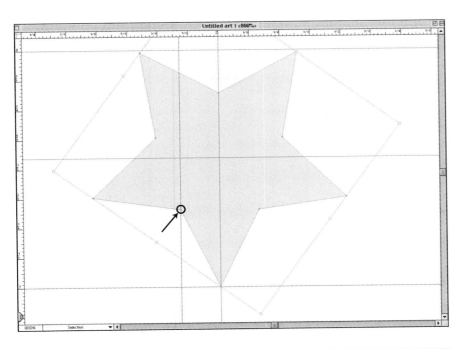

Figure 4.24
Drag a vertical guide to the control point marked by the arrow.

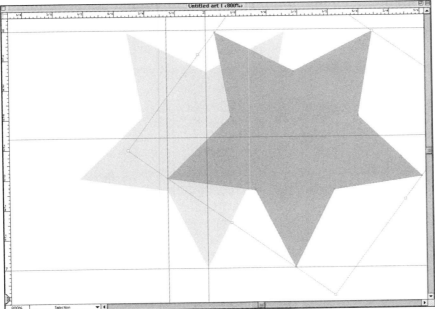

Figure 4.25
You now have two stars.

6. Zoom out to 300% and Transform Again (Command/Ctrl+D). A third star moves the same distance away. Fill it with light purple and Transform Again. Fill the new star with pink and Transform Again. Fill this star with yellow, but leave it selected. Figure 4.26 shows the five stars that you have created.

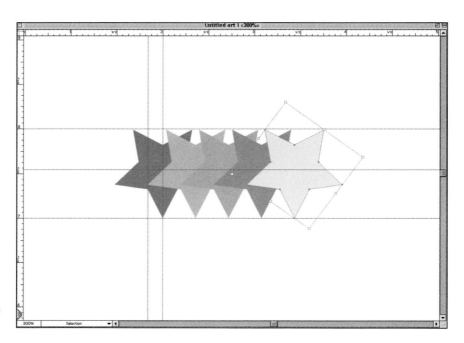

Figure 4.26

You have made a five-star lineup.

7. The tile that you are creating is to be seamless. Therefore, you need to repeat the five-star sequence to obtain one complete repeat (because the design is overlapping). Therefore, Transform Again. Use the Eyedropper tool to set the fill to the *same* green as you used for the first star. To be totally safe and sure of a good repeat, Transform Again and fill the final star with the same cyan used in the second star. You now have seven stars.

8. Select all the stars, press Option/Alt, and drag a duplicate of these stars for safekeeping to the pasteboard area of your image. Lock the guides if they want to come along for the ride when you drag and copy the stars. Deselect the stars after you make the copy and return to the 300% view of your pattern-in-process.

9. Drag a vertical guide from the left ruler until it intersects the control point at the bottom of the rightmost *green* star (that's one in from the last star on the right). Figure 4.27 shows the position of the guide.

10. Unlock the guides (if they're locked). Drag the leftmost vertical guide off the image. (This action leaves the two vertical guides that intersect the bottom points of the stars.)

11. Select the Rectangle tool. Make sure that Snap To Point is selected in the View menu. Draw a rectangle between the two vertical guides and the 7- and 8-inch marks (the top and bottom horizontal guides). Figure 4.28 shows the drawn rectangle.

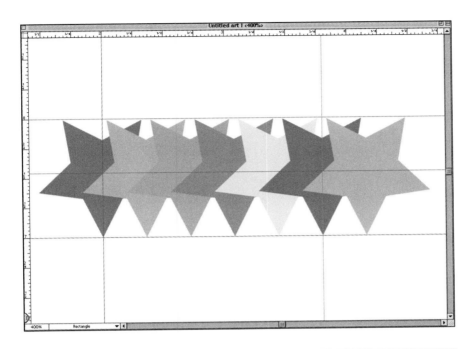

Figure 4.27
Place another vertical guide.

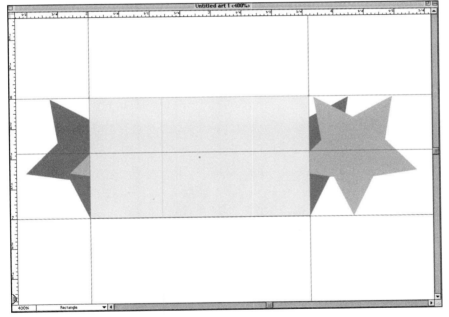

Figure 4.28
This rectangle sets the size for
the finished pattern tile.

12. Select the stars and the rectangle in the image area. Click on Crop in the Pathfinder palette. The stars are trimmed to an exact repeat size. Group the stars (Command/Ctrl+G). Figure 4.29 shows the cropped stars.

13. Drag the grouped stars into the Brushes palette. Click on the Pattern Brush radio button to define a Pattern brush (let's not worry about corner tiles right now). Accept all the default settings. Click on OK.

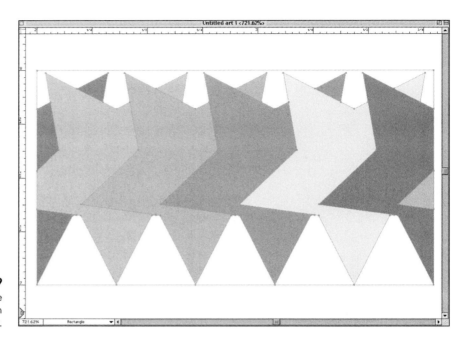

Figure 4.29

The Crop command uses the rectangle to trim the stars to an exact repeat.

Deselect the grouped stars (clicking on the stars a second time applies the new brush to *them*—which is not what you want to do).

14. Select and drag the grouped stars into the Brushes palette again. This time, select the Art Brush radio button. Again, accept the defaults, as shown in Figure 4.30.

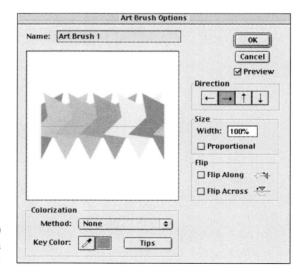

Figure 4.30

The New Art Brush Options dialog box.

15. Deselect the grouped stars. Select and drag the grouped stars into the Brushes palette. Select the Scatter brush. Accept the defaults, as shown in Figure 4.31, and then deselect.

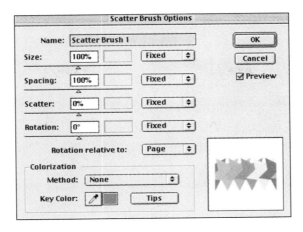

Figure 4.31
The New Scatter Brush Options dialog box.

16. Drag the original cropped tile to the pasteboard area of your image. Clear the guides (View|Guides|Clear Guides). In the image area, draw as large a star as will fit. Set the Fill to None. Click on the Stars Pattern brush to apply it. Figure 4.32 shows the result. Because you didn't define a corner tile, the points of the star are empty.

Figure 4.32
The star pattern decorates the large star.

17. Let's fix that problem. Select the yellow star in the seven-star pattern that you copied prior to cropping the stars. Drag it (with Option/Alt pressed *after* you start to drag) to the first box—the outer corner box—in the Stars Pattern brush that you created. Accept the defaults in the Brushes dialog box and click on Apply To Strokes. Then, select the pink star and follow the same procedure, except that you need to drag it to the fourth box in the Brushes palette entry for the Stars Pattern brush. Again, click on Apply To Strokes. Figure 4.33 shows that the star now has a whole star at each point.

18. The pattern is still too big for the size of the star. Double-click on the Star Pattern brush and change the Size to 60%. Figure 4.34 shows the result. If you want a smaller star for the corner, you can scale a copy of

Figure 4.33

The single stars fill the corners of the large star.

the individual yellow star (on the pasteboard) to 60% and replace the corner star by pressing Option/Alt and dragging the scaled yellow star into slot 1 of the Star Pattern brush. Figure 4.35 shows this effect.

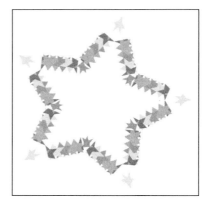

Figure 4.34

(Left) Scale the star pattern to 60 percent to better fit the proportions of the object to which it is applied.

Figure 4.35

(Right) The corner element is scaled to 60 percent in Illustrator and replaces the original corner star in the Pattern brush.

19. With the large star still selected, click on the Star Scatter brush entry near the top of the Brushes palette. The image changes to look like Figure 4.36. This image is not very attractive and does not show that it was applied to a star.

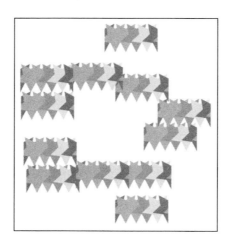

Figure 4.36

The Scatter brush scatters the stars in such a way as to completely obscure the star-shaped path.

20. Double-click on the Star Scatter brush entry to open the Brush Options dialog box. Set the Size to 30% (or 31% as it shows up in my screen capture in Figure 4.37). Set the Spacing to 30%. Click on OK and Apply To Strokes. Figure 4.38 shows the changed star. Now, you can see that the image elements are applied to a star shape.

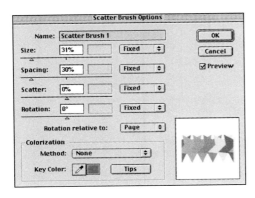 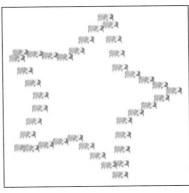

Figure 4.37
(Left) Change the Size and Spacing in the Scatter Brush Options dialog box.

Figure 4.38
(Right) When you change the brush options, the result is much more attractive.

21. Open the Scatter Brush Options dialog box for the star again. This time, play with all the controls until you are sure that you know how each control affects the result. Switch the Rotation Relative To setting from Page to Path. Figure 4.39 shows some changes in the settings from Figure 4.37, and Figure 4.40 shows the result. The star sets march around the larger star as if they were band members at a half-time maneuver. Explore some other settings. Figures 4.41 to 4.44 show two other sets of settings and their matching stars.

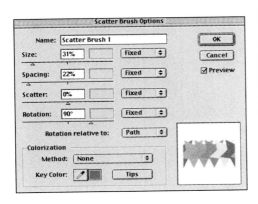 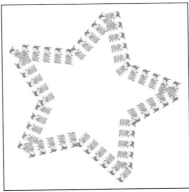

Figure 4.39
(Left) Change the Angle of Rotation and the Rotation Relative To settings in the Scatter Brush Options dialog box.

Figure 4.40
(Right) The tiles march around the star.

22. With the large star shape selected, click on the Star Art brush that you created to apply the brush to the large star. Figure 4.45 shows the somewhat less than wonderful result. The single tile of five stars is stretched and elongated over the length of the star path.

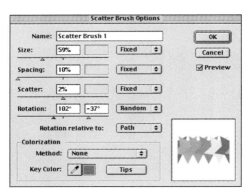

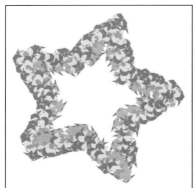

Figure 4.41
(Left) Set some random parameters in the Scatter Brush Options dialog box.

Figure 4.42
(Right) With random rotation and a tight spacing, the star looks stamped with a linoleum block.

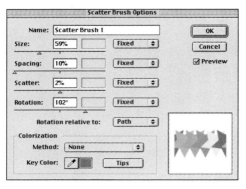

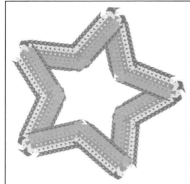

Figure 4.43
(Left) Set a fixed Angle of Rotation in the previous settings in the Scatter Brush Options dialog box.

Figure 4.44
(Right) A regular pattern emerges that could not easily be achieved with the Pattern brush.

Figure 4.45
The default settings on the Art brush aren't the best look for the star shape.

23. You can change the look of the Art brush by adjusting its Brush options. In Figure 4.46, I changed the direction in which the tile is stretched and applied. I also changed the Size to 40%. If you click on Proportional, the image tile keeps its aspect ratio as it stretches around the shape. Except for short strokes, this setting is rarely practical. Figure 4.47 shows the result of the settings changes. Experiment with the settings until you find some that you like.

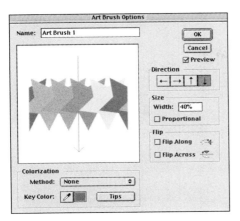

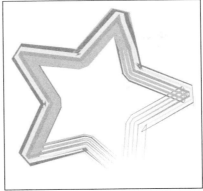

Figure 4.46
(Left) You can change the direction in which the tile is applied.

Figure 4.47
(Right) Changing the apply direction and the size results in a totally different design.

24. You can also split large strokes to take control of how the Art brush is applied. To do so, select the Scissors tool. With the large star selected, click on every control point to split the star into 10 separate paths. With all the segments selected, set the Width in the Brush Options dialog box to 40% and the Direction to Stroke From Left To Right. (The tile also looks good Stroked From Bottom To Top.) Figure 4.48 shows the results.

Figure 4.48
Splitting the star into segments reduces the stretch on the image tile.

25. What else can you do with this brush and the star shape? So that you can get more wiggle for your stroke, you can apply the Roughen filter (Filter|Distort|Roughen). Try it. Select all the segments. Use the filter settings shown in Figure 4.49. By using relatively few new smooth points but a significant amount of change, you can create interesting waves in the star shape that are automatically followed by the Art brush. Figure 4.50 shows the result. (I also could not resist showing you the same image stroked from bottom to top. See Figure 4.51.)

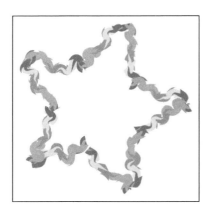

Figure 4.49

(Left) Use these settings for the Roughen filter.

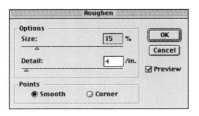

Figure 4.50

(Right) The Roughen filter adds interest to the strokes that use the Art brush.

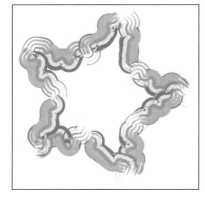

Figure 4.51

This is the same image as Figure 4.50 but is stroked from bottom to top.

If you have to decide when to use which brush type, you need a clearer idea of the strengths and weaknesses and the possibilities of each. The following are some very general guidelines:

- If you want to apply a uniform tile that repeats end to end without variation, use the Pattern brush. The length of the stroke is not a factor.

- If you want to randomize where the elements are applied, or if you want to change the angle of their application, use the Scatter brush. The length of the stroke does not matter here, either.

- If you want to apply a single element along an entire stroke, use the Art brush. If the element is pictorial in nature, it will remain recognizable only if the path is fairly short. However, if the design element is abstract, the path length becomes much less significant.

- If your path contains many corner points that are a significant element in the design, a Pattern brush is suitable only if you also design corner elements for it.

- If the start and endpoints of a stroke need to be rounded or contain a special element, you can do that only with a Pattern brush. The Scatter brush makes no accommodation whatsoever, and the Art brush can

change only the start and end of a stroke if you define the brush shape
that way from the start (such as an arrow).

A Painterly Stroke

Corel Painter contains a series of wonderful brushes that are designed for use by
Web artists. The brushes are optimized for Web use because they aren't anti-
aliased. In other words, they have hard edges that paint in a solid color. Although
the edges produce a single color that doesn't fade to the background color, the
shape of the edges differs with each brush and is quite interesting. I thought that
it would be fun to use some of these Painter brushes in a project to create strokes
that could be applied with Illustrator's Art brush (ergo, Project 4.3). For those of
you who don't have Painter, I've included a Photoshop document that contains
sample brush strokes. (If you don't have Photoshop either, you can start with the
Illustrator path documents created in Photoshop.)

PROJECT 4.3 Abstract Art Strokes

1. Open the image STROKES2.PSD in Photoshop. If you don't have
    Photoshop, skip to Step 8. Figure 4.52 shows the original image of
    several strokes created using some of Painter's new Web brushes.

2. Although several strokes are available for you to try, you can start with
    the thick stroke that is second from the bottom. Select the rectangular
    marquee tool. Draw a marquee around the stroke. Figure 4.53 shows
    the selection.

How Do I Send Paths from Photoshop?

In Chapter 11, I cover ways to
get Photoshop paths into
Illustrator. If you cannot follow
the instructions here, try brows-
ing through Chapter 11 and
then come back to this project.

Figure 4.52
Web brush strokes created in
Corel Painter.

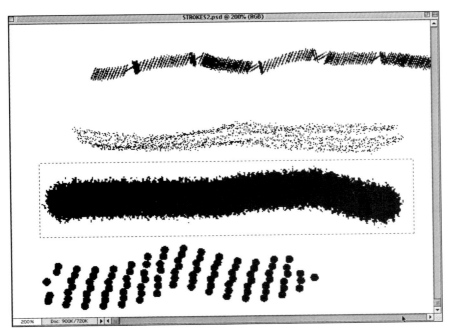

Figure 4.53
Select the stroke that is second
from the bottom.

3. Copy the selection to the clipboard (Command/Ctrl+C). Create a new document (File|New). Accept the defaults. Paste in the selection from the clipboard (Command/Ctrl+V).

4. Choose Image|Image Size. Select the Constrain Proportions checkbox. Select the Resample Image checkbox. Change the Size to 800%. Change the Interpolation Method to Nearest Neighbor so that you can keep the image aliased and sharp while you resize it large enough to capture an adequate path (which is why you copied the original stroke to a new image).

5. Double-click on the Magic Wand tool to open the Options palette. Set the Tolerance to 0 and deselect the Anti-Alias checkbox. Click on a black pixel in the new image. Choose Select|Similar. All the black pixels in the image are selected.

6. Make the Paths palette active. Choose Make Work Path from the sidebar menu on the Paths palette. Select a Tolerance of 1, as shown in Figure 4.54, to draw a tight path around the selection. Double-click on the Work Path entry in the Paths palette to save it. You can use the default name of Path 1.

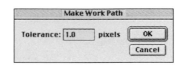

Figure 4.54
Enter a Tolerance of 1 to draw a tight path around a selection.

7. Choose File|Export|Paths To Illustrator. Save the file as BIGSTROKE.AI.

8. In Illustrator, open the file BIGSTROKE.AI (it is also on your CD-ROM). Because it's a Photoshop export file, it looks empty. Select the entire image (Command/Ctrl+A). Change the Fill to black. Choose Object|Crop Marks|Release and delete the empty rectangle around the large filled stroke object.

9. Because the stroke is gigantic, select the entire image, double-click on the Scale tool, and enter a Uniform Scale of 20%. Click on OK.

10. Choose the Selection tool. Group all the objects in the image (Command/Ctrl+G).

11. Change the Fill to 50% gray. Figure 4.55 shows the reduced-in-size stroke in gray.

Figure 4.55
The stroke is colored gray and reduced to 20 percent.

12. Press Option/Alt and drag a duplicate of the stroke. Fill the duplicate with 20% gray and overlap the lighter gray stroke near the bottom of the original stroke.

13. Press Option/Alt and drag a duplicate of the light gray stroke. Set its Fill to 80% black. Let this stroke overlap the top of the medium gray stroke but send it to the back (Object|Arrange|Send To Back). Figure 4.56 shows the three overlapping strokes.

Figure 4.56
Three copies of the original stroke overlap one another.

14. Group the three strokes. Drag them onto the Brushes palette and define a new Art brush, as shown in Figure 4.57. Remember to change the Colorization method to Tints And Shades.

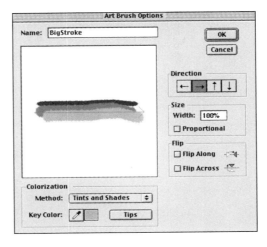

Figure 4.57

The Art Brush settings for the BigStroke brush that you have just created.

15. Drag the original stroke into the pasteboard area for safekeeping. With nothing selected, change the Fill color to None and the Stroke color to a soft pink.

16. Choose the Paintbrush tool and click on the BigStroke Art brush. Draw an object. Figure 4.58 shows a fast sketch that I did just to let you see how the brush looks.

Figure 4.58

A fast sketch made with the BigStroke Art brush.

Obviously, we have just started to scratch the surface of possibilities with this technique, but we need to move on. Try applying the strokes top to bottom and bottom to top as well as horizontally.

Something's Fishy

As you can see, you can easily create strokes that look like watercolor by using the Art brush. The Art brush also is a wonderful tool when you want to create an object that can be enhanced by bending and stretching along its length. Leaves come to mind as an almost perfect application. Figure 4.59 shows a bare tree (from Ultimate Symbol's Nature Icons collection) to which I have added leaves (from the same clip art set). I defined a single leaf as an Art brush to be stroked from bottom to top. Every leaf in the image looks different because the shape of the leaf as an Art brush follows the shape of the stroke used to paint it. The time saved is tremendous—if I had to draw each leaf, it would have taken much longer than the five minutes that I spent putting the image together.

Although I changed the colors of the individual leaves, most natural leaves have gradations of color in them. An Art brush that uses a gradient would be lovely. Unfortunately, it is also impossible—at least if you try to define a shape

Figure 4.59
A bare tree (from the Ultimate Symbol Nature Icons collection) stroked with the Leaf Art brush.

containing a gradient as an Art brush. None of the object-defined brushes can contain masks, compound paths, gradients, patterns, or gradient meshes. They need to be simple objects. In Project 4.4, you learn how to get around the lack of support for gradients and compound paths, and so on in the object-defined brushes, and you learn how to define any brush that you want.

PROJECT 4.4 Expand Your Horizons

1. In Illustrator, open the image FISH.AI or draw your own simple fish outline. Figure 4.60 shows the starting image.

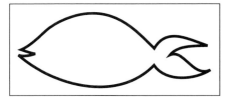

Figure 4.60
The fish is the starting place.

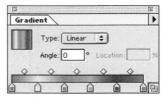

Figure 4.61
Select the Rainbow gradient and activate the Gradient palette.

2. Select the fish. Press Option/Alt and drag a duplicate to the pasteboard area for safekeeping.

3. Change the Units preferences to points. Create a new layer. Select the Rectangle tool and click inside the image area. Create a rectangle that is 250 points wide by 10 points high (this size gives you approximately nine stripes in the fish). Set the Stroke of the rectangle to None. Set the Fill of the rectangle to the Rainbow Linear gradient. Figure 4.61 shows the Gradient palette with the Rainbow gradient selected.

4. In the Gradient palette, drag the last four colors on the right (purple, pink, blue, and green) off the palette to remove them. Removing these colors leaves only the orange and the yellow, as shown in Figure 4.62. Drag the yellow pointer to the right edge of the color slider, as shown in Figure 4.63.

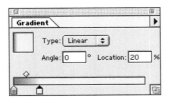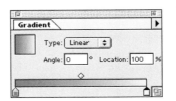

Figure 4.62
(Left) Remove all of the colors except for orange and yellow.

Figure 4.63
(Right) Drag the yellow pointer to the right edge of the color slider.

5. Drag the gradient rectangle to a position just above the top of the fish. Lock the Fish layer (Layer 1). Choose Object|Transform|Move. Move the rectangle horizontally 0 points and vertically –9 points (one height distance). Click on Copy. Transform Again (Command/Ctrl+D) until you have covered the fish. You should have about 12 gradient rectangles, as shown selected in Figure 4.64.

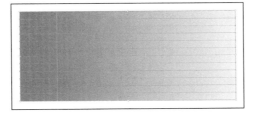

Figure 4.64
Cover the fish with gradient rectangles.

6. Select the bottom rectangle and every other rectangle (select one, skip one until you select six). In the Gradient palette, exchange the placement of the yellow and orange points by sliding them toward the center. Then, put the yellow pointer at the left end and the orange pointer at the right end. Drag the Position slider to 70% to lengthen the yellow transition area. Figure 4.65 shows the result.

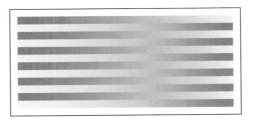

Figure 4.65
Edit the yellow-orange gradient.

7. Select the fourth rectangle from the bottom and the fifth rectangle from the top (they are both orange-on-the-left gradients). Drag the yellow pointer from its position at the right edge of the slider to the 50% mark

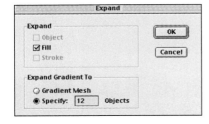

Figure 4.66
Stagger the transition areas to make the gradients less regular.

to keep the yellow in the gradient solid for a longer time. Figure 4.66 shows the new transition areas. You are making this change to stagger the position of the transition area so that it is less regular.

8. Select the entire image (Command/Ctrl+A). Because you have Layer 1 locked, only the gradient bands should be selected. Choose Object|Expand. Expand the fill to 12 objects. Expanding posterizes the gradient, but it also prevents any printing problems that might occur and adds a bit of sparkle to this particular image. In the fish, I feel that the banding can actually enhance the design—which wouldn't be the case in other situations. You might not have any printing problems even if you used the full 256 objects to describe the gradient, but you don't need to put that theory to the test right now. Figure 4.67 shows the Expand dialog box.

Figure 4.67
Expand the object.

9. Group the objects (Command/Ctrl+G) and deselect them.

10. Remove the lock on Layer 1 and drag it above Layer 2. You can now see the outline of the fish on top of the gradient squares, as shown in Figure 4.68.

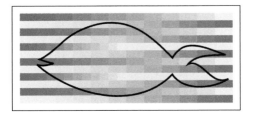

Figure 4.68
The fish shows up on top of the gradient.

11. Select the fish outline. Double-click on the Scale tool and enter a Uniform Scale of 100%. Click on Copy. Hide the selection (Command/Ctrl+3). You'll need this extra copy in a little while.

12. Select the fish and all gradient squares beneath it. In the Pathfinder palette, click on Crop. Figure 4.69 shows the cropped fish. You need to use the Crop command if you want to make the rectangle conform to the shape of the fish. The only other way to get the fish shape is to use the fish as a mask, but if you did that, you wouldn't be able to define the result as an Art brush because masks aren't allowed.

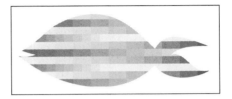

Figure 4.69
Here's the cropped fish.

13. Show the hidden selection (Command+Option+3/Alt+Ctrl+3). Now, the fish has a stroke around it. Change the Stroke weight to 1 point.

14. Lock Layer 1. Drag Layer 2 above it in the Layers palette (Layer 2 is now empty because cropping the fish moved everything onto Layer 1).

15. Select the Circle tool. Set the Fill color to white and the Stroke color to None. Press Shift+Option/Shift+Alt and draw a circle as large as you want for the white of the fish's eye. Select the fish outline. Double-click on the Scale tool and enter a Uniform Scale of 35%. Click on Copy. Change the Fill of the copy to black. Figure 4.70 shows the finished fish.

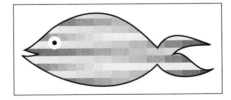

Figure 4.70
Finally—a finished fish.

16. Select all the pieces of the fish and drag the fish into the Brushes palette. Create a new Art brush using the settings shown in Figure 4.71. This is the first time that I have instructed you to choose the Hue Shift method of Colorization. When you use this method (which works like the Hue slider in Photoshop's Hue/Saturation command to move all the colors around the color wheel), you need to select a key color from the Art brush. This color is used as the controlling color to calculate the distance of the shift around the color circle. Use the Eyedropper tool inside the Art Brush dialog box and click the solid yellow of the stripe that you see third from the bottom of the fish. Click on OK to exit the dialog box.

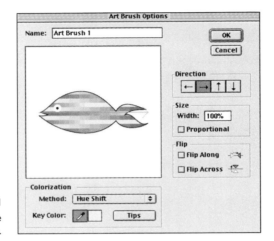

Figure 4.71
Use these settings to create the fish art brush.

On Using Strokes and Fills

You could also make the fish's eye by using a black fill with a very large white stroke around it. That approach would seem to be more efficient. However, when you make an Art brush from the fish and apply it to a short stroke, the black center of the eye disappears because no room exists for it any longer in the image. When you define the eye as two filled shapes, both shapes appear, regardless of the length of the stroke that you make with the Art brush.

17. Deselect the fish, and then select and drag it to the pasteboard area for safekeeping.

18. Deselect everything. Pick a strong yellow for the Stroke and None for the Fill. Choose the Paintbrush tool and the Fish brush and draw a school of fish. Select some of the fish and change their Stroke colors. Select some of the fish and use the Selected Object icon on the bottom of the Brushes palette to change the Colorization method to Tints And Shades only for the selected strokes. The two fish that are swimming against the crowd in Figure 4.72 were able to do so because I selected the Flip Along checkbox in the Selected Object Art Brush Options dialog box. The two hot pink and orange fish were stroked from top to bottom in a copy of the Fish brush.

Figure 4.72
Notice the two fish that swim to a different wave pattern.

Let It Snow

The Expand command might be one of the best tools for creating interesting brushes that seem to make use of "forbidden" elements such as gradients, but you can play additional tricks with brushes. The Expand command also allows you to create brushes *from* brushes (as you will in Chapter 5, where you'll use the Celtic knot brush as the corner element in a Celtic knot design).

The computer term for this process is *recursion*. Recursion is something that calls or refers to itself. A good example in "common" language is a company named MAGIC, where MAGIC is the acronym for MAGIC Auto Glass Installation Company, and the MAGIC in MAGIC Auto Glass Installation Company stands for MAGIC Auto Glass Installation Company and—you have the idea. It goes on forever. I'm fascinated by the possibilities of recursion in artwork. One of the most entrancing first tricks I learned in Photoshop from Kai Krause was how to turn an image into a custom bitmap to use it as the halftone for the same image (so that when you looked closely at the printed image, it was printed with smaller copies of itself).

My attraction to recursive images was sparked by the book *Gödel, Escher, Bach,* written in 1979 by Douglas Hofstadter. In this incredible book of mind games and wordplay, Hofstadter frequently creates words that use embedded letters to spell out other words (a *yes* made up of tiny copies of the word *no*, or the word *holism* sort of written twice but in such a way that reading the letters that make up each major letter spells *reductionism*).

Project 4.5 is my playful tribute to recursion and to the infinite ways in which recursion can recurse.

Smart Guides and Dumb Behavior

Do not try to create the circle by dragging the mouse along the top edge of the rectangle. I will not vouch for all computer systems, but on mine, this action seems to confuse the program and no circle gets drawn. Because I'm having problems, it's only fair to also alert you to them. If you drag away from the top line, however, you can still see when the circle has reached the edges of the rectangle, and you will be able to create your circle.

PROJECT 4.5 Recursive Play: Scatter Brushes from Scatter Brushes and Images from Pattern Brushes

1. Create a new document in Illustrator. You are going to draft a large snowflake.

2. Neither the stroke nor the fill color nor the exact size of the shapes matters in this step, but for consistency, set the Fill to None and the Stroke to black. Select the Rectangle tool. Press Option/Alt and click in the image window in the center about a quarter of the way down from the top of the page to open the Rectangle Options dialog box. Enter a width of 1.5 inches and a height of 2 inches.

3. Turn on Smart Guides (Command/Ctrl+U). Select the Ellipse tool. Move the cursor over the rectangle until you can see the Smart Guide that says Align 90°. Move your cursor up until it is still on the Align 90° line and the word "intersect" appears as you reach the top of the rectangle,

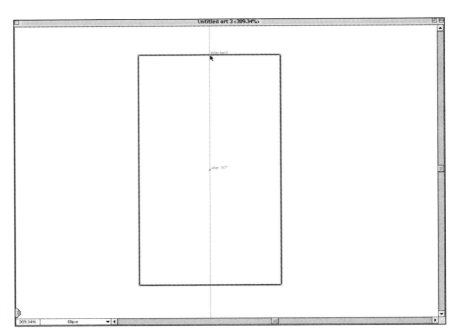

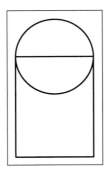

Figure 4.73

Align your cursor over the rectangle and move it up until the word "intersect" appears at the rectangle's top edge.

Figure 4.74

Move the circle on top of the rectangle so that the center of the circle matches (when the word "path" appears to the right).

Figure 4.75

Delete half of the form.

as shown in Figure 4.73. Press Option/Alt and the mouse button and drag the circle toward the right side of the rectangle. Press Shift after you begin to drag and release the mouse button when the word "path" appears by the right edge of the rectangle. Figure 4.74 shows the circle on top of the rectangle.

4. Select both the rectangle and the circle and click on Combine in the Pathfinder palette. You now have a shape that looks unfortunately just like a tombstone (but it won't for long). Your next step is to divide the shape in half vertically.

5. Select the tombstone and choose the Pen tool. You need to place another point in the exact center of the bottom edge of the object. Move your mouse until the Smart Guide reads both Align 90° and Intersect when you are over the bottom line, and then click to add a point. Now, you know where to divide the shape.

6. Turn off Smart Guides (Command/Ctrl+U), or you might not be able to accurately use the Scissors tool. Select the Scissors tool. Click on the control point at the center top of the object. Click on the control point that you added at the bottom center of the object. Press Delete/Backspace until half the tombstone has disappeared. If you prefer, you could instead sweep-select half the object with the Direct Selection tool and then press Delete. That way, you would not need to use the Scissors tool. Figure 4.75 shows the new form—now looking somewhat like half a feather (which is a much happier description).

7. Why did you need to split the shape? Most snowflakes are formed from six identical spokes, and each spoke exhibits bilateral symmetry (that is, one half is the mirror image of the other). You are now in the process of creating the "master" spoke (or half spoke). Let's add some interest to this half spoke. Select the shape. Choose Filter|Distort|Zig-Zag. Be conservative in your settings (don't use too much of the filter). Figure 4.76 shows the settings that I used.

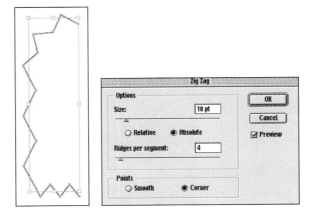

Figure 4.76
Use these settings to distort the form.

8. Choose Filter|Distort|Roughen. Figure 4.77 shows the settings that I used. The Roughen filter is completely random. If you do not like the preview, keep moving the sliders until you do. If you come back to a previous setting, the result will differ from what you saw before. Do not let the line cross itself if you can avoid it. In Figure 4.77, you can see a small area of overlap at the bottom of the shape. This overlap is okay at the bottom edge but not anywhere else in the shape.

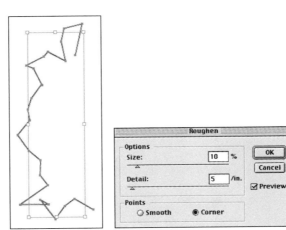

Figure 4.77
The Roughen filter creates a small area of overlap that's acceptable only at the bottom edges of the shape.

9. Leave the shape selected. Choose the Reflect tool. Place your cursor on the bottom endpoint of the path, press Option/Alt, and click to open the Reflect Tool Options dialog box. Select Vertical Axis and click on Copy to make a mirror image of the half spoke. Figure 4.78 shows the result of the Reflect command.

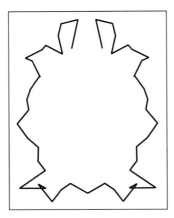

Figure 4.78
Reflect the snowflake.

10. You now need to join the two halves of the shape. Choose the Direct Selection tool. Draw a small marquee around the two bottom points where the Reflect tool placed the right half of the shape. Average the points (Command+Option/Alt+Ctrl and press J) both vertically and horizontally and then join the points (Command/Ctrl+J) with a corner point.

11. Select the two endpoints at the tops of the shapes. They are probably not touching. Average the points (Command+Option/Alt+Ctrl+J) both vertically and horizontally. Join the points (Command/Ctrl+J) with a corner point. You now have one shape, as shown in Figure 4.79.

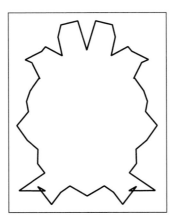

Figure 4.79
Edit the points to create a single flake shape.

12. Select the entire shape by using the Selection tool and then choose the Rotate tool. Press Option/Alt and click on the point at the bottom center of the shape (where the two halves meet). Enter an Angle of 60 degrees in the Rotate Tool Options dialog box and click on Copy. Transform Again (Command/Ctrl+D) four more times. You now have a snowflake.

13. Even though the snowflake form is endlessly fascinating and the snow-flake probably looks best as an outline, you need to put these spokes together into one shape for this project (see Figure 4.80). Select the entire image (Command/Ctrl+A). Drag a copy of the combined form to the pasteboard area of the document for safekeeping. Press Option/Alt to make a copy as you drag. Create a new layer and move the extra snowflake's "selected rectangle" from Layer 1 to Layer 2 in the Layers palette. Lock Layer 2.

Figure 4.80
The uncombined snowflake is a thing of beauty.

14. Select the entire image (Command/Ctrl+A). Because you locked Layer 2, only the snowflake in Layer 1 is selected. Click on Combine in the Pathfinder palette. Figure 4.81 shows the single outline that results.

15. My snowflake now looks solid; yours probably will, too. However, even if you can't see it, the snowflake is part of a compound path. The next step: Release the compound path and remove the extra bits and points. With the snowflake selected, choose Object|Compound Paths|Release. The object is not grouped, so you don't need to ungroup it. Do not deselect.

16. Press Shift and click on the outer edge of the snowflake outline to dese-lect the main shape. Delete whatever is left.

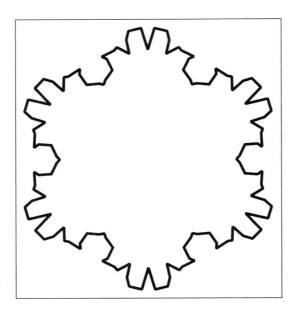

Figure 4.81
You need to combine all of the flake sides into a single shape.

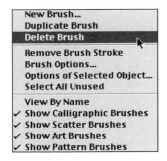

Figure 4.82
Choose Delete Brush from the menu.

17. The output of this portion of the project is a Brush library that you will use a bit later. You need to empty the current brushes out of the Brushes palette so that you are not saving duplicates. In the Brushes palette sidebar menu, choose Select All Unused. Because you have not used any brushes in this image, all the brushes are selected. From the same sidebar menu, select Delete Brush, as shown in Figure 4.82. Click on OK in the Delete Selected Brushes box. The Brushes palette is now empty.

18. Select the snowflake and give it a Fill of 50% gray and a Stroke of None. Drag the snowflake into the Brushes palette and define it as a Scatter brush. Leave the Size and Spacing at 100% and the Scatter at 0%. Change the Rotation to Random and set the sliders from –180 degrees to 180 degrees to allow for maximum rotation. Set the Rotation Relative To option to Path. Click on OK to accept the settings that are shown in Figure 4.83. Deselect the snowflake.

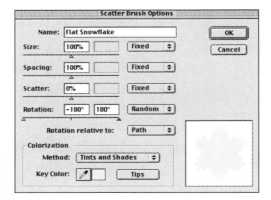

Figure 4.83
Use these Scatter Brush Options settings.

19. You are going to create some variations in the snowflake to make a variety of brushes. Let me tell you an easy way to reuse the settings that you have just made. Drag the thumbnail for the Simple Snowflake brush to the New Brush icon at the bottom of the Brushes palette to make a copy of the brush.

20. With the Selection tool, select the original large snowflake that you used to create the first brush (hereafter, I will just call it the "snowflake shape"). Change the Fill to 30% gray and give it a Stroke of 60% gray with a Stroke weight of 4 points. Drag the snowflake shape into the Brushes palette—pressing Option/Alt after you start to drag the shape— and drop onto the thumbnail of the copy of the Simple Snowflake brush that you just created. This action reopens the Scatter Brush Options dialog box and changes the brush itself to the new version. Because you want to use the same settings, change the name to "30 Percent Outline" and click on OK to close the dialog box.

> ### Why Would Anyone Color a Snowflake Gray?
>
> Does gray seem an odd choice of color for a snowflake? Probably. However, by coloring the snowflake a shade of gray, you gain the ability to change the Colorization method and have it matter. If your brush is white (or black), no Colorization methods (except Hue Shift) affect it at all. However, if you use shades of gray, you give your brush the maximum flexibility.

21. You can make other variations using other combinations of gray values for fill and stroke (or for only fill or stroke). Make a snowflake brush that uses a radial gradient in shades of gray from 10% to 75%. Build it exactly as you did in the Fish exercise (using Expand and Crop). Expand the gradient to about 50 shades. Unlock the "safety" copy of the snowflake on the pasteboard and change the Stroke of the uncombined shapes to white with a Stroke weight of 9 points and Miter Limit of 5 points. Option/Alt+drag this shape into another copy of the Simple Snowflake brush. You can even create some other snowflakes if you want. If you choose to create snowflakes with smooth rather than corner points, do not use the Combine command on them. Instead, just select all six spokes and drag them to the Brushes palette. They can be either filled or stroked (but not both—stroking the uncombined spokes does not create a symmetrical snowflake).

22. Re-create several of the variants—a plain filled snowflake, a stroked and filled snowflake, a stroked snowflake, and an uncombined stroked snowflake as Pattern brushes. Remember to save corner snowflakes for these Pattern brushes.

23. You need another element that I have already created for you. It is a brush made out of the word *Snow* from FFEricRightHand (another of my favorite FontFont fonts). You might just as well save it into the library that you are building. Choose Window|Brush Libraries|Other and negotiate to the Chapter 4 Starts directory. Choose the file SNOW.AI. To transfer the brush to your document's own Brushes palette, just use the brush in the image. Even if you toss away the brush stroke, the brush remains in your Brushes palette. The SNOW.AI document has two brushes; if you like the snowflake, you can transfer it as well.

24. Save the document as SNOWFLAKES.AI and then close it. You will use it (or its Brushes palette) shortly.

So, what happens now? Where do you go from here? (Yes, you can ask.) You created a variety of snowflake brushes and placed them into a document that can be used as a Brush library. In the next project, you will modify a Japanese snow scene that I created for this book (from diverse elements redrawn but taken from *Japanese Border Designs*, Theodore Menten, Dover Books, 1975; this volume is part of the Dover Pictorial Archive of royalty-free images).

In Project 4.6, you will turn the snow scene into a brush so that you can select a monochromatic color scheme for it. You will then use the snowflake brushes that you created earlier to decorate the image. I have saved two versions of the snow scene. SNOWSCENE.AI contains mostly white elements (the sails and houses are all white). In SNOWSCENE2.AI, these white elements have been colored. I think SNOWSCENE.AI is the more attractive design, but the colors in SNOWSCENE2.AI allow themselves to be colorized. It is your choice which version to use.

PROJECT 4.6 The Big Brush Switch

1. Open the image SNOWSCENE.AI (or SNOWSCENE2.AI) on the enclosed CD-ROM. Figure 4.84 shows the original SNOWSCENE.AI.

Figure 4.84
This is the starting snowflake image.

2. To prepare the image to be used as a brush, you need to rid it of any illegal elements, such as gradients, masks, and dynamic brushes. The image, by design, has no masks or compound paths. However, the mountains (in the Houses layer) and the flat waves (in the Flat Waves layer) contain Calligraphic brushes. The Whitecaps are a Pattern brush. You need to expand these elements. To do so, lock all the layers *except* for the Houses layer. Select the entire image (Command/Ctrl+A). Choose Object|Expand. Expand the Object, the Fill, and the Stroke. Lock the layer.

3. Unlock the Whitecap layer. Select the entire image (Command/Ctrl+A). Choose Object|Expand. Expand the Object, the Fill, and the Stroke. Lock the layer again.

4. Unlock the Flat Waves layer. Select the entire image (Command/Ctrl+A). Choose Object|Expand. Expand the Object, the Fill, and the Stroke. Lock the layer again.

5. Unlock the Boats layer. Calligraphic strokes were applied here as well. Select the entire image (Command/Ctrl+A). Choose Object|Expand. Expand the Object, the Fill, and the Stroke. Lock the layer again. The image looks no different, but Illustrator will now permit you to create a Pattern brush from it.

6. In the sidebar menu for the Brushes palette, choose Select All Unused. Then, from the same menu, choose Delete Brush. Click on OK in response to the warning message.

7. Unlock all the layers. Select the entire image (Command/Ctrl+A). Drag the entire image into the Brushes palette. Select the Pattern Brush radio button. Name the brush "Image Brush". Leave the Scale at 100% and change the Colorization method to Tints And Shades.

8. Save the document as SSBRUSH.AI and close it.

9. Create a new Illustrator document. Choose File|Page Setup to change the orientation of your document to Landscape mode (wider than long).

10. Turn on the Rulers (Command/Ctrl+R). Drag a guide from the top ruler to the 5 1/4-inch mark on the left vertical ruler. Set the Fill color to None and the Stroke color to 50% black. Select the Pen tool. Click on the left side of the guide where the guide meets the image margin. Press Shift and click again on the guide where it meets the right edge of the document (you are going past the margin on the right side). Turn off the Rulers (Command/Ctrl+R). Choose View|Clear Guides.

11. Choose Window|Brush Libraries|Other Library. Select the SSBRUSH.AI that you created in Step 8. Select the stroke that you created. Click on the Image Brush brush. Use the arrow keys to move the image into position top to bottom (it should be close). If necessary, stretch the path a bit to make the image fill the document area within the margin guides. Figure 4.85 shows the SNOWSCENE2.AI applied back to the image as a brush. The image has changed very little.

12. Experiment with changing the Stroke color to change the coloring of the entire image. As you drag the Stroke selection slider, you see a variety of monochromatic color schemes appear. I eventually set my Stroke color to CMYK: 0,50,70,21 (a light, grayed peach).

Why Create a Pattern Brush?

Of the three available types of pictorial brushes, why did I choose to have you create a Pattern brush from the entire image? The Pattern brush is the only type of brush that can easily be applied to a straight line without distortion. The Art brush is not a good choice because it easily distorts. The Scatter brush would work, but why give it a chance to create multiple copies? Of course, if you wanted to shrink the image and apply multiple copies of it over a background, the Scatter brush would be a very good choice. There is no really fixed rule. The Pattern brush was the safest choice for this project.

Figure 4.85

The entire image can be used as a brush with almost no change to the image.

13. Lock Layer 1 (with the image in it). Create a new layer.

14. Choose Window|Brush Libraries|Other Library and open the SNOWFLAKELIB.AI that you created (or mine, if you did not complete Project 4.5).

15. Select the Paintbrush tool and scatter one or two large, simple snowflakes about the page. Choose Object|Expand. Expand the Object, the Fill, and the Stroke. Ungroup (Shift+Command/Shift+Ctrl and press G) two times. With Shift pressed, click on the snowflakes to deselect them and then delete the skeleton stroke. Figure 4.86 shows the image—somewhat overwhelmed by two overly large flakes.

Figure 4.86

These snowflakes are not exactly true to scale.

16. You can now use these large snowflakes as the path for more snow-flakes. They are now just regular paths. Apply the SNOW text brush as a Scatter brush to one of the snowflakes (see Figure 4.87). Change the Stroke to white and then change the brush settings to Accept Tints And Shades. You also can change the other brush settings. If the snowflake is too large for your image, resize it by pressing Shift as you move a corner control handle on the bounding box. The brush that has been applied automatically conforms to the new object size.

Figure 4.87
Apply a brush to the snowflake path.

17. Press Option/Alt and drag a duplicate of the snowflake object. You can resize it as you want, but this method is an easy way to grab the stroke. You can then apply any brush that you choose. Try the various brushes. Keep the snowflakes either white or light blue or light pink-purple. Figure 4.88 shows my solution in grayscale here. On the CD-ROM, you can see it as FLAKESDONE.AI (so you can poke around and see my settings).

Figure 4.88
The image with no whitecaps has been manipulated in Photoshop to control the visual impact of the snowflakes on the village.

Moving On

You covered a lot of information in this very long chapter and completed some very challenging projects. You should have both an excellent idea of how to create Calligraphic, Pattern, Scatter, and Art brushes and a good appreciation for the pitfalls and strengths of each brush type. You also learned how to use the Combine and Expand commands to help create brushes that would otherwise not be possible.

The ability to define an image as a brush and to use Tints And Shades to recolor it is a powerful color effect. With this technique, you can turn an image into sepia tones (or shades of gray). If you define Hue Shift as your Colorization method, you can move the colors in the original around the color wheel. After you have your color scheme set in the brush, you can render it by expanding the brush back into individual shapes. The colors are then "set." You can still alter them globally (or individually) by using the Adjust Colors filter or the Negative or Complement option on the Color palette's sidebar menu. We didn't have the time to try those tricks in this chapter.

In Chapter 5, you learn how to create a variety of effects based on dashed strokes.

Chapter 5

A Bit of Dash

By Sherry London

Dots and dashes can really spice up a stroke. Illustrator 9 allows you to create multiple strokes on each object. This chapter looks at some ways to make the most of this feature.

I really enjoy playing with the dashes and gaps that change the look of strokes. I'm fascinated by the changes that dotted lines can make in a design. The creativity allowed by the changes in Illustrator 9 are breathtaking and show up quite well in this chapter. In addition to creating dotted and dashed lines (which you could do before), you can now create paths with multiple dotted or dashed strokes and make these strokes interact with one another by using Blend modes and opacity as well.

In this chapter, you work through five projects, including one simple project, one practical project, and two fanciful projects. I hope that you'll enjoy the never-ending variety of dashes and gaps.

Workin' on the Railroad

You can create a variety of strokes by using dashed lines. In Project 5.1, you'll create a circle of railroad tracks. Of course, the tracks aren't important, as you probably don't have much call for them on a regular basis. However, when you get the idea of how to create dashed lines, you can take your train in many new directions.

PROJECT 5.1 Basic Dashes and Gaps

Here, you'll learn how to create dashed lines and align additional strokes to them.

1. Create a new document in Illustrator.

2. Change the Fill to None and the Stroke to black. Figure 5.1 shows the Stroke palette before I created any objects.

Figure 5.1

The settings shown here are typical default settings for strokes in Illustrator. However, the Stroke palette usually shows the last settings you used.

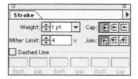

3. Select the Ellipse tool. Click once in the center of your image and enter a width of 6 inches and a height of 4 inches, as shown in Figure 5.2. Move the resulting ellipse back into the center of your image if necessary.

Figure 5.2

Illustrator makes it easy to create an ellipse at exactly the size you want.

4. Change the Stroke width to 40 in the Stroke palette, as shown in Figure 5.3.

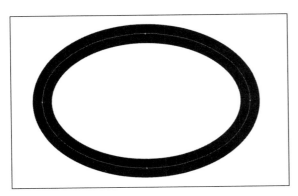

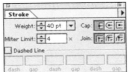

Figure 5.3
A Stroke width of 40 points makes a thick outlined edge on the ellipse.

5. Select the Dashed Line checkbox in the Stroke palette. Enter a dash of 2 points and a gap of 6 points, as shown in Figure 5.4 (which also shows the result). Instant pickup sticks!

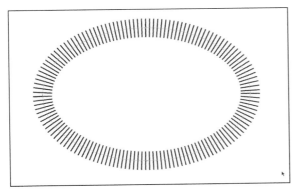

Figure 5.4
You can create parallel straight lines by using a wide stroke on a dashed line.

6. Leave the dashed ellipse selected and double-click on the Scale tool. With the Uniform Scale radio button selected and the scale amount set to 100%, click on Copy. Figure 5.5 shows the dialog box. Change the Stroke weight to 2 points and deselect the Dashed Line checkbox.

7. Double-click on the Scale tool again, and then click on Copy with the same settings used in Step 6. This step makes another copy of the ellipse.

Help! Blob Alert!

If the dash and gap patterns that you select don't divide evenly into the perimeter of your shape, you might see an unusually thick dash somewhere in the object. If your object must be the specified size, then you need to do some math to make everything come out right. However, the easiest fix is to simply scale the object a bit up or down until the unintended dash disappears.

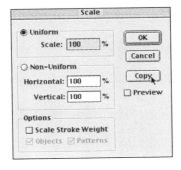

Figure 5.5
You can make an in-place copy easily by simply clicking on Copy with the Scale tool set to 100%.

8. Leave the new copy selected. Change the Stroke weight to 30 points (about 10 points smaller than the original stroke) and uncheck the Dash checkbox.

9. Choose Object|Path|Outline Stroke. Although the image looks as if nothing has changed, if you look at the Fill/Stroke Swatches in the Toolbox, you'll see that you now have a filled shape instead of a stroked shape. Click on the double-headed arrows next to the Fill/Stroke Swatches in the Toolbox to swap the Fill and the Stroke. Now, you have train tracks. In this case, the tracks are a compound path, which you may release if you prefer (Object|Compound Path|Release). Change the Stroke weight to 2. Figure 5.6 shows the result.

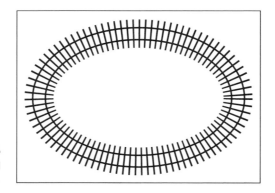

Figure 5.6
The train can now go around the tracks.

This project illustrated a simple technique. You can spin it out in many directions. You can even use this technique to create wiggly lines. I want to thank David Xenakis for this simplified version of my original instructions. To make a wiggly line, you simply need to follow the original instructions with a different stroke. Illustrator treats open and closed objects somewhat differently when you outline a stroke. If you outline an ellipse, you get a compound path. If you outline an open stroke, you do not. If you want separate paths from an open outlined stroked path, you need to cut the outlined stroke apart. Figure 5.7 shows train tracks that wiggle along an open path.

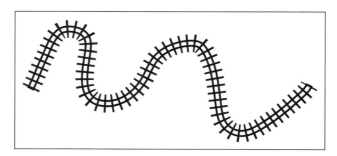

Figure 5.7
Here, you can see some wiggly tracks.

Illustrator 9 can play some wonderful tricks with adding multiple strokes to a path, as shown in Project 5.2. You could actually create your train tracks as a single stroked path.

PROJECT 5.2 On the Same Track

This project shows how to create a "track" style that you can use to stroke any path.

1. Create a new document in Illustrator.

2. Change the Fill to None and the Stroke to black.

3. Select the Ellipse tool. Click once in the center of your image and enter a width of 6 inches and a height of 4 inches. Move the resulting ellipse back into the center of your image if necessary.

4. Change the Stroke width to 32 in the Stroke palette.

5. Make the Appearance palette active. Choose New Stroke from the side drop-down menu. Change the Stroke color to white and change the Stroke width to 28 points. The image now looks as if you have a 2-point double black line (which is the illusion that you want to create).

6. Choose New Stroke from the side drop-down menu in the Appearance palette (you need to keep the object selected throughout this process). Change the Stroke width to 40 and the color to black.

7. Select the Dashed Line checkbox in the Stroke palette. Enter a dash of 2 points and a gap of 6 points. Your railroad tracks are now complete.

8. To be able to use them again, drag the stroke into the Styles palette. You can double-click on the style thumbnail and change the name to "Tracks".

9. Draw a curvy path with the Pen tool or the Pencil tool and try out the style.

The only potential problem with this stroke occurs if you want to be able to see the background behind the tracks. Where you had transparency using the first construction method, you now have a white line. Illustrator provides a solution, however. When your path object is complete, deselect all the attributes in the Appearance palette by clicking underneath them so that nothing in the Appearance palette is highlighted; then change the Object Blend mode to Multiply. Now, the white will drop out everywhere.

The following examples take the dash-and-gap technique a bit further.

La Vie en Danse

A dashed line has long been the symbol for "cut here" on a coupon. However, no rule states that a coupon has to be rectangular. In Project 5.3, you'll create a coupon that incorporates its topic (a ballet dancer) into the coupon itself. The dotted line both adds to the design and shows a more playful treatment for the traditional coupon.

PROJECT 5.3 Cut Here: A Dotted-Line Coupon

I've divided this project into several distinct parts. You'll create the basic coupon shape, add the text and a text pattern, and then add a watercolor stroke behind it.

Clipping Coupons

The first part of the project shows how to create the coupon.

1. Open the image DANCER.AI from the companion CD-ROM. It looks like a blank image (because it was saved as paths from Photoshop), but it isn't. Select the entire image (Command/Ctrl+A). Change the stroke to black. Make sure that the Dashed Line checkbox is not selected in the Stroke palette. Set the Stroke width to 4 points. Figure 5.8 shows the original dancer stroked in black.

Figure 5.8
The image of a dancer, stroked with black to make it visible, is the starting point of this illustration.

2. Choose Object|Crop Marks|Release to remove the crop marks placed in the image when it was created by the Photoshop Paths To Illustrator command. Delete the invisible object that appears in the bounding box (the crop marks, when released, turn into a rectangle with no stroke and no fill).

3. Double-click on the Scale tool, select the Uniform radio button, and enter a scale percentage of 70. Click on OK (don't make a copy). Move the dancer toward the left of the document so that you have room to create the coupon. Figure 5.9 shows the dancer, reduced in size.

Figure 5.9
Scale the dancer and move her to the left of the document.

4. Double-click on the Scale tool. Select the Uniform radio button and enter a scale percentage of 100. Click on Copy. With the new copy selected, create a new layer (click on the Create New Layer icon at the bottom of the Layers palette). Move the selected object to the newly created layer by dragging the tiny rectangle at the right of Layer 1 in the Layers palette from Layer 1 to Layer 2. Click on the Eye icon in the Layers palette to hide Layer 2.

5. Create a new layer (Layer 3). Drag it below Layer 1 in the Layers palette. Protect Layer 1 from changes by clicking on its Lock toggle. Figure 5.10 shows the Layers palette as it should now look. Layer 3 is the active layer.

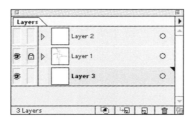

Figure 5.10

The Layers palette with three layers created, including one hidden and one locked.

6. Select the Rectangle tool. Make sure that the Dashed Line checkbox is not selected in the Stroke palette. Set the Stroke width to 4 points. Click in the image and set the rectangle's width to 4.26 inches and height to 2.461 inches, as shown in Figure 5.11.

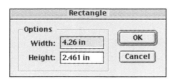

Figure 5.11

Set the width and height of the rectangle that will become the body of the coupon.

7. Now that the coupon rectangle is created, you need to get it into position and size it properly. This procedure is a bit tricky. Figure 5.12 shows an enlargement of the dancer with circles placed to show the exact intersection points for the coupon and the dancer. I've also changed the strokes to light gray so that you can clearly see the black circles.

   Use the Selection tool to move the rectangle into position by the dancer's leg that forms the left edge of the coupon. Then, pull up on the control point at the top center of the bounding box to correctly size the height of the coupon until it intersects with the dancer's outstretched leg.

   The hardest point to set is the place where the lower-left corner of the rectangle meets the dancer's toe. You need to ensure that the rectangle doesn't overlap the outside edge of her weight-bearing leg. To make it easier to see where you're placing the rectangle, toggle Artwork mode on (Command/Ctrl+Y) and turn on Smart Guides (Command/Ctrl+U). You can then move the lower-left corner of the rectangle to the dancer's toe and easily snap it into place. Figure 5.13 shows a close-up of the left side of the dancer's legs and location of the rectangle.

8. You'll fuse the dancer and the rectangle a bit later to form the body of the coupon. In the process, you'll remove the inside portion of the dancer's legs. However, you need to save this area for reuse. Here's the easiest way: Lock Layer 3 (the rectangle layer) and unlock Layer 1 (the dancer). Leave Smart Guides and Artwork mode turned on. Choose the

About Paste In Front

David Xenakis reminds me that I need to tell you that Paste In Front or Paste In Back are also viable commands. You can certainly use them rather than my method of either duplicating the layer or scaling the object at 100 percent and making a copy. I use the alternate approaches because I dislike using the clipboard. Although this technique probably dates back to the days of limited RAM (and I'm a long-time Photoshop user, which only reinforces my concern about copy-and-paste), I almost never use the clipboard or copy-and-paste if another way is equally reasonable.

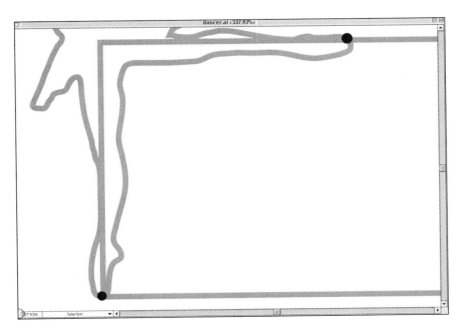

Figure 5.12
The black circles show the points at which the coupon needs to intersect with the dancer's legs.

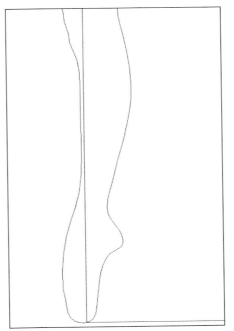

Figure 5.13
You need to watch the position of the rectangle along the left edge of the dancer's leg very carefully to make sure that it doesn't overlap (which would give the dancer an unnaturally straight edge to the front of her leg).

Direct Selection tool. Drag the tool from the lower-right corner of the locked rectangle to the upper-left corner of the locked rectangle to select the area of the dancer inside the rectangle (use the Smart Guides to let you know you're in the right place). Figure 5.14 shows the selected points as filled squares.

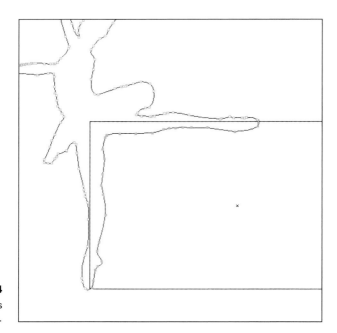

Figure 5.14
Select the area of the dancer's legs that are within the rectangle.

9. Turn off Smart Guides (Command/Ctrl+U). Toggle Artwork mode off (Command/Ctrl+Y). Copy the selected area to the clipboard. Lock Layer 1, and then create a new layer (Layer 4). Choose Edit|Paste In Front (yes, I use the Copy and Paste commands when it's really necessary). Hide Layer 1. Figure 5.15 shows the area inside the rectangle pasted into Layer 4 with the dancer on Layer 1 hidden. Use the Direct Selection tool to clean up stray points outside the rectangle. Lock and hide Layer 4 for now. Make Layer 1 visible again.

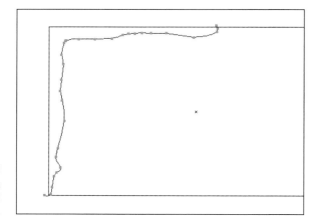

Figure 5.15
Check the pasted area for points that lie outside the rectangle and remove them.

10. Remove the locks from Layers 1 and 3. Select both the dancer and the coupon. The easiest way to join them into one shape is to click on Unite in the Pathfinder palette. If the shapes are properly aligned, the Unite command forms one seamless shape, as shown in Figure 5.16.

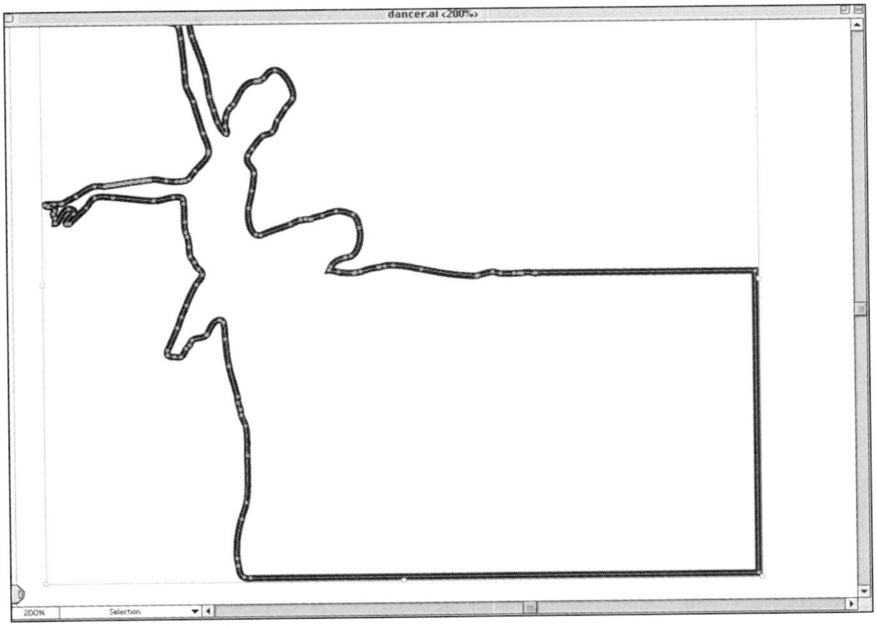

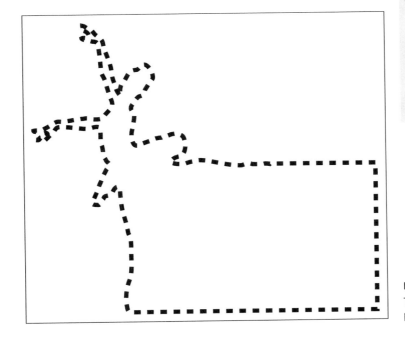

Figure 5.16
The dancer and the coupon form one seamless shape when you use the Unite command on the Pathfinder palette.

11. Coupons typically use dotted or dashed lines to show where to cut. With the dancer/coupon selected, select the Dashed Line checkbox on the Stroke palette. Set both the dash and the gap to 6 points. Figure 5.17 shows the result.

The Unite Command and Extra Points

You get the most efficient use from the Unite command if you check the Remove Redundant Points box before you use the command. You'll find this setting in the Pathfinder palette's side drop-down menu. Unfortunately, this setting isn't sticky, and you'll need to reset it every time you start Illustrator.

Figure 5.17
The dancer/coupon with a 6-point dash and gap.

12. Experiment with a variety of dash-and-gap settings. Experiment with the Stroke width as well. When you're finished playing, use these settings: Stroke Weight: 4 points, Dash: 2 points, Gap: 6 points, Cap: Round, Join: Round. Figure 5.18 shows these settings, and Figure 5.19 shows the result.

Figure 5.18
These Stroke settings create an elliptical dotted line around the coupon.

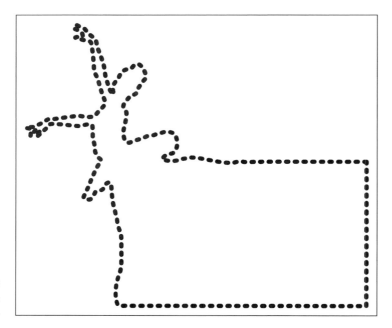

Figure 5.19
The coupon with the settings from Figure 5.18.

13. Make Layer 4 active and make its Eye icon visible so that you can see what is on the layer. Lock Layers 1 and 3 (although Layer 3 should contain nothing). Figure 5.20 shows that you have managed to salvage the "cut" portion of the dancer's legs so that she is whole again.

Troubleshooting the Unite Command

What happens if the shapes don't intersect properly? You might get an unwanted line segment when you use the Unite command. If you get this result, you can select the unwanted area with the Direct Selection tool and delete it, or you can unite the two shapes manually.

To unite the shapes manually, use the Direct Selection tool and select the last point on the dancer's weight-bearing leg and the closest point on the coupon. Choose Object|Path|Average (Command/Alt+Option/Ctrl+J) and select the Both radio button. Click on OK. Then, select Object|Path|Join (Command/Ctrl+J). Select a Smooth Join. Repeat the same process for the points on the dancer's outstretched leg and the closest coupon point. This technique makes the same seamless shape as the Unite command, but it's not as easy.

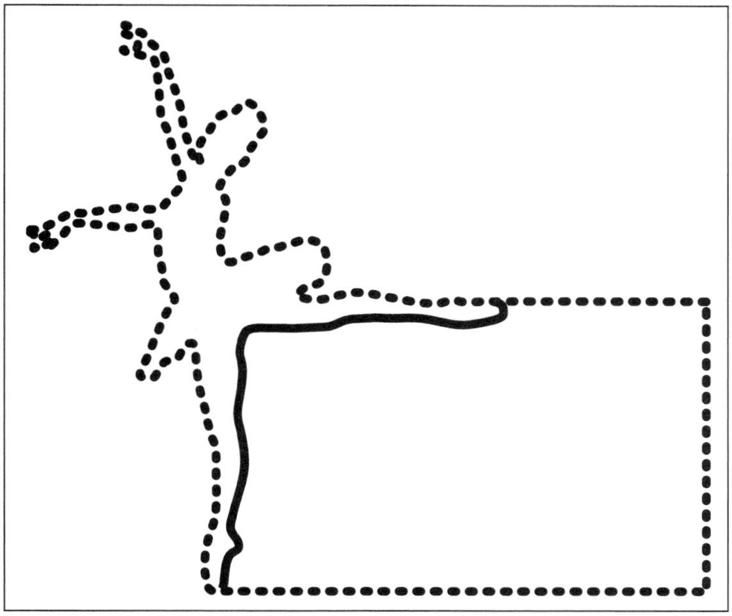

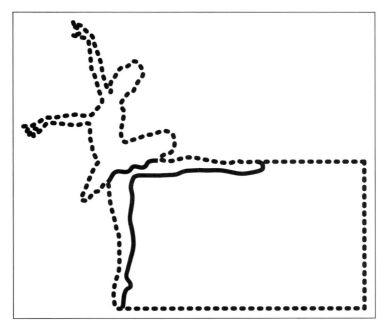

Figure 5.20
You need to replace the missing portions of the dancer's legs, but they should not be part of the dotted "cut here" lines.

14. Select the Pencil tool. With Layer 4 still active (but with no objects selected), draw a wavy line that finishes the bottom of the dancer's tutu (her skirt for those of you unfamiliar with ballet dress). This too is a 4-point black solid stroke. Figure 5.21 shows the dancer with her skirt completed.

Figure 5.21
Use the Pencil tool to finish the dancer's tutu.

Text and Pattern

In this part of the project, you'll import the text and create a pattern fill for the dancer.

1. Now, it's time to import the text of the coupon. You can create your own if you prefer. I liked the way that the Image Club (now EyeWire) Fajita Picante font looked. I have changed the text to outlines so that you can use it. Make Layer 3 active, visible, and unlocked. Currently, nothing should be on this layer (the coupon, which was originally on this layer, was moved to Layer 1 when you combined the coupon and the dancer). Choose File|Place. Select the Show All Files checkbox so that the BALLET.AI file on this book's companion CD-ROM is selectable. Click on Place to bring the text into your working image. Use the Selection tool to center the text in the coupon. Figure 5.22 shows the result. (By the way, if this were a real ad, adding an address and phone number would be a lovely gesture for the prospective customer.)

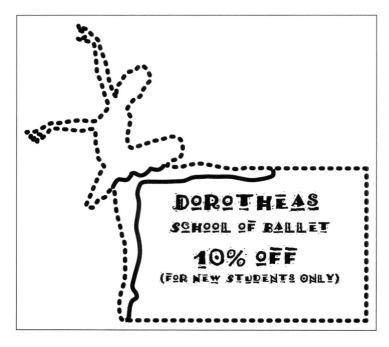

Figure 5.22

The Place command is used to add the text to the coupon.

2. Remember that copy of the dancer that you've hidden in Layer 2? You're going to fill it with a text pattern that you need to create now. Use Adobe Garamond bold for the font if you have it; if not, Times Roman will suffice. Set the point size to 12. Enter "Dance Dance Dance". Leave a space between each word. Press Return/Enter and type "Dance" four times on the next line. Press Return/Enter again and repeat line 1. Select all the

Dance Dance Dance Dance Dance Dance Dance Dance Dance Dance

Figure 5.23
This image shows the start of the text pattern fill.

text. Click on Align Center in the Paragraph palette. Reduce the leading between the lines until almost no space appears between the lines. On my version of Adobe Garamond, 10-point leading looks best. Figure 5.23 shows the way the text should look.

3. Select the text object with the Selection tool. Choose Text|Create Outlines. Group the text (Command/Ctrl+G).

4. Select the Rectangle tool with no fill and a black stroke with a width of 1 point. Place your cursor between the first "a" and "n" in the second line of text. Draw a rectangle that extends up over the first line of text and ends between the last "a" and "n" on the second line. Figure 5.24 shows the correct placement of the rectangle.

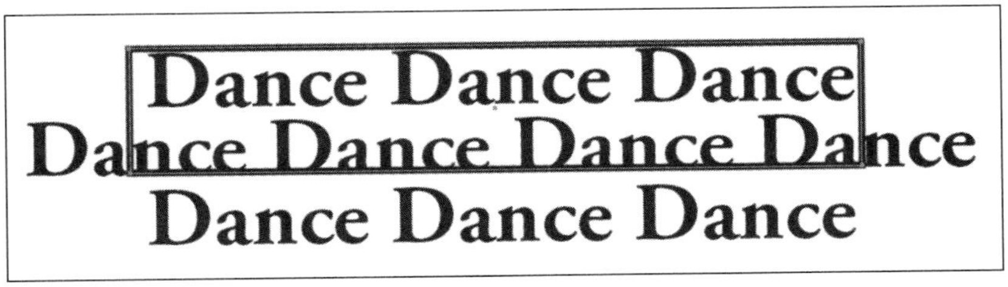

Dance Dance Dance Dance Dance Dance Dance Dance Dance Dance

Figure 5.24
This rectangle sets the final size for the pattern.

5. Move the control handle in the center of the bottom side of the rectangle to resize the rectangle so that it ends just above the lowercase letters in the third line. Move the center-top control handle so that the rectangle starts just above the lowercase letters in the first line. Figure 5.25 shows this location.

Dance Dance Dance Dance Dance Dance Dance Dance Dance Dance

Figure 5.25
The rectangle now encloses exactly one pattern repeat.

6. Because it is difficult to be sure that the rectangle is positioned so perfectly that the letter *D* will repeat seamlessly, you can take advantage of the room for error that the white space between the lines provides. Use the Selection tool to move the rectangle up, until the horizontal edges are not touching any text. Press Shift after you start to move the rectangle to constrain movement to the vertical direction only. Figure 5.26 shows a good position for the rectangle.

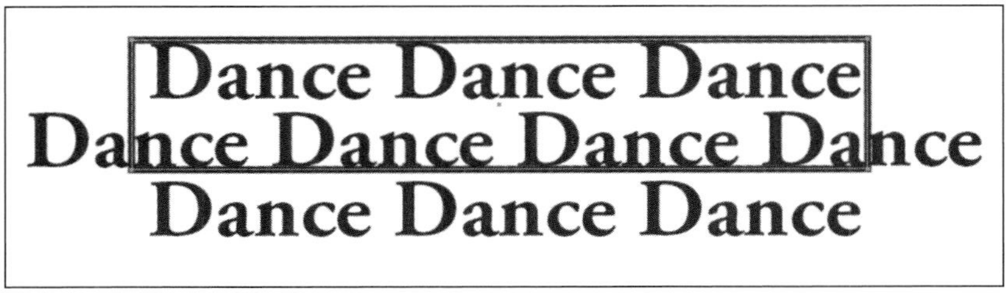

Figure 5.26
The rectangle is moved to ensure that the letters do not show a seam.

Dance Dance Dance
Dance Dance Dance Dance
Dance Dance Dance

7. You only need the portion of the text encircled by the rectangle as your pattern (shown in Figure 5.27). You might think that the logical next step would be to create a mask from the rectangle. Unfortunately, a pattern tile cannot contain a mask. You could ungroup the text and, using the Selection tool, select each letter that is outside the rectangle and delete it. However, there's an easier way. Make sure that the rectangle is selected. Choose Object|Arrange|Send to Back. Change the stroke on the rectangle to None (remember, it also has no fill). The rectangle, as the bottom shape in a pattern, clips the pattern to the shape of the rectangle. Figure 5.28 shows the finished pattern as it looks to Illustrator.

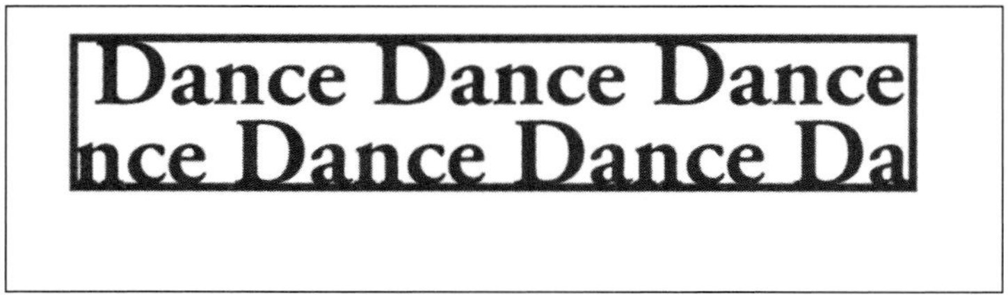

Figure 5.27
This is the area that will be the actual pattern.

Dance Dance Dance
nce Dance Dance Da

Figure 5.28
The finished pattern tile (the text inside of the invisible rectangle).

Dance Dance Dance
nce Dance Dance Da

8. Select the invisible rectangle and the text. You can group it all together for easier transport if you want. Drag the pattern into the Swatches palette.

9. Make Layer 2 visible. Drag the layer to the bottom of the Layers palette. Select the dancer. Change her Stroke to None and click on the new pattern in the Swatches palette to make it the fill. Figure 5.29 shows the almost-finished coupon.

Figure 5.29
The coupon is almost complete.

Some Coupon Color, Please...

If you were creating this coupon for a newspaper, it would now be adequate for an inexpensive run. In basic black and white, not much can be done to mess up the printing. However, you might want to add some color to it. Custom brush strokes provide the perfect background. In this part of the project, you'll add some color.

1. Add a new layer (Layer 5) and drag it to the bottom of the Layers palette. Write-protect Layers 1 to 4 by turning on their lock icons.

2. Choose a pastel yellow for your Stroke color. Choose Windows|Brush Library|Artistic Sample. This library is provided with Illustrator 9. If, for some reason, it does not show up in your library list, you should have it on the Illustrator 9 installation CD-ROM. Select the Paintbrush tool and click on the last brush in the library (it is called Watercolor-Wet), as shown in Figure 5.30. Paint a squiggle behind the dancer.

Figure 5.30

Use the Watercolor-Wet brush to add some excitement and color to the coupon.

3. Change the Stroke color to a pastel green and paint another squiggle. Make one stroke each in pastel blue, light lavender, and pastel pink. Each stroke should be a bit larger than the previous one and should finally cover the entire area occupied by the coupon.

4. Because each stroke is higher in the layering order than the previous one, your final stroke in light pink might tend to dominate the image. In my original, I decided that I preferred the strokes in reverse order. If you would too, select your first stroke (the yellow one) and send it to the back (Object|Arrange|Send To Back). Then, select the green stroke and send it to the back. Select and send to the back the blue stroke, then the purple stroke, and finally the pink stroke. This way, you rearrange the layering order, and now the smallest of the strokes is the one that is fully visible. Figure 5.31 shows the finished coupon, in grayscale. It looks better in the color Illustrator Studio.

> **An Easier Way to Rearrange the Strokes**
>
> You might find it easier and more convenient to use the new Layers palette features in Illustrator 9 to rearrange the order of the strokes. Because all the brush strokes should be on Layer 5, you can twirl down the arrow on Layer 5 and then simply change the stacking order of the strokes by dragging their Layers palette entries into the desired stacking order.

You might want to use some of Illustrator 9's new features on this coupon. You can experiment with the Feather effect on the brush strokes and with changing the opacity for the strokes. Although you can certainly change the Blend modes for the strokes, I didn't feel that this change added much to the image. (Multiply was the only Blend mode that I felt gave at least an acceptable result.)

A Dash of This and a Dot of That

By using dashed and dotted lines, you can create exciting overlapped strokes. The new multiple stroke capability of Illustrator 9 really shines here. You can create amazing complexity and pattern using a single path with multiple strokes.

Figure 5.31
The finished coupon has soft brush strokes of color in it.

In the Cityscape project, you'll learn how to create textures using dotted and dashed lines on open paths. The textures that combinations of dashes and gaps can create are truly spectacular. You'll practice a few different methods of working with these stroked patterns and learn the various trade-offs that are necessary when deciding which method to use.

Architecture 101—Design and Construction

I had a very difficult time writing this chapter. The dash strokes are easy to create, but I was having so much fun that I couldn't stop to actually write the material. Be warned. You could spend a number of semi-pointless hours simply playing with the capability to create many strokes on a single path and watching the new patterns form as you change the dash-and-gap specifications.

There actually is a method to the madness. To make multiple strokes with dashes and gaps line up with one another, you need to make sure that the sums of all the dashes and gaps add up to the same amount or to even multiples of that amount. For example, in the dancer coupon that you created above, you used a dash of 2 points and a gap of 6 points. That gives you a total of 8 points. Any other dash-and-gap pattern that adds up to 8 points or to a multiple of 8 points will repeat evenly along the same path. Figure 5.32 shows a close-up of a multiple-stroked path with several variations of stroke that add up to 8 points. It also shows the Appearance palette. In Project 5.4, you'll decorate a series of buildings with a variety of compound strokes.

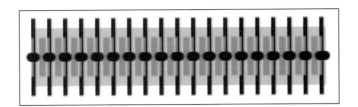

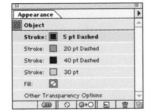

Figure 5.32
You can create multiple strokes
on a single object or path.

PROJECT 5.4 Cityscape

I've divided this project into several sections. You'll learn how to manually fill a shape with strokes, how to create a fill pattern from a stroke, and how to save a compound stroke as a style.

City Style

In this first part of the Cityscape project, you'll learn how to create multiple strokes on a path and define them as styles for later use. First, you'll build four stroke sequences and save them as styles into a separate file.

Pattern 1

Follow these steps to create Building Pattern 1:

1. Create a new document in Illustrator.

2. Select the Pen tool. Click to set the first point. Press Shift and click to set a second point about 2 inches away in a straight line. Change the Stroke weight to 8 points. Use black as the Stroke color (you'll change it later).

3. In the Stroke palette, select the Dashed Line checkbox and enter the values Dash: 3 points, Gap: 7 points, Dash: 8 points, Gap: 5 points, as shown in Figure 5.33. Select a Butt Cap and a Miter Join.

Figure 5.33
Creating the first
dash-and-gap pattern.

4. In the Appearance palette, choose Add New Stroke from the side drop-down menu.

5. Change the Stroke color to white. In the Stroke palette, change the Stroke weight to 2. Enter the values Dash: 0 points, Gap: 1 point, Dash: 1 point, Gap: 9 points, Dash: 6 points, Gap: 6 points for the dashed line. Figure 5.34 shows an enlargement of the combined stroke.

Figure 5.34
The first building stroke is complete.

6. Make sure that the path is selected. If you add up the number of points in the dash-gap sequence, you'll notice that a "repeat" is 23 points long. In the Transform palette, change the W field (the Width) to 46 points to make two full repeats. Drag the path onto the Styles palette. Deselect the path and double-click on the new style that you just created. Change the name of the style to "Building Pattern 1".

Pattern 2

Follow these steps to create Building Pattern 2:

1. Select the Pen tool. In a different area of the same document, click to set the first point. Press Shift and click to set a second point about 2 inches away in a straight line.

2. Set the Stroke weight to 20 points and the Stroke color to black. Create a dashed line with Dash: 10 points, Gap: 2 points, Dash: 6 points, Gap: 2 points.

3. In the Appearance palette, choose Add New Stroke from the side drop-down menu.

4. Use white as the Stroke color for the new stroke and give it a Stroke weight of 7 points. Create a dashed line with this sequence: Dash: 2 points, Gap: 2 points, Dash: 5 points, Gap: 3, Dash: 6, Gap: 2 points. Figure 5.35 shows a close-up of this stroke.

> **A Dash of 0 Points?**
>
> You might want to offset the dashes-and-dot pattern and start your pattern (especially on the second stroke of a path) with a gap instead of a dash. Illustrator doesn't let you begin with a gap, but you can "trick" the software. Enter a zero as the value for the first dash. When you do so, the first item that Illustrator displays is the gap. However, you need to have a balanced display. In this instance, you can end with a gap of 6 points (which allows the pattern to correctly wrap around). In many cases, you need to end the sequence with a gap of 0 points as well, so that you have an even number of dashes and gaps in the sequence.

Figure 5.35
The second building stroke is complete.

5. Make sure that the path is selected. This repeat is 20 points long. In the Transform palette, change the W field (the Width) to 40 points. Drag the path onto the Styles palette. Deselect the path and double-click on the new style that you just created. Change the name of the style to "Building Pattern 2".

Pattern 3

Follow these steps to create Building Pattern 3:

1. Select the Pen tool. In a different area of the same document, click to set the first point. Press Shift and click to set a second point about 2 inches away in a straight line.

2. Select the Dashed Line checkbox in the Stroke palette. Create a Dash: 6 points, Gap: 2 points, Dash: 8 points, Gap: 2 points sequence. Set the Stroke width to 6 points using black as the Stroke color.

3. Change the Stroke color to white. Change the Stroke width to 2 points. Create a dashed line pattern of Dash: 4 points, Gap: 4 points, Dash: 8 points, Gap: 2 points. Figure 5.36 shows the finished stroke.

Figure 5.36
The third building stroke is complete.

4. Make sure that the path is selected. This repeat is 18 points long. In the Transform palette, change the W field (the Width) to 36 points. Drag the path onto the Styles palette. Deselect the path and double-click on the new style that you just created. Change the name of the style to "Building Pattern 3".

Pattern 4

Follow these steps to create Building Pattern 4:

1. Select the Pen tool. In a different area of the same document, click to set the first point. Press Shift and click to set a second point about 2 inches away in a straight line.

2. Set the Stroke width to 40 points. Mark the Dashed Line checkbox in the Stroke palette. Create a sequence of Dash: 2 points, Gap: 2 points, Dash: 8 points. Notice that you are using only three slots on the dash-and-gap area. Figure 5.37 shows the stroke that results. See whether you can figure out what is strange about it.

Figure 5.37
Using only three spots on the dash-and-gap list makes the sequence of dashes and gaps reverse. You have a dash of 2, gap of 2, and dash of 8 and then a gap of 2, dash of 2, and gap of 8 before the sequence repeats.

Unbalanced Dash-and-Gap Sequence

When you create a dash-and-gap sequence, you normally have an even number of dashes and gaps. If you enter only one value (such as placing 12 points in the first Dash field and leaving the others blank), you get a stroke with a pattern of a 12-point dash and then a 12-point gap.

If you extend the sequence to include more values but end with an uneven number of values, Illustrator reads the sequence twice, but the second reading exchanges the dash and gap values. So, for the sequence of Dash: 2 points, Gap: 2 points, Dash: 8 points, you get a 2-point dash, 2-point gap, 8-point dash, and then a 2-point gap, 2-point dash, and an 8-point gap. On the next repeat, Illustrator is back to the original sequence again, and the cycle continues for the length of the stroke.

3. In the Appearance palette, choose Add New Stroke from the side drop-down menu.

4. Change the Stroke color to light gray. Because you want the light gray to "fill in the blanks," enter this sequence for dashes and gaps: Dash: 0 points, Gap: 2 points, Dash: 2 points, Gap: 8 points, Dash: 0 points. Notice that you managed to move the pattern sequence by adding "dummy" zero values at the front and back of the sequence. Figure 5.38 shows this effect.

Figure 5.38
When you add a 0-length dash to the beginning and a 0-length gap to the end, the dashes in the gray line appear in the gaps in the black line.

5. Make sure that the path is selected. This repeat is 24 points long (remember, it takes two cycles to complete the pattern). In the Transform palette, change the W field (the Width) to 48 points. Drag the path onto the Styles palette. Deselect the path and double-click on the new style that you just created. Change the name of the style to "Building Pattern 4". When you start to fill in the buildings, you'll make a much more complex pattern from this example.

6. Finish up this section by saving the file as BLDGPAT.AI.

City Building

In this section of the project, you'll try out four construction methods, using the stroke styles that you just created.

The Navy Office

You'll use Building Pattern 1 to cover this office with copies of the original stroke.

1. Open the image CITYSCAPE.AI from this book's companion CD-ROM. Figure 5.39 shows this abstract image of city buildings. Lock all the layers.

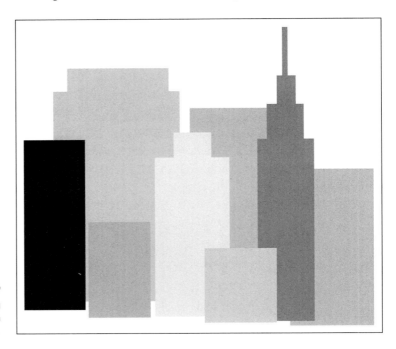

Figure 5.39

An abstract series of building shapes is the starting point for a texture exploration.

2. Unlock the Navy Bldg layer. Select the object on the Navy Bldg layer. The Fill color changes to navy. Drag the Fill swatch into your Swatches palette to save the color so that you can change the color of your stroke pattern to match this building.

3. Choose View|Guides|Make Guides. Toggle the View|Guides|Lock Guides menu item so that a checkmark appears in front of it on the menu. The navy object loses its fill, but you can now snap points to it. Toggle the Snap To Point option on the View menu to select it as well.

4. Select the Pen tool. Click to place a point on the bottom-left corner of the building guides. Press Shift to constrain the next point to the horizontal and place it on the bottom-right point of the building guides. (Zoom in so that you can see the building well enough.)

5. Choose Window|Style Libraries|Other Libraries. Locate and open the BLDGPAT.AI image that contains your saved stroke styles. From the BLDGPAT library, click on the Building Pattern 1 style to apply it to your new stroke.

6. Choose the 8-point dashed line in the Appearance palette, as shown in Figure 5.40. Make sure that the Stroke color is the selected swatch in the Toolbox. Then, click on the orchid swatch in the Swatches palette to change the color of the black dashes to the navy of the original building.

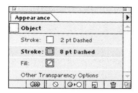

Figure 5.40
Change the color of the 8-point dashed stroke to navy.

7. Choose Object|Transform|Move. Set the Vertical field to 10 points and the Horizontal field to 0. Setting the fields in this order (which is backward in the dialog box) automatically sets the Distance and Angle correctly (and, if your Units preferences were set to inches, it also calculates the points specified in inches). Click on Copy. Because the widest part of the stroke is 8 points, copying the line 10 points away gives you a pleasing amount of white space between the strokes. You now have two strokes in your building.

8. Use the Transform Again command (Command/Ctrl+D) to copy and move the stroke to cover the rest of the building guides.

9. Select all the component strokes in the building and group them (an easy way to do so with all the other layers locked is to choose Edit|Select All).

10. The stroke pattern that you created is partially transparent; the gaps allow whatever is behind them to show through. Although a transparent building is okay, let's put a solid fill behind this one. With no objects selected, change the current Fill color to an orange-brown (CMYK: 50, 85, 100, 0) and set the Stroke to None. Choose the Rectangle tool and draw a rectangle that snaps to the building guides. Select Object|Arrange|Send Backward to put the fill behind the stroke pattern. Figure 5.41 shows the building filled with the pattern.

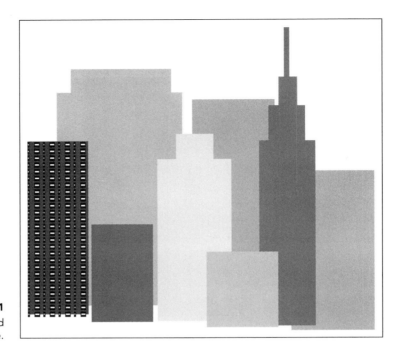

Figure 5.41
You can duplicate a dashed
stroke to fill an entire rectangle.

The Orchid Office

In this portion of the project, you'll fill another building with Building Pattern 2 and shorten the pattern line to conform to the shape of the building.

1. Lock the Navy Bldg layer. Unlock the Orchid Bldg layer and select the orchid building. To make it easier to see this building, hide the other layers in the image. Save the orchid color in your Swatches palette. Repeat Steps 3 and 4 from the preceding section, "The Navy Office," to make guides and draw the foundation line stroke.

2. Choose View|Guides|Make Guides. Toggle the View|Guides|Lock Guides menu item so that a checkmark appears in front of it on the menu. Make sure that the Snap To Point option on the View menu is also selected.

3. Select the Pen tool. Click to place a point on the bottom-left corner of the building guides. Press Shift to constrain the next point to the horizontal and place it on the bottom-right point of the building guides.

4. Set the Fill color to None. Apply Building Pattern 2 from BLDGPAT library.

5. Select the 20-pt stroke in the Appearance palette and change its Stroke color to the orchid of the original building.

6. Choose Object|Transform|Move. Set the Vertical field to 22 pt and the Horizontal field to 0. Click on Copy.

7. Use the Transform Again command (Command/Ctrl+D) to copy and move the stroke to cover the rest of the building guides. The top strokes will be larger than the tapered top of the building.

8. Select the two stroke groups that cover the top of the building (where it diminishes in size). Drag the control handles on each side of the selection so that the stroke covers only the shape of the building (drag the bounding box until it snaps to the guides). Figure 5.42 shows the finished building.

The Green Building

The small green building is your next "victim." You've completed two buildings so far, and the only difference between them is that one gets smaller at the top. On both patterns, you've left white space between the strokes. It would be faster to fill the building shape if you could simply define the stroke as a pattern swatch and be done with it. As it happens, you can—and you will.

1. Remove the lock from the Green Bldg layer (and lock all the other layers). Select the green building (an easy way to make the correct green your current Fill color). Save the color in your Swatches palette. Deselect the green building and choose the Pen tool. Set the Fill color to None. Use an area of your image under the buildings. Click to create a point, press Shift, and create another point about 4 inches to the right of the first point (you don't need to measure; just make the stroke wider than the green building).

2. Apply the Building Pattern 3 to the stroke.

3. Select the darker stroke in the Appearance palette. Change the Stroke color to the saved green swatch. Drag the stroke into the Swatches palette. After the stroke is safely in the Swatches palette, delete the original stroke from the document.

4. Select the short green building. Change the Fill color to the pattern that you just created (make the Fill the active swatch in the Toolbox and click on the new pattern in the Swatches palette). Figure 5.43 shows the cityscape with three buildings textured.

The Yellow Building

The yellow building is next on your list. For this building, you'll create a more complex series of strokes based on Building Pattern 4 to use as a pattern fill.

1. Make the Yellow Bldg layer the only unlocked layer. Select the yellow building to set the current Fill color and drag the swatch into the Swatches palette. Deselect the yellow building and choose the Pen tool. Swap the Fill and Stroke colors. Working in the bottom portion of the image, click to create a point, press Shift, and create another point about 4 inches to the right of the first point (make the stroke wider than the building).

2. Apply Building Pattern 4 to the stroke.

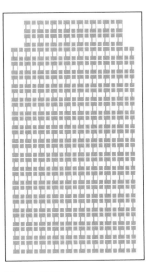

Figure 5.42
The orchid building is finished, and the strokes at the top are shorter to conform to the original shape.

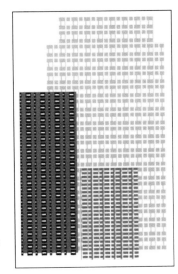

Figure 5.43
Three buildings are now complete.

3. Change the colors of the stroke. Make the black stroke in the Appearance palette the same yellow as the original building. Make the gray stroke CMYK: 50, 0, 50, 0. Drag the light green swatch into the Swatches palette.

4. Choose Object|Transform|Move and move the line 40 points vertically and 90 degrees. Click on Copy.

5. You now need to reverse the colors in the copied line. Select the yellow stroke in the Appearance palette and change the Stroke color to the same green as the other part of the line. The entire stroke now looks solid. Then, select the other green stroke in the Appearance palette and change its Stroke color to the original yellow.

6. Lock both copies of the stroke on the Layers palette (don't lock the layer—lock only the paths).

7. Select the Pen tool. Draw a stroke that is exactly at the bottom of the two strokes. After you set the first point, press Shift to keep the stroke straight. Click on the No Style style in the Styles palette. (I don't think that I want to say *that* aloud five times quickly!)

8. In the Stroke palette, change the Stroke width to 5 and the dash pattern to Dash: 1 point, Gap: 6 points. Select a Round Cap. You may leave the Miter Join setting as is. Contract the line, if needed, so that the dots start and end within the larger stripe. Figure 5.44 shows the current stroke pattern.

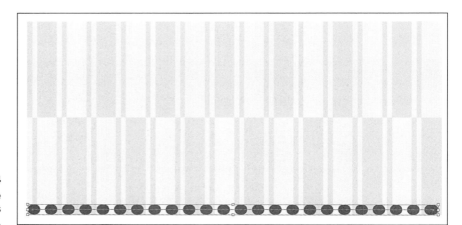

Figure 5.44
Adding a dotted line to the dashed pattern provides some spice.

9. In the Appearance palette, choose New Stroke. Drag the new stroke below the original one. Set the Stroke color to yellow and the Stroke width to 7 points. Deselect the Dashed Line checkbox (you now have a solid yellow stripe). Change the Cap to Butt. Shorten the line if it now extends beyond the sides of the wider yellow/green stripes. If the stroke is lower than the wide stripes, press the up-arrow key to move the stroke so that it is totally on top of the wide strokes.

10. Select the dotted brown and solid yellow line. You need to make three more copies across the pattern. Choose Object|Transform|Move and move the line vertically 20 points (one-half of the 40-point width of each stripe). Click on Copy. Use the Transform Again command two more times (Command/Ctrl+D). Figure 5.45 shows this finished pattern.

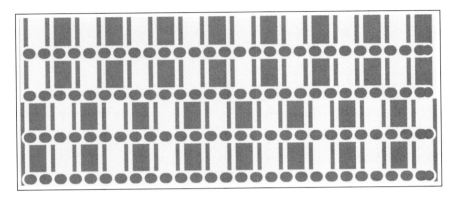

Figure 5.45
The complex stripe pattern is complete.

11. Unlock the two wide stripes.

12. Select the entire stripe and drag it into the Swatches palette. Change the fill of the yellow building to the new pattern. You can delete the pattern, but I recommend instead that you cut it from this image and paste and save it to a new file. There is no good way to reconstruct the starting pattern by using only the pattern swatch because Illustrator simplifies the shapes when it makes a pattern. Figure 5.46 shows the four buildings completed.

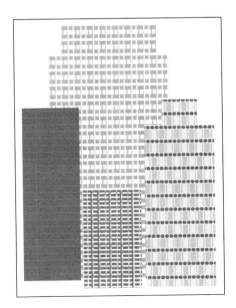

Figure 5.46
Four buildings are now complete.

Architecture 102—Windows and Paint

You have now applied two stroke sequences and two complete patterns to buildings. It was undoubtedly easier to make the pattern fill conform to the uneven shape of the yellow building than it was to make the stripes conform to the shape of the orchid building. You can create a pattern from a stripe so that no space remains between strokes. You can also create a pattern that allows for white space by simply adding an unstroked, unfilled rectangle to the selection as a spacer. You'll try this next as you continue the "Cityscape" project.

Spaced-Out (and Pulled-In) Strokes

Follow these steps to complete the fifth building:

1. Make the Salmon Bldg layer the only unlocked layer. Select the salmon building to make its fill the active Fill color. Save the Fill color in your Swatches palette. Deselect the building and use the Pen tool to make a straight line somewhere on the bottom of the image. Swap the Fill and Stroke colors. Set the Stroke width to 10 points, with a Butt Cap. Select the Dashed Line checkbox and create a pattern of Dash: 10, Gap: 6, Dash: 4, Gap: 2. (This project illustrates a reverse Fibonacci progression with a base of 2 points—if you want to follow the logic of the line.)

2. In the Appearance palette, create a new stroke. Change the Stroke color to white and the Stroke width to 6 points. Reverse the stroke pattern (Dash: 2 points, Gap: 4 points, Dash: 6 points, Gap: 10 points). Deselect the stroke. Select the Rectangle tool. Set both the Fill and the Stroke color to None. Create an invisible rectangle around the stroke that is a bit taller than the stroke. Select the stroke and the rectangle and drag them into the Swatches palette. Select the salmon building and set the fill for the building to the newly defined pattern. Figure 5.47 shows the image with five buildings completed. Don't delete the original pattern stroke.

SeaGreen Building

In this part of the project, you're going to see what happens when you create a pattern with overlapping transparent areas. Continue using the same stroke as the one that you created for the salmon building.

1. Select the no-stroke-no-fill rectangle around the stroke and delete it.

2. Unlock the SeaGreen Building layer (don't lock the Salmon Bldg layer, however, or you will also lock your pattern-to-be). Select the building to make its fill the Current Fill color. Deselect. Drag the Fill color into the Swatches palette. Select the salmon stroke in the Appearance palette. Change the Stroke color to the green that you just dragged into the Swatches palette.

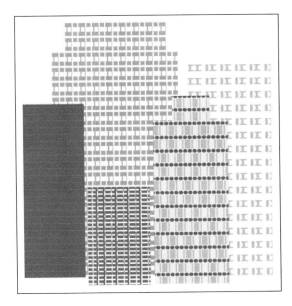

Figure 5.47
The fifth building created shows how you can leave white space in a pattern.

3. Choose Object|Transform|Move and set the vertical amount to 10 points. Then, click on the Angle field and make sure that it defaults to 90 degrees. Click on Copy. Choose Transform Again (Command/ Ctrl+D) two more times. (You'll have four strokes.)

4. In the Layers palette, you can easily select the top and the third-down strokes.

5. Leave the two strokes selected. Choose Object|Transform|Reflect and select the Vertical Axis radio button. Select the Objects checkbox and not the Patterns checkbox. Then, click on OK.

6. Select all four stroke sets and group them (Command/Ctrl+G).

7. You can easily define this four-stroke combination as a pattern. However, let's see what happens if you want to overlap this "set" about three-quarters of the way up. Select the grouping. Make sure that you have enough room to repeat the pattern once. Choose Object|Transform|Move, set the vertical position to 30 points, and click on the Angle field to set it to 90 degrees. Click on Copy.

8. Select both groups. Drag the two groups onto the Swatches palette to make a pattern tile. The overlapped stroke makes a subtle pattern variation.

9. Select the SeaGreen building and fill it with the new pattern.

You have two remaining shapes. I chose to leave the pink building solid and to create only a small blue and white pattern to the aqua building in the foreground. Finish the two shapes with any stroke pattern you want. This is an excellent opportunity for you to apply the lessons in this chapter. Figure 5.48 shows the final Illustrator image.

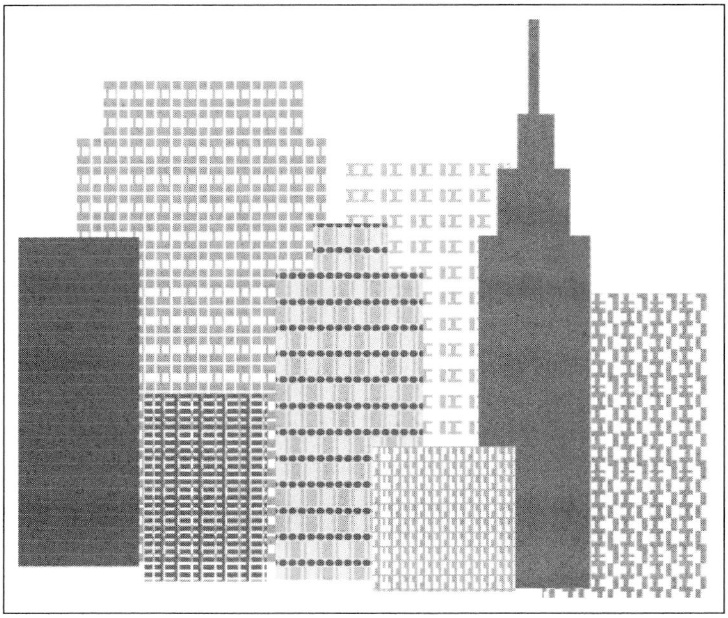

Figure 5.48
This is my finished Illustrator cityscape.

I also saved this image as a layered Photoshop file. I added to it a scan of turtles swimming in a sea (taken from *Japanese Stencil Designs*, by Andrew W. Tuer, Dover Books, 1967). I embossed both the sea design and the buildings and added some gradients and layer masks. You can inspect the Photoshop layered file as it is on the companion CD-ROM (CITYSCAPE2.PSD). Figure 5.49 shows the finished Photoshop image (and, of course, it looks better in the color Illustrator Studio).

Knotting Up Loose Ends

You've seen several of the possibilities and uses for dashed lines in this chapter. Some limitations exist as well. You can't slice (Object|Path|Slice) an open path to sever it, although the Slice command works as expected on a dashed, stroked object that is closed. The Expand command (which I use repeatedly throughout this book) doesn't work well on dashed strokes. When you expand a stroke with a dashed line in it, you get a solid line (not the little boxes that I hoped would magically appear).

However, you've seen that you can create patterns from dashed stroked paths. You can also create pattern brushes, which expand into shapes. In this chapter's final project, you'll create a pattern brush out of a dashed path. This technique is excellent for the combined dash patterns that you've made (even though it's a bit redundant because you can directly stroke an object's path with multiple strokes from the Styles palette). Overlaid dash patterns are attractive when placed on printer's ornaments and curlicues (you can find several examples in this book's CD-ROM clip art sample from Ultimate Symbol). Figure 5.50 shows an

Figure 5.49
The cityscape image can be finished in Photoshop to allow you to add special effects.

Figure 5.50
Printer's flourish and ornament design using clip art from Ultimate Symbol's Design Elements collection.

example that I created using flourishes and a circle design from Ultimate Symbol's Design Elements collection. I stroked all the flourishes with a Pattern brush made from a dashed stroke.

You, too, can play with a Pattern brush. To save you the hours it took me to create this image (and I didn't do nearly as good a job as the monks in Ireland did by hand in the Middle Ages), you'll use a Celtic knotwork image as your starting point, along with a dash pattern you created for the previous cityscape image.

PROJECT 5.5 Tying Knots

In this project, you'll have a chance to create a pattern and use it to create another pattern, which you'll use to create a different pattern until you build a knot from a knot.

1. Open the image CELTIC.AI from the CD-ROM that accompanies this book. Figure 5.51 shows the starting image. The image contains three layers—a green continuous knot and a black knot that has been cut apart to show the weaving of the continuous line. (Using this layered image allows those of you who want to try it the opportunity to see whether you can do a better job of weaving the ribbon than I did—and I'm sure that, with patience, you can.) It also contains a layer that has on it the simple I-beam stroke that you created earlier in this chapter. The stroke is also defined as a Style.

Figure 5.51
The original Celtic knot image.

2. Select the dash stroke and choose Object|Expand Appearance.

3. Drag the selected dash pattern onto the Brushes palette and select the New Pattern Brush radio button in the resulting dialog box. In the New Pattern Brush dialog box that appears, name the pattern "I-Beam Dash" and change the Colorization method to Tints And Shades, as shown in Figure 5.52.

4. Hide the layer that contains the green continuous knot. Select the broken knot. Click on the I-Beam Dash brush in the Brushes palette. Change the Stroke color to dark green. Figure 5.53 shows the result.

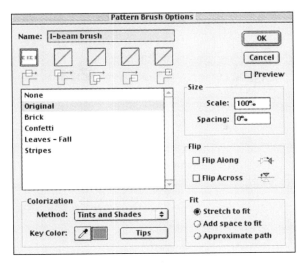

Figure 5.52
Setting the options for the
Pattern brush.

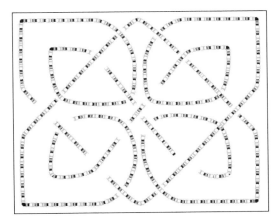

Figure 5.53
Stroke the broken knot paths
with the Pattern brush.

5. Click on the Eye icon next to the Continuous Knot layer to turn it back
   on. Notice that you can see the green of that layer right through the
   brushed path. Therefore, the Pattern brush has areas that are transparent because of the gaps in the original dashed line. Transparent areas
   are fine, unless they annoy you. They annoyed me as I was doing this
   example, so you are going to add an opaque background to the stroke
   and resave the Pattern brush.

6. Deselect everything in the image. Hide the Continuous Knot layer
   again. Choose a Stroke of None and a Fill of dark blue. Select the Rectangle tool. Draw a rectangle over the dashed line on the pasteboard
   area so that it's as close as possible in size to the dashed line. Choose
   Object|Arrange|Send To Back. Figure 5.54 shows the new stroke pattern.

7. Select the entire stroke pattern and drag it onto the Brushes palette.
   Make it a Pattern brush and give it the same options as you did in Step 3.
   Name the brush "Dash Pattern 2". Select the Broken Knot and click on

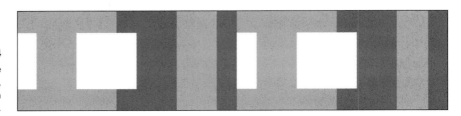

Figure 5.54
When you place an opaque object behind a dashed line, the entire line becomes an opaque pattern.

Dash Pattern 2 to apply it. Were you to reveal the Continuous Knot layer now, it would show through much less than it did before (you don't need to do this, however).

8. If you look carefully at the outer corners of the knot, you'll notice gaps in the line. The Pattern brush allows you to create special tiles for the corners of a line. Let's do that now. Select the entire dash pattern that is still on the pasteboard. Press Option/Alt and drag it to make a duplicate. Work in the duplicate. Ungroup it (Shift+Command/Ctrl+G), and then deselect.

9. With the Selection tool, click on the dashed line in the center of the line pattern. You will know that you have selected the desired piece if the Fill color in the Toolbox is set to None and the Stroke to white. (It's much easier to twirl down the layer and select the path directly.) You should be able to see the dashed-line pattern in the Stroke palette. Choose the Scissors tool and click on the path line about the same distance from the left edge as the line is high (the idea is to end up with a mostly square chunk that you can use as a corner). Delete the *selected* chunk of line (that's the part of the line to the right).

10. Select the medium-blue dashed line by clicking at the center of the line where no white is visible. Use the Scissors tool and click in the same spot as you did in Step 9. Delete the selected portion to the right. Only the deep-blue rectangle is left at the original length. Figure 5.55 shows the line pattern after the two pieces have been removed.

Figure 5.55
The small chunk to the left of the line is all that will be left when the corner tile is complete.

11. Select the deep-blue rectangle and drag its right bounding box handle toward the left until it is only a tiny bit larger than the blue and white stripe. Select all three pieces and group them.

12. Press Option/Alt after you start to drag the square tile to the Brushes palette. Continue to drag the tile and then drop it into the first division on the Brushes palette on the entry that contains the Dash Pattern 2 brush. The arrow in Figure 5.56 shows the square on which to drop the tile. The square is outlined in black if you drag it with Option/Alt pressed. If you drop it in the wrong place, you will not get the expected results.

13. Figure 5.57 shows the Pattern Brush Options dialog box with the new tile placed in slot 2 in the dialog box (this is the outside corner slot, and the confusing thing is that it is at a different position than the slot onto which you dragged the tile). Click on OK. Then, click on Apply To Strokes when that dialog box appears.

Figure 5.56
Drag the corner tile into the first slot on the Brushes palette in the Dash Pattern 2 brush (the location of the arrow).

Figure 5.57
The Pattern Brush Options dialog box shows you whether you dragged the tile to the right spot.

14. Repeat Steps 12 and 13. This time, however, press Option/Alt and drag the corner tile to the fourth division (out of six) on the Brushes palette. You need to watch it carefully. The pattern itself occupies two slots. Figure 5.58 shows the correct place to drop the tile. Again, select Apply To Strokes. All your corners now have tiles in them.

15. Now, you can have some fun with this image. Select the pattern-brushed knot, press Option/Alt, and drag a copy of the knot to the pasteboard. Work on the copy on the pasteboard.

16. Select the pattern-brushed knot on the pasteboard and make the Transform palette active. Type ".773" for both the height and the width of the knot. Press Return/Enter to accept the values. The knot becomes tiny, and the pattern is all mixed up.

Figure 5.58
Drag the same corner tile to the Inner Corner tile location in slot 4 (where the arrow is located).

17. With the tiny knot still selected, click on the second icon from the left at the bottom of the Brushes palette. By doing so, you can customize the options for a selected item. Change the scale to 35%, as shown in Figure 5.59, and then click on OK. Figure 5.60 shows the knot with the scaled pattern.

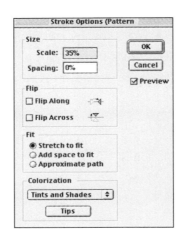

Figure 5.59

(Left) You can set specific options for each item to which you apply a custom brush.

Figure 5.60

(Right) The pattern fits much better now on the tiny knot.

18. Select the tiny knot and Option/Alt drag to make a duplicate of it. Choose Object|Expand and expand the object, its stroke, and fill. Group it. (You cannot create a Pattern brush from something that contains a Pattern brush. Expanding the object makes all its attributes "real" and removes the brush pattern by re-creating it in permanent objects.)

19. Select the tiny expanded knot group and drag it onto the Brushes palette to create a new Pattern brush. Name it "Knot Pattern". Set the Colorization to Tints And Shades. Click on OK. Press Option/Alt and drag the tiny expanded knot group back on the Knot Pattern entry in the Brushes palette in slot 1 (to make an outside corner). Click on OK. Press Option/Alt and drag the tiny expanded knot group back on the Knot Pattern entry in the Brushes palette in slot 4 (to make an inside corner).

20. Select the large knot in the center of your image. Click on the Knot Pattern brush to apply it to the large knot. Click on the second icon on the left at the bottom of the Brushes palette to open the options for the selected object. Set the Scale to 75%. You might need to do some cleanup. If stray points or lines in the image show up as blobs of dark color, you can use the Direct Selection tool to find and delete them. You might also want to space the breaks in the knot differently. Edit the shape as you see fit. Figure 5.61 shows the image at this point (after some cleanup has been done).

Figure 5.61
The Celtic knot after a bit of cleanup.

21. Unfortunately, although you made the original brush pattern fully opaque, in this knotted version, the areas where the knot is not are not opaque (sorry about that). To rectify this situation, select the large center knot (your image area). Copy it to the clipboard (Command/Ctrl+C). Choose Edit|Paste In Front.

22. Change the Stroke to None to remove the brush (or click on the first icon on the left at the bottom of the Brushes palette). Select white as the Stroke color and change the Stroke width to 45 points. Choose Object|Arrange|Send To Back.

23. With the white knot still selected, repeat Step 21. Change the Stroke color to black. Choose Object|Arrange|Send To Back. Do not deselect. Press the right-arrow key two times and the down-arrow key three times to move the black shadow and then deselect.

24. Select the topmost large center knot in the image area. Choose a medium green for the stroke. If the image doesn't change, open the selected item options and set the Colorization to Tints And Shades.

25. Double-click on the Scale tool and select a uniform scale of 100%. Click on Copy to place a copy of the knot directly on top of the first one. Click on the Dash Pattern 2 brush to change the brush stroke back to the thinner brush. Click on the second icon from the left at the bottom of the Brushes palette and set the scale for the pattern to 100%. Change the Colorization to Tints And Shades and click on OK. Choose a gold for the stroke.

26. Double-click on the Scale tool and select a uniform scale of 60%. Click on Copy. Click on the second icon from the left at the bottom of the Brushes palette and set the scale for the pattern to 90%. Change the Colorization to None and click on OK. Figure 5.62 shows the finished image (which looks better in the color Illustrator Studio).

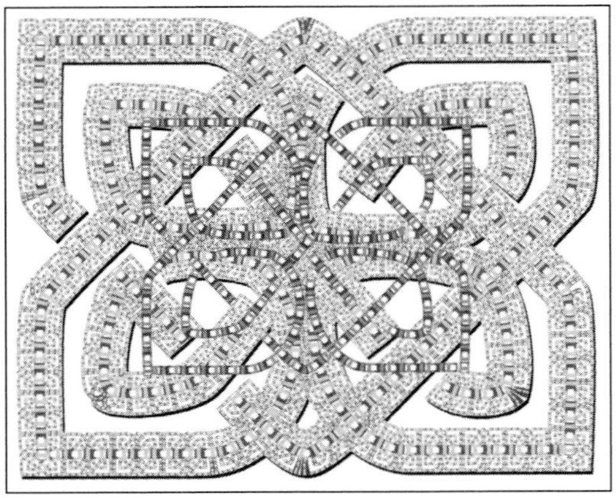

Figure 5.62
The completed image.

Moving On

You should now be an expert in making patterns from dashed and dotted lines. You learned how to use dash-and-gap patterns to create decorative lines such as train tracks. You also used a variety of dashed lines to make a coupon and a group of textures. In this chapter, you learned how to create patterns and Pattern brushes from dashed lines and learned about some of the commands (such as Expand) that might not work as expected on dashed open strokes.

In Chapter 6, you'll learn about making transformations in your images—using all the Transform commands in new and interesting ways.

Illustrator 9 Studio

*This studio showcases the results of several of the
projects you will find in this book that feature the
exciting new functions and capabilities of Illustrator 9.*

A new feature of Illustrator 9 is the Transform effect. This tool lets you create complex, multiple-copy forms "on the fly," using only one shape, and it also rotates and scales them. You can change the entire look of an object with a single edit by changing the underlying shape. Introduced in Chapter 1, the Transform effect allows you to build this necklace from a single gradient-filled circle.

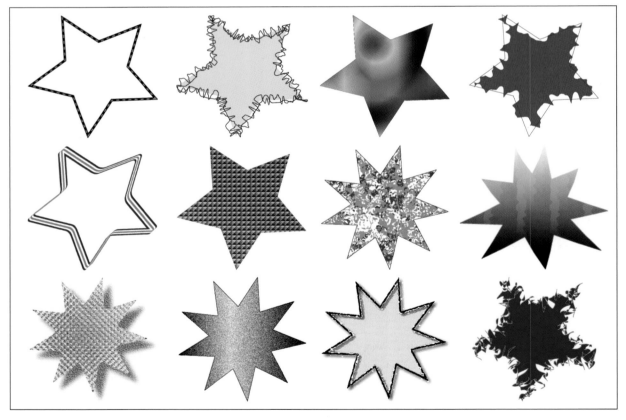

Illustrator 9 now allows you to save Styles. Styles are a combination of fills, strokes, transparency, and effects that can be applied to a new object with a single click. Here you see only a few of the many styles now possible in Illustrator 9. You'll learn more about using these effects in Chapter 2.

You can also use styles to turn a few dots into a grape leaf stroke that you can apply around the border of a pattern-filled rectangle. After adding a number of filters and text, you can see the result. If you save these specifications as a style, with one click, you can create decorated capital letters that any medieval monk would have died for!

You can take a simple logo and add an Offset path effect to create a gradient fill to enhance backgrounds. Add the Roughen Effect to fancy-up the comet tails and create the appearance of glow and motion (bottom-left). Applying a few additional filters can produce variations to reproduce, onscreen, the desired result (bottom-right). Chapter 2 introduces and familiarizes you with these techniques.

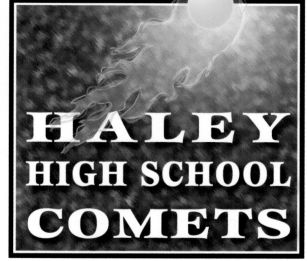

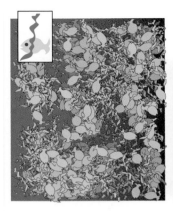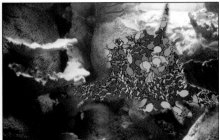

You can create a tiny fish-and-seaweed element and repeat it multiple times. You can randomly move the elements and finally use Blend Front To Back to add a gradient wash of color from the foremost object to the one at the back of the stack.

Here is the the result. With further manipulation, you can add a rasterized version of the fish into a fish-shaped mask, color a background scene, and produce a new illustration. This image (sharkreefdone.psd) was produced from the Illustrator files in Photoshop. You can find this file on this book's companion CD-ROM, in the Chapter 3 Ends folder.

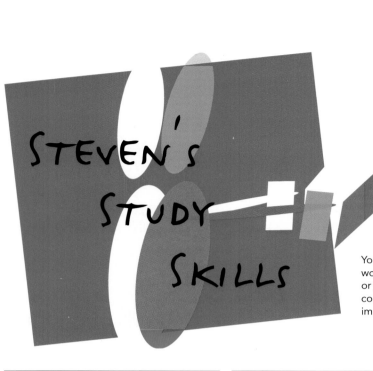

You can use Illustrator 9's new Blend modes that work exactly as the same modes work in Photoshop, or you can still use the Mix Hard and Mix Soft commands. This is how the Steven's Study Skills image was created (see Chapter 3).

Three steps to a cup of coffee: Take a wire frame outline of the cup (top-left) and add the gradients needed to add realism to the shape, mixed in with a few blend modes (bottom-left). Stir some smoke and a triple shadow—courtesy of the Offset path and the Transform effects—you have a realistic cup of coffee (right). Learn how this image was created in Chapter 3.

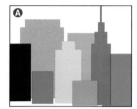

In Chapter 5, you learn a variety of ways to create patterns as well as an incredible new feature in Illustrator 9—how to layer strokes on top of each other in a single path. The base set of patterned buildings (**Ⓐ**) was created totally in Illustrator. Dashed and dotted lines were added to create an interesting effect for each building. The image was then placed into Photoshop, where additional effects and the sky were added to unify the color and create a complete composition (**Ⓑ**).

A coupon doesn't always need to be square. A simple dotted line in an interesting shape works well. In Chapter 5, you learn how to use the image of a ballet dancer as the basis of the coupon and how to layer watercolor strokes behind it for effect.

This Victoria's Garden Restaurant example shows how to use clip art motifs (here, a printer's swash from the Ultimate Symbol Design Elements Collection) as the path that you'll stroke with a dash pattern. The gradient mesh behind the image adds color to the simple scheme of the image. See Chapter 5.

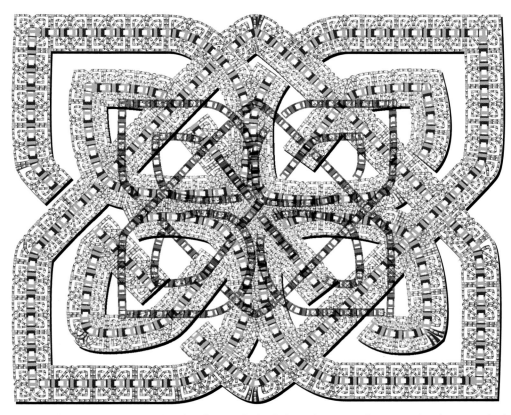

Chapter 5 shows you how to create pattern brushes from multiple dash strokes. Here, the pattern brush was applied to a Celtic knot motif to make an ornament that, in turn, becomes a pattern brush. Using this brush again, you can create a Celtic knot stroked with many Celtic knots of the same shape. Arrange the knots in different ways and use the Multiply blend effect to create interaction between the top and lower shapes.

Illustrator 9 has all the tools needed to make a great pizza—Roll out a circle and add sauce, apply a dash of Scribble and Tweak; create cheese with the Duplicate command, cook up some gradient-filled meatballs, mix it up with Transform Each and bake. See Chapter 6 for this pizza recipe.

This image shows what you can do with concentric stars and boxes. You can add a stroke to the edges of objects using a gradient as a pattern brush. The stars' colors are blended from closest to farthest objects in the stack (see Chapter 6.)

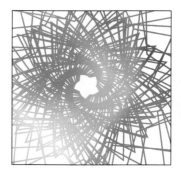

The creation of this image originated in Illustrator from a series of concentric stars (top-left). In Chapter 6, you'll learn how to create this image using features that are completely new in Illustrator 9. The top-right version of the image was built mostly in Photoshop due to program limitations in Illustrator 8—the large image was built totally in Illustrator 9.

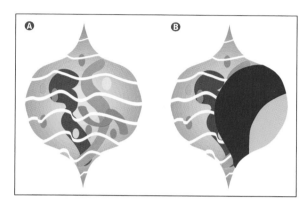

Take an ogee-shaped object (Ⓐ) and cut it into three parts using a rotation template (Ⓑ).

Rotate all three layers to make it look as though each ogee sits somewhat behind the other one. This image is the lowest rotation layer in the mandala.

Add a background and two more rotational objects—the center layer on the final image.

Distress the background and add another rotated object in front...then contemplate the amount of time you've just spent learning how to create this 60's-style design! For the complete details, see Chapter 6.

Gradient meshes (see Chapter 5) can be difficult to control. Here, one is used as a simple background of a stroked object with an abstract fill behind it.

A distorted star with an inverted point is used to create the body of this girl. In Illustrator, you can draw a path that touches three sides of a rectangle to form infinite, interlocking patterns. You can fill your images with the pattern, as I have done here with the girl's dress (see Chapter 7).

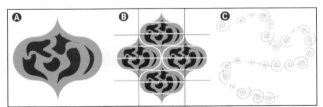

In Chapter 7, we'll use an ogee (Ⓐ) to build a pattern shape. An ogee tiles seamlessly (Ⓑ) when you construct the repeating pattern. Create a randomly sized pattern brush from a simple spiral and expand it to create a texture (Ⓒ).

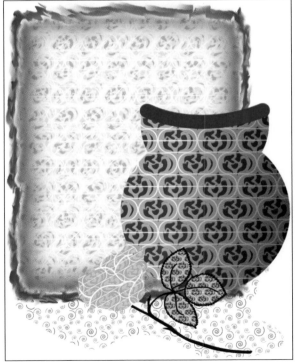

The final image (see Chapter 7) uses variations of the ogee pattern on the flower, leaf, and vase, and uses the texture as a shadow under the objects. The backdrop uses the same ogee pattern, with an opacity mask constructed from a rotated version of the pattern fill.

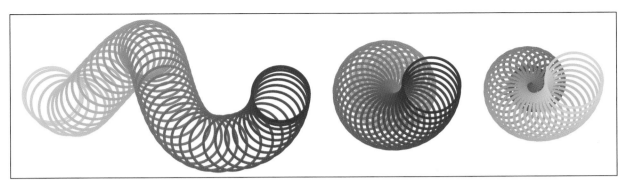

A blend along a wavy spine (left) twists when you replace the spine with a spiral (center). You can switch the front-to-back orientation of the blend by choosing Blend|Reverse Spine or, reverse the colors of the blend (right). See Chapter 8.

In Chapter 8, you learn how to create incredible realism with gradients. The flat spray can on the left almost jumps off the page after custom gradients are applied (right).

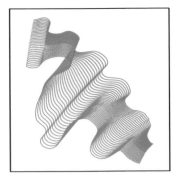

The two blended line ribbons (top-left) were the original inspiration for this stylized illustration of turtles patterned after a Japanese woodcut. Learn how to create water from blended line ribbons (bottom-left) in Chapter 8.

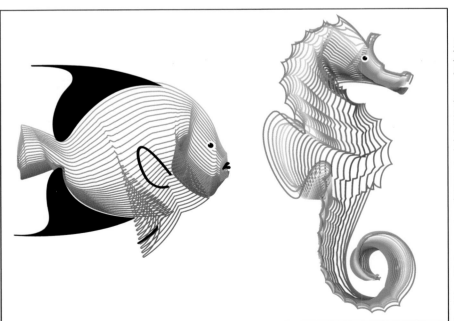

You can use any piece of clip art as the basis for creating intricate line blends. The Make Blend command adds the intermediate lines and also makes the color mixes. The fish features a single blend across its body, and the seahorse features a blend between an existing, expanded blend. Learn about the Make Blend function in Chapter 8.

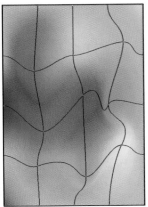

Change a rectangle into a gradient mesh object, then fill various portions of the mesh with different colors.

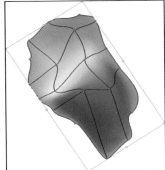

Using the sub-group selection tool to move the points of the rectangle, you can push the object into the shape of a petal.

In Chapter 8, you learn learn how to create this flower from several gradient mask objects, change the Blend modes, and add a drop-shadow effect.

The pen, by David Xenakis, is great example of realism using gradients.

You'll learn how to take a length of clip-art fabric like the one I used here from the *Direct Imagination* Racinet's Le Costume Historique CD-ROM, and miter it to fit inside of a kimono. You'll also learn how to use a portion of the image to create a background pattern and how to place and rasterize Illustrator art. See Chapter 10 for more information.

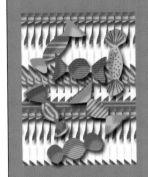

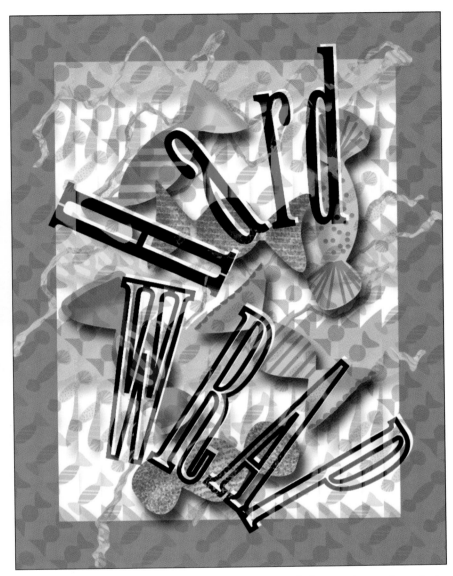

In Chapter 10, you'll learn how to work with Illustrator images inside of Photoshop. The top left Illustrator image shows the basis of a Photoshop composite. You can build complex patterns in Illustrator to add texture and visual appeal to the final image. Because you can save Illustrator files in Photoshop format with layers intact, you can easily hide part of the original image while arranging and coloring the candy to create one of the several patterns you'll need.

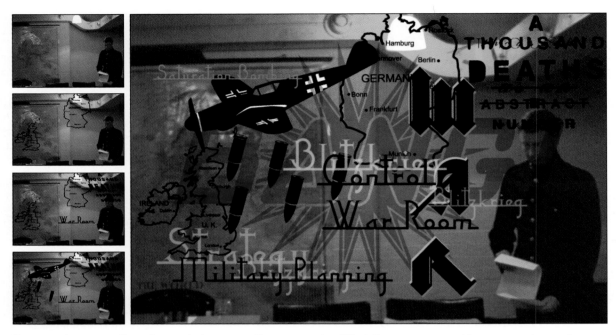

Knowing when to use Photoshop and when to use Illustrator can be difficult if you want to combine raster and vector images. All the objects in this composite image (plane and text) were created in Illustrator and placed into Photoshop. In Chapter 10, you learn how to import, scale, and rotate Illustrator objects by using Photoshop as your compositing program.

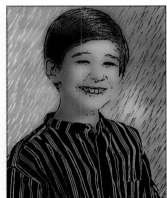

You can take a photograph (as I did with my nephew) and prepare it in Photoshop to get woodcut-looking paths in Illustrator. When filled with black, these paths provide an interesting stylized look to a blurred copy of the original image. You can also create a hatch pattern to use as texture for the image.

You can also take a raster image and change it into a stylized piece of artwork by changing it into a gradient mesh object (see Chapter 8). The original used in this example was a color photograph of a Halloween street scene.

Chapter 6

Transformations

Transformations are what happen when you take simple shapes and, using only Illustrator commands, turn them into something else. This chapter looks at some of my favorite ways of turning simple things into complicated ones.

By Sherry London

Illustrator is bursting at the seams with commands to change one shape into another. You can use the Transform palette, the Pathfinder palette, the Transform tools (Free Transform, Rotate, Reflect, Skew, and Scale), and a host of other Path commands and filters. New to Illustrator 9 is the ability to select the point of transformation in the Transform palette. You've already used some of these tools in previous projects, yet there are too many of them to try to use everything here. Instead, I've somewhat arbitrarily picked out techniques that I like and developed three major projects for this chapter.

Extra Cheese (Transformations in Action)

It's difficult to believe that I never tasted a "real" pizza until I was in high school. Pizza shops did exist, but I was a fussy eater, and I really hated the pizzas served by the Philadelphia school system (a slice of stale bread topped with a spoonful of tomato sauce and a slice of cheese, which was cooked until the cheese was nicely browned). If that was a pizza, I wanted no part of it!

How Do You Like Your Pizza?

The pizza that you're going to create in Project 6.1 is more appetizing (if not totally realistic). While you are building its ingredients, you'll also learn about the Free Transform tool, perspective text, the Add Points command, and the Transform Each command. Because the project is quite long, I've divided it into a number of subprojects.

Transforming an Advertisement

6.1 In this project, you'll build a pizza from component parts and then distort it, create a border, and turn it into an ad for a pizza shop.

Building the Perfect Pizza

In this first segment of the project, you'll build the entire pizza.

1. Create a new document in Illustrator.

2. Choose the Ellipse tool. Create an oval or circular shape in your image. It doesn't matter where or how large—we'll fix that in the next step.

3. Although I could have had you create the circle at the correct size, you'll use the Transform palette because this is the Transformations chapter. Leave the circle selected. Enter 4.6 inches into both the width and the height fields in the Transform palette. Press Return/Enter to execute the transformation, as shown in Figure 6.1.

4. Change the Stroke to None and the Fill to a warm, crusty golden-brown (I used CMYK: 20, 42, 70, 7). Double-click on the Layer entry in the Layers palette and change the Layer name to "Pizza Dough". You'll use a lot of layers in this example.

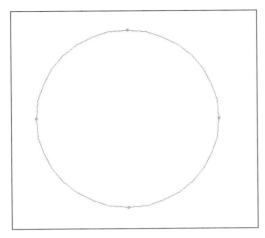

Figure 6.1

You can use the Transform palette to make changes in the size and position of your objects.

5. Lock the Pizza Dough layer. Change your Fill color to CMYK: 20, 75, 70, 7 (or your favorite tomato-sauce color). Drag the Pizza Dough layer entry in the Layers palette to the New Layer icon at the bottom of the Layers palette. (Or you can choose Duplicate from the side drop-down menu in the Layers palette. Either method will make a fast "copy in place" without needing to physically copy and paste in front.) The layer is named "Pizza Dough Copy". Double-click on the layer entry and change the name to "Sauce".

6. Unlock the Sauce layer. Drag the Fill color swatch from the Toolbox (or the Color palette) onto the unselected circle. The circle immediately changes to the new color. You can drag any color swatch onto an unselected object—a useful technique when you have the desired color in the Toolbox but know that it will disappear as soon as you click to select another object.

7. Select the circle. Double-click on the Scale tool and enter a Uniform Scale amount of 80%. Click on OK (not on Copy).

8. Choose Object|Path|Add Anchor Points. The circle had four points; now it has eight because the Add Anchor Points command places one point midway between every original pair of points in the object. Choose Object|Path|Add Anchor Points again. Now, the circle has 16 points, as shown in Figure 6.2, and your object is much more malleable if you want to apply filters or effects that tweak the points.

9. Choose Effect|Distort|Scribble And Tweak. Select the Preview checkbox. All three option checkboxes should be selected by default, as shown in Figure 6.3. Change the Horizontal and Vertical sliders as you want, but don't let the sauce spill out of the pizza dough. The filter produces random effects, and moving the sliders back to a setting that you've looked at previously will give you different results. When you like what you see, click on OK. Figure 6.4 shows the sauce—now spread out nicely on the dough.

Efficiency

Copying the Pizza Dough layer is probably not the most efficient way to create a scaled copy of an object. A more direct route to this end is to simply double-click on the Scale tool and create an 80-percent copy. Then, fill it with sauce color. However, Illustrator has a variety of paths to the same end. Efficiency isn't everything. You should also know the side roads.

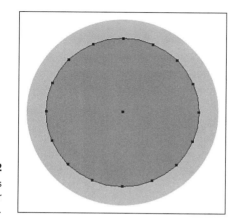

Figure 6.2

The Add Anchor Points command doubles the number of points in an object.

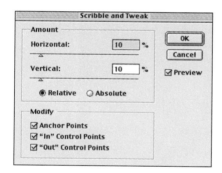

Figure 6.3

(Left) Using the Scribble And Tweak dialog box, you can control how random changes are applied to the control points in the selected object.

Figure 6.4

(Right) Instant tomato sauce (after adding a dash of Scribble And Tweak).

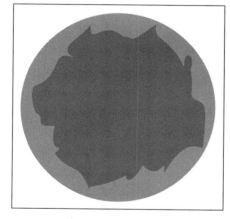

Using Live Effects

When you apply a filter using the Effect menu, you can go back and tweak it any time you want. As you learned in Chapter 2, Live Effects are new to Illustrator 9, and they are very powerful. Remember that you can apply the *same* effect multiple times. Therefore, when you alter the effect, you need to reopen it from the Appearance palette.

10. Do you like meatballs? They're tasty on a pizza, so you'll add some now. Create a new layer and name it "Meatballs". Lock the other two layers. Select the Ellipse tool and click somewhere on top of the sauce. In the dialog box, enter both width and height dimensions of 0.6. Leave the meatball selected.

11. Set the Stroke color to None. Set your Fill color to CMYK: 20, 59, 96, 6 (a light meat-brown). Drag the Fill swatch to the left end of the Gradient slider in the Gradient palette. If your Gradient palette contains any other color stops, drag them off the palette to get rid of them (except for the one at the far right). Click on the color stop at the far right of the Gradient slider and change its color to CMYK: 20, 70, 75, 42 (a darker meatball color). Change the gradient Type to Radial.

12. Press Option/Alt and use the Selection tool to drag copies of the meatball and scatter them over the sauce. Figure 6.5 shows the pizza in progress.

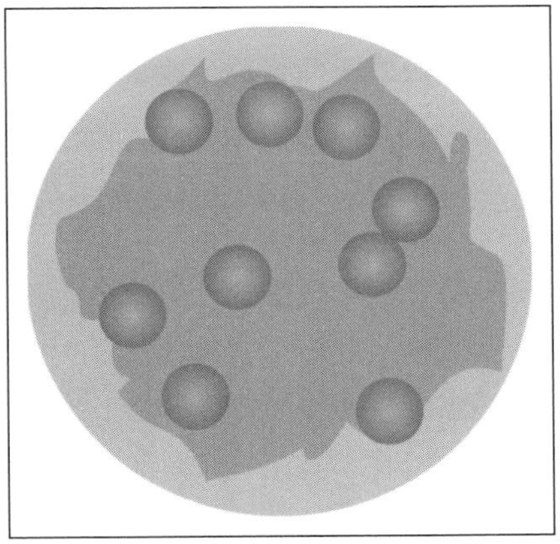

Figure 6.5
Meatballs add a nice flavor to a pizza.

13. You're now going to create the crusty rim on the pizza. You have four choices as to how you like your pizza:

    - Neat sauce, light crust

    - Neat sauce, dark crust

    - Messy sauce, light crust

    - Messy sauce, dark crust

    The general steps for all options are the same. You first need to create the crust itself. Make the Pizza Dough layer active and lock all the layers (including the Pizza Dough layer). Duplicate the layer as you did in Step 5 and name it "Crust".

14. Remove the lock from the Crust layer. Select the circle. Use the Transform palette to change the width and height of the circle to 4.45 inches. Press Return/Enter to execute the transformation. Visually recenter the crust object.

15. Double-click on the Scale tool and enter a Uniform Scale amount of 80%. Click on Copy. Select the unlocked shapes in the image (Command/Ctrl+A). Create a Compound path (Command/Ctrl+8). You now have a doughnut shape with a huge hole.

16. Choose the Eyedropper tool and click on a meatball. This action makes the gradient that you used for the meatball the current Fill color. Press Option/Alt and click inside the compound path that you created in Step 15 to transfer the gradient to the crust.

17. The crust has a slight problem with this gradient—it isn't really showing up at all. First, you need to define a highlight color for the crust. Click just under the 50% location on the gradient slider to create a color stop. Click on the new color stop and give it a value of CMYK: 3, 21, 45, 0. The gradient still doesn't appear. The problem is that the crust is in the default part of the gradient, where no large color change occurs.

18. The easiest solution is to create a pizza with a dark crust. To do so, drag the highlight color stop (now at the 50% location) toward the right until it nears the last color stop. The highlight is now visible in the crust. Position the color stop so that the highlight is in approximately the center of the crust edge. On my image, its location is 91.01%. Then, drag the leftmost color stop until it also nears the right edge (85.39%). Figure 6.6 shows the Gradient palette, and Figure 6.7 shows the pizza.

Figure 6.6

The Gradient palette shows the locations of the three color stops needed to create a gradient for the crust.

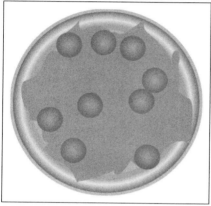

Figure 6.7

The pizza now has a dark, messy crust.

19. Creating a light-crust pizza is a bit trickier. One way is to simply move the two color stops on the left toward the left until both the highlight and the leftmost brown are farther from the right edge. This action lightens the crust. However, it still leaves a browned outer crust. If you like your pizza less well done, you need to move all three color stops toward the center of the Gradient slider, as shown in Figure 6.8. Choose the Gradient tool. To get the center highlight to appear in the middle of your crust, you need to first position the Gradient tool in the center of the crust shape (that is, in the middle of the "hole") and press and hold the mouse button. Press Shift and drag the Gradient line past the right edge of the document. Doing so makes the gradient think that its center is in the center of your crust and gives you the lightly toasted look shown in Figure 6.9.

Figure 6.8

Use these Gradient settings for a light crust.

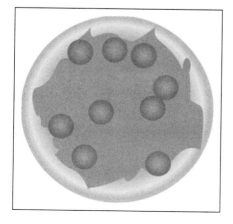

Figure 6.9

By employing the Gradient tool, you can get a lightly toasted pizza crust.

20. If you prefer a neat pizza with no messy sauce on the crust, move the Crust layer up until it is just under the Meatballs layer. If you also want your meatballs to look as if they are cut off at the crust, move the Crust layer until it is above the Meatballs layer, as shown in Figure 6.10.

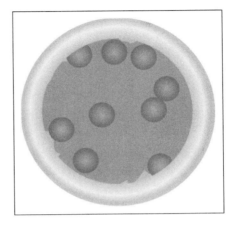

Figure 6.10
You can achieve a neat pizza by moving the Crust layer above the Meatballs layer.

21. Let's create the cheese. Lock all the layers. Create a new layer and name it "American Cheese". Set your Stroke color to None and the Fill color to CMYK: 2, 6, 38, 0 (a medium-light yellow).

22. Choose the Rectangle tool and click near the top-left corner of the bounding box for the pizza (or where it would be if the pizza were selected). Create a rectangle that is 0.1 inch wide and 0.7 inch high. Choose the Selection tool. Press Option/Alt and drag a copy of the cheese shred to the right about one cheese shred width away. Press Shift after you begin to drag to constrain movement to the horizontal. Transform Again (Command/Ctrl+D) until you have created an entire horizontal row that covers the pizza, as shown in Figure 6.11.

> **Baking a Dark Crust**
>
> If you prefer the dark-crust pizza, you might want to stroke the crust in the same color as the outer edge of the crust. A 5- or 6-point stroke works well to blend the dark color into the outer lip of the pizza that you created in Step 14, when you reduced the size of the original pizza dough circle.

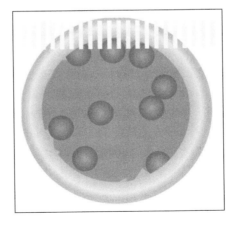

Figure 6.11
Create a horizontal row of shredded cheese.

23. Select the unlocked shapes (Command/Ctrl+A). Press Option/Alt and drag a copy of the cheese shred down about one cheese shred width away. Press Shift after you begin to drag to constrain movement to the vertical. Transform Again (Command/Ctrl+D) until you have created an entire vertical row that covers the pizza, as shown in Figure 6.12.

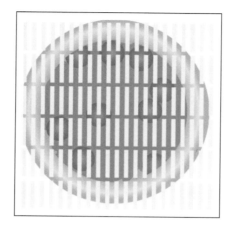

Figure 6.12

Create vertical rows of shredded cheese across the pizza.

24. The arrangement of the cheese shreds is unnatural; you need to fix that now. Select the unlocked cheese shreds (Command/Ctrl+A). Choose Object|Transform|Transform Each. Leave the Scale at 100%. Allow movement between −0.7 inch horizontally and 0.7 inch vertically. Set the Rotation to 359 degrees and select the Random checkbox, as shown in Figure 6.13. Preview the effect to make sure that you like it; what you see is what you get. When you are satisfied, click on OK. Figure 6.14 shows the layer of scattered cheese. Do not deselect.

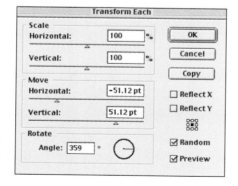

Figure 6.13

Use these settings in the Transform Each dialog box.

25. You need to create a layer of cheddar cheese (I think I forgot to mention that you are creating a three-cheese pizza). Choose Object|Transform| Transform Each. The previous settings should still be there. Accept these settings and click on Copy. Do not deselect. Create a new layer named

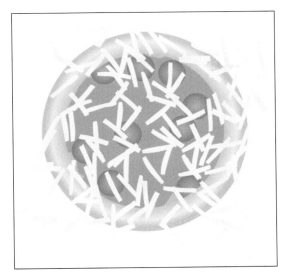

Figure 6.14
This arrangement of cheese is more natural.

"Cheddar Cheese". Move the selected object rectangle from the American Cheese to the Cheddar Cheese layer (thus moving the newly dispersed layer of cheese onto the new layer).

26. Select a more orange color for the Fill. I used CMYK: 2, 30, 38, 0. Now, the cheese looks more like cheddar (or Colby).

27. Let's add a bit of curve to the cheese. Unlock the American Cheese layer. Now, you can select both cheese layers. Choose Effect|Distort|Twirl and enter an amount of 30 degrees. Because this filter works from the center of the selection to the edges, it applies just a gentle curve. Figure 6.15 shows the pizza with two layers of cheese.

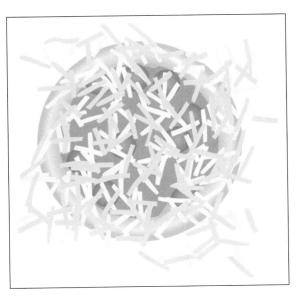

Figure 6.15
The pizza now has two layers of cheese scattered about.

28. The cheese is really a mess. It's all over the table. You need to clean it up. Lock all the layers. Drag the Layer entry for the Pizza Dough layer to the New Layer icon at the bottom of the Layers palette. Change its name to "Cheese Mask". Drag the layer to the top of the Layer stack. Unlock the American Cheese and Cheddar Cheese layers. Select all the unlocked objects (Command/Ctrl+A). Make a mask (Object|Masks|Make; Command/Ctrl+7). Lock the Cheddar Cheese and American Cheese layers again.

29. You need to decide how much cheese you want on your crust. If you don't scale the cheese mask, you have cheese all over the crust. If that's the way you like your pizza, that's fine with me. If you want the crust to be somewhat free of cheese, you can double-click on the Scale tool and enter a Uniform amount of 85%. If you don't like cheese on the crust at all, you can scale the Cheese mask uniformly at 80%. If you want some scattered cheese on the crust, you can apply the Add Anchor Points command to the mask and use the Roughen effect (but you need to be sure that the filter doesn't remove any of the cheese from on top of the sauce). I scaled the mask to 85%, as you can see in Figure 6.16.

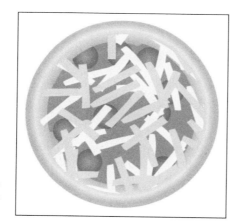

Figure 6.16
The pizza's cheese is now mostly on top of the tomato sauce.

30. The top layer of cheese looks a bit flat. To add some depth, drag the icon for the Cheddar Cheese layer to the New Layer icon at the bottom of the Layers palette to make a copy. Name the copy "Cheddar Cheese Shadow". Move the layer under the Cheddar Cheese layer. Lock all the layers except for the Cheddar Cheese Shadow layer. Select the entire image (Command/Ctrl+A). Set the Fill to CMYK: 11, 43, 92, 2 (a sort of Velveeta color). Press the down-arrow key two times, and then press the right-arrow key two times to offset the shadow.

31. You need to create a layer of Parmesan cheese. This grated cheese tends to stick in clumps (or else can be very coarsely added in small chunks). Create a new layer named (surprise) "Parmesan Cheese". Drag it below the Cheddar Cheese shadow layer. Lock all the other layers, and hide all the cheese and mask layers (except for the Parmesan Cheese layer). Set your Stroke to None and your Fill color to a very pale, light yellow (almost white). I used CMYK: 5, 8, 23, 0. Create an ellipse (by using the Ellipse tool) that is approximately 0.5 inch wide by 0.3 inch high somewhere on top of the sauce.

32. Press Alt/Option and drag-copy 20 to 30 of these little clumps and scatter them about in the sauce. Select all the cheese clumps (Command/Ctrl+A). Choose Object|Transform|Transform Each. Allow the shapes to scale horizontally by 85% and vertically by 115% and rotate up to 356 degrees. If you like your arrangement, set the horizontal and vertical movement to zero. Select the Random checkbox and click on OK.

33. Use the Roughen effect (Effect|Distort|Roughen) to add some irregularity to the shapes. Use Smooth Points. Figure 6.17 shows the settings that I used. If the blobs are too thick, use the Transform Each command to scale only the vertical direction about 75%. Figure 6.18 shows the Parmesan cheese on top of the tomato sauce and meatballs. The other cheese layers are hidden.

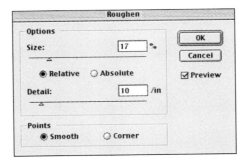

Figure 6.17
You can use the Roughen effect to add randomness to the control points in a shape.

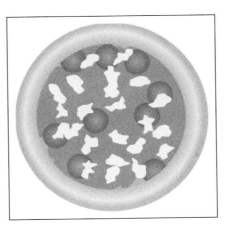

Figure 6.18
The Parmesan cheese blobs.

What Is the Roughen Effect?

Illustrator 9 gives you two ways to apply most filters. You can use the Filter menu, which makes the changes permanent, or you can use the Effect menu, which allows you to change your settings at any point in the process.

34. The pizza needs a few more meatballs. Lock the Parmesan Cheese layer and unlock the Meatballs layer. Select one meatball. Create a new layer named "More Meatballs" and move it to the top of the Layer stack. Move the selected object rectangle from the Meatballs layer to the More Meatballs layer. Lock the Meatballs layer.

35. Press Option/Alt and drag a duplicate of the meatball until you have three meatballs on this layer. Lock the More Meatballs layer.

36. Now, you need to add some extra cheese. Drag the icon for the American Cheese layer to the New Layer icon at the bottom of the Layers palette. Name the layer "Extra Cheese" and drag it to the top of the Layer stack. Dragging the layer pops the cheese out of the mask, which is fine for now.

37. Select the unlocked cheese shreds (Command/Ctrl+A). Choose the Rotate tool. Rotate the layer about 45 degrees from its center point (which means that all you need to do is drag the mouse until the image rotates as much as you want it to). Deselect everything.

38. Use the Selection tool to select rectangular areas of cheese that go outside the crust. If you also select some of the cheese inside the crust at the same time, that's fine. The cheese layer is too thick, and selecting it helps to thin it out. Feel free to leave a few odd strands of cheese on the crust. Anything too perfect screams that it was drawn by computer. You're also welcome to add a few more meatballs if you see the need. Figure 6.19 shows the pizza that is now fully assembled.

Figure 6.19
One meatball pizza with extra cheese, hold the pepperoni.

39. Save your work; it would be a shame to lose it now.

From a New Perspective

Now that you've built a pizza, you're going to use it in an ad for a pizza parlor called Pizza Pizza. In this section of the project, you'll change the angle from which you view the pizza.

1. You're going to make the pizza look as if it's on a table that's being viewed more from in front than from the top down. To keep the mask around the cheese layers, you need to group the mask and the cheese layers first (if you don't group the layers, the mask won't scale when you scale the rest of the image). Unlock the Cheese Mask, Cheddar Cheese, Cheddar Cheese Shadow, Parmesan Cheese, and American Cheese layers. Select all the unlocked objects (Command/Ctrl+A) and group them (Command/Ctrl+G). All the objects move to the Cheese Mask layer, so you can delete all the other unlocked layers because they're now empty. Figure 6.20 shows the Layers palette after the cheese layers are deleted.

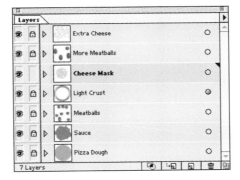

Figure 6.20
After you group the cheeses with the mask, these layers still contain objects.

2. Unlock all the layers. Double-click on the Scale tool. Select Non-Uniform and choose a Horizontal Scale of 100% (no change) and a Vertical Scale of 46%. Click on OK. Lock all the layers.

3. The perspective of the pizza has dramatically changed. Some of it looks a bit flat—as if everything has melted. Let's add a bit of punch back into it. Unlock the More Meatballs layer. Click on a meatball, press Option/Alt, and drag the top-center handle on the bounding box to make the meatball a bit more round. It should not flatten out as much as the rest of the pizza because the meatballs are a bit higher. Then, select the Gradient tool. Move the highlight of the radial gradient back to the place where the new top of the meatball would be. Fix as many meatballs as you want.

4. Lock the More Meatballs layer. Unlock the Cheese Mask layer. Using the Group Selection tool, choose about 10 slices of cheese. With these slices still selected, add a new layer (name it "Top Cheese") and transfer the selected objects to the new layer by moving the selected object rectangle from the Cheese Mask layer to the Top Cheese layer. Lock the Cheese Mask layer again.

5. Drag the icon for the Top Cheese layer to the New Layer icon at the bottom of the Layers palette. Place the duplicate layer under the original and name it "Top Cheese Shadow". Lock the Top Cheese layer.

6. Select everything on the Top Cheese Shadow layer and change the fill to an orangish color similar to the Velveeta cheese shadow color that you previously used. Press the down-arrow key two times and the right-arrow key two times to offset the shadow.

7. Unlock the Top Cheese layer. Select the two unlocked layers (Command/Ctrl+A). Choose Effect|Distort|Punk And Bloat and move the slider to 50%. Click on OK. Now, you have a bit more depth in the image, as you can see in Figure 6.21. Lock all the layers.

Figure 6.21
The pizza with a change in perspective now looks a bit less flat.

Border Crossings: How to Turn a Neat Square Corner

You're now ready to construct the border for the pizza advertisement. You'll use the Pathfinder commands and learn how to manipulate a pattern tile to build a mitered corner unit.

1. You need to build a border around the pizza for the ad. Because I didn't give a specific location in the image as your starting point, you need to create the border from wherever your pizza is currently located. Create a new layer named "Border". Turn on the Rulers (Command/Ctrl+R). Drag a guide to the top of the pizza. Drag guides from the side ruler until they just touch the right and left sides of the pizza. Place the mouse cursor on the zero-point where the two rulers meet at the top of the image. Drag the zero-point until it hugs the upper-left edge of the virtual rectangle that you have made with the guides.

2. Drag a vertical guide from the side ruler until it is halfway between the left and right guides. Drag a horizontal guide from the top ruler approximately one-quarter of the height of the pizza lower than the top guide. Select the Rectangle tool and use a Fill of None with a Stroke of any color that you want for now. Press Option/Alt and click with the Rectangle tool at the intersection of the center guide and the one-quarter-distance guide. In the dialog box that pops up, enter a rectangle width of 6 inches and height of 4 inches. Click on OK.

3. Drag another guide from the top ruler until it lies on top of the top stroke of the new rectangle. Drag down another guide and place it 1 inch higher than the top of the rectangle.

4. Choose the Ellipse tool. Move your cursor to the intersection of the top-of-the-rectangle guide and the center vertical guide. Press Option/Alt and drag an ellipse until its top reaches the highest guide in the image and its sides reach the guides that mark each side of the pizza. Release the mouse button. Figure 6.22 shows the image with the guides placed as requested and both the rectangle and the ellipse in place.

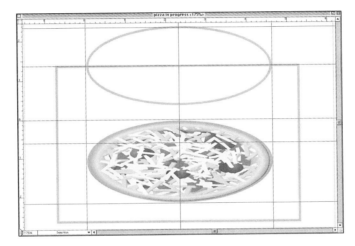

Figure 6.22
The border elements are now drawn.

5. Select both the rectangle and the ellipse. Click on the Unite command in the Pathfinder palette. You now have a shaped panel that acts as a border. I've already created the border Pattern brush for you. You'll create the corner motif by mitering the pattern unit.

6. Open the file PATTERN.AI on this book's companion CD-ROM. It contains one pattern tile and the same border structure that you're using in the pizza example. Figure 6.23 shows a many-times enlargement of the pattern tile for the border.

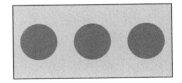

Figure 6.23
The pattern tile is an orange rectangle that contains three green circles.

7. Select the pattern tile, press Option/Alt, and drag a duplicate of the shape. Make another, pressing Shift after you begin to drag to constrain movement to the horizontal.

8. Select the last copy and Ungroup (Shift+Command/Ctrl+G). Delete the three circles, leaving only the rectangle. Change the Fill color to any other dark contrast color. Figure 6.24 shows the arrangement. Leave the rectangle selected.

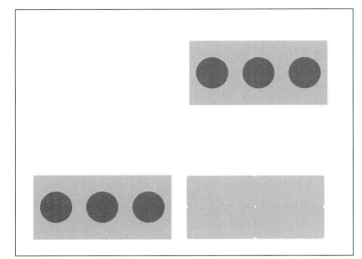

Figure 6.24

Ungroup the center tile and delete the circles.

9. Turn on Smart Guides (Command/Ctrl+U) and select the Pen tool. Drag your mouse cursor over the upper-left corner of the rectangle. You will then see a line that says "on" and "align 135 degrees," as shown in Figure 6.25. Click the Pen to leave a point on that guideline above the rectangle. Follow the Align On 135 Degrees guideline below the rectangle and click to set another point. You now have a stroke that cuts the top-left corner of the rectangle at a 45-degree angle. It is your miter line to create a corner for a border.

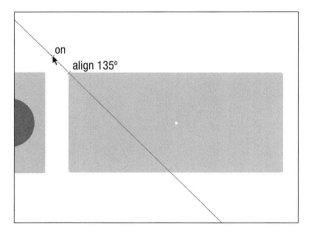

Figure 6.25

Using the Smart Guides, you can easily find the proper angle needed to miter a corner.

10. Turn off Smart Guides (Command/Ctrl+U). Select *only* the miter line stroke. Choose Object|Path|Slice. You now have a triangle and an object that looks like a knife blade. Select the "knife blade" object and delete it.

11. Select the triangle and the remaining pattern tile copy. Click on Horizontal Align Left in the Align palette and then click on Vertical Align Bottom. The triangle needs to be on top of the pattern tile. With both shapes selected, click on Crop in the Pathfinder palette. You now have a 45-degree corner cut from the original pattern tile, as shown in Figure 6.26.

12. To make a mitered corner, you need to create a mirror image of the corner. The entire miter takes two transformations: a flip and a rotate. Neither rotating nor flipping alone can produce the miter. Therefore, the first step is to flip the shape horizontally. You can do so in two ways. You can duplicate the shape, open the Transform palette sidebar menu, and select the Flip Horizontal command, or you can do both a flip and copy in one step by using the Reflect tool. If you use the Reflect tool, Alt/Option-click on the bottom-right point of the triangular shape. Select Vertical Axis and click on Copy. Figure 6.27 shows this process.

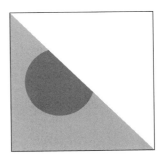

Figure 6.26
You have created one-half of the corner tile.

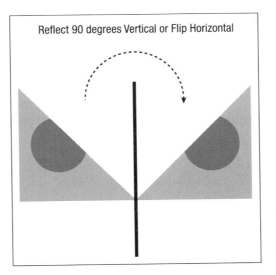

Reflect 90 degrees Vertical or Flip Horizontal

Figure 6.27
To make a mitered corner, you must first flip or reflect the corner tile.

13. The next step in building the mitered corner is to rotate the flipped unit by 90 degrees. To start, select the flipped copy. Alt/Option-click on the lower-left corner of the flipped triangle. Enter 90 degrees into the dialog box. Click on OK. To make certain that the copies are exactly aligned, select both triangles, click on Horizontal Align Left in the Align palette, and then click on Vertical Align Bottom. Group the two shapes (Command/Ctrl+G). Figure 6.28 shows the process and the final corner.

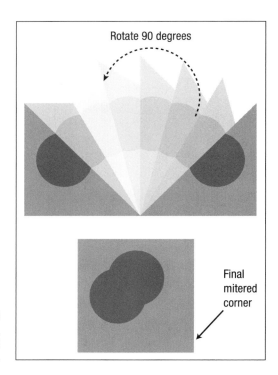

Figure 6.28
To make the mitered corner tile, you need to rotate the flipped copy 90 degrees.

14. If you look carefully at the Brushes palette in Figure 6.29, you see that the Brush icon occupies the second and third squares of a six-square row. The two squares show the brush to be applied to the straight and curved portions of a stroke. Squares 1 and 4 are reserved for the two types of corner tiles. Therefore, you need to drag the grouped corner tile onto the first square in the brush entry in the Brushes palette. Important: Press Option/Alt *after* you start to drag the object. Click on OK. Drag the shape *again* (with Option/Alt, as you did before) into the fourth square on the brush. Click on OK in the dialog box.

Figure 6.29
The Pattern brush "lives" in a six-square entry in the Brushes palette.

15. Select the border shape by using the Selection tool, and then click on the Pattern brush to apply it to the stroke. Figure 6.30 shows the border, and it looks as if the corner tiles are flipped so that they don't merge properly with the straight pattern.

16. The secret of designing a corner tile is to set it up the way the upper-left corner of a Pattern-brushed rectangle should look. Your instructions didn't bother asking you to do that before you defined the corner. Let's do it now. First, deselect all image elements. Then, click on the brush entry and drag the entry into the image. The pattern tiles appear as objects (this technique is an excellent way to obtain the pattern elements if all you have kept is the brush). Ungroup (Shift+Command/Ctrl+G) the objects.

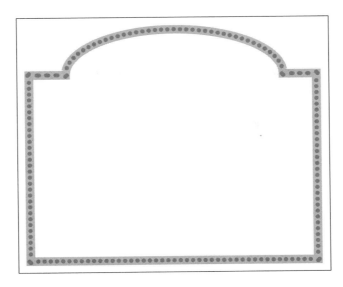

Figure 6.30
Applying the pattern to the border shows a problem with the way the corner elements are oriented.

17. Position the straight edge to the right of a corner. Duplicate the straight edge, rotate it 90 degrees, and place it under the corner, as shown in Figure 6.31.

18. It is even more obvious from Figure 6.31 that something is amiss. The solution is simple: Flip the corner tile until it is placed where you prefer it to be. Select the corner tile. From the Transform palette sidebar menu, choose Flip Vertical and choose Flip Horizontal. The tile lands in a much happier place. Figure 6.32 shows its new position.

Flip or Rotate?

You can use the Rotate box in the Transform palette to save yourself a step. Set the angle of rotation to 180 degrees. The result is the same as flipping vertically and horizontally.

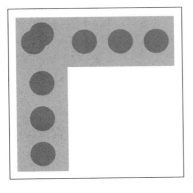
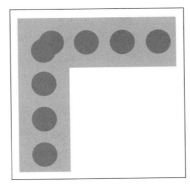

Figure 6.31
(Left) Simulating a border that contains a corner tile.

Figure 6.32
(Right) Flipping the corner tile both horizontally and vertically points it in a much better direction.

19. Repeat Step 14 to drag a copy of the corner into squares 1 and 4 of the Pattern brush entry. Click on Apply To Strokes each time you are asked. Figure 6.33 shows the border correctly cornered.

20. Save the PATTERN.AI file to your hard drive as BORDER.AI and close the document. Return to the document that contains the pizza.

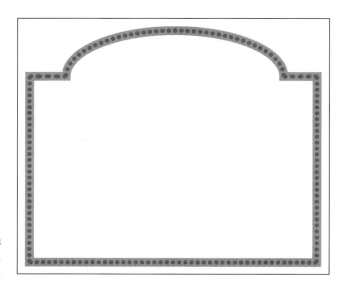

Figure 6.33

The border looks much better now.

21. In the pizza image, choose Window|Brush Libraries|Other Libraries. Select BORDER.AI as the library to open. With nothing selected, click on the brush in the BORDER.AI library. From the sidebar menu on the BORDER.AI Brush library, select Add To Brushes. Close the library. The brush is now added to the Brushes palette for your document.

22. Select the border panel, and click on the new Pattern brush to apply it.

23. Save your work again.

Distortions of Meaning: Putting Type in Perspective

An ad has to have some text to let you know whose product to buy. In this section of the project, you'll use imported text and create a distorted shadow for it. I set the word "Pizza" using ICGChoc. I used a copy of the pizza dough ellipse as the path. I changed the text to Outlines, and I then used the Free Transform Perspective tool (which you'll also use later) to make the word larger at the left than at the right. I reflected a copy of the word across a 90-degree vertical axis and then saved the file.

1. Open the file PIZZATEXT.AI from the this book's companion CD-ROM. This file contains the saved pizza text.

2. Use the Selection tool to drag the text (which is grouped) from the PIZZATEXT.AI file into your working pizza file.

3. Turn on the Rulers (Command/Ctrl+R) if they aren't already visible. If any guides currently show in your image, choose View|Clear Guides. Drag a horizontal guide from the top ruler to just underneath the top horizontal edge of the border (formed from the original rectangle in

Step 9 of the "Border Crossings" section). Drag the vertical guides from the left-side ruler so that they are at the inner corners of the border where the rectangle meets the ellipse.

4. Select the Rectangle tool with a black Stroke and a Fill of None. Draw a rectangle that begins at the left intersection of the vertical and horizontal guides, extends to the intersection of the horizontal guide and the rightmost vertical guide, and continues down not quite as far as the start of the pizza.

5. Turn on Smart Guides (Command/Ctrl+U). Click on the Pizza Pizza text at the upper-left point of the letter *P* and drag this point until it intersects with the upper-left corner of the rectangle you just drew. Turn off Smart Guides (Command/Ctrl+U). Select both the text and the rectangle and click on Align Horizontal Center in the Align palette. Deselect. Select the rectangle and delete it. Clear the guides. Figure 6.34 shows the text before clearing the guides so that you can see their position.

An Alternate Approach

David Xenakis suggests a way that might be easier than my approach: With the Direct Selection tool, sweep select the node at the top of the arc. Copy and paste in front. Set the stroke to None. On the Attributes palette, set this arc to show a center point. Drag out a vertical guide. Unlock the guides. Select the guides and release them. Center vertically with the text. With both the text and guide selected, drag so that the guide lines up with the center point of the arc. Sweep select across the center point of the arc and press Delete (which deletes the guide and the no-stoke arc).

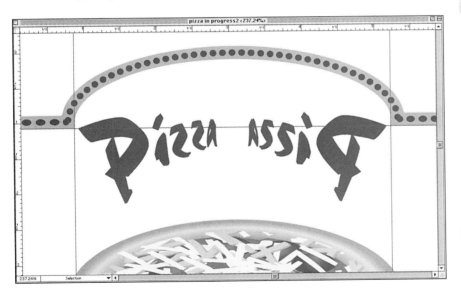

Figure 6.34
Position the text by centering it on a "dummy rectangle" created along the guidelines shown.

6. Duplicate the text layer by dragging the Pizza Pizza layer entry to the New Layer icon at the bottom of the Layers palette. Lock the Pizza Pizza layer. Rename the copied layer "Pizza Pizza Shadow". Change its Fill color to 30% black and drag the layer below the Pizza Pizza layer in the Layers palette.

7. Grab the top-center handle of the text's bounding box and drag it down until the bounding box is just under the small letter *a* in *pizza*, as shown in Figure 6.35.

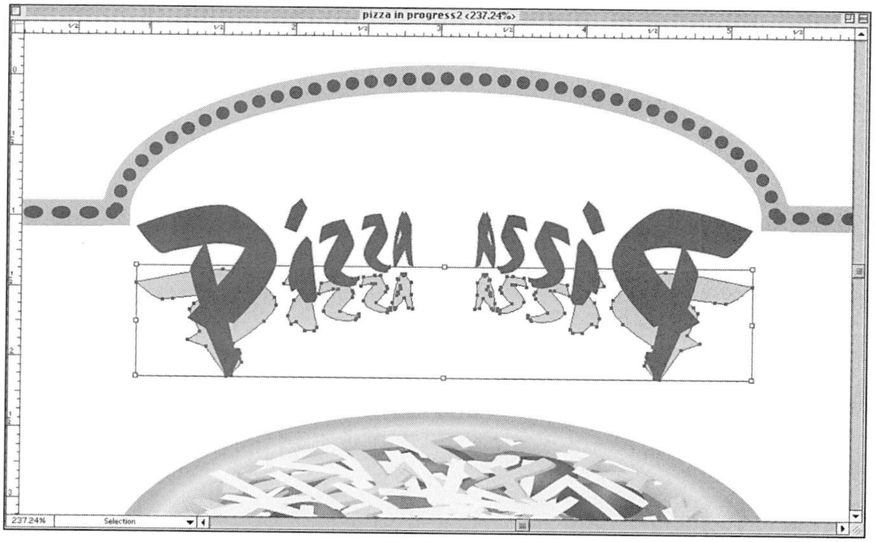

Figure 6.35
Resize the text shadow as shown.

8. Choose the Free Transform tool. Place your cursor over the control handle at the top-left corner of the shadow text and start to drag the handle to the left. Just after you begin to drag the control handle, press Command/Ctrl+Option/Alt+Shift in the order that I've listed them. Watch what happens to your shape as you add each additional key. Using the Command/Ctrl key, you can distort the image by moving a single corner. By adding Option/Alt, you can skew the shape, and by adding Shift, you can apply perspective.

Drag the handle (with the three keys still pressed) until it reaches the center of the border. Release the mouse button before you release the keys. Lock the Pizza Pizza Shadow layer. At this point, only one more task remains.

Green Plate Special

You need to create a tray to hold the pizza. The Punk And Bloat Effect makes short work of this task.

1. Lock all the layers. Drag the entry for the Pizza Dough layer to the New Layer icon at the bottom of the Layers palette. Double-click on the copied layer and name it "Plate". Drag the Plate layer to the very bottom of the Layer stack.

2. Unlock the Plate layer and select the elliptical object. Choose Object|Path|Add Anchor Points. The ellipse receives four new points.

3. Double-click on the Scale tool and enter a Uniform amount of 120%. Click on OK (do not make a copy).

4. With the ellipse selected, choose Filter|Distort|Punk And Bloat and move the slider to 12%, as shown in Figure 6.36. This creates a flower shape for the tray beneath the pizza.

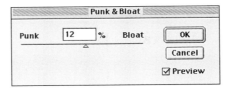

Figure 6.36
The Punk And Bloat effect controls the shape of curved path segments so that you can create flowers or a wide variety of unusual forms.

5. Click on the Stripes pattern swatch (the last one on row 2 of the Default Swatches palette) to set the Fill for the tray. Figure 6.37 shows the finished pizza ad in grayscale here and in color in the Illustrator 9 Studio.

Figure 6.37
You have created an advertisement for a pizza parlor using a variety of transformation commands.

String Art and Transparency

When I was little, I used to love drawing with the Spirograph toy. I still enjoy it enough that I bought one for all my nieces and nephews. A tiny—almost a throwaway—note in Deke McClelland's book, *Real World Illustrator 7*, inspired this next project. Deke just happened to mention that pressing the tilde (~) key as you use any of the shape tools in the Toolbox causes you to draw multiple copies of the shape. That gave me an idea, and you now have the opportunity to profit from it.

In this next project, you'll create a series of string art stars and use them to build an illustration. I'll also show you a variety of new Illustrator 9 techniques that will enable you to create Photoshop-like effects with the shapes while keeping them in Illustrator.

The Shape Tools

The Ellipse pop-out in the Illustrator Toolbox contains four tools: the Ellipse, the Polygon, the Star, and the Spiral. The Rectangle pop-out has two tools: the Rectangle tool and the Round-Corner Rectangle tool. All the shape tools have certain similarities in the way in which they are applied. Before we create a finished piece, let's just play a bit with these tools in Project 6.2.

PROJECT 6.2 Get into Shape

This project takes you on a brief tour of the shape tools and the amazing effects you can get from them just by holding the tilde (~) key as you draw. (If you have no interest in string art, this project is a good reminder about the other options available in each shape tool.)

1. Create a new document in Illustrator.

2. Select the Ellipse tool. Choose a Fill of None and a black Stroke of 1 point. Click the mouse button and draw an ellipse. As you draw, press and hold the tilde key. Figure 6.38 shows one of the doodles I created by using the Ellipse tool. You can produce amazing sculptural forms.

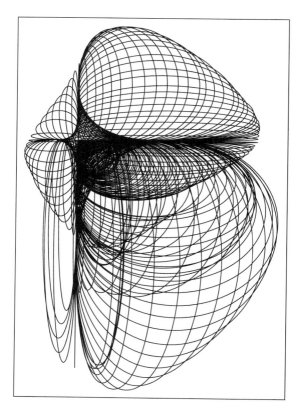

Figure 6.38
This form almost resembles a seashell.

3. If you press Shift in addition to the tilde key as you draw, you can create interlocking circles. However, the effect is much harder to control because Shift also acts as a constrain key, and the copies tend to go in lines at a 45-degree angle, as you can see in Figure 6.39. The free-form ellipses occurred when I released Shift.

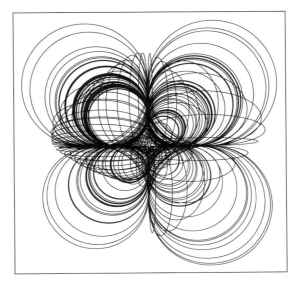

Figure 6.39
The Shift key makes it harder to draw circles where you want them to be.

4. The Rectangle tool and the Round-Corner Rectangle tool work the same way. You can interactively control the radius of the rounded corner by pressing the up- and down-arrow keys as you draw the shape. I don't think I could coordinate that with using the tilde key (at least not without three hands). Try drawing some shapes and changing the roundness of the corners. Then, try using the tilde key as you draw.

5. The Polygon tool also lets you use the up- and down-arrow keys as you draw. The arrows increase and decrease the number of sides to the shape. The Polygon makes wonderful string art. Figure 6.40 shows a form that resembles a rose.

6. The Spiral tool has even more options. With this tool, as with the Polygon tool, you can rotate as you draw. You can also change the number of segments by pressing the up- and down-arrow keys. If you use the Spiral tool's options dialog box to set the size, you can change the tightness of the wraps on the spiral (decay) and the direction in which the form spirals. Figure 6.41 shows the options available, and Figure 6.42 shows a variety of different spirals. Try drawing some spirals. Before you change the settings in the dialog box, make sure you know what they were. You can much too easily create a spiral that won't spiral, and after you've changed the options, they remain in effect until you use the dialog box to change them again (so recovering the original settings isn't easy).

Figure 6.40

"Rose is a rose" is a series of interlocked polygons.

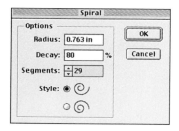

Figure 6.41

Using the Spiral tool's options dialog box, you can control some elements that you cannot set interactively.

Figure 6.42

A variety of spirals.

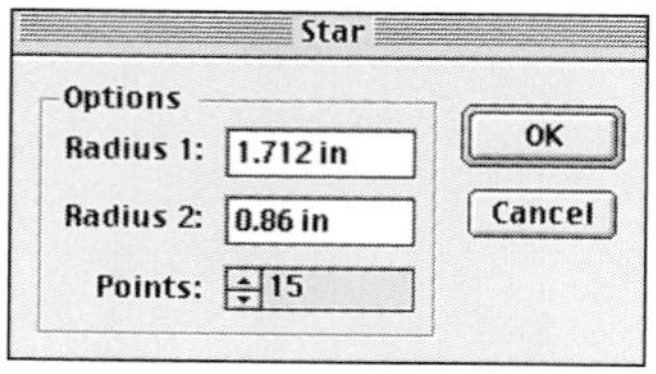

Figure 6.43

In the Star Options dialog box, you can set the inner and outer radius of the star as well as change the number of sides.

7. When you use the Star tool, you can change the number of points on the star by pressing the up- and down-arrow keys. You can move the location of the star (and the other shapes as well) as you draw by pressing the spacebar. You can also change the sharpness of the points by setting the inner and outer star radius, but you need to click in the image to open the Star options dialog box to make changes to the radius. Figure 6.43 shows the Star Options dialog box, and Figure 6.44 shows some stars. You will create stars using the tilde key later in the chapter in Project 6.3, but practice making a variety of stars right now.

Figure 6.44
You can draw an infinite variety of star forms.

The Astronomer's Eye

When you create string art with the help of the tilde key, you can create lovely, complex forms. They are stunning as black-and-white compositions. If you want to add color to these creations, you'll find it to be a bit more difficult. Because so many shapes are available, Illustrator can take a long time to redraw the screen—even if you have a fast machine and a lot of RAM. If you add to that complexity, the redraw times get worse.

You might also have an issue with patience. I don't have enough patience to individually select each shape and recolor it. You can make a global change, but you cannot, for example, add a gradient to the strokes—which would be a wonderful effect—because Illustrator doesn't do gradients on strokes. You can laboriously hand-select some stars and change their stroke weight or color. That is what I did in Figure 6.45, but this job is really quite tedious.

To create the image in Figure 6.46, I used the Front To Back color filter to color the stars and created a gradient that I expanded into a pattern brush so that I could stroke the stars with multiple colors. Don't try this technique on a slow system!

Selecting with the Layers Palette

If you want to make a random selection of shapes to recolor, you can quickly select them by clicking on the select buttons in the expanded view of the Layers palette. Just keep the Shift key pressed as you add to the selected objects.

PROJECT 6.3 String Art Stars

There are probably a thousand ways to do this project. The project begins as a series of concentric stars similar to the ones you've just created. Figure 6.47 shows the image as it appeared in the first version of this book written for Illustrator 8. In that version, I took the stars into Photoshop so that I could use apply modes and opacity, and add drop shadows to the foreground elements.

Figure 6.45

(Left) You can hand-select certain stars and change their stroke color or weight.

Figure 6.46

(Right) You can apply a gradient to a stroke if you make it into a pattern brush first. Creating this complex image was much easier than it looks.

Figure 6.47

"Through A Telescope" was started in Illustrator and finished in Photoshop.

The jury is still out, as I write this chapter, as to whether it is still more practical to continue to create this project in a combination of Illustrator and Photoshop; however, it's now possible to use only Illustrator to achieve the desired results. You can find the original instructions on the CD-ROM for this book in the file ASTRONOMER.PDF. I'm going to live dangerously and show you how to create it in Illustrator.

Why *dangerously*? This image is very complex. If you experience problems of slowness or crashing as you work through this project, you need more memory allocated to Illustrator. If you cannot do that, work smaller and simplify the stars that you create at the beginning of this project. You can also build this project in individual files and rasterize any portion that becomes too time-consuming.

This project, however, affords you the opportunity to use some of Illustrator's newest and most exciting features—Opacity Masks, transparency, and Live Effects.

Building the Background Image

In this section of the project, you will learn how to create the multiple stars and use them both as the layer object and as an opacity mask. In addition, you'll have the opportunity to change opacity settings and create a gradient object with multiple fills.

1. Create a new document in Illustrator. Set the document size to 5 inches by 5 inches.

2. Select the Star tool. Use a traditional 5-point star (with Radius 1 at about 2 inches and Radius 2 at about 1 inch).

3. Set the current Stroke to None and the current Fill to black.

4. Start in the center of the lower-right quadrant of the image and draw a star. Press tilde (~) as you draw to draw out multiple copies. As you are drawing the multiple copies, drag the mouse cursor (with the mouse button still down) in a large spiral around your original star. You might need to try several drawings or undo and try again a few times until you like the results. Try to leave a distinct, visible star in the center of the image. Make the points fall outside the borders of the image as you reach the end of your drawing. If you are going to follow the "all-Illustrator route" for this project, make the star as quickly as you can so that you leave fewer copies. In this instance, "simple" is much better. Figure 6.48 shows my starting image.

5. Save the image as STRINGART1.AI. Select the entire image (Command/Ctrl+A). Copy it to the clipboard (Command/Ctrl+C).

6. Create a new image that is 5 inches square.

7. You first need to create a background of blue sky for this image. To start, select the Rectangle tool. Choose a Stroke of None and a Fill of light blue. Create a square that is exactly the dimensions of the image.

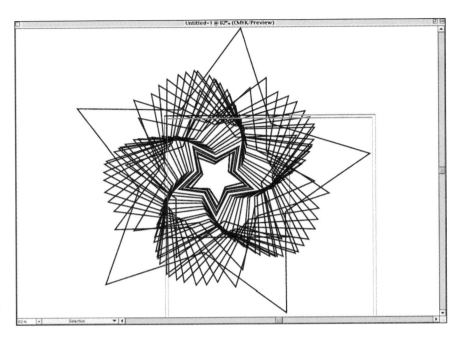

Figure 6.48

This is my starting star image.

8. You have a variety of choices as to the color of the image. The easy thing is to leave it a solid blue. You could also create a gradient of light to medium blue (either linear or radial). In Chapter 8, I'll describe a number of gradient techniques. After you've worked through that chapter, you could even create a gradient mesh object with a variety of blue shades. The background only peeks through the final image, so the choice is yours.

9. After you have colored your background image, double-click on the layer in the Layers palette and change the name of the layer to Background. Then, lock the layer by clicking on the second column to reveal the lock icon.

10. Create a new layer. Double-click on it to change its name to "Bright". With the Rectangle tool, draw another 5-inch rectangle in the image (this time on the Bright layer). Fill this rectangle with the Rainbow gradient from the Swatches palette.

11. In the Gradient Options palette, change the Angle to 45 degrees.

12. Make the Appearance palette active. Choose Add New Fill from the side drop-down menu. Use the Partial Spectrum from the Swatches palette as the new fill, but change the angle to -45 degrees. Change the Opacity of the fill to 50 percent and set the Mode to Hard Light. You can also experiment with the Gradient tool and dynamically change the angle by dragging the cursor over part of the image. In addition, you can change the Gradient type to Radial and see whether you can get the colors to show up in a more exciting manner (I dragged the Gradient tool a short distance near the top-left quadrant of the image with the

Gradient type set to Radial). I would show the result here, but you cannot see the result well enough in grayscale to make it useful. Save this image as GRADIENT.AI.

13. In this Bright layer, you're going to actually mask the rectangle with the stars that you created in the previous image. Using the stars as the mask has the advantage of not needing to make a clipping path to keep the stars inside the 5-inch bounding box of the image (or of trying to crop them to the correct shape). To make the mask, first open the Transparency palette. From the side drop-down menu, choose Show Options. You then can see all the options for the palette.

14. Choose Make Opacity Mask from the side drop-down menu in the Transparency palette. Select the empty thumbnail on the Transparency palette (the right slot). That is the location for the mask. With the mask as the active image, paste in the selection from the clipboard (Command/Ctrl+V).

15. Make black your Stroke color and change the Fill to None. Set the Stroke width to 3 points. This number is variable. If you have many stars close together, you can make the stroke width smaller. A stroke that is too large will cover the entire image.

16. Select the Invert Mask checkbox in the Transparency palette. Then, click on the image thumbnail rather than the mask thumbnail. Change the object Opacity to 50 percent and the Mode to Multiply. Figure 6.49 shows the Transparency palette with the mask in place.

17. Save the file as GRADMASK.AI, and then lock the Bright layer.

18. Add a new layer to the image. Drag this new layer between the Background and the Bright layer. Change its name to "Red".

19. Paste the copied stars (the same ones you used for the mask) into this layer and position them so that they match the masked image in the Bright layer.

20. Change the stroke width to 9 points and the stroke color to red. Change the fill to None. Drag the Transparency slider to 35 percent. Change the blend mode to multiply. Figure 6.50 shows the Appearance palette with the correct settings. This layer functions as a soft red shadow for the gradient stars.

21. Your image now contains stars that are larger than the image size. You need to clip the stars to the same size as the image. Choose the Rectangle tool. Exchange the fill and stroke so that you have a Fill of Red and a Stroke of None. In the same Red layer, create a rectangle that is 5 inches square. Make it conform to the boundaries of the image.

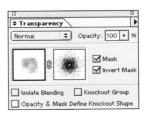

Figure 6.49
You can use the stars as a mask in the Transparency palette.

Figure 6.50
The Appearance palette shows the correct settings for the red shadow-glow layer.

Why Save So Many Files?

I am asking you to save the files in pieces because that gives you the best chance of backing off to an earlier state if you don't like something or you have problems with the complexity of the image.

22. Select the entire layer by clicking on the radio button in the Red layer on the Layers palette. Choose Object|Clipping Mask|Make (or Command/Ctrl+7). The image that extends beyond the 5-inch area should disappear.

23. Lock the layer. Save the file as 3LAYERS.AI.

24. Now that you have the full background built (the three layers), you can evaluate the result. If you feel that the gradient layer is too bright, you can select the object, highlight the Object Opacity line in the Appearance palette, and reduce the object opacity to 80 percent. Figure 6.51 shows the image thus far.

Figure 6.51
The three-layer image forms the background for this project.

Finishing Up

In this last section of the project, you'll add your background to the foreground elements in the image and use the new Drop Shadow effect.

1. Make sure that your background image is open and all layers are locked. Create a new layer by clicking on the Add New Layer icon at the bottom of the Layers palette. Double-click on the layer name in the Layers palette and change the layer name to "Telescope". This layer needs to be the top layer in the image. Choose File|Place and place the file SCOPE.AI from this book's companion CD-ROM. The image is sized to exactly fit the 5-inch boundary of the background. Lock the layer.

2. The next element to be placed is the eye. The eye is taken from the Ultimate Symbol Design Elements collection. I have already sized it correctly and added a pillow emboss to it using Photoshop. I haven't found an easy way to duplicate the pillow emboss effect in Illustrator

(emphasize *easy*). Therefore, I used Photoshop. Create a new layer above the Telescope layer. Name the layer "Eye". Choose File|Place and place the SMALLEYE.PSD image at the default size. Uncheck the Link and Template checkboxes. Click on Place. In the next dialog box, select the Convert Photoshop Layers To Objects radio button and click on OK.

3. Position the eye image so that the bottom right of the eye (which has a diagonal stem) lines up to the left and slightly above the start of the telescope and looks as if the eye is coming out of the telescope. (You can see this position on the finished image in Figure 6.53.) Lock the layer.

4. Create a new layer. Name this layer "Text". It should be the topmost layer in the image. Choose File|Place and place the file TEXT.AI from the CD-ROM for this book.

5. Choose Effects|Stylize|Drop Shadow. Choose an X-Y offset of 0.1 inch and a Blur of 0.02 inch. Set the Darkness to 50 percent, as shown in Figure 6.52. Click on OK. Lock the layer.

> **How Else Can I Combine the Images?**
>
> You have a choice between placing the telescope into the background image or copying the background elements into the telescope image. If you have any trouble placing the telescope into the main image, you can copy each of the background layers, one at a time, into the telescope image and build your final image there. Because of the complexity of each of your background layers, don't copy them all at once. Copy one at a time and lock each layer after it's copied. Then, create a new layer for the next element before you try to paste the image data into it.

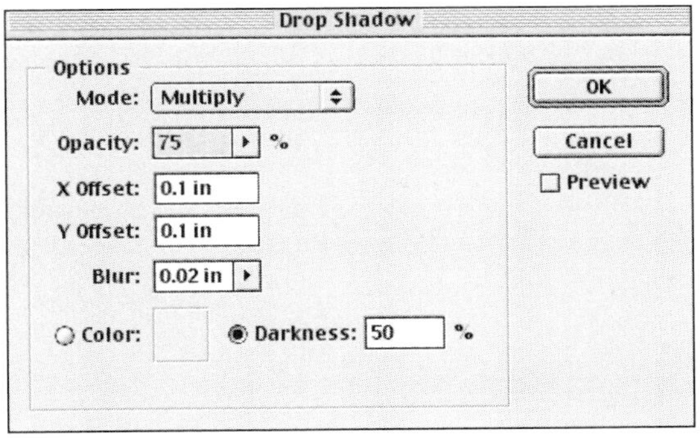

Figure 6.52
Use these settings to apply a drop shadow effect to the text.

6. Unlock the Telescope layer. Drop down the arrow on the Telescope layer in the Layers palette to see the objects on the layer. Click on the radio button by the telescope group to select it.

7. Choose Effects|Stylize|Drop Shadow. Choose an X-Y offset of 0.1 inch and a Blur of 0.07 inch. Set the Darkness to 50 percent. Click on OK. Lock the layer.

8. Open the STRINGART1.AI image that you created and saved in the first part of this project. Select the entire image and copy it to the clipboard.

9. In your working image, create a new layer that is placed above the Red layer and below the Telescope layer. Paste the string art stars into this layer. You should see a bounding box. Position the bounding box so that its bottom-right corner is in the bottom-right corner of the image. Scale the image from the top-left corner until it's about one-quarter as large as the image.

10. Drag it upward until you can see the center star form just above the telescope.

11. Select the same green that is in the "Eye" as your stroke color. Make sure that the Fill color is set to None. Give the stars a stroke of 5 points.

12. Change the Apply mode to Multiply. Reduce the Opacity of the layer to 65%. Figure 6.53 shows the final image in grayscale. You can see it in color in the Illustrator 9 Studio.

Figure 6.53

The string art stars have been combined with other Illustrator elements in Illustrator.

Mandalas

A mandala is a complex circular image that can help you to restore peace and inner harmony if you contemplate its center. Because I love kaleidoscopes, I'm also attracted to mandalas and other circular design forms (I'm also a child of the 1960s who forgot to grow up—as long as I have tie-dye in my world, I'm happy). The mandala that you'll work on in Project 6.4 can bring you peace and inner harmony when you contemplate it—but only after it's done. It is a bit of a nasty project; it was a bear to create the first time, until I got all the kinks out, but I have tamed it so that you at least should not throw this book through your computer screen.

If this is a nasty project, why put it in the book? I like the results, although you might not need to create mandalas on a daily basis. I also think that once you work through it, you'll have a better understanding of how some of the Path-finder commands work, and you'll learn ways to search for a solution when the command doesn't work—but you think that the command should be working. Even if you never create a full mandala, you might very well need to create rotated objects that share many of the same characteristics.

In this project, you'll create two levels of revolving objects, and you'll also learn how to transform the straight edge of an image into a ragged border.

PROJECT 6.4 A Tale of Over and Under

In the first part of this project, you'll rotate a decorated ogee around its bottom edge to create the start of a mandala. The challenge of the project is to make part of the last object rotated (the one on top) tuck under the first object so that the pattern is maintained throughout the entire rotation. The only way to do that is to cut the ogee into the necessary segments before you rotate it. To make sure that the cut ogee stays in its proper position, you must do all the original cutting "in place" with objects locked and/or hidden so that you can select the correct ones. Although the process might seem confusing at first, work each step carefully in order, and it will come out right.

Slice and Dice

Part one of this project shows you how to slice up the ogee into the number of pieces needed so that the final rotation looks as if it is tucked under the first rotation.

1. Open the file OGEEDESIGN.AI. It contains a number of layers, but only one (the one shown in Figure 6.54) is visible. Figure 6.55 shows the Layers palette.

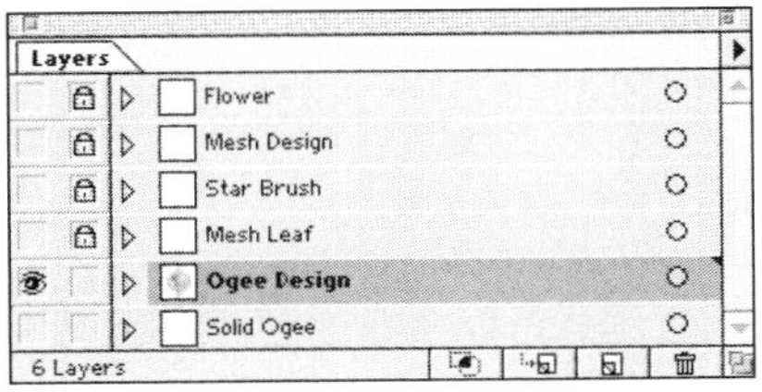

Figure 6.54
(Left) The decorated ogee forms the basis of this project.

Figure 6.55
(Right) The Layers palette for OGEEDESIGN.AI contains a number of layers that are not visible.

2. You'll need only the Solid Ogee and Ogee Design layers for the first part of this project. To begin, turn on the Rulers (Command/Ctrl+R).

3. Select the Ogee Design. Drag a horizontal and a vertical guide so that they intersect at the bottom-center control handle on the object's bounding box, as shown in Figure 6.56.

Building an Ogee

I have already created the ogee for you because I don't want this project to occupy the entire book, but I want to explain how it was created and show you the files that you can use to build your own version.

In Chapter 7, you'll build an ogee from scratch to use as a pattern. An ogee is a geometric object that can interlock because all its sides use rotated copies of the same stroke. However, OGEEPLAIN.AI, which is on this book's companion CD-ROM, gives you an already-built shape to use if you don't like my design (or simply want to make one of your own). You may divide the ogee with any lines that you want or use the ones that I've placed in the image file for you.

Figure 6.54 shows a close-up of the single ogee design. This design is the major element that you'll rotate. I filled the solid ogee with a radial gradient that I expanded into 25 steps. I then placed a variety of shapes on top of the ogee. I used the lines in the OGEEPLAIN.AI file along with the Divide command on the Pathfinder palette to cut the ogee into strips. I then moved each section apart to create the white spaces.

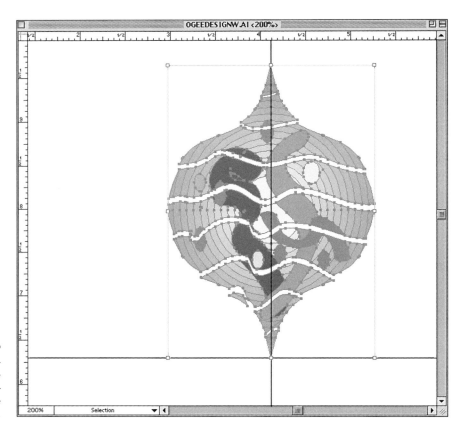

Figure 6.56

Drag guides so that they intersect at the bottom point of the ogee (which is also the bottom-center control handle on the bounding box).

Why Make the Guides on the Ogee Design Layer?

You need to create your guides based on the bottom point of the Ogee Design layer because it is not the same as the bottom point of the Solid Ogee layer.

4. Lock the Ogee Design layer. Reveal the Solid Ogee layer. Select the entire image (Command/Ctrl+A). Only the solid ogee is selected.

5. Zoom into your image until you can very clearly see the intersection of the guides. Choose the Rotate tool. Press Option/Alt and click on the point where the guides intersect. Enter -30 degrees in the Rotate Tool Options dialog box and click on Copy.

6. Change the fill of the copy to dark blue.

7. When objects cross one another, the Pathfinder commands do not always work as expected. Select the Pen tool. Place the Pen over the bottom point on the dark blue ogee (you know that you are over a point when you see a minus sign next to the Pen icon). Click to remove the bottom point from the shape. Figure 6.57 shows a close-up of the lower points of the objects. Figure 6.58 shows the objects after you have deleted the bottom point. Deselect.

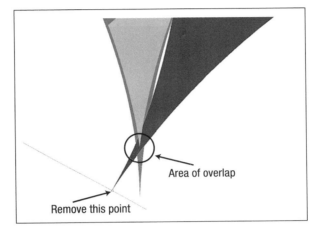

Area of overlap

Remove this point

Figure 6.57
Delete the bottom point on the dark ogee to remove the area where the two points overlap.

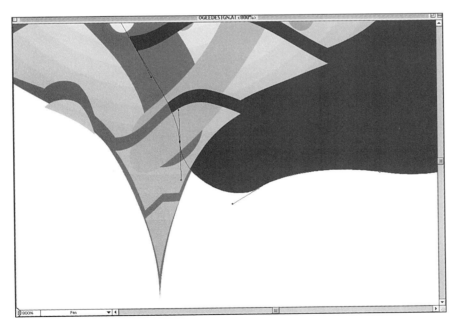

Figure 6.58
The shapes no longer cross one another.

8. Hide the Ogee Design layer. Select the entire image (Command/Ctrl+A). Click on Divide in the Pathfinder palette.

9. Ungroup (Shift+Command/Ctrl+G) and then deselect.

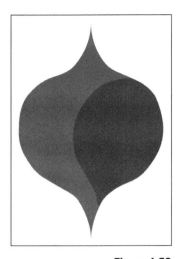

Figure 6.59

The original solid ogee is now divided into two segments.

Another Way to Duplicate the Layer

You can also duplicate the layer by selecting the Ogee Design layer and then choosing Duplicate Ogee Design from the drop-down menu in the Layers palette.

10. Select the right portion of the dark blue ogee and delete. This action leaves only the two sections that form the original ogee (one magenta and one dark blue, as shown in Figure 6.59).

11. Turn on the Ogee Design layer again (don't unlock it) and zoom in to your image until you can very clearly see the intersection of the guides. Select the dark blue segment of the solid ogee.

12. Choose the Rotate tool. Press Option/Alt and click on the point where the guides intersect. Enter –30 degrees in the Rotate Tool Options dialog box and click on Copy.

13. Change the Fill color of the copy to yellow. Hide the Ogee Design layer.

14. Select both the yellow copy and the dark blue ogee segment. Click on Divide in the Pathfinder palette.

15. Ungroup (Shift+Command/Ctrl+G) and then deselect. Select the right segment of the yellow ogee and delete it. Figure 6.60 shows the finished template.

16. Drag the icon for the unlocked Ogee Design layer to the New Layer icon (the center icon at the bottom of the Layers palette). Drag the new layer to the bottom of the layer stack.

17. Lock and hide the original Ogee Design layer.

18. Choose the Selection tool. Select the dark blue and the yellow segments of the solid ogee. (Alternatively, you can always use the radio buttons on the Layers palette to select the object.) Choose Edit|Select|Select Inverse. Now, the magenta segment and the ogee design on the bottom layer are selected.

19. Click on Crop in the Pathfinder palette. Figure 6.61 shows the result.

Figure 6.60

(Left) You have divided the original solid ogee into three pieces.

Figure 6.61

(Right) Cropping the magenta segment and the designed ogee leaves the designed ogee in the area originally occupied by the magenta cutting template.

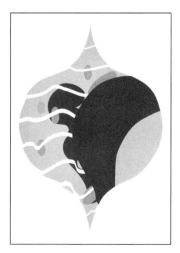

How Many Pieces Do You Need?

If this were a project of your own and you were using a different shape, how would you know the number of pieces that you need in the final cutting template? You need to cut your original shape into as many pieces as required for your rotation to rotate out of the original image. When you rotated the shape the first time, the copy overlapped. When you rotated the *copy*, it still overlapped the original. If you were to rotate that third piece, it would completely clear the original—showing that you need only three pieces.

Examine Figure A. It shows a differently shaped object that you are planning to rotate at 15 degrees. That would move it in the opposite direction from the ogee and take 24 copies to complete a circle (360 degrees/15 degrees=24 rotations). You can see in the figure that it takes four additional shapes before the rotation clears the starting object. Figure B shows the cutting template that you would need. To make something this complex, you would just repeat Steps 11 through 15 with the newest copy until you have divided your original shape into the needed number of elements.

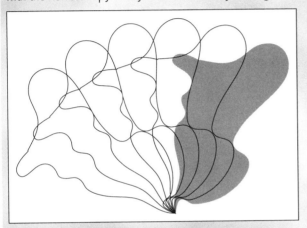

Figure A
This object needs five cuts for the rotation to clear the original shape.

Figure B
The cutting template for the complex shape.

As you will see a bit later, you need the cutting template only because the rotated ogee design is a grouped shape. If it were solid, the area of overlap would not show anyway (but the example would be much less interesting). Figure C shows the finished rotation of the hypothetical shape with the cut shapes left in the template colors. In the color Illustrator 9 Studio, you can see a version of this sample image that was filled with a Rainbow gradient and then rotated. All the cuts were needed to make the shape come out right. I've also included the original shape file (SHAPE.AI) on the CD-ROM so that you can try it or play with it if you want.

Figure C
After the pieces are put in order, the rotated cutting shape shows the complexity of the design.

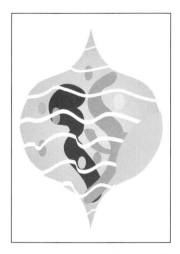

Figure 6.62
Cropping the dark blue segment
and the designed ogee leaves
the designed ogee in the area
originally occupied by the dark
blue cutting template.

20. Only the Solid Ogee layer contains an active selection. Drag the selected object rectangle from the Solid Ogee layer to the Ogee Design copy layer. Lock the Ogee Design copy layer.

21. Unlock the Ogee Design layer. Drag the icon for the unlocked Ogee Design layer to the New Layer icon (the center icon at the bottom of the Layers palette). Drag the new layer just under the Solid Ogee layer.

22. Lock and hide the Ogee Design layer.

23. Choose the Selection tool. Select the yellow segment of the solid ogee. Choose Edit|Select|Select Inverse. Now, the dark blue segment and the ogee design on the Ogee Design Copy 2 layer are selected.

24. Click on Crop in the Pathfinder palette. Figure 6.62 shows the result.

25. Only the Solid Ogee layer contains an active selection. Drag the selected object rectangle from the Solid Ogee layer to the Ogee Design Copy 2 layer. Lock the Ogee Design Copy 2 layer.

26. Reveal and unlock the Ogee Design layer. Drag its thumbnail in the Layers palette underneath the Solid Ogee layer. (Because this is the last cut, you don't need to make a copy.)

27. Select the entire image (Command/Ctrl+A). The ogee design and the yellow solid segment are selected.

28. Click on Crop in the Pathfinder palette. Now, the ogee design looks exactly as it did when you first opened the file—except that the ogee is in three parts. Move the selected object rectangle from the Solid Ogee layer to the Ogee Design layer. Drag the Solid Ogee layer (which has nothing on it) to the trashcan on the Layers palette.

29. Unlock the two other ogee design layers. Now, you're ready to rotate the shape.

Let's recap what you did before we move on. You took the template shape and created enough rotations to see that you needed to slice the shape into three parts. You then created the three cutting templates and used these templates to crop copies of the ogee design into the same three segments. Why not just use the originals, rotate them, and use the Divide command as you did when making the templates? If the shapes were solid, you could. However, when you use the Divide command and then Ungroup to delete the extra areas, all the shapes in the segment are also ungrouped. This approach becomes very ugly if you need to decide, on a piece-by-piece basis, which shapes to keep and which to toss. I selected the easiest method that I could manage in the hope that my logic makes sense to you.

In theory, you could also have used the Minus Front command and a different set of templates. However, the Minus Front and Minus Back commands in the Pathfinder palette work in a much different way than you might think they do (or than *I* think they should). If you have a group of objects and a single shape, and the single shape is on top, I feel that it is logical to expect that the Minus Front command would remove the top shape from the grouped object below it. Not so. Rather, the command removes everything but the very bottom object in the group from the very bottom object in the grouping. Therefore, the command is less than useful when you try to use it with a grouped object. Because the Minus Back command works the same way, it too is worth using only on solid objects.

As the Ogee Turns

In the next portion of this project, you'll create the actual mandala form and learn why you had to make mincemeat out of the ogee shape in the first place.

1. Rearrange the layer order so that the Ogee Design layer is on the bottom of the layer stack, the Ogee Design Copy 2 layer is on top of that, and the Ogee Design layer copy is the top of the three layers. With this reordering of layers, your mandala will be perfect when you rotate it.

2. Select the entire image (Command/Ctrl+A) to select all three parts of the ogee.

3. Choose the Rotate tool. Press Option/Alt and click on the intersection of the two guides at the bottom point of the ogee. Enter –30 degrees into the Rotate Tool Options dialog box. Click on Copy.

4. Transform Again (Command/Ctrl+D) 10 times to complete the circle. Figure 6.63 shows the perfectly seamless mandala. Because you kept each segment of the shape on its own layer, when you rotated the shape, the stacking order was correctly maintained. Compare this version to Figure 6.64, where the shapes were not sliced up (I have darkened the last rotation on Figure 6.64 and added a circle at its tip so that you can more clearly spot the area that is not seamless).

5. Just for fun, switch the order of the Ogee Design layers and see the different patterns that emerge. Leave it with your favorite setting exposed. Save the file.

Around the Mandala Again

You still have four layers in the mandala that you haven't seen. These four layers contain additional elements to build a second layer of the mandala. No trick is involved here. You'll only rotate the shapes. However, one of these shapes, the element on the Mesh Leaf layer, is a gradient mesh. I've created it

Figure 6.63

(Left) When you create a mandala from a sliced and layered shape, you get a perfectly seamless rotation.

Figure 6.64

(Right) When you create a mandala from a whole shape, the last rotation sits on top, and you cannot tuck part of it in to make it look like every segment is on top of every other one.

so that it doesn't overlap. If it did, all you could do is learn to live with it. You cannot use any Pathfinder filters on a Mesh object, and you can't expand a Mesh object. If you had to make it overlap and then make it layer properly, your only recourse (other than slicing the object before you make it into a gradient mesh) would be to put it into Photoshop and force it to work there.

The other layers are complex as well, but they don't touch one another. The Flower layer is built from several radial gradients, the Mesh Design layer contains another gradient mesh, and the Star brush layer is a Scatter brush. Now, on to Project 6.5.

PROJECT 6.5 A Framed Mandala (and Some Distort Filters)

Finishing this particular design will be easy. The ogee was the most difficult piece, and that is now done. However, rotating the remaining layers does slow down Illustrator quite a bit. Because of that, you'll hide the ogee mandala that is already drawn until the other layers are rotated.

The Revolving Door

In this section of the project, you'll learn how to revolve the other elements in the mandala file.

1. Choose View|Clear Guides to remove the original guides. They're on the Ogee Design layer that you need to hide (but not yet).

2. Reveal the four hidden layers and unlock them.

3. Make the Mesh Leaf layer active by clicking on its name in the Layers palette.

4. Drag a horizontal and vertical guide into the image so that they intersect at the center of the mandala.

5. Lock and hide the Ogee Design layers (all three of them).

6. Select the entire image (Command/Ctrl+A).

7. Select the Rotate tool. Press Option/Alt and click on the intersection of the guides. Enter 30 degrees in the Rotate Tool Options dialog box to send the new elements in the opposite direction.

8. Transform Again (Command/Ctrl+D) 10 times. You can either wait for the screen redraw or press the command keys 10 times as you count to make sure you've got it right. This is a very slow screen redraw. Figure 6.65 shows the new mandala.

Figure 6.65
Create a secondary mandala in your image.

9. Reveal the Ogee Design layers to see what you've drawn.

10. Unlock all the layers. Select the entire image. Double-click on the Scale tool and enter 80% in the Uniform Scale box. Click on OK. This action reduces the size of all the elements and gives you enough room to create a starburst and a background. Lock all the layers.

On the Edge

In this final part, you'll create several starbursts behind the mandala and create an interesting edge treatment for the image.

1. Create a new layer. Drag it to the bottom of the Layer stack. Name it "Starburst1".

2. Select yellow as your Fill color and set the Stroke to None.

3. Choose the Ellipse tool. Place your mouse cursor at the intersection of the two guides, press Shift+Option/Alt and drag a perfect circle from the center until the outline reaches the center of the mesh designs in the mandala. Release the mouse button before you release the modifier keys.

Filter and Effects

In the remaining steps, I ask you to apply several filters. If you want to be able to rearrange the effects afterward, you may use the Effect version of the filters instead.

4. Although you cannot see the circle, you can still see the selection's bounding box. Choose Object|Path|Add Anchor Points. Choose the Add Anchor Points command two more times. The circle now has 32 points.

5. Select Filter|Distort|Punk And Bloat. Use a setting of –59. This action drags the points into a nice starburst. Check to make sure that you can see the starburst and adjust the settings if you cannot. Click on OK.

6. To keep your sanity as the screen redraws, hide all the layers except the Starburst1 layer.

7. Select the entire image (Command/Ctrl+A). (Only the starburst is selected.) Double-click on the Scale tool and enter 90% in the Uniform Scale box. Click on Copy.

8. Choose the Rotate tool. By eye, rotate the copy so that its points fall between those of the first starburst.

9. Select the larger starburst. Fill it with a Rainbow gradient. Figure 6.66 shows the two starbursts. Lock the Starburst1 layer.

Figure 6.66
Two starbursts.

10. Make the Mesh Leaf layer visible (though locked) if that is where your guides are located (if not, view the layer where the guides are).

11. Create a new layer. Name it "Background". Drag it to the bottom of the Layer stack.

12. Choose the Rectangle tool. Set your Fill color to black with a Stroke of None. Place your mouse cursor at the intersection of the two guides, press Shift+Option/Alt, and drag a perfect circle from the center until the outline reaches a bit past the ends of the starbursts. Release the mouse button before you release the modifier keys. Figure 6.67 shows the visible image with the background in place.

Figure 6.67
Create a black square to act as
the background of the image.

13. With the black rectangle selected, choose Object|Path|Add Anchor
    Points three times.

14. Choose Filter|Distort|Roughen. Select a Size of about 4, an Amount of
    about 10 or 12 per inch, and Corner points, as shown in Figure 6.68.

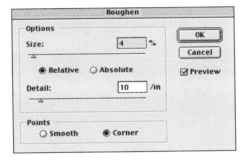

Figure 6.68
The Roughen filter dialog box
allows you to create a rough
edge to the background panel.

15. Double-click on the Scale tool and enter a Uniform amount of 110% in
    the dialog box. Click on Copy. Change the Fill of the copy to magenta
    or hot pink. Send the copy to the back.

16. Select the Rotate tool and drag the magenta copy to rotate it a little bit.

17. Select Filter|Distort|Punk And Bloat and drag the slider to about –6.
    Click on OK and then deselect.

18. Turn on all the layers. Your mandala is finished. Figure 6.69 shows the
    finished image in grayscale.

You can build up very complex edge effects by the combination of filter and
layers of background that you use. Although you copied the inner edge to
make the outer edge, you certainly could have used a totally different filter or
filter setting on the outer edge.

Figure 6.69
The finished mandala.

Moving On

In this chapter, you learned to use nearly every transformation command that Illustrator contains. You worked a very complex design in Illustrator to use the string art paths as the basis for a masked design. You applied effects and filters, and you also reduced the opacity of selected areas and used the new Blending modes. You learned how to miter the corner of a border on a Pattern brush. You also learned how to cut apart a shape so that it will seamlessly rotate.

In Chapter 7, you'll explore the world of patterns and textures.

Chapter 7

Patterns and Textures

In this chapter, you'll look at different patterning systems and some ways that you can use patterns. You'll also try out and tame the Photo Crosshatch filter.

By Sherry London

Patterns are all around us: on our clothes, on floors and walls, and on furnishings and household items. So often, Illustrator is used to create patterns with only rectangular repeats because they are all that most artists know how to create. The possibilities for using patterns are endless, and some of the best uses of patterns are almost subliminally subtle.

I have a confession—if you haven't already guessed, I'm a pattern junkie. For many years, I designed knitwear and needlework. I still do in my "spare" time. My first introduction to personal computers was to use them to automate the pattern-design process. So, this is more than "just another chapter" to me.

The Language of Pattern

People created patterns long before computers were developed. Patterned fabric and pottery remains predate the written word by hundreds of centuries. The word *pattern* has several meanings. Although it's commonly used to refer to the template used to cut fabric for clothing or to instructions to knit or stitch something, it also refers to design elements that repeat across a surface. It's this context in which the word *pattern* is used in this chapter.

Language can certainly be imprecise, and I can make the words mean whatever I say they mean, so I want to define the following terms before I take you into this world of largely unknown terminology:

- *Motif*—The subject of the pattern, the design to be repeated (and a more popular term that means much the same thing as *repeat unit*).

- *Pattern*—A recognizable motif that repeats at regular and predictable intervals along an invisible grid or lattice.

- *Texture*—A series of nonrepresentational motifs that repeat at regular and predictable intervals along an invisible grid but are arranged in such a way as to look completely random. You cannot easily distinguish where each repeat begins or ends in a properly done texture. In addition, a true texture has no distinguishing feature that would allow you to locate the motif from which it's constructed.

- *Symmetry*—The ways in which an arbitrary motif can be manipulated to form a repeat. This is a mathematical concept. It's possible to repeat a motif to cover a surface in only 17 ways (and 7 ways to repeat a pattern on a band or border).

- *Generating Unit*—The smallest area of a motif from which an entire repeat unit can be constructed.

- *Repeat Unit*—The smallest area that can be used to create the repeat pattern (it can contain multiple copies of the pattern-generating unit). I'm also inclined to call this a *tile*. Because Illustrator can create only rectangular block repeats, the repeat unit (as used here) will always be the smallest rectangle that can be defined as a pattern to re-create the selected symmetry and grid structure.

- *Pattern Skeleton*—This is my own term (see, I told you that I make them up). This is the no-stroke, no-fill rectangle that sits behind a pattern repeat unit in Illustrator and defines its boundaries.

- *Grid*—The invisible geometric construct on which the pattern is based. A block repeat, for example, uses a rectangular grid. A grid can also be a parallelogram, a triangle, a diamond, or a hexagon. The terms *lattice* and *network* are also used to refer to the grid and are actually somewhat more accurate, if not as commonly understood.

This list might already be more information than you wanted to know about patterns, but after you really get into working with patterns, they become entrancing and addictive. Don't worry about the dry terminology used in this section; I'm just setting the stage.

Dropping Patterns

Most patterns use a rectangular grid network as the repeat structure. Figure 7.1 shows a simple motif with a visible pattern skeleton behind it, repeated along a rectangular grid. The rows and columns are lined up like soldiers. It doesn't have to be that way. Figure 7.2 shows the same motif using a brick repeat (look at the pattern skeleton—it resembles the pattern formed by bricks). The rows are all even, but the columns don't line up. Figure 7.3 shows the pattern varied in another way. This example illustrates the classic *half-drop* repeat beloved of wallpaper designers around the world. The columns line up, but the rows don't.

Figure 7.1
A standard rectangular grid makes this pattern comfortingly familiar.

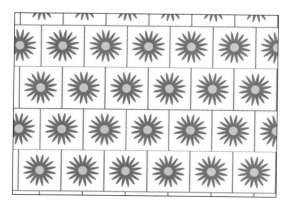

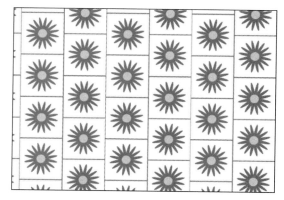

Figure 7.2

(Left) This example uses a brick repeat where the rows are even but the columns aren't.

Figure 7.3

(Right) The half-drop repeat creates the impression of vertical lines and is a common wallpaper repeat structure.

Figure 7.4 shows a repeat that uses a *diaper network*. I'll bet you thought that a diaper network was a support group for wet, young bottoms! Seriously, it's a traditional pattern design term that refers to a structure that repeats on the diagonal. Many other repeat networks are possible—circles and hexagons are behind many Celtic, Chinese, and Arabic patterning systems. Although these structures are beyond the scope of this book, look at the Rectangular Repeats project to see how the basic pattern structures are created.

Figure 7.4

A repeat that uses a *diaper network*.

PROJECT 7.1   Rectangular Repeats

In this project, you'll create a plain, rectangular repeat:

1. Open the image GUITAR.AI. It doesn't look much like a guitar, but you get the idea. It's small, and it tiles nicely.

2. Select the guitar and drag it into the Swatches palette. This is the easy way to create a pattern (though, as you'll see, not the best way). Double-click on the new pattern tile in the Swatches palette and name it "Too Close To Play".

3. Choose the Rectangle tool. Click near the bottom of the image and enter a width of 7 inches and height of 4 inches. Click on OK. Make the Fill color swatch active and click on the Too Close To Play pattern.

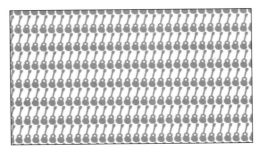

Figure 7.5
Because the guitar had no space around it when you dragged it to the Swatches palette, the motifs are very close together in the pattern itself.

Guess what? Those guitars really are too close together, as you can see in Figure 7.5. Of course, if you like it this way, there's nothing wrong with this method of defining a pattern.

4. You can control the distance between the guitars by using a pattern skeleton. This invisible rectangle sits behind your motifs and defines the boundary of the repeat. Deselect the test pattern rectangle. Select the Rectangle tool. Set the Fill and Stroke to None. Click near the small guitar motif and enter 1 inch for both the height and the width.

5. Choose the Selection tool. Drag the rectangle so that it surrounds the guitar motif. Choose Object|Arrange|Send To Back. Press Shift and add the guitar to your selection. Drag both the guitar and the pattern skeleton to the Swatches palette and then deselect. Double-click on the new pattern swatch and name it "One Inch". (If you name it with the repeat unit selected, you'll fill the objects with the new pattern.)

6. Select the test pattern rectangle. Click on the One Inch pattern to fill the rectangle. Figure 7.6 shows this image. Now, the pattern is too far apart.

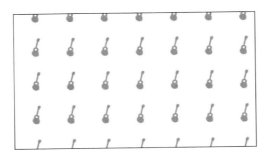

Figure 7.6
One inch is probably too far apart for this guitar motif to repeat; however, a pattern skeleton rectangle of one inch sets the distance.

7. You'll probably have an easier time setting your desired spacing by eye. Draw a no-stroke, no-fill rectangle around the guitar as I did in Figure 7.7. You can easily center the motif by clicking on Horizontal Align Center and Vertical Align Center in the Pathfinder palette, but it isn't necessary—the pattern will repeat just fine as long as the entire repeat unit is inside the pattern skeleton. You should send the pattern skeleton to the back, however (though as long as the repeat unit is totally inside it, the stacking

order of the pattern skeleton doesn't matter either). Select the guitar and the pattern skeleton and drag them to the Swatches palette. Then deselect. Name the swatch "Right Size". You can drag the swatch directly from the Swatches palette onto the test pattern rectangle to change the fill. Figure 7.8 shows the Right Size pattern.

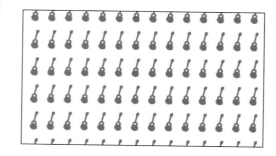

Figure 7.7
(Left) Draw a rectangle around your motif to provide the needed spacing.

Figure 7.8
(Right) The pattern looks much better when you control the spacing of the repeat.

8. You might find it easier to visualize your spacing (though the construction is trickier) if you attach the motif to the top-left corner of the pattern skeleton. Zoom in as closely as possible to the guitar motif and the pattern skeleton. Toggle Outline mode (Command/Ctrl+Y). Bear with me; although this process might seem Byzantine, it becomes a timesaver when you try to create the other pattern network types. You'll also get a better understanding of what happens when you tile a motif, as you follow along.

9. Deselect everything. Turn on Smart Guides (Command/Ctrl+U). Select the guitar motif. Place your cursor over the center point of the guitar (the spot right in the center of the "hole") and drag it to the top-left corner of the pattern skeleton (you'll see the word *anchor* when you're at the right spot).

10. Select both the guitar and the pattern skeleton. Press Option/Alt and drag the objects to the right (from the center of the guitar's hole) until the copy snaps to the original (press Shift after you begin to drag to constrain movement to the horizontal). You need to be closely zoomed in for the tolerances to be tight enough to work. Figure 7.9 shows the two guitars.

11. Zoom out so that you can see both repeats with room to spare. Select both guitars and their invisible boxes. Again, drag from the center of the guitar's hole (whichever one you prefer) to move a copy of the motifs. This time, drag downward (with Alt/Option and, after you start to drag, Shift pressed) until the copied objects snap to the bottom of the originals. Figure 7.10 shows this step.

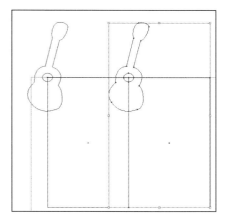
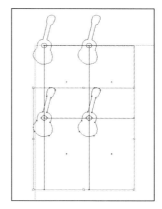

Figure 7.9
(Left) Notice how the selected guitar overlaps the pattern skeleton rectangle of the first motif.

Figure 7.10
(Right) Drag a copy of both guitars and their invisible rectangles downward until the copies snap to the bottom of the originals.

12. Deselect everything. Select and delete the three copied rectangles (leave the original and leave all the guitars). Figure 7.11 shows the remaining pattern skeleton and the four guitars. Zoom in to about 4800% on each corner of the pattern skeleton where it meets a guitar. Double-check to make sure that all the guitars are exactly snapped to the points of the rectangle. Turn off Smart Guides (Command/Ctrl+U). Toggle Outline mode (Command/Ctrl+Y).

13. Select the entire repeat unit (the four guitars and the pattern skeleton). Drag it to the Swatches palette and then deselect.

14. Name the pattern swatch "Four Guitars". Zoom out to Fit In Window (Command/Ctrl+0). Select the test pattern rectangle and apply the Four Guitars pattern. It should look no different than it did before (although the start of the pattern will probably shift). The four corner elements should meet seamlessly. If you feel the need to check out the image, zoom into the test pattern and examine it. Don't close your practice image; you'll use it in the other projects in this section.

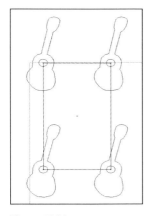

Figure 7.11
The repeat unit consists of four guitars and a pattern skeleton.

The screen display of the pattern might look more ragged than it did when you simply surrounded the single motif with a rectangle. Not to worry: That is only screen artifacting and will not show up in print (unless, of course, you really misaligned the tiles).

The following two questions might come to mind as you finish this first exercise:

- *Should I use the Crop command to make the repeat unit the same size as the pattern skeleton?* No. You could crop, and it wouldn't change things—in theory. In practice, I've seen cropping cause the pattern to meet improperly. The "sure bet" is to drag the pattern skeleton and all the stuff hanging onto it and let Illustrator determine the pattern boundaries. This approach also makes it easier to edit the pattern again, if needed.

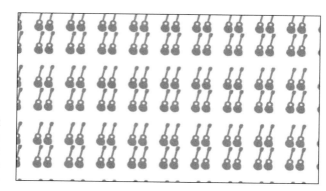

Figure 7.12

The pattern looks like this if you forget to make the pattern skeleton the base object in your repeat unit.

- *What happens if the pattern skeleton isn't the bottom object in the repeat unit?* The short answer: Your tile won't tile properly. Figure 7.12 shows this best.

After you go through the agony of figuring out the complex way to make a single motif repeat, it's simple to make a brick or half-drop repeat out of it, which is your next task.

PROJECT 7.2 Brick It Up

In this project, you'll create a brick pattern:

1. Select the four-guitar repeat and drag a copy of it to another location in your image. Zoom in to the copied pattern repeat unit. To make a brick repeat, you need two guitars on top and one on the bottom—dead center between the two top guitars.

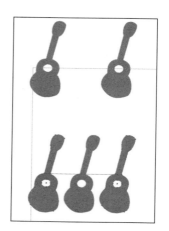

Figure 7.13

To place an object dead center between two others that are identical, use the Blend tool with a step of 1.

2. The next step seems odd, but it really works. It's a technique recommended many years ago by Luanne Seymour Cohen in her landmark work on Illustrator patterns (the manual for the original Adobe Collector Series patterns, long out of print). How do you create an object in between two others? Use the Blend tool. Select the two bottom guitars. Then choose the Blend tool. In the Blend Options dialog box (Object| Blends|Blend Options), set the Specified Steps to 1. Click on the center point of the leftmost guitar on the bottom and then click on the center point of the rightmost guitar on the bottom. Figure 7.13 shows you the five guitars (four and a blend).

3. Because Illustrator 9's blends are "live," you need to expand the blend (Object|Blends|Expand) so that the blended object can live on its own. After you've expanded the blend, deselect it, select it again, and ungroup it (Shift+Command/Ctrl+G). Deselect.

4. Select the two end guitars (the start and endpoints for the blend that you just expanded) and delete them. Look carefully at Figure 7.14. It shows the three remaining guitars and the pattern skeleton (all selected

so that you can see the pattern skeleton rectangle). If you look inside the pattern skeleton, you'll notice that the pieces of the guitars are not enough to make a repeating pattern. The rectangle itself doesn't contain even one complete guitar. Therefore, you need to enlarge the pattern skeleton.

5. Toggle Outline mode (Command/Ctrl+Y). With the Selection tool, select the pattern skeleton. Double-click on the Scale tool and select Non-Uniform. Enter a Horizontal scale amount of 100% and a Vertical scale amount of 200%. Click on OK. Figure 7.15 shows the Outline view. Now, the pattern skeleton encompasses one complete guitar and two halves (which can join together to form another whole).

6. Toggle Outline mode (Command/Ctrl+Y). Zoom out to Fit In Window (Command/Ctrl+0). Select the entire repeat unit (if necessary, first send the pattern skeleton to the back) and drag it into the Swatches window. Deselect the repeat unit and name the new pattern "Bricked Guitars". Select the test pattern rectangle and fill it with the Bricked Guitars pattern. Figure 7.16 shows the pattern applied to the rectangle.

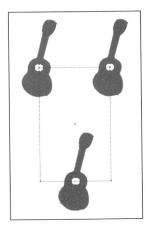

Figure 7.14
The pieces of guitar that fall within the pattern skeleton are not enough to reconstitute an entire guitar.

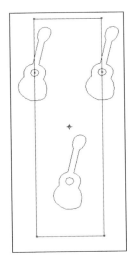
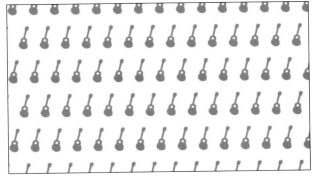

Figure 7.15
(Left) When you double the vertical measurement of the pattern skeleton, it becomes large enough to hold a full brick repeat.

Figure 7.16
(Right) The guitars are now in a brick repeat.

PROJECT 7.3 The Half-Drop Repeat

Let's create a half-drop repeat so that you can see the differences:

1. Zoom in to your image on the original four-guitar repeat. Select the four guitars and the invisible pattern skeleton. Drag a copy of the selection to another location.

2. Select the top-right and bottom-right guitars. With the Blend tool, click on the center points of the top and then the bottom selected guitar. The Blend Options should be set to a specified step of 1.

3. Expand the blend (Object|Blends|Expand), deselect, select again, and ungroup.

4. Select and delete the top-right and bottom-right guitars. Figure 7.17 shows the almost-ready repeat unit. Again, you'll notice that the pattern skeleton is not large enough to hold a whole repeat unit.

5. Select the pattern skeleton rectangle only. Double-click on the Scale tool. Select Non-Uniform. Enter a Horizontal scale amount of 200% and a Vertical scale amount of 100% (this is the exact opposite of the procedure to create a bricked repeat). Click on OK. Figure 7.18 shows the finished repeat unit.

Figure 7.17
(Left) After you create a blended top-to-bottom guitar, remove the two originals on the right of the repeat unit.

Figure 7.18
(Right) The finished half-drop repeat unit is wider than it is long (whereas the bricked repeat unit was longer that it was wide).

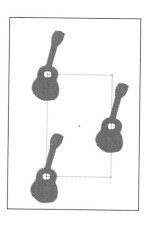
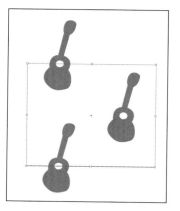

6. Zoom out to Fit In Window (Command/Ctrl+0). Select the entire repeat unit (if needed, send the pattern skeleton to the back first) and drag it into the Swatches window. Deselect the repeat unit and name the new pattern "Half-Dropped Guitars". Select the test pattern rectangle and fill it with the Half-Dropped Guitars pattern. Figure 7.19 shows the pattern applied to the rectangle.

Figure 7.19
The Half-Dropped Guitars pattern shows straight columns and alternating rows.

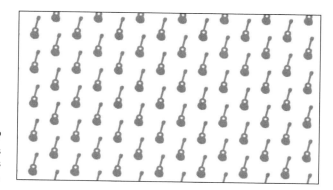

PROJECT 7.4 Diapering Patterns

Now, that you've made brick and half-drop repeats, the diaper pattern you'll create next is easy. Because this is the third time through on similar instructions, I made these instructions brief. Review the earlier projects if you have trouble remembering a command or shortcut.

1. Make another copy of the original four-guitar pattern repeat unit.

2. Switch to Outline mode. Turn on Smart Guides. Drag a copy of one of the guitars from its center point to the center point of the pattern skeleton.

3. Turn off Outline mode and turn off the Smart Guides.

4. Select the center guitar. Choose the Rotate tool and rotate the center guitar until it's leaning slightly in the opposite direction.

5. Select the entire pattern repeat, drag it to the Swatches palette, and deselect. Name the new pattern "Diapered Guitars". Select the test pattern rectangle and fill it with the diaper pattern. Figure 7.20 shows the pattern repeat unit, and Figure 7.21 shows the tiled pattern.

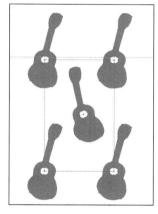

Figure 7.20
This is the repeat unit for the diapered guitars.

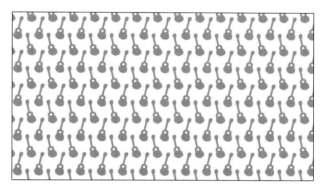

Figure 7.21
Guitars arranged in a diaper pattern (a pattern structure that repeats diagonally in both directions).

PROJECT 7.5 Honey Bees—A Variation on a Plane

Before you leave this topic, try one of the slightly more complex patterns—one of the 17 symmetries. If you have the Terrazzo filter from Xaos Tools for Photoshop (one of my favorite plug-ins), you can see that this is the symmetry called "Honey Bees." It involves two rotations and a reflection, but it's easy to do if you follow along:

1. Make a copy of one of the guitars and the original pattern skeleton. Drag it to a new location in the image. With both objects selected, click on Horizontal Align Center and Vertical Align Center in the Pathfinder palette to center the guitar inside the pattern skeleton rectangle. Toggle Outline mode (Command/Ctrl+Y). Select just the pattern skeleton. Resize the pattern skeleton (press Shift and Option/Alt to constrain the aspect ratio and scale from the center) so that it hugs the guitar more closely, as in Figure 7.22.

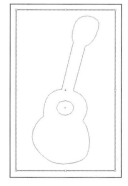

Figure 7.22
Resize the pattern skeleton to fit more tightly around the guitar.

2. With both objects selected, choose the Rotate tool. Press Option/Alt and click on the lower-right corner of the pattern skeleton. Enter 180 degrees in the Amount field. Click on Copy. Figure 7.23 shows the result.

3. Select both guitars and pattern skeleton rectangles. Double-click on the Reflect tool. Select the Vertical radio button and click on Copy. Figure 7.24 shows the pattern in progress.

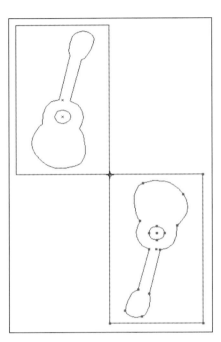 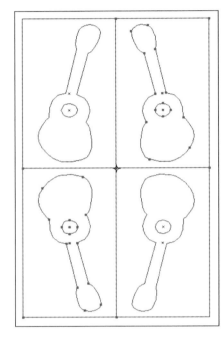

Figure 7.23

(Left) Rotate a copy of the motif and the pattern skeleton 180 degrees from the bottom-right corner.

Figure 7.24

(Right) Reflect the two guitars and the two pattern skeletons vertically.

4. The next step is the only tricky one. Leave only the two reflected guitars selected (they were selected at the end of Step 3). Choose Object|Transform| Transform Each. Set the Horizontal and Vertical scale to 100%, move the objects vertically and horizontally 0 points (in other words, *don't* move them), and change the Angle of Rotation to 180 degrees. Deselect the Random checkbox. Click on OK (not Copy). Figure 7.25 shows the correctly filled-in dialog box, and Figure 7.26 shows the pattern repeat unit.

5. Toggle Outline mode off (Command/Ctrl+Y). Because you can see white space around the guitars, simply select all four pattern-generating units and drag the entire repeat unit to the Swatches palette. Name the pattern and fill your test rectangle as you've done before. Figure 7.27 shows the tiled pattern. (If the pattern was more complex and some of the elements crossed over pattern skeleton rectangles, you would need to unite the four pattern skeleton rectangles that actually form the skeleton of the pattern.)

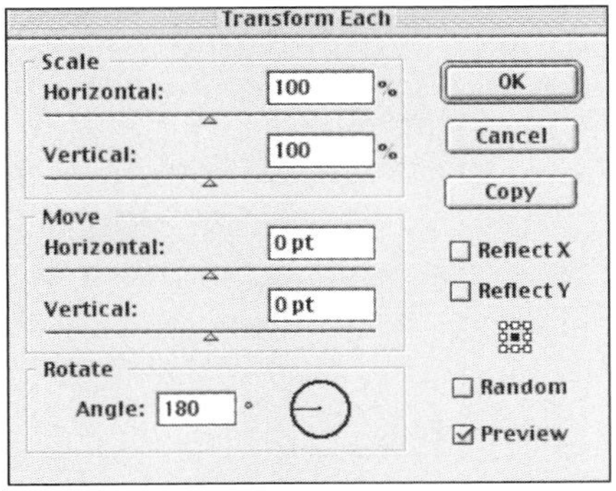

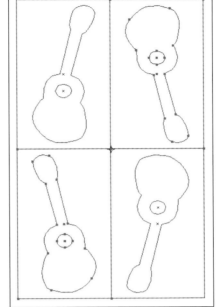

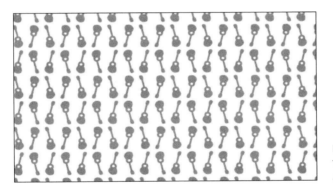

Figure 7.25
(Left) In the Transform Each dialog box, you can rotate each guitar individually.

Figure 7.26
(Right) The final pattern repeat unit.

Figure 7.27
The Honey Bees repeat shows another version of the guitars.

The Pattern Brush

You're going to use the guitar again to create an interlocking Pattern brush—a bit more challenging but still simple. A Pattern brush is a special type of brush, introduced in Illustrator 8, that allows you to paint a pattern along a path. The same procedures that work for creating a pattern also work when you're creating a Pattern brush. The only difference is that you need to exercise a bit of care when defining a Pattern brush pattern because it needs to fit along a path. Therefore, a wide pattern is better for a Pattern brush than a tall one. A side benefit of the next project is that it will segue nicely into our discussion of creating interlocking patterns.

A Long Line of Guitars

In this project, you'll change the guitar pattern into a Pattern brush:

1. Drag a copy of one of the guitars in the original pattern repeat unit to a new location in the image. Toggle Outline mode on (Command/Ctrl+Y). Don't copy the pattern skeleton because you need to make a new one.

2. Choose the Rotate tool. Press Option/Alt and click on the top-right anchor point of the guitar (it's actually on the right side of the fret, but it's the highest point on the right side). Enter 180 degrees as the angle of rotation and click on Copy. Group the two guitars (Command/Ctrl+G).

3. Draw a pattern skeleton around the double-guitar object, giving it a bit of white space. With the pattern skeleton and the two guitars selected, click on Horizontal Align Center and Vertical Align Center in the Align palette to center the guitars in the rectangle. (Of course, if you draw the pattern skeleton from the center—the point where the two guitars join—the rectangle will automatically be centered.) Figure 7.28 shows the pattern-generating unit.

4. Select the guitars and the pattern skeleton. Press Option/Alt and move the selection to the right (press Shift after you begin to drag to constrain movement to the horizontal) until the left edge of the pattern skeleton rectangle copy clears the guitar, as shown in Figure 7.29.

5. Transform Again (Command/Ctrl+D) two more times. Figure 7.30 shows the four pattern-generating units in a row.

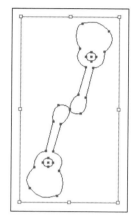

Figure 7.28

The rotated guitars and the new pattern skeleton form the pattern generating unit from which the new repeat unit is created.

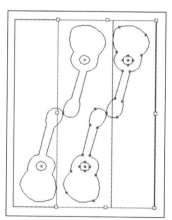
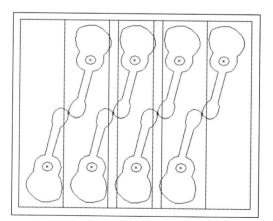

Figure 7.29

(Left) Move a copy of the guitars and the pattern skeleton to the right.

Figure 7.30

(Right) Create two more copies of the guitars and pattern skeleton with the same spacing by using the Transform Again command.

6. Select the second pattern skeleton rectangle from the left. Hide it (Object|Hide Selection). You could also turn off the Eye in the Layers palette. Select and delete the remaining pattern skeleton rectangles. Show All (Object|Show All). Zoom in closely to the selected pattern skeleton rectangle and drag each side of the rectangle toward the center until the sides are precisely between the two connected guitars, as shown in the circled side control handles in Figure 7.31.

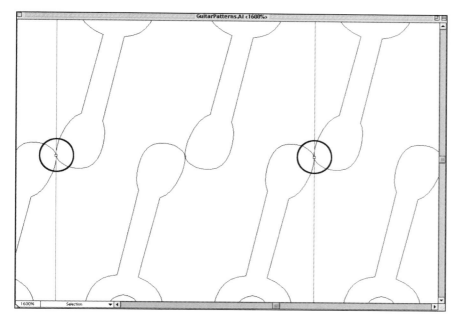

Figure 7.31
Move the control handles of the bounding box of the pattern skeleton toward the center until each side lies between two connected guitars.

7. Select the pattern skeleton and send it to the back.

8. Select and drag the pattern repeat unit into the Brushes palette. Figure 7.32 shows the dialog box that pops up. Select New Pattern Brush.

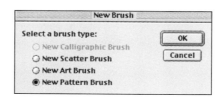

Figure 7.32
You can use the New Brush dialog box to create a Pattern brush.

9. Figure 7.33 shows the next dialog box. Name the Pattern brush "Rotated Guitars" and click on the Inner Corner icon. Select the Honey Bees pattern that is in the list as the corner element. Click on the Outer Corner icon and select the Honey Bees pattern again. Click on OK.

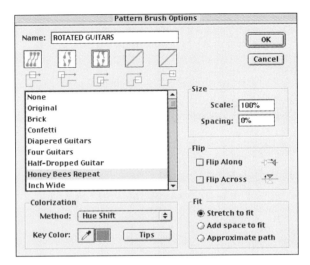

Figure 7.33
The New Pattern Brush
dialog box.

Creating Patterns with Backgrounds

You've used a pattern that has no fill in the background—its "white spaces" are clear. Should you want to place a background of a specific color behind the pattern, you still need to define a no fill-no stroke rectangle as your bottom object on the pattern. This is the only sure way (especially if pattern elements hang outside of the filled background rectangle) to be sure that you have properly defined your pattern to Illustrator.

10. Select your test pattern rectangle. Change its Fill to None. Choose the Paintbrush tool. Click on the new Pattern brush to use the brush as the stroke for the rectangle. Figure 7.34 shows the rectangle and some painted strokes.

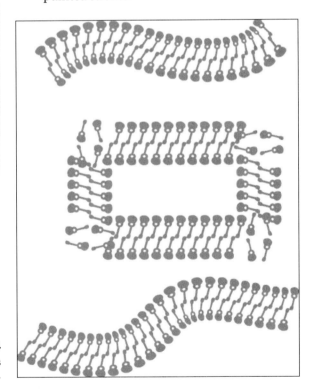

Figure 7.34
The rotated guitars are applied as a stroke using the Pattern brush.

Having learned how to define patterns, you now know the basics of the Pattern brush as well. Of course, you also met some Pattern brush tricks in Chapters 4 and 8. You can close the guitar image now; it has served you well.

Escher Patterns

M. C. Escher created some of the most exciting patterns the world has ever seen. He was a master at making hands look like they were drawing each other and at making two-dimensional lizards pop out of the canvas and seem to walk away. He created interlocking patterns in which geese faced in alternate directions. The incredible thing about many of his patterns was the way in which they interlocked to form animals and plants, yet they tiled seamlessly.

Escher was a master at the mathematics of symmetry. I can't even begin to imagine how he worked out most of his effects (and I certainly couldn't duplicate them), but I do have a few interlocking tricks up my sleeve.

The Three-Corner Trick

If you draw a line of any shape that hits three corners of a rectangle, when you repeat the rectangle, the shapes will seamlessly interlock. This can be a bit of a fiddly project, but its worst offense is that once you master the technique, it can easily become addictive.

One thing that I love about Illustrator is the large number of ways in which you can construct an object. It allows me to exercise my propensity for getting (as my tenth-grade geometry teacher once put it) "to New York by way of Chicago"—and I grew up in Philadelphia, so New York is only 90 miles away. If there's a short, easy way to do something, my natural inclination (and first tries) will be anything but that. However, I promise that I tried (and rejected) at least 12 other ways of constructing this effect until I developed the procedure shown next. This way is as easy as I can find to explain it.

PROJECT 7.7 Creating Interlocking Patterns

In this project, I'll show you one way to create irregular-looking pattern shapes that interlock with one another:

1. Create a new document in Illustrator.

2. Select the Rectangle tool. Click on the intersection of the top and left margins in the document. In the Rectangle Options dialog box, enter a width of 2 inches and a height of 1 inch. Click on OK. Choose View|Make Guides.

3. Turn on Smart Guides (Command/Ctrl+U). Select the Pencil tool. Toggle Outline mode on (Command/Ctrl+Y).

4. Begin in the lower-left corner of the rectangle guide and draw any type of squiggly line that you want. It must do three things:

   - It must start in the lower-left corner.

   - It must touch the upper-left corner.

   - It must end at the upper-right corner.

Potential Stroke/Fill Problem

Be careful when you select a pattern fill. It's possible to fill a stroke with a pattern, but it's not bright. You might not see that you've applied a pattern to your stroke on screen (unless it has a wide stroke width), and you'll probably get a long wait and, perhaps, an error when you go to print (and trapping the stroke is not an amusing day's task). Always make sure that you are actually changing the Fill swatch when you click on a pattern because it's much too easy to get this wrong.

The line can go outside the rectangle a bit as long as it meets these three criteria. As you gain more experience, you'll notice that it's even possible to break the "it must touch the upper-left corner" rule if you obey the other rules. Figure 7.35 shows the line that I drew.

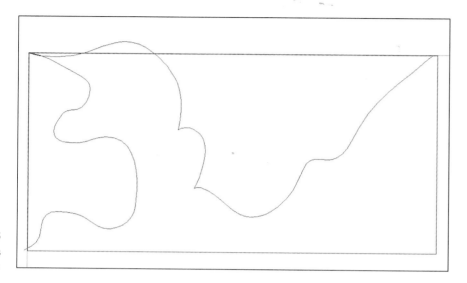

Figure 7.35
Draw a squiggly line that touches three corners of the rectangle.

5. If you zoom in on the corners of the rectangle, you'll probably discover that you didn't quite get the path to exactly touch the corners. Use the Direct Selection tool to attach both endpoints to their respective corners of the guides. Unfortunately, for this technique to work correctly, you must be exact.

6. When you fix the endpoints of the path, take a closer look at how the path hits the upper-left corner of the guides. It has a nasty tendency to form a loop rather than a point, which is what happened in Figure 7.36. As you can see in the selected corner tip, the two parts of the path cross over each other. You need to use the Direct Selection tool and move the direction lines so that the path no longer overlaps and loops. Figure 7.37 shows the problem area fixed. Now, you're ready to play.

7. Choose the Scissors tool. Click on the top-left corner point of the path (the point that you just fixed) to break your line into two separate paths.

8. If it is not already selected, select the lower-left-to-upper-left corner path. Choose Object|Lock or click on the Lock icon in the Layers palette.

9. Zoom in to the image as closely as you can while still seeing the entire path. Choose the Selection tool and deselect everything. Position your cursor at the top-left corner of the top path. The Smart Guides should tell you that it is an anchor point. Press Shift+Option/Alt and keep the

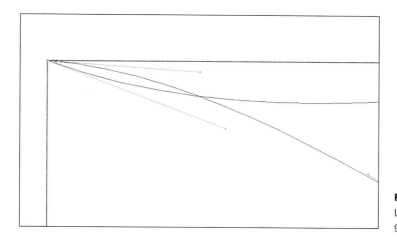

Figure 7.36
Leaving a loop in a corner is a good way to make a mess.

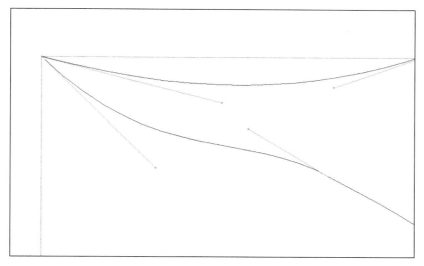

Figure 7.37
The loop is untangled and looks much better now.

keys pressed. Click on the anchor point (still holding down the modifier keys) while dragging the path downward. Drag the copy down until the word "intersect" appears along the left margin. Release the mouse button and then the modifier keys.

10. Choose Object|Unlock All and then Edit|Select Inverse. Then, choose Object|Lock Selected to prevent yourself from accidentally selecting the top or bottom paths—an easy thing to do in this instance.

11. Position your cursor at the top-left corner of the side path. The Smart Guides should tell you that it is an anchor point. Press Shift+Option/ Shift+Alt and keep the keys pressed. Then, click on the anchor point (while still holding down the modifier keys) while dragging the path to the right. Drag the copy to the right until the word "intersect" appears along the top margin. Release the mouse button and then the modifier keys. Figure 7.38 shows the puzzle piece that I created. Your's should be somewhat similar.

Average Alert

Watch carefully when you average the two points. If you are doing this procedure quickly, you might have selected more than two points. If you do, Illustrator will try to average them all. If you see any points move when you average them, undo the command, reselect the points, and try again.

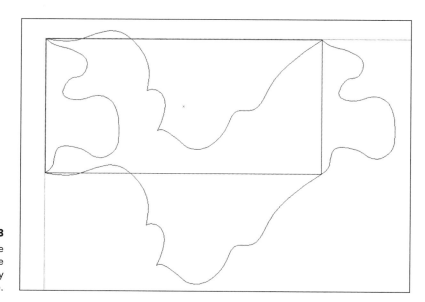

Figure 7.38

By copying the top and side segments of the path, you have created a completely interlocking shape.

12. Choose Object|Unlock All and then deselect. Turn off Smart Guides (Command/Ctrl+U). Although you can work with them on, I find them unpleasant and in my face when I don't really need them, so I leave them active for as short a time as possible.

13. You now need to join all four corners so that you form a closed, filled shape. To do so, use the Direct Selection tool to select the two points that intersect to form the corner of the shape. Average the points (Command/Ctrl+Option/Alt+J) both vertically and horizontally. Join the points (Command/Ctrl+J) with a corner point (unless, as in the lower-right corner of my example, you feel that a smooth point would work better). Repeat this procedure for each of the four "corners" (the places where the cut paths meet).

14. Select a Fill color for the shape. Toggle Outline mode off (Command/Ctrl+Y). Turn on Smart Guides (Command/Ctrl+U).

15. Choose the Selection tool. Position your cursor at the top-left corner of the shape. The Smart Guides should tell you that it is an anchor point. Press Shift+Option/Alt and keep the keys pressed. Then, click on the anchor point (while still holding down the modifier keys) while dragging the path downward. Drag the copy down until the word "intersect" appears along the left margin. Release the mouse button and then the modifier keys.

16. Transform Again (Command/Ctrl+D) two more times. You have four of the shapes in your document. Select shape 2 and change its Fill color. Select shape 4. Use the Eyedropper tool to give it the same Fill color as shape 2.

17. Select the entire image (Command/Ctrl+A). Choose the Selection tool. Position your cursor at the top-left corner of the top shape (this is not the same as the bounding box control handle, so you are less likely to have problems). The Smart Guides should tell you that it is an anchor point. Press Option/Alt and click on the anchor point (while still holding down the modifier key). After you start to drag the shapes to the right, press Shift to constrain the movement to the horizontal. Drag the copy to the right until the word "intersect" appears along the top margin. Release the mouse button and then the modifier keys.

18. Transform Again (Command/Ctrl+D). You have a grid of shapes four rows by three columns deep. You need to flip the colors of the center column of shapes. The easiest way is to select the Eyedropper tool. Use Command/Ctrl to access the Selection tool to select the object and then release the key to pick the color for the shape. Figure 7.39 shows the finished group of interlocking shapes.

Figure 7.39
You've created an interlocking grid of shapes using counterchange coloring (that is, alternating colors).

19. Select the Rectangle tool and choose a Fill and a Stroke of None. Press Option/Alt and click near the center of the group of shapes. Enter a width of 4 inches and a height of 2 inches into the Rectangle Tool Options dialog box. Click on OK. Choose Object|Arrange|Send To Back. You don't have to try to find the exact center of the image. As long as the rectangle is over the solidly filled shapes, your pattern will tile properly.

20. Select the entire image (Command/Ctrl+A). Press Shift and drag the lower-right-corner control handle on the bounding box up and to the left to make the pattern tile smaller. Don't decrease its size too much because you can always scale the pattern after it's applied. However, we created the pattern at a size that's probably too large for comfort.

21. Select the entire object again and drag it to the Swatches palette. Make a test rectangle and try your new pattern. Figure 7.40 shows my pattern applied to a clothing shape in a very stylized image.

Figure 7.40

The young lady in the image is wearing a jumper that sports the latest fashion in interlocking patterns.

How does this effect work? Why does it work? The "secret" is that you are really creating an odd-shaped rectangle with identical parallel sides. When you take a rectangle and make changes to a side, as long as you make the same changes to the opposing side, the rectangle will always tile. You merely created two very strange-looking sides for a rectangle and repeated them.

The other trick in this exercise is that you must know your starting tile size. Even though you reduced the pattern repeat before making it into a pattern, up until the last moment you knew the original repeat size (it was the 2-by-1 rectangle that started the procedure). Your final tile must be an even multiple of both directions of that first rectangle. If you had wanted only to repeat your single-colored tile (though I don't see much point in doing that), the tile size would have been the same as the original. Because you used two colors, the full repeat was twice the original rectangle size.

You can also use this technique to create wonderful Pattern brushes. If you want to define your interlocking pattern as a Pattern brush, you can use the irregularly shaped top and bottom edges as they are and, for a two-color pattern, make a pattern skeleton that is 4 inches wide (twice your original rectangle).

The Ogee

You can also create interlocking patterns that aren't based on rectangles. Hexagons tile seamlessly just as they are; diamonds also tile by nature, and the ogee form is another shape that always tiles if constructed properly. So, you've never heard of an ogee? You've seen it even if you didn't know it had a name. It's a pattern long used in Arabic, Islamic, and Persian design. It also looks like an old-fashioned Christmas-tree ornament—the ones that were pointed on top and bottom and round in the middle. That's an ogee. As a motif, it frequently appears in wallpaper design. (Too frequently—we lived for much too long with a green velvet flocked ogee pattern on a metallic gold background that a previous owner of our house put up on the bedroom walls. Yes, it was as awful as it sounds.) However, the ogee has a respectable lineage and can be quite lovely as a pattern device when used in good taste.

PROJECT 7.8 O, Gee What a Beautiful Morning

In this project, you'll create and decorate an ogee:

1. Create a new document in Illustrator.

2. Choose a Fill color (I used a soft green) and set the Stroke to None. Select the Ellipse tool. Click near the center of the image and enter 1.5 into the Width and Height fields of the Ellipse Tool Options dialog box. Click on OK.

3. Turn on the Rulers (Command/Ctrl+R). Turn on Smart Guides (Command/Ctrl+U). Drag a horizontal and vertical guide so that they intersect in the exact center of the filled circle. (Does your circle lack a center point? Click on the square-with-a-period-in-it icon on the Attributes palette.)

4. You need only one quarter of the circle. Choose the Rectangle tool. Draw a rectangle to the right of the vertical guide so that it completely covers the right side of the circle, as shown in Figure 7.41.

5. Select the entire image (Command/Ctrl+A). In the Pathfinder palette, click on Minus Front. Now, you have a half-circle.

6. Draw another rectangle. This time, let it cover the bottom half of the half-circle, as shown in Figure 7.42.

7. Swap the Stroke and the Fill for the quarter-circle so that it's stroked but not filled. Toggle Outline mode on (Command/Ctrl+Y). Choose the Scissors tool. Click on the two points of the circle where the arc intersects the guides. Figure 7.43 shows the quarter-circle cut with direction lines coming from the cut anchor points. For the screen capture, I also changed stroke colors so that you could see the two pieces that come from the scissors cut.

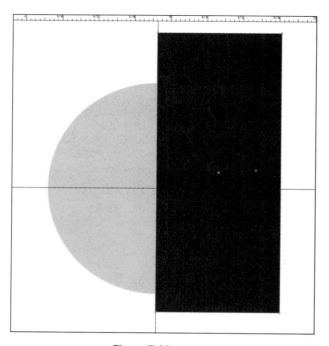 

Figure 7.41
(Left) Cover the right side of the circle with a rectangle.

Figure 7.42
(Right) When you subtract the rectangle from the half-circle, you leave only a quarter of the original circle.

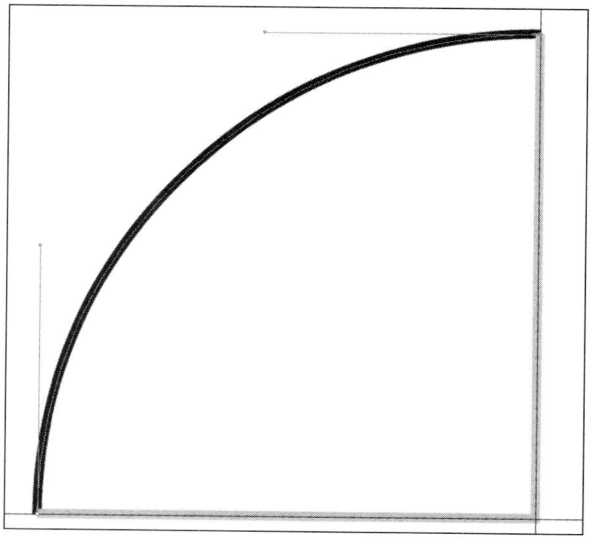

Figure 7.43
Cutting the arc from the bottom and side of the quarter-circle leaves only the arc.

8. Select the right-angle portion of the quarter-circle and delete it. Only the arc remains.

9. Select the arc. Choose the Rotate tool. Press Option/Alt and click on the top endpoint of the arc (the one that touches the vertical guide) to set the top point as the center of the transformation. Watch the Smart Guides to make sure that you are clicking in the right place. Enter 180 degrees into the Rotate Tool Options dialog box. Click on Copy. Figure 7.44 shows the path that becomes the template for all sides of the ogee.

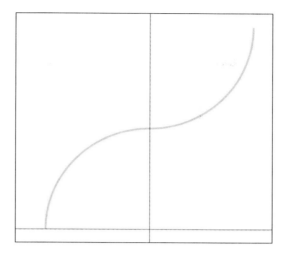

Figure 7.44
The ogee tiles because its side is made from a path that is rotated to form the second half, and all its sides are flipped or rotated copies of the original path.

10. Choose the Direct Selection tool. Drag a marquee around the two points on the arc where the copy joins the original (on the vertical guide). Average the points (Command/Ctrl+Option/Alt+J) both vertically and horizontally. Join the points (Command/Ctrl+J) with a smooth point. Figure 7.45 shows the almost lyrical picture of the curved arcs with perfectly straight direction lines. Deselect.

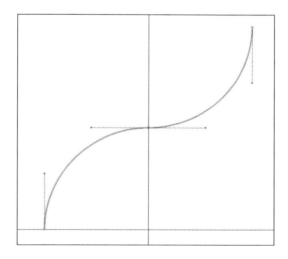

Figure 7.45
The curve of the joined ogee with its direction lines is almost magical.

11. Choose the Selection tool and select the curved line. Choose the Reflect tool. Press Option/Alt and click on the top endpoint on the curved line. Select the Vertical radio button in the Reflect Tool Options dialog box. Click on Copy. Use the Direct Selection tool to select the top points on the ogee-to-be. Figure 7.46 shows this point as a screen capture of the line after the Reflect tool was used. Average the points (Command/Ctrl+Option/Alt+J) both vertically and horizontally. Join the points (Command/Ctrl+J) with a corner point.

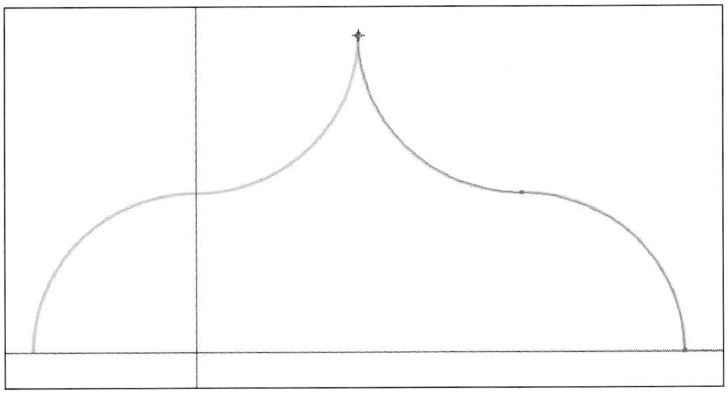

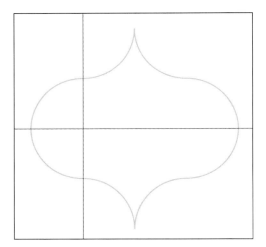

Figure 7.46

Select the top points of the two curves; then average and join them.

12. Select the entire image (Command/Ctrl+A). With the Reflect tool, press Option/Alt and click on either of the endpoints of the path that lies along the horizontal guide. Select the Horizontal radio button in the Reflect Tool Options dialog box. Click on Copy. Figure 7.47 shows the finished ogee outline.

Figure 7.47

The finished ogee outline.

13. With the Direct Selection tool, select the two points that form the left side of the ogee and touch the horizontal guide. Average the points (Command/Ctrl+Option/Alt+J) both vertically and horizontally. Join the points (Command/Ctrl+J) with a smooth point.

14. With the Direct Selection tool, select the two points that form the right side of the ogee and touch the horizontal guide. Average the points (Command/Ctrl+Option/Alt+J) both vertically and horizontally. Join the points (Command/Ctrl+J) with a smooth point. Select the entire image (Command/Ctrl+A). Toggle Outline mode off (Command/Ctrl+Y). Swap the Fill and the Stroke so that the ogee is filled. Move the ogee so that its bottom point snaps to the intersection of the guides, as shown in Figure 7.48.

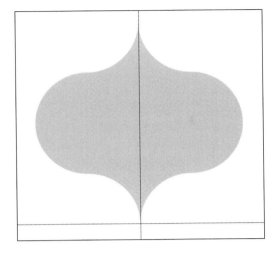

Figure 7.48
Snap the bottom point of the filled ogee to the intersection of the guides.

(Deselect everything and move your cursor over the bottom point until the Smart Guides indicate the anchor point. Press the mouse button and drag to select the object at the same time.)

15. Hide the guides. Decorate your ogee with designs or squiggles as you wish. (You might want to turn off Smart Guides if they annoy you.) Figure 7.49 shows my very abstract decoration. (You're going to be cutting apart the ogee and its decoration, so don't get too carried away.) Don't use gradients, patterns, meshes, or the Paintbrush tool (or masks or compound paths).

16. Select the entire image (Command/Ctrl+A). Drag a copy of the ogee into the pasteboard area for safekeeping. Create a new layer and move the copied ogee's selection rectangle onto the new layer. Lock and hide the layer. Now, it's not in your way, but it's there if you need it. Make Layer 1 active.

17. Select the entire image (Command/Ctrl+A). Click on Merge in the Pathfinder palette.

18. Show the guides (View|Show Guides). Turn on Smart Guides (Command/Ctrl+U). Select the entire image (Command/Ctrl+A). Drag a horizontal guide to the first set of anchor points below the top point of the ogee. Drag a horizontal guide to the last set of anchor points before the bottom point of the ogee, as shown in Figure 7.50.

19. Deselect. Choose the Pen tool. The color doesn't matter, but you need to select a Fill of None and a Stroke of whatever. Draw a straight line across the ogee using the top horizontal guide as your ruler. The line must be wider than the ogee. Press Option/Alt and drag a copy of the line (press Shift after you begin to drag to constrain movement to the vertical) down to the next horizontal guide, as shown in Figure 7.51.

Figure 7.49
Decorate the ogee using whatever and however many colors you want.

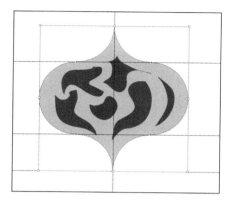
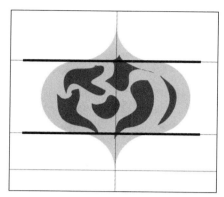

Figure 7.50

(Left) Create two more guides that are horizontal at the second from the top and second from the bottom points on the ogee.

Figure 7.51

(Right) You need to have a line that runs across the width of the ogee on both guides that you added to the image. I've deliberately thickened the lines in this figure.

20. Select both lines. Select Object|Blends|Blend Options and set the Specified Steps to 1. Choose the Blend tool and click on the leftmost endpoint of each line. Select the blend. Choose Object|Blends|Expand (see Figure 7.52).

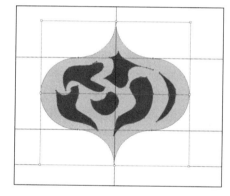

Figure 7.52

Three lines are used to cut the image apart.

21. Select the entire image (Command/Ctrl+A). Click on Divide in the Pathfinder palette. The lines disappear, leaving a cut-up ogee behind. If you look closely (and if it's not beyond the limitations of this book's printer, you should be able to see the cut lines in the selected image shown in Figure 7.52.

Figure 7.53

The color bands show the objects to be grouped to form horizontal strips.

22. Now, you need to put the ogee back together again across horizontal strips. Select all the pieces in a strip and group them. Figure 7.53 shows the reconstructed ogee. I've changed the color for each strip so that you can see it. Don't change the colors in your own ogee. You might need to zoom in close to the tiny cuts if any of the tiniest pieces fall near a horizontal cut. Select the small pieces on a strip first to make it easier to see which ones have been selected. You also might find it easier to hide the guides until you have rebuilt the ogee.

23. Show the guides if you have hidden them and turn on Smart Guides if they are off. Drag a horizontal guide to about 1 inch above the first

horizontal guide in the image. With nothing selected, place your cursor over the top point of the ogee. Press the mouse button and drag the ogee up to the new guide. Press Shift after you begin to drag to constrain movement to the vertical.

24. Select the entire image (Command/Ctrl+A). Click on Vertical Distribute Center in the Align palette. (If the command doesn't work, you've got a tiny ungrouped cut somewhere that's gumming up the works.) Figure 7.54 shows the cut and parted ogee.

25. Select the entire image (Command/Ctrl+A). Group the shapes (Command/Ctrl+G). Press Shift after you begin to drag to constrain movement to the vertical and drag the ogee up slightly along the vertical guide. Move it about the same distance as the space between the strips of the ogee.

26. Drag a small square from the intersection of the horizontal and vertical guides to act as a spacer. It should be about twice the size as the space between the strips of the ogee. I haven't found any good automated way to complete this step without measuring precisely and driving everyone bonkers. Just work by eye and drag the bottom point of the ogee to the top of the spacer square. Then, drag a copy of the ogee directly down until the top of the copy touches the bottom of the spacer square. Drag another copy to the left of the original so that it's centered on the left side of the spacer square. Drag a copy of the left side to the right side of the spacer square. Your image now should look like Figure 7.55.

Figure 7.54
The ogee has been cut and the pieces moved apart.

Figure 7.55
Four copies of the ogee frame a spacer square in the center.

27. Delete the spacer square. Clear the guides. It's time to create new ones. Zoom in closely. You need to frame the ogee with four guides; from the top and bottom points of the side ogees, you need horizontal guides. From the same top and bottom points on the side ogees, you need vertical guides. The Smart Guides help you place them accurately by reporting on "anchor point" and/or "intersect." Figure 7.56 shows the ogee with its four new guides.

Figure 7.56
You'll use the four new guides to make a pattern skeleton.

> **How Do I Know Whether I've Got Them All?**
>
> The easiest way to make sure that you have selected all the little cuts in the horizontal strip is to hide the selected objects after you've selected a group of them. You can keep selecting and hiding until none of them are left in the strip. When you choose Object|Show All, all the hidden objects appear selected. You can now easily group them.

28. Select the Rectangle tool with no Fill and no Stroke. Drag a rectangle from the top-left intersection of the guides to the bottom-right intersection of the guides. You might want to turn off Smart Guides before you make this move. I find Smart Guides more trouble than they're worth when I already have guides in the image. Send the new rectangle to the back so that it can act as a pattern skeleton.

29. Select the entire image (Command/Ctrl+A). Drag it to the Swatches palette. Drag your pattern repeat unit to the pasteboard for now. Create a test rectangle and fill it with the new pattern. Double-click on the Scale tool and deselect the Scale Objects checkbox, leaving the Patterns checkbox selected. Set a Uniform Scale amount of 40%. Click on OK. Figure 7.57 shows the tiled pattern used in an image in a variety of ways.

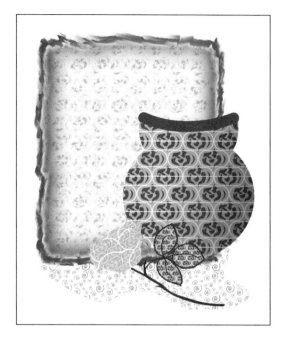

Figure 7.57
The ogee pattern makes an interesting tile and can be varied to produce a number of different effects.

Manipulating Patterns

Illustrator gives you a large number of manipulations and functions that you can use on patterns. Although the online help and the manual list all of them, I wanted to give you this mini-list as well:

- You can recover the objects from which the pattern is created by dragging the pattern from the Swatches palette directly into your document.

- You can change the starting point of your pattern in the object by either changing the zero point on the rulers or using the Move command from the Transform menu and selecting the Pattern Only option.

- You can perform any transformation on your pattern after it is applied to an object by using any and all of the transformation commands on the Transform menu with the Patterns Only option selected. Don't go too crazy with this capability because it will haunt you when you print the image. Patterns, in general, can be difficult to image because they can be so complex. Therefore, a word of caution is in order.

- You can change the color of a pattern by dragging it out of the Swatches palette, editing the objects, and then dragging it in again under a new name.

- Although Illustrator 9 has no new pattern-specific features, the newfound capability to use transparency, blend modes, and opacity masking gives you a totally untapped source of new and exciting pattern effects.

Embossed Patterns

When you define a pattern with a no-stroke, no-fill pattern skeleton, the background of the pattern is transparent. Having such a background allows you to create effects such as layering one pattern on top of another and making the pattern look embossed.

PROJECT 7.9 Jazz Band Is Coming

This project presents a fast poster that you can create from one of the guitar patterns from earlier in this chapter:

1. Create a new document in Illustrator.

2. Choose Window|Swatch Libraries|Other Library and select the GUITARPATTERNS.AI file from this book's CD-ROM.

3. Drag the Half-Drop Guitar pattern from the Swatches palette to the document.

4. Make three copies of the pattern tiles.

5. Decide what color you want the background to be. Drag the new background color swatch into the Swatches palette.

6. Select the guitars in one copy of the pattern (use the Group Select tool) and change their Fill to the background color (name it "BGK One"). Make another group of guitars a light tint of the background color (named "Light One") and make the third copy a darker shade of the background color (to keep the pattern subtle, I used a medium tone; name it "Dark One").

7. Drag each newly colored pattern group back into the Swatches palette and name it appropriately.

8. Create a poster-sized rectangle and fill it with the background color.

9. On a new layer, create another rectangle the same size on top of the first one. Set its Fill to the darkest pattern.

10. On another new layer, create a rectangle of the same size on top of the others. Set its Fill to the white or the lightest pattern. Don't worry right now that the new pattern is covering up the original. You'll fix that problem in a few moments.

11. Create a new layer. Make a final rectangle and fill it with the background color pattern. Again, the pattern is in the same location.

12. Lock all the layers except for the darkest pattern layer. Twirl down the layer arrow and select just the pattern-filled rectangle. Click on the radio button to select the object. Choose Object|Transform|Move. In the

dialog box, select the Patterns checkbox. Make sure that the Object checkbox is not selected. Enter "-2" in both the horizontal and vertical distance fields. Click on OK.

13. Lock all the layers except for the lightest pattern layer. Twirl down the layer arrow and select just the pattern-filled rectangle. Click on the radio button to select the object. Choose Object|Transform|Move. In the dialog box, select the Patterns checkbox. Make sure that the Object checkbox is not selected. Enter "+2" in both the horizontal and vertical distance fields. Click on OK.

14. If the dark layer looks too dark to you, unlock the layer and select the object. In the Opacity palette, reduce the opacity of the object.

15. Open the file JAZZBAND.AI from the enclosed CD-ROM. Create a new layer. Drag the contents into the poster file and position as you want. Figure 7.58 shows the final effect.

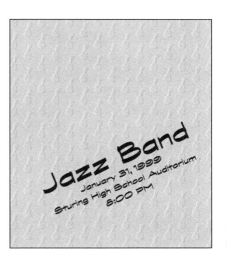

Figure 7.58
You can create an embossed look to patterns through layering.

You can also take your patterns into Photoshop, though you need to crop them before you save the tile for transfer (unless you apply the pattern in Illustrator and then bring the filled shape into Photoshop). Photoshop requires a rectangular tile and doesn't recognize Illustrator's convention of the transparent pattern skeleton. However, after you have the pattern in Photoshop, you can easily recolor it, use it with Apply modes, control the transparency, or filter it. In Photoshop, you can get an interesting embossed look by applying the Emboss filter to the pattern and then using Hard Light mode on the embossed layer to add texture to the layer beneath.

Shadows

The Jazz Band poster is a bit anemic and could use a bit of spice. Let's use some patterns in a slightly different way to jazz it up a bit.

Patterns to Photoshop

Another, perhaps faster, way to prepare a pattern tile for transfer to Photoshop is to bring the background "skeleton" rectangle to the front of the pattern unit and choose Make Mask. You can copy the masked rectangle into Photoshop. There's no need to crop the pattern if you make a mask.

PROJECT 7.10 Pattern Play—Adding Some Jazz

In this project, I'll show you how to create a pattern to be used as a shadow:

1. Drag the Light One pattern from your Swatches palette to the pasteboard area of the image. Ungroup (Shift+Command/Ctrl+G).

2. Create a new layer. Drag Layer 3 between Layers 1 and 2 in the Layers palette list. Lock Layers 1 and 2.

3. Drag one tiny light guitar to the center of your image. Press Shift+Option/Alt to resize the object from its center and maintain the aspect ratio. Make the guitar quite large and rotate it to a pleasing angle, as shown in Figure 7.59.

Figure 7.59
Enlarge the tiny guitar from the pattern to use it as a soft background element, and rotate it to work better in the design.

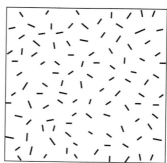

Figure 7.60
The original Confetti pattern (darkened).

4. You'll now create a patterned shadow for the guitar. Drag a copy of the Confetti pattern (one of the patterns in the GUITARPATTERS.AI library) from the Swatches palette onto the pasteboard of your image. Figure 7.60 shows the original pattern. It's very light—even lighter than the image shown in the figure because I felt that it wouldn't show up enough in print at its original weight.

5. Ungroup the pattern. The pattern consists of a number of straight lines and a pattern skeleton rectangle that's smaller than the combined shapes. Deselect. Select just the pattern skeleton. Look at the Fill and Stroke swatches on the Toolbox. The pattern skeleton rectangle has no Stroke, but it has a Fill of white. This means that it will also have an opaque white background, so it cannot be used, as it is currently, to texture an object. Change the Fill to None. Now, the pattern is transparent and can be applied over another color.

6. Select the entire pattern again and deselect the pattern skeleton. Only the short strokes in the pattern should be selected. Change the weight of the strokes to 3 points. Change the Fill color to a shade slightly darker than the one that you used on the Dark One pattern. Figure 7.61 shows the altered pattern.

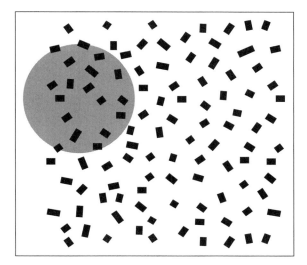

Figure 7.61
The "new" version of Confetti has thicker lines, a medium gray Fill, and is transparent (as you can see from the shape that I placed underneath for purposes of this figure—the base rectangle is not in your image).

7. Select the new pattern repeat and drag it onto the Swatches palette. Deselect. Name the pattern "Transparent Confetti".

8. Press Option/Alt and drag a copy of the large guitar to the left and slightly toward the top of the image. It will be your drop shadow. In the Layers palette, drag the sublayer for the shadow below the original guitar sublayer. Change the Fill to the Transparent Confetti pattern that you just created. Figure 7.62 shows the image.

Figure 7.62
You can use a transparent pattern as a shadow element.

9. The image still needs more pizzazz. Create a new layer above the current layers. Select the Rectangle tool and drag a wider-than-it-is-high rectangle across the center of the image. Use the Rotate tool to interactively rotate it so that the right end is higher than the left. Figure 7.63 shows my rotated rectangle.

Figure 7.63
Add a rotated rectangle to the image.

10. You should have two tiny guitars "left over" from the pattern that you dragged onto the pasteboard. Change the Fill color of one of them to the same color that you used in the Transparent Confetti pattern. Don't enlarge the size of the tiny guitar. Drag the recolored guitar to the Brushes palette. Define it as a Pattern brush. Click on OK.

11. Select the rotated rectangle and, with the Stroke as the active Toolbox swatch, click on the guitar Pattern brush to apply it to the rectangle. I think that the guitars need to be smaller and spaced farther apart. Double-click on the guitar Pattern brush in the Brushes palette to reopen the Brush Options dialog box. Change the Scale to 70% and Spacing to 10% (to leave a bit more room between elements). Click on OK. When asked, click on Apply To Strokes.

12. As a final task, you need to mask out the corners of the guitar-stroked rectangle. The rotated rectangle is likely to extend over the edge of your image. Although the pieces near the page boundary might not print, and the areas outside the boundary definitely won't print, it's a good idea to control things so that only what you really want to print shows up on the page. Anything that falls within the page margin will definitely print.

Make Layer 1 (the bottom layer) active. Choose Duplicate Layer 1 from the side drop-down menu on the Layers palette. Drag the new layer to the top of the stack.

13. Select the background rectangle on the top layer and change its Fill and Stroke to None.

14. Lock all layers except for the top layer and the guitar pattern brush rectangle. Make a mask (Object|Masks|Make; Command/Ctrl+7). Figure 7.64 shows the finished poster.

Figure 7.64
The jazzed-up Jazz Band poster.

Textures: Splotches, Spatters, and Spots

You can also create random splotches, spatters, and dot textures (and any other type of texture that you dream up) in Illustrator. The following sections show you how to do this.

Creating Random Textures

The confetti pattern that you used in the Jazz Band Shadow project is a good example of a texture. It certainly fits the definition that you were given at the start of this chapter.

You can add wonderful subtlety to your images by applying either a pattern or a texture with a transparent background over an object—especially if you keep the color of the texture close to the value of the object (the closer it is in value, the more subtle the effect). You can add flair to your image by controlling where the shapes contain texture. Figure 7.65 shows an example using simple shapes.

Texture

Texture consists of a series of nonrepresentational motifs that repeat at regular and predictable intervals along an invisible grid (but are arranged in a way that looks totally random). You cannot easily distinguish where each repeat begins or ends in a properly done texture. In addition, a true texture has no distinguishing feature that would allow you to locate the motif from which it is constructed.

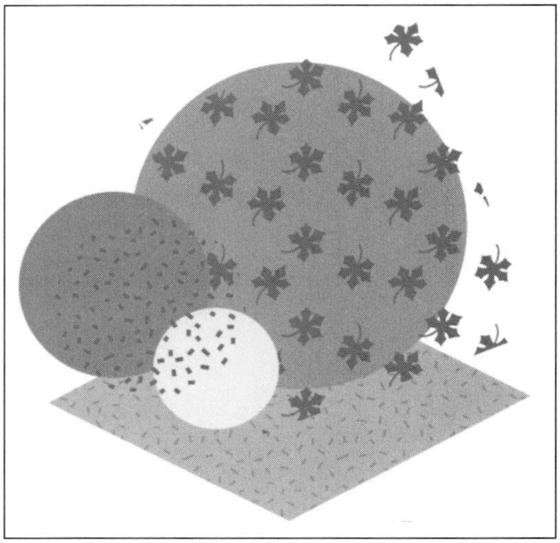

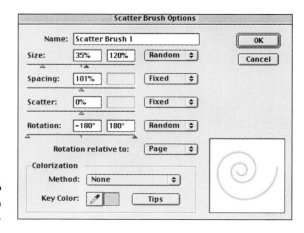

Figure 7.65

A simple composition is enhanced by the use of texture that doesn't quite conform to the confines of the main shapes.

 A Random Stroll

7.11 Project 7.11 shows how to create a randomly spaced texture that tiles seamlessly:

1. Create a new document in Illustrator.

2. Select a Stroke of light blue (or whatever color you want) and a Fill of None.

3. Choose the Spiral tool. Click in your image to open the Spiral Tool Options dialog box. Enter a radius of .25-inch and click on OK.

4. Select the spiral and drag it to the Brushes palette. Click on New Scatter Brush. Complete the dialog box as shown in Figure 7.66. Click on OK. Deselect.

Figure 7.66

Use these settings to create a new Scatter brush.

5. Select the Paintbrush tool. Click on the spiral Scatter brush to select it. Draw a curvy path as shown in Figure 7.67.

Figure 7.67
Because of the random settings, you have many different sizes and angles of spirals when you paint a curvy line.

6. With the brush stroke selected, choose Object|Expand and expand the object. Ungroup (Shift+Command/Ctrl+G).

7. Select just the skeleton stroke and delete it. You are left with a wide choice of sizes and angles for the spiral motif.

8. Choose the Rectangle tool. Select a Fill and Stroke of None. Click in your image and enter a width and height of 2 inches in the Rectangle Tool Options dialog box. Click on OK.

9. Toggle Outline mode on (Command+/Ctrl+Y).

10. Drag some of the spirals onto the rectangle so that they intersect the left and top edges only. Don't cover any corners. Figure 7.68 shows my developing texture.

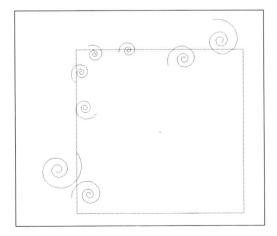

Figure 7.68
Place spiral motifs over the top and left sides of the rectangle so that they intersect the rectangle but don't cover any corners.

11. Turn on Smart Guides (Command/Ctrl+U). Select the entire texture-in-progress. Press Option/Alt and drag the objects to the right from the left side of the rectangle (press Shift after you begin to drag to constrain movement to the horizontal) until the word "intersect" appears as you drag over the right side of the original rectangle.

12. Select both rectangles and their spirals. Repeat Step 11, dragging a copy of the assembly down from the top of the rectangle until the copy intersects the bottom of the original rectangle. Figure 7.69 shows the four rectangles and their spirals.

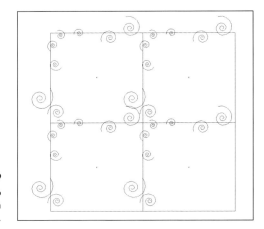

Figure 7.69

Copy the texture in progress to the right and then to the bottom of the original unit.

Using Layers

You may find this technique easier: You can make a new layer that contains the original set of spirals and drag the entire layer to the edges of the pattern to test the seams.

Random Texture Design

If you have trouble visualizing how the pattern will tile, turn on Smart Guides and drag a copy of the tile to the right; then drag both repeat units down so that you can preview the tiling behavior.

---

13. Turn off Smart Guides (Command/Ctrl+U). Delete the three copied rectangles. Move the extra spirals that don't cover the edges of the original rectangle into the center of the rectangle. Scatter them randomly but try to space them so that they don't bunch up. *Don't move any spiral that touches an edge and don't place any of the new spirals over an edge.* Following this key rule allows your pattern to tile seamlessly. You can place anything else anywhere within the rectangle, but the edges are sacred. If you have trouble, select the pattern skeleton and the edge spirals and lock them. That way, you cannot move them accidentally. Figure 7.70 shows my texture. Notice that the bottom-right corner shows two edge spirals that overlap.

14. You need to fix the spirals because no other pairs of spirals overlap, and allowing it to remain would create a break in the texture. However, the top and bottom edges of the rectangle are matched pairs. They need to remain identical. The solution is to select the *matching* spiral along opposite edges. Figure 7.71 shows the improved spacing achieved by moving *pairs* of edge spirals.

15. Select the pattern skeleton. Send it to the back.

16. Select the spirals and the pattern skeleton. Drag the texture into the Swatches palette. Deselect. Select and drag the original repeat unit to the pasteboard. Create a test pattern rectangle and fill it with your texture. Figure 7.72 shows the texture tiled.

Figure 7.70

(Left) The almost-completed texture has a problem of two overlapping edge spirals.

Figure 7.71

(Right) Fix the spacing of your spirals if necessary by moving pairs of edge spirals. Adjust the inner spirals because you want to compensate for the edge changes.

Figure 7.72

The spirals form a random texture.

The Photo Crosshatch Filter

Adobe's marketing literature for Illustrator 8 touted the then-new Photo Crosshatch filter (first introduced in version 8) as an easy way to create *Wall Street Journal*-type graphics. Certainly, the *Wall Street Journal* is known for its wonderful textured line drawings. The crosshatched patterns show the image detail and value through the weight and spacing of the lines. That's what the Photo Crosshatch filter is also supposed to do.

I'm sure you just caught the word *supposed*. In theory, the filter takes a continuous-tone photo and uses the values in the image as a basis for creating a textured line drawing. Okay, it actually does precisely that. I'm just not very happy with the usual result. The Photo Crosshatch filter is easy to use but diabolically difficult to make look good. The default settings on the filter produce marginal to unsatisfactory results.

You can find other ways to make the filter yield decent results. I have. The next project presents the results of my exploration.

The problem with the filter, oddly enough, is that it almost gives you too many choices. It's powerful but slow to apply, and complex images take a long time to redraw (the filter is also prone to the same printing ghoulies as the Pen And Ink filter). Because the best way to discover optimal settings is to experiment, you need a lot of time and patience to get good results. The Photo Crosshatch filter actually changes the bitmapped image into a vector drawing. Each line created by the Photo Crosshatch filter is a separate object. You end up with so many objects that you cannot see the image with all of them selected.

Before you start the project, I want to show how some simple cleanup in Photoshop can vastly improve even the default settings. Figure 7.73 shows a photograph taken by a friend several years ago in Frankfurt, Germany. Figure 7.74 shows the same scene with the Photo Crosshatch filter applied in Illustrator using the default settings (which you'll see shortly) and five layers. Notice that the sky posterizes badly (and the electric wires don't add anything to the scene, either). Figure 7.75 shows the same settings in Illustrator after I cleaned up the image in Photoshop to fill the sky with solid color.

You can get more abstract looks with the Photo Crosshatch filter, but the longer the lines you use, the less detail you see. Figure 7.76 shows the Frankfurt scene heavily edited and posterized in Photoshop (actually, I practically redrew the scene in order to control the values in the buildings). Figure 7.77 shows a finished image from Illustrator using longer line settings than the default and changing the angles of the lines.

Figure 7.73
A street scene in Frankfurt.

Figure 7.74
The default settings in the Photo Crosshatch filter are applied in five layers to the Frankfurt street scene.

Figure 7.75
I reused the default settings to the Frankfurt street scene but made the sky a solid color in Photoshop before I reapplied the filter.

Figure 7.76
A posterized and redrawn Frankfurt street scene.

Figure 7.77
The Photo Crosshatch filter with a border added.

To use the Photo Crosshatch filter, place a raster image into Illustrator and select it. Then, choose Filter|Pen and Ink|Photo Crosshatch. The dialog box shown in Figure 7.78 appears. It also shows the default values (unless, of course, you changed them during a previous session).

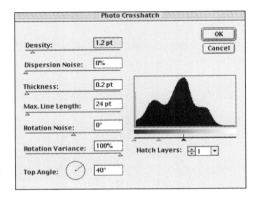

Figure 7.78
You get these default values for the Photo Crosshatch filter.

The following is a brief explanation of how the filter works:

- According to Illustrator's manual, the Density slider adjusts the number of hatch elements applied to the image, from .5 point to 10 points. A more useful explanation of density is that this setting controls the amount of coverage that you get from the filter. A low-density setting (.5) results in a heavy coverage that nearly obscures the shape. At a setting of 10 points, the hatch elements are far apart.

- The Illustrator manual states that the Dispersion Noise setting controls the spacing of hatch elements (0% to 300%). It does, but not in the same way that the density does. The Dispersion Noise setting controls the variance in the spaces between the hatch elements. The higher the Dispersion Noise setting, the more random-looking the lines become. Although they keep the same angle (if you don't change the angle setting), they are scattered about the object.

- Thickness controls the stroke weight of the hatch elements (minimum: .1 point, maximum: 10 points).

- You can set the Max. Line Length of the hatch elements (5 points to 999 points). You'll see more detail with a shorter line length.

- Rotation Noise sets the amount of random rotation of objects within the hatch layers, from –360 degrees to 360 degrees.

- Rotation Variance sets the amount that each layer is rotated from the previous layer, from 0% to 100%.

- Top Angle sets the angle of rotation for the topmost hatch layer, from –360 degrees to 360 degrees.

Posterizing in Photoshop

When you posterize an image in Photoshop, you'll almost always have some white in the final image. Areas of solid white jump out at you when you apply the Photo Crosshatch filter. If you don't want to see the sharp tonal variations, make sure that you put a light (but not white) color into your image in the white areas before you save it and place it in Illustrator. If the image has at least a 10-percent area of color, you can change the histogram in the Photo Crosshatch filter so that all the areas in the image contain some tone.

It's time for you to try out the filter. The image that you'll use is an old photograph of the mother of a friend. This image is a good choice because it has simple lines and a reasonable range of values.

PROJECT 7.12 Crosshatching Photos

In this project, I'll show how to create your own crosshatched photo:

1. Create a new document in Illustrator. Place the image RITASMUM.PSD from the enclosed CD-ROM. Figure 7.79 shows the original photograph.

Figure 7.79
A photograph taken in the 1930s is the basis for the Photo Crosshatch filter.

2. Choose Filter|Pen and Ink|Photo Crosshatch. Accept the defaults and click on OK. Except for the lightest areas of the image, the entire image is covered in a uniform mass (or mess) of lines. Undo. Try it again with five layers—that's better. Undo. Figure 7.80 shows the image with one layer and the default settings, and Figure 7.81 shows it with five layers and the default settings.

Figure 7.80
(Left) Default settings, one layer.

Figure 7.81
(Right) Default settings, five layers.

3. Try it *again*. This time, enter the settings shown in Figure 7.82. All the settings, except for Rotation Variance and Top Angle, have been modified. This image is much more successful, as you can see in Figure 7.83.

Figure 7.82

(Left) New settings for the Photo Crosshatch filter.

Figure 7.83

(Right) These settings produce a nicely shaded image that resembles a mezzotint because of the short line length and reduced density.

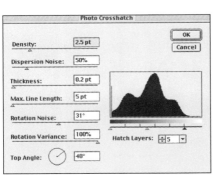

4. Undo and then apply the filter again. This time, choose a line length of 100 points. Figure 7.84 shows the enormous difference that this change causes in the image. The line length reduces the image detail, but for a different image, it could produce an appropriate and exciting effect.

Figure 7.84

Changing the line length to 100 points reduces the detail in the image.

5. You can also help the Photo Crosshatch filter find the correct values in the locations where you want them by posterizing the photograph in Photoshop before you place it in Illustrator. Delete the placed file RITASMUM. Instead, place your Illustrator image 5TONE.PSD. It is the same image, but it's posterized by Photoshop into five values and then

reworked a bit. Experiment with a variety of settings on this image as well. When you posterize an image, it loses detail. Because of the loss of detail, the image becomes a perfect candidate for abstract and stylized treatments.

Figure 7.85 shows the finished image that I created using the 5TONE.PSD version of the photograph. I used the settings shown in Figure 7.86 to filter the posterized photo. I then locked the layer, created a new one beneath it, and placed the 5TONE photo again. I adjusted the colors in the photo by using the Filter|Colors|Adjust Colors filter to remove 50 percent of the black. I then locked that layer and created another new one below it. I filled the layer with a dark brown and turned it into a three-by-three Gradient Mesh object with 70% Highlight To Edge. I added a no-stroke, no-fill rectangle around it to give it some growing room, selected both rectangles, and rasterized them. I unlocked Layer 2 (the photo) and applied the Auto F/X Photo/Graphic Edges filter to both raster objects at the same time. The edge treatments in the Photo/Graphic Edges filter are wonderful and add so much to an image. The filter is among my favorites. I also used a smaller version of the filtered layer as an opacity mask for the main image (I had to take this image into Photoshop to prepare and color it black).

Figure 7.85
The 5TONE photo is used as a basis for this image, which is finished off with an edge treatment from Auto F/F applied to a rasterize Gradient Mesh object and then used as a border and as an opacity mask.

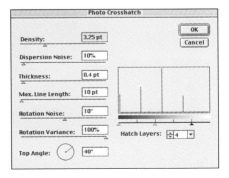

Figure 7.86
The Photo Crosshatch filter settings used.

Moving On

You learned several different techniques in this chapter for creating and using patterns and textures. You can create rectangular, half-drop, and brick repeats and make diaper patterns. You also learned how to create patterns that interlock and how to apply them to a path using a Pattern brush. Now, you can even create interlocking geometric patterns, such as ogee forms.

You also learned how to create seamless, seemingly random textures, and you learned to use the new Photo Crosshatch filter. You also learned some tricks about that filter.

We've played only with simple, one-motif patterns, but you can combine multiple motifs to create ever more complex and interesting patterns. You can, for example, combine multiple motifs in the diaper pattern that you created or color each spiral in the texture differently (as long as the edge spirals match) to form a seamless pattern. I hope that I also managed to communicate my love for pattern and the excitement that it generates.

In Chapter 8, you'll learn about the many uses of gradients, blends, and meshes.

Chapter 8

Gradients, Blends, and Meshes

Illustrator contains such a wealth of color gradation tools that you never need to settle for flat just because you're using an illustration program. This chapter looks at the variety of techniques at your disposal.

By Sherry London

A Short Introduction

You can use blends, gradients, and gradient mesh objects to add glowing color and depth to your Illustrator projects. I could say a huge amount about each of these topics in this chapter, but space limitations prevent it (we can't publish the *Encyclopedia Illustratannica* here). To cover everything would require at least another book! Therefore, I need to keep this chapter brief (you do, after all, want to learn more about Illustrator than how to make blends and gradients). In most of my chapters, I have tried to give you complete projects. In this chapter, however, you will simply work with several pieces of projects (with a few full projects interspersed). In this way, I should be able to cover more effects using blends, gradients, and gradient mesh objects.

Blends

In the beginning, there were blends. Using a blend, you could change colors from shape A through shape B. Illustrator had no gradients in its earliest incarnations. To simulate gradients, you had to blend from one rectangle to another and then mask the result to get it into the shape that you wanted. Times have changed.

The blends have also changed. The live blend was introduced in version 8. Live blends allow you to change the way the shape blends after you apply the blend. Version 9 adds no new features that change the structure of the blends, but you can now add transparency to the blends and use a blend as an opacity mask.

Basic Blends

Because this is an intermediate-to-advanced-level f/x book, I really don't want to cover very much that you can just as easily find in the Illustrator manual or the online help. However, I'll quickly review some of the most basic operations here.

The Fundamentals

You can use the Blend tool to create intermediate objects from two objects. The objects are blended by color and by shape so that you can change a black square into a gray circle, for example. You can control the number of steps in the blend so that you can blend smoothly (as in Figure 8.1) or do it in discrete steps (as in Figure 8.2).

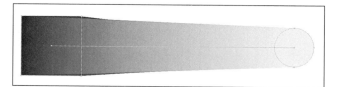

Figure 8.1
You can create a smooth blend between two differently shaped and colored objects.

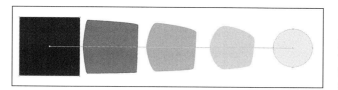

Figure 8.2
You can create a stepped blend between two differently shaped and colored objects.

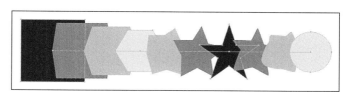

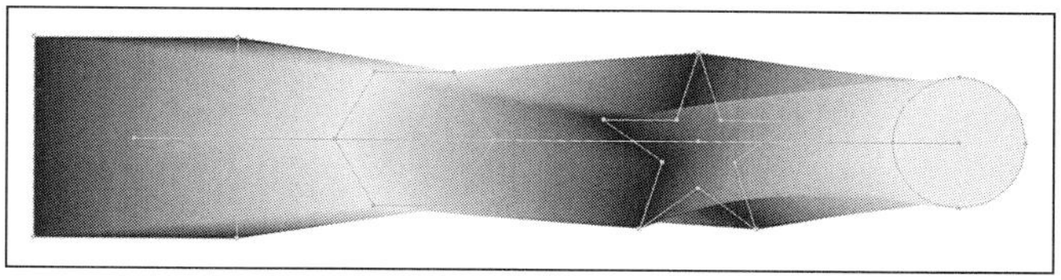

Figure 8.3
You can create a smooth blend between multiple differently shaped and colored objects.

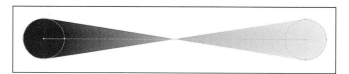

Figure 8.4
You can create a stepped blend between multiple differently shaped and colored objects.

You can also blend multiple objects together smoothly (as shown in Figure 8.3) or in discrete steps (as shown in Figure 8.4).

You can edit the starting or ending shapes in the blend and select the point on each object from which to blend. The starting point for the blend is significant because it affects the shape of the finished blend. For example, two circles blended from their top points look like Figure 8.5, whereas the same two circles blended from the top point on circle 1 to the bottom point on circle 2 look like Figure 8.6, where the blend shrinks to nothing and then thickens again.

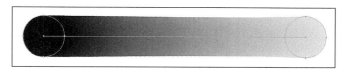

Figure 8.5
You need to carefully select the points to blend. These two circles are blended from their top points, resulting in a smooth blend.

Figure 8.6
This blend moves from the top point on circle 1 to the bottom point on circle 2.

Because the blends are now "live" (you can see the line between the starting and ending shapes on any of the figures shown so far), you can change the blended objects without having to re-create the blend. You can use the Direct Selection tool or the Group Selection tool to choose one of the blend participants. You can then change the object's color or shape.

If you blend between two stroked objects, the Stroke color, as you can see in Figure 8.7, is blended as well. If you try to blend between two patterned objects, Illustrator gets confused and is not able to produce the blend, as you can see in Figure 8.8. However, if you blend between a solid object and a gradient, Illustrator does a much better job.

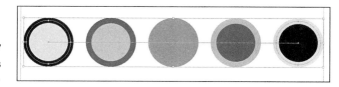

Figure 8.7
You can blend strokes as well as fills.

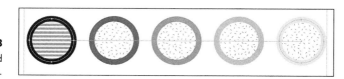

Figure 8.8
Blends between two patterned objects are not very successful.

Of course, most blends don't occur in a straight line. Before the gradient mesh objects debuted in Illustrator 8, a blend was the only way to create chiaroscuro (realistic highlights and shadows) on an object. Using a blend, you can put the shine on an apple—a very primitive example of which shows up in Figure 8.9. By making the blend 75 percent opaque, you can control the intensity of the colors.

Figure 8.9
By creating a blend whose ending shape is on top of the starting shape, you can create a highlight in an object.

The Spine Switch

One of the more interesting (if possibly less-than-useful) things that you can do with a blend is to change the shape of its *spine*. This line connects the shapes in the blend. Try this short project just for fun.

PROJECT 8.1 New Vertebrae

This project shows you what happens when you change the shape of the spine that controls a blend.

1. Create a new document in Illustrator.

2. Change your Fill to None and your Stroke color to yellow. Select the Ellipse tool. Click once near the upper-left corner of the image. Enter 1.5 inches in the height and width fields in the dialog box.

3. Press Option/Alt and drag a duplicate of the circle to the top-right edge of the document directly across from the original, as shown in Figure 8.10. Press Shift after you begin to drag to constrain movement to the horizontal. Change the Stroke color to purple.

Figure 8.10
Two circles waiting to be blended.

4. Select the entire image (Command/Ctrl+A).

5. Choose the Blend tool. Click on the control point at the top of the yellow circle; then click on the control point at the top of the purple circle. A straight, smooth blend appears.

6. Choose Object|Blends|Blend Options and select Specified Steps in the Spacing pop-down. Enter "45" as the number of desired steps, as shown in Figure 8.11. Now, the blend consists of interlocked circles.

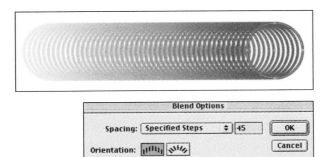

Figure 8.11
You can create a specific number of objects in a blend.

Ways to Get Smooth Points

You can also use the Convert Point tool and drag handles out of the end nodes of the spine. If you do, all points that you add to the line are automatically smooth points (because you made the spine into a curved path).

7. After you create the blend, you can change the shape of the spine. One way to do so is to edit the spine itself. Deselect the blend. Choose the Direct Selection tool. Click approximately on the center of the blend to select only the spine.

8. Choose the Pen tool. Use the Pen tool to add control points to the spine, and then use the Direct Selection tool (or the Pen tool with Command/Ctrl pressed) to move the control points. You can use the Pen tool (with Alt/Option pressed) to change the corner points that you added into smooth points. Figure 8.12 shows the slinky that results.

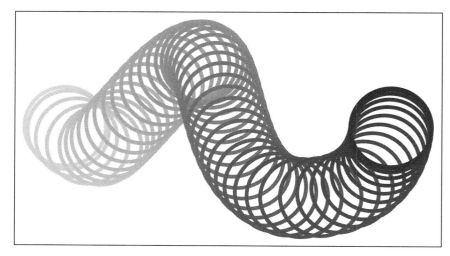

Figure 8.12
You can change the tube into a slinky by adding and manipulating the control points along the spine of the blend.

9. You can also create an object in isolation and replace the original blend spine with it. To perform this process, select the Spiral tool. Click once inside the drawing area. In the dialog box that appears, enter a Radius of 1 inch, a Decay of 80%, and 10 segments. Then, select the top Style radio button, as shown in Figure 8.13.

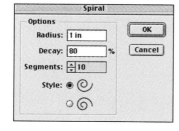

Figure 8.13
The Spiral tool options dialog box.

10. Select the entire image, which is the blend and the spiral (Command/Ctrl+A). Choose Object|Blends|Replace Spine. Figure 8.14 shows the result.

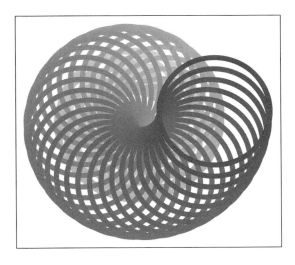

Figure 8.14
When you replace a linear spine with a spiral, the entire blend curls up on itself.

11. You can coax this blend into a snail-shell shape. To start, deselect the blend. Select just the purple circle with the Group Selection tool. Double-click on the Scale tool and enter a Uniform value of 30% in the dialog box. Click on OK. Figure 8.15 shows what happens.

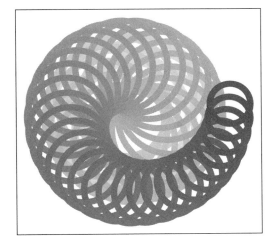

Figure 8.15
Now, you have a curl.

12. With the blend selected, choose Object|Blends|Reverse Front To Back. As you can see in Figure 8.16, you can almost picture the little snail inside.

13. You can also reverse the direction of the blend. To do so, choose Object|Blends|Reverse Spine. Now, you have a seashell (see Figure 8.17).

14. If you need to "set" the blend so that it is no longer live, or if you want to manipulate any of the objects that the blend has created, you can select the Object|Blends|Expand command. Try it.

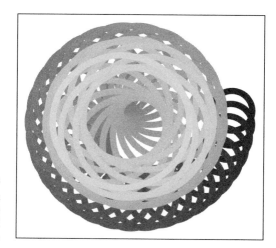

Figure 8.16
Switching the front-to-back orientation of the blend makes the spiral blend resemble a snail in its shell.

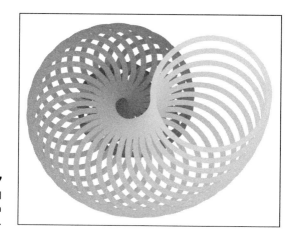

Figure 8.17
You can create a conch shell by reversing the direction of the blend.

Stroke Blends

Although you might normally associate the Blend command with filled shapes, as you saw in the "New Vertebrae" project, you can also blend strokes. In the first project, you used stroked, closed objects. In Project 8.2, you'll use open paths. In Project 8.3, you'll blend shapes that contain multiple strokes.

Weaves

You can use stroked line blends to mimic grids and woven goods. The following project is a fast example—and I'm not even going to attempt to suggest a "real world" use for it.

PROJECT 8.2 Waffle Weave

Follow these steps to experiment with stroked line blends:

1. Open a new document in Illustrator.

2. Turn on the Rulers (Command/Ctrl+R). Drag a guide to the 4-inch mark and another guide to the 8-inch mark along the side ruler. Create vertical guides at the 2- and the 6-inch marks on the top ruler.

3. Select the Pen tool. Click at the top-left intersection of the guides, press Shift, and click at the top-right intersection of the guides. The result is a perfectly straight line. Set the Fill to None and the Stroke color to green, and then set the Stroke weight to 6 points.

4. Press Option/Alt and drag a duplicate of the stroke to the lower horizontal guide. Press Shift after you begin to drag to constrain movement to the vertical. Change the Stroke color for the duplicated line to yellow.

5. Select both lines and choose the Blend tool. Click in the leftmost point of both lines to set the blend points.

6. Choose Object|Blends|Blend Options and set the Specified Steps Spacing option to 20. Click on OK. Figure 8.18 shows the venetian blind effect that results.

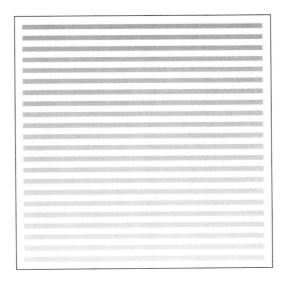

Figure 8.18
When you blend one straight line into another in specified steps, you can create venetian blinds that show a gradation of color.

7. With the blend selected, double-click on the Rotate tool. Enter 90 degrees as the Angle of rotation and click on Copy. Figure 8.19 shows the resulting waffle weave.

8. You can do the same thing with wavy dashed lines (and if you rotate the final result and mask it, you can make a graduated square). To start, open a new document in Illustrator.

9. Use the Pencil tool to create a wavy green stroke that is 6 points wide. In the Stroke palette, select the Dashed Line checkbox and enter 12 points, 8 points, 6 points, and 4 points, respectively, in the first four boxes, as shown in Figure 8.20.

10. Press Option/Alt and drag a duplicate of the stroke (press Shift after you begin to drag to constrain movement to the vertical) down about four inches. Change the color of the copied stroke to gold.

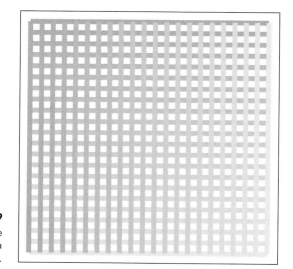

Figure 8.19
When you rotate a copy of the open blend, you can produce a fake weave.

Figure 8.20
Enter the dashes and spaces as shown.

11. Select both lines and click on the leftmost point of each line with the Blend tool. Figure 8.21 shows the blend. The white spaces in the blend are caused by the dashed line.

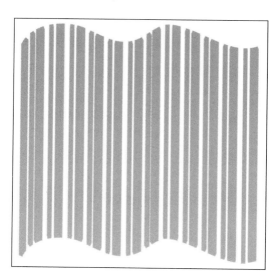

Figure 8.21
Blending two dashed lines yields stripes.

This technique has some intriguing possibilities. Try creating a blended dashed line with a spiral spine. Try overlapping the objects. Try placing various colored or gradated backgrounds behind the weaves.

Concentric Star Strokes

If you apply one of the new styles that contain a multiple stroke to two objects, you can create a shape blend between them. This technique is quite effective when you use it on concentric objects. Try this project to see how it works.

PROJECT 8.3   Stars within Stars

In this project, you'll create two stars, apply the same stroked style to both of them, and blend to create additional copies of the stars.

1. Create a new image in Illustrator.

2. Choose the Star tool (it's in the Ellipse tool slot). Set the star so that it draws the desired number of points (I used a 5-pointed star).

3. Turn on the Rulers (Command/Ctrl+R).

4. Drag a horizontal and vertical guide into the approximate center of your image.

5. Place your cursor at the intersection of the two guides. Press Option/Alt and then Shift to create a star from the center and constrain its orientation. Make the star as large as you can.

6. Repeat Step 5 but make the star fairly small this time.

7. Select the entire image (Command/Ctrl+A). Apply the Black-Red Dashes style that comes installed in the Illustrator Style palette.

8. Choose Object|Blend|Blend Options and set a Specified Step of 3. Click on OK. Then, choose Object|Blend|Make. Figure 8.22 shows the result.

> **About Specified Step Blends**
>
> When you specify a number of steps, you get that number of steps even if you don't have enough room for each step. You can use this capability to your advantage. Leaving less room than needed to accommodate the number of steps gives you overlapped multiple strokes and, in the concentric technique that you just used, makes the shape look as if it is filled with dashed lines.

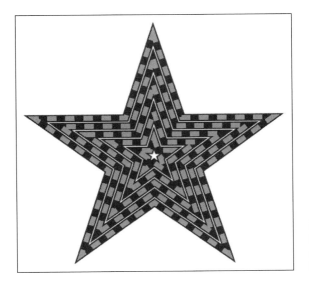

Figure 8.22
Create two objects and give them the same style, and then blend them.

The Great Ribbon Fantasy

One of my favorite tricks with linear blends is "The Great Ribbon Fantasy." This simple technique is the first technique that I ever learned for using blends, and it fascinated me when I saw it—probably in a Mac magazine—so many years ago in the days of Freehand 2 or 3.

As you can see throughout this book, anything that involves a lot of colors or looks tie-dyed appeals to the latent hippie in me. In any case, this technique is interesting and, with some additional new twists that I've not seen written about before, bears repeating.

PROJECT 8.4   Irregular Line Blends

In this project, you'll learn how to create two or more lines and blend them into one another to create a wavy, very dimensional ribbon.

1. Create a new document in Illustrator.

2. Using the Pencil tool with no Fill and a color that you like as the Stroke (I chose cyan), draw a very wavy line either straight across the page or at a diagonal. The line that I used is shown in Figure 8.23.

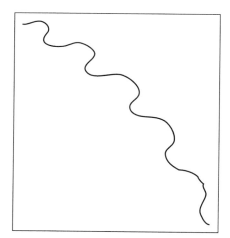

Figure 8.23
This figure shows the starting line for my ribbon fantasy.

3. Pick a different Stroke color and draw another wavy line, but make it very different from the first line. Figure 8.24 shows my second line.

4. Select both lines. Select Object|Blends|Blend Options and enter a Specified Steps Amount of 30. Click on OK. Choose the Blend tool and click on the left points on both lines. Figure 8.25 shows the result in grayscale, and you can see the color in the Illustrator 9 Studio. Also in the Illustrator 9 Studio is a second version of the image. This one is twisted out of shape by replacing the spine of the blend with a short, wavy line.

I could go on about the different effects you can get by changing the lines and changing the shape of the spine. However, as I prepared this image for

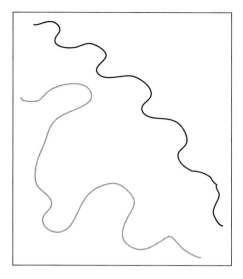

Figure 8.24
This figure shows both lines before the blend is created.

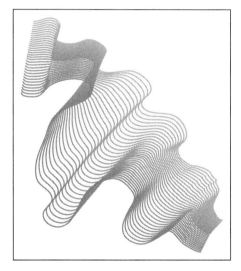

Figure 8.25
The Great Ribbon Fantasy.

publication, it occurred to me that this could be an interesting technique to use with clip art—to cut apart a simple shape and then blend the top line against the bottom one. I prepared two more short examples, using clip art from Ultimate Symbol's Nature Icons collection. The stylized shapes of the clip art in this collection work beautifully in the treatment that I have in mind.

PROJECT 8.5 Clip Art Blends

In this project, you'll learn how to cut apart a piece of clip art and apply a blend to the lines that define its structure.

1. Open the file ANGELFISH.AI from the this book's companion CD-ROM. Figure 8.26 shows the fish, which has already been split apart into the layers shown in Figure 8.27.

Figure 8.26
The Angel Fish from the Ultimate
Symbol's Nature Icons collection.

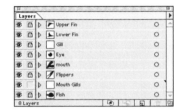

Figure 8.27
The Layers palette shows how I
have divided the fish into layers.

2. Hide all the layers except for the Fish layer. Swap the Fill and the Stroke so that the fish now has no Fill and a black Stroke.

3. Choose the Scissors tool. Click on the two points that are circled in Figure 8.28 to cut the fish apart.

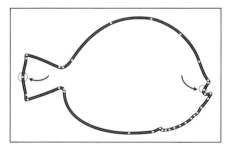

Figure 8.28
The arrows show the two circled
points on which to click to sever
the fish into two parts.

4. Deselect and then select the top half of the fish with the Selection tool. Change the Stroke color to orange. Press the up-arrow key several times to move the top half a bit away from the bottom half.

5. Select the bottom half of the fish and change its Stroke color to yellow.

6. Choose Object|Blends|Blend Options. Set the Specified Steps number to 30. Click on OK.

7. Select both lines that make up the fish. With the Blend tool, click on the leftmost endpoints of the two lines. Figure 8.29 shows the result.

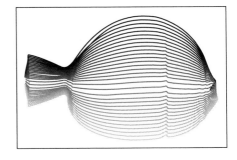

Figure 8.29
The blended lines re-form the body of the fish.

8. Turn on all the layers. You'll notice that the objects on the Gill and Mouth Gills layers are white, which doesn't show up too well. (Forgive me, by the way, if I am verbally mutilating fish anatomy. Biology was never my thing.) Select the objects on both those layers and change the Fill to a more appropriate color. Black is fine; orange or yellow should work as well.

9. Select the fin on the Upper Fin layer and lock all the other layers.

10. Swap the Stroke and Fill colors on the fin so that it has no Fill and a black Stroke.

11. Select the Scissors tool. Click on the leftmost of the two circled points on Figure 8.30 with the Scissors tool. Then, click on the circled point on the right (the two arrows make these points easier to find). Delete the selected line at the bottom of the fin. You'll need to press Delete twice.

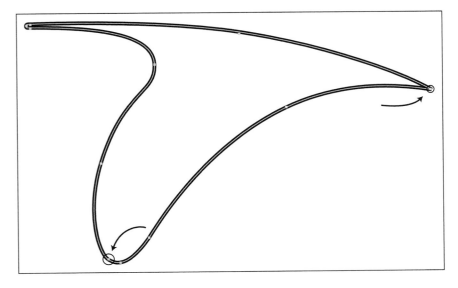

Figure 8.30
Use the Scissors tool to "fin-tune" the fish.

12. With the Scissors tool, click on the point that is at the tip of the fin (where the two "arms" come together).

13. Deselect. With the Selection tool, select the upper line and press the up-arrow key twice to move the top fin far enough away to be able to select both points.

14. Select both lines. With the Blend tool, click on the two points at what was originally the sharp tip of the fin.

15. Deselect the blend. With the Group Selection tool, click on the top line (the one that you moved). Press the down-arrow key twice to move it back into its original place. Figure 8.31 shows the fish with all its layers turned on. You can also see it in color in the Illustrator 9 Studio. The color Illustrator 9 Studio also shows a variation of the fish created in the same way. The difference is that I did not separate the objects on the Mouth Gills and Flippers layers from the original fish body, so I got a dramatically different blend.

Figure 8.31
The finished Angel Fish.

16. You can blend more than two lines at a time. To see how, open the SEAHORSE.AI image, which is another image in Ultimate Symbol's Nature Icons collection. As I did with the Angel Fish image, I cut the original shape into component parts and put each part (only three here) on its own layer.

17. Keep only the Seahorse layer visible. Swap the Stroke and the Fill on the seahorse so that it has a black Stroke and a Fill of None.

18. With the Scissors tool, cut the seahorse at the tip of its tail and the center of its snout (in both cases, no control points exist; you need to click on the stroke itself).

19. Choose Object|Blends|Blend Options and set the Specified Steps number to 4. For this technique, you need six paths in total. The Specified Steps number counts the *extra* paths to add. Click on OK.

20. Move one of the paths a little bit away from the other one so that you can find the endpoint on which to click. Select both paths. With the Blend tool, click on the two endpoints that are on the seahorse's snout. You should end up with six lines, as shown in Figure 8.32.

Figure 8.32
Blending the two main lines on the seahorse with a Specified Step amount of four yields a total of six lines.

21. Choose Object|Blends|Expand. Ungroup (Shift+Command, Mac; Ctrl+G, Windows) and then deselect.

22. Start with the leftmost path by selecting it. Change its stroke to red-orange. Change the remaining paths (in left-to-right order) to yellow, green, cyan, purple, and hot pink. You have made a color wheel of the strokes.

23. Select the entire image (Command/Ctrl+A). With the Blend tool, carefully click on the endpoint of each path near the seahorse's snout—from the red-orange to the yellow, green, cyan, purple, and hot-pink paths. The Blend tool turns black and shows a plus sign (+) when it is over a path. You will need to wait for the blend to be calculated as you click on each path.

24. If you have more than four paths between each of your six colors, choose Object|Blends|Blend Options and fix the number of Specified Steps.

25. Choose Object|Blends|Reverse Front To Back. Figure 8.33 shows the rainbow result in a grayscale rainbow; you can see a color version in the color Illustrator 9 Studio.

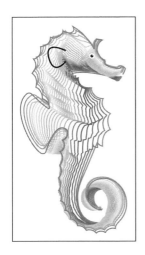

Figure 8.33
The rainbow seahorse in grayscale—with four blends between each color line.

Gonna Build a Mountain

You can use linear blends to create scenery. I can picture this technique being used with the stylized clouds, mountains, and seas of traditional Chinese art, but in the "Linear Landscapes" project, I'll demonstrate it in a form more suited to a science fiction or fantasy project. You can build a mountain from a single line.

Linear Landscapes

8.6 This project shows you how to blend lines to simulate a filled shape.

1. Create a new document in Illustrator.

2. You need to draw a line to define the top of the mountain first. Use the Pencil tool to create an irregular line. Give it a Fill of None and a Stroke of at least 5. For now, the color doesn't matter (as long as it isn't white). Figure 8.34 shows my starting line.

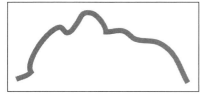

Figure 8.34
This line will become the top of a mountain.

3. Choose the Selection tool. Press Option/Alt and drag a duplicate of the stroke toward the bottom of the image, as far down on the page as you want your mountain to be high.

4. Press Option/Alt and use the center control handles on the top and sides of the bounding box to flatten and widen the stroke to form the base of the mountain. Figure 8.35 shows the two lines.

Figure 8.35
The bottom line is a flattened and widened version of the first line.

5. Choose Object|Blends|Blend Options and set the Specified Steps number to between 3 and 7 (your choice). Select the entire image (Command/Ctrl+A); both lines will be selected. With the Blend tool, click on the leftmost endpoints of top and bottom lines to create a stepped blend. Figure 8.36 shows the five intermediate steps that I created.

Figure 8.36
This blend has five intermediate steps.

6. Choose Object|Blends|Expand to free the seven lines from one another. Ungroup (Shift+Command/Ctrl+G) and then deselect.

7. You can now rearrange the lines as you wish—to get a less even blend than would otherwise occur. Your next step will be to color the lines and reblend them smoothly to form the mountain. Now is your chance to redecorate. You can remove some of the lines, widen or shorten the space between them, or stretch or shorten some of the lines. The changes that you make here determine the shape of your mountain. I tossed away the bottom two intermediate lines, stretched the remaining lines, moved them, and duplicated the lowest line. Figure 8.37 shows the new arrangement before coloring and blending.

Figure 8.37

The altered structure lines for the mountain are ready to be re-colored and blended again.

8. Change the stroke color on the lines to create the coloring for the mountain. My choices are (starting at the top) a snowy gray-white, a pebbly gray dirt, golden pebbles and dirt, rich green trees, dark-green leaves, to golden dirt again.

9. Choose Object|Blends|Blend Options and set the Spacing to Smooth Color. Click on OK.

10. Select the entire image (Command/Ctrl+A). With the Blend tool, click on the leftmost endpoint of each line in turn to include it in the blend. Instant mountain! Figure 8.38 shows the result.

Water, Water, Everywhere

The next project shows you how to create a stylized Japanese-type wavy-water scene using identical wavy lines and a Specified Step blend. Because you already know how to do the "technical" aspects of the blend, I created most of

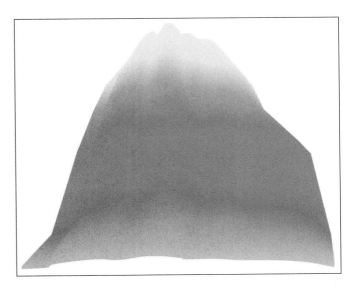

Figure 8.38
You have created a single mountain, and you can, with a bit of imagination, expand on it to create an entire landscape.

the pieces for you. After you work through this project, you can change the shape of the line, the gradient, or any other aspect of the image to see how the changes affect the final result. This project ties together all that you've learned in this section.

PROJECT 8.7 Creating Turtle Water

This example is mostly a blend-and-go project. Repeating multiple copies of the blended objects, masking the result, and placing it over a shaded background create the water effect.

1. Open the image TURTLES.AI from the this book's companion CD-ROM. Figure 8.39 shows the two lines that are visible when you open the file.

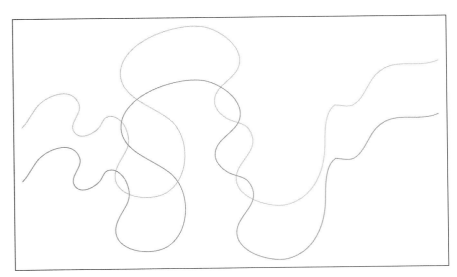

Figure 8.39
Wavy water lines are all that's visible when you open the file TURTLE.AI.

2. Choose Object|Blends|Blend Options and set the Specified Steps number to 9.

3. Select the entire image (Command/Ctrl+A).

4. Choose the Blend tool. Click on the leftmost endpoint of the top line to set the start of the blend. Click on the leftmost endpoint of the bottom line to end the blend. Figure 8.40 shows the blended lines.

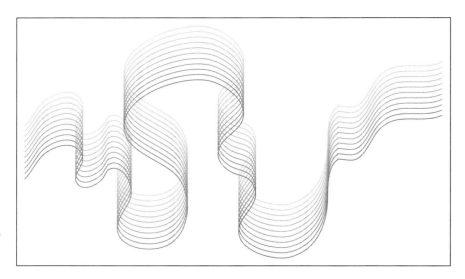

Figure 8.40
The wavy line makes a beautiful ribbon.

5. With the Selection tool, drag the blend up to the top of the page.

6. Press Option/Alt and drag a copy of the blend down directly under the first blend (press Shift after you begin to drag to constrain movement to the vertical). Leave as much space between the objects as there is space between the lines in the blend. Figure 8.41 shows the second blend in place.

7. Transform Again (Command/Ctrl+D) until the blend reaches the bottom of the image.

8. Turn on the Background layer by clicking in the first column in the Layers palette next to the entry for the Background layer. Don't remove the lock on the layer. The Background layer contains a gradient.

9. Delete any of the blends that fall totally outside the areas occupied by the background rectangle. I'm asking you to delete these blends to optimize print speed. There's no point in having the rip rasterize a blend, only to toss it away. Figure 8.42 shows the rectangle with the blends that fall on top of it.

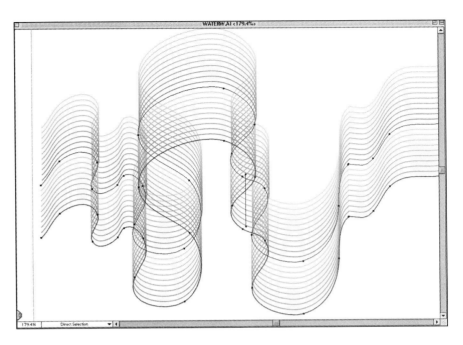

Figure 8.41

Drag a copy of the blend down so that it looks like a continuation of the original ribbon.

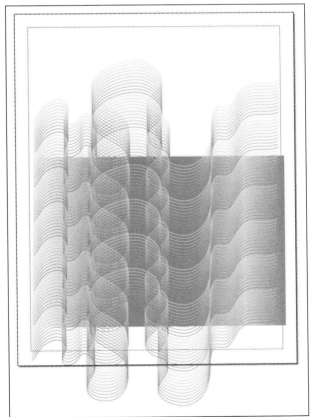

Figure 8.42

All the remaining blends overlap the gradient on the Background layer.

10. Select the Rectangle tool. Choose a Fill of None. The Stroke color (or whether there is a stroke) doesn't matter. Place your mouse cursor at the top-left corner of the Background layer gradient (though the Water layer is the active layer). Drag out a rectangle from the upper-left corner of the Background layer gradient to the lower-right corner, where the blends end. Figure 8.43 shows this rectangle stroked in a very wide black stroke so that you can see it.

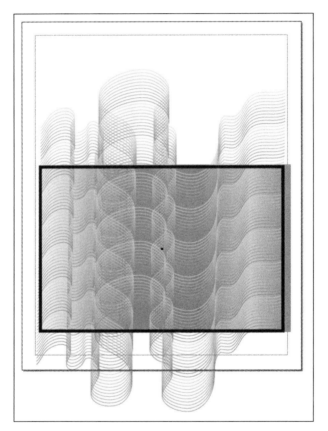

Figure 8.43
Draw a rectangle that will become a mask.

11. Select the entire image (Command/Ctrl+A). Because only the Water layer is unlocked, it will be the only layer selected. Make a mask (Object|Masks|Make; Command/Ctrl+7).

12. Lock the Water layer and make visible the remaining layers. Each of the turtles is on its own layer—two turtles are above the water and five are below it. In each turtle layer, you'll see a group within the group. This subgroup selects the lines on the turtle's back. Figure 8.44 shows the Layers palette with the subgroup selected on the Main Turtle layer. I changed the Blending mode on each turtle's back. You need to unlock each layer before you can make the changes, but lock each layer when you are done with it. Table 8.1 lists the changes that I made to each turtle layer.

Table 8.1 Blend modes for the turtle layers.

Layer	Blending Mode
Top-Left Turtle	Difference
Middle-Right Turtle	Difference
Bottom-Left Above	Soft Light
Top-Right Turtle	Soft Light
Main Turtle	Overlay
Bottom-Left Turtle	Overlay
Bottom-Right Turtle	Overlay

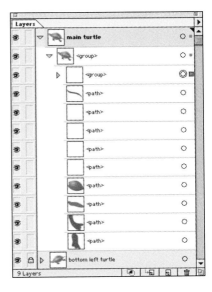

Figure 8.44
The subgroup is selected on the Main Turtle layer of the Layers palette.

13. Create a new layer and name it "Large Border". Make this layer the top one on the Layer list. Choose the Rectangle tool with a white stroke of 50 points and no Fill. Drag the rectangle tool so that it is the same size as the Background layer. Change the Blend mode to Soft Light. On a new layer (named Smaller Border) above the Large Border layer, create another rectangle. Draw this one at the inside edge of the stroke on the Large Border layer. Change the stroke to 8 points and the Blend mode to Overlay. Save your work.

14. The final change that you might want to make is to remove some of the water blend groups near the top of the image. You can select each group individually on the Layers palette by twirling down the layer. Turn off the eye icon on the groupings that you want to remove to preview the effect first. Figure 8.45 shows the final result in grayscale. It's also shown in the Illustrator 9 Studio (in color, of course).

What makes this effect work? The shape of the line itself plays a big part in the success of the water scene. I tried a number of different lines before I found one that I liked. The spacing of the lines (that is, the number of intermediate steps)

Figure 8.45

The finished water scene—turtles and all.

also matters. One big factor, however, is the closeness of the colors that I chose for the starting and ending lines. I had to strike the finest balance to find shades that were obviously different, but still close enough that they didn't cause the water to form an obvious pattern.

Gradients

One fervent cry of Illustrator users was for real gradients—ones that worked like the gradients in Macromedia Freehand—where you didn't have to create a blend and mask it. CorelDRAW users already had that gradient (or Fountain) tool. Several versions ago (frankly, I forget which one), Adobe obliged. Gradients made it easier to control the direction and angle of the color ramp. Because a gradient was a type of fill, no mask was necessary—which also simplified things quite a bit. In this section, after we cover the basic steps needed to create a gradient, I'll move on to some gradient "tricks." Because this book is really aimed at an intermediate level, I think that most of you have already used gradients.

Gradient Basics

When you apply a gradient to an object, you can control several attributes, such as the color ramp, the angle of the ramp, and whether the ramp is linear or circular. At its most basic, a gradient is applied by simply clicking on a square in the Swatches palette that contains a gradient. You can modify this gradient as you wish.

You can also create your own gradient. If you haven't used any other gradient within Illustrator's memory, you'll see the basic black-to-white linear gradient.

The following is a fast recap of how to create a gradient:

- *To change a color*—Click on a Color Stop to select it. Use the Colors palette to change the Stop to another color.

- *To pick up a color*—Click on a Color Stop to select it or add a Color Stop. Choose the Eyedropper tool. Press Shift and click on the desired color from anywhere in the image.

- *To add a color*—Click under the Color Slider where there is not currently a Color Stop tab. A new Color Stop will appear.

- *To remove a color*—Drag the Color Stop off the Gradient palette by dragging it downward.

- *To copy a Color Stop*—Press Option/Alt and drag the Color Stop to a new location.

- *To change the spacing*—Drag the Color Stop closer to or farther away from its neighboring stops to change the distance over which Color A changes to Color B.

- *To set the Gradient Type*—Change the pop-down menu from Linear to Radial and vice versa.

- *To set a new global angle*—Enter a number into the Angle field.

Using the facilities on the Gradient palette, you can create gradients that are quite complex and exciting and that move to many colors. You can also create sharp stripes or color changes by setting the location of two colors directly next to one another, as shown in Figure 8.46.

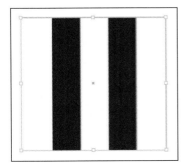

Figure 8.46
You can create stripes by placing two Color Stops next to one another and placing two stops of the same color a distance apart.

You can change linear gradients into radial gradients and vice versa by changing the gradient Type in the pop-down menu. You can also change the angle of the gradient either by entering into the Angle field or by interactively using the Gradient tool—which works exactly like the Gradient tool in Photoshop. Project 8.8 shows how to control the Gradient tool using multiple objects.

Angled Moves

I discovered an entertaining curiosity when I was fiddling with gradients. Although you can get some of the same results just by carefully using the Gradient tool, my technique is easily repeatable. Stated simply, if you change a radial gradient that has been individually placed into multiple objects into a linear gradient (with all the objects selected at the same time), the angle at which the radial gradient was applied remains the same. This technique can create interesting angled text.

PROJECT 8.8 Working the Angles

You can create this gradient effect as follows:

1. Open the image WELCOME.AI on this book's companion CD-ROM. The image simply says "WELCOME" in 72-point Adobe Copal Solid type that has been converted to outlines. I like the Copal typeface for lettering effects because the letterforms are so wide that a lot of room is left for decoration. You should also see guides in the image. If you don't, choose View|Show Guides. Figure 8.47 shows a screen capture of the image so that you can see the placements of the guides.

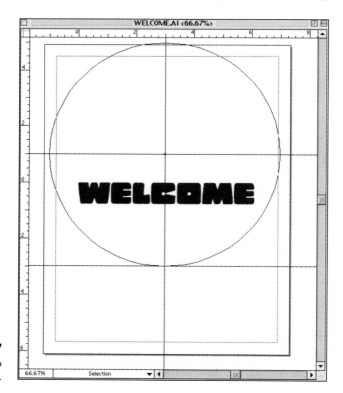

Figure 8.47
"WELCOME" text shows up surrounded by guides.

A Guided Explanation

You might wonder why the guides are set up in the WELCOME image as they are and how I got that circle in place. First, I created the text and changed it to outlines. I then turned on the rulers. I selected the text objects and dragged the origin point of the rulers to the top-left corner of the bounding box. The text was just a bit wider than 6 inches (6.102, to be precise). The halfway point was a bit beyond 3 inches, where I placed the one vertical guide. The guide marks the vertical center of the text.

I changed my fill to the MODI RAINBOW radial gradient (which you'll use soon) and, with all the text selected, used the Gradient tool to find the starting and ending points where I liked the gradient fill. I made note of those points along the side ruler and dragged guides to those points. They're the two horizontal guides in the image.

I then selected the Ellipse tool and placed the cursor at the intersection of the vertical guide and the top horizontal guide. This intersection becomes the center of a circle drawn from the intersection to the bottom guide with Shift and Alt/Option pressed to constrain the Ellipse tool to draw a circle from the center. I changed the selected circle to a guide by selecting View|Make Guides. I now have a circle that allows me to control the angle of the Gradient tool as I apply a gradient individually to several objects.

2. Choose Window|Swatch Libraries|Other Libraries and locate the KAIGRAD.AI file on the companion CD-ROM. This file loads a palette that contains two swatches. Click on each swatch in the palette (MODI RAINBOW and KAI GRADIENT) to transfer these swatches to the Swatches palette attached to the WELCOME.AI image. You may close the KAIGRAD.AI swatch library after you've transferred the swatches.

3. Select the entire image (Command/Ctrl+A). Click on the MODI RAINBOW swatch in the Swatches palette. Figure 8.48 shows the text with the radial gradient applied.

Figure 8.48
Text with radial gradient applied to all objects.

4. Deselect everything. Select only the letter *W*.

5. Choose the Gradient tool. Place your mouse cursor on the intersection of the vertical and horizontal guides (which from now on I'll call *center circle*). Press and hold the mouse button. Drag the Gradient tool line from the center circle through the letter *W* until it reaches the circular guide. Release the mouse button. Although you could draw a number of lines with those directions, aim for the lower-left corner of the *W*.

6. Select the letter *E*—the second letter in WELCOME. Again, drag the Gradient tool line from the center circle to the circular guide. This time, drag it through the *E*. As you drag the Gradient tool line, try to keep the

line going though only one letter on its passage to the circular guide. If possible, in each letter, aim for the lowest point on the letter that both misses another letter and is closest to the left side of the letter (for "WEL") or the right side of the letter (for "OME"). Drag the Gradient tool directly down for the letter *C* that is in the center of the word.

7. Select each of the remaining letters in turn and apply the radial gradient with the Gradient tool. For each letter, drag from the center circle through the selected letter to the circular guide. Figure 8.49 shows the text after all the letters have been filled. Even though each letter was filled individually, the gradient looks even because you have used a consistent starting point and drag length.

Figure 8.49
Each letter is filled with the same radial gradient applied at a different angle.

8. Select the entire image (Command/Ctrl+A). Change the Gradient Type in the Gradient palette from Radial to Linear. Figure 8.50 shows the result.

Figure 8.50
Now you have a linear gradient.

9. If you like the way the linear gradient falls, you're done. However, you can play out this technique a bit more. If you select a different linear gradient, your letters will keep the same gradient angles (if you apply a gradient defined as radial, all bets are off). With the letters still selected, click on the KAI GRADIENT swatch that you transferred into your Swatches palette (the gradient name is explained in the sidebar "What's a 'Kai Gradient'?"). Figure 8.51 shows the new look for the text.

Figure 8.51
Change the fill for the text to the KAI GRADIENT swatch.

10. Repeat Steps 4 through 7, using the new linear gradient. Your result, shown in Figure 8.52, looks like a radial gradient, but it's not. However, should you need to expand the gradient for some reason, it would be easier to handle than a true radial gradient. Figure 8.53 shows a before

Figure 8.52

Applying a linear gradient to multiple objects from a consistent starting point with a consistent line length makes the linear gradient look radial.

Figure 8.53

The top text object shows the MODI RAINBOW gradient applied to the entire word at one time. The bottom text object shows what happens when you change the gradient type from radial to linear.

and after image of the text if you apply the MODI RAINBOW radial gradient to all the text at once and then change it to a linear gradient. As you can see, you lose the angled application of the linear gradient—everything becomes the same angle. If you want to play some more, import the Swatches palette from the YELLORGRN.AI image on the companion CD-ROM. The custom radial gradient that it contains also looks good with this technique.

Metallic Looks

Metallic-looking images are always very popular—especially on text. Project 8.9 shows a fast technique to create metallic letters from a linear gradient.

PROJECT 8.9 All That Glitters

Here's how to create a metallic gradient:

1. Open the document METAL.AI on this book's companion CD-ROM. It contains the word *METAL* in Adobe Copal Solid, which was changed to outlines and scaled to fit the page width. The tracking is opened a bit. I set the type originally at 72 points with 60 thousandths of an em tracking.

2. Select the entire image (Command/Ctrl+A).

3. Make sure that the Fill swatch is active. Click on the Metal Gradient swatch in the Swatches palette (it might be the last swatch in the palette).

4. With all the letters selected, choose Object|Transform|Transform Each. Set both the Horizontal and Vertical Scale amounts to 80%, as shown in Figure 8.54. Click on Copy, but do not deselect.

What's a "Kai Gradient"?

If you own Kai's Power Tools from Corel, you can use the wonderfully complex gradient presets that come with the product. Of course, you can use KPT to create gradients in shapes that are impossible in Illustrator, but you can also find very interesting linear or radial gradient presets—or you can modify a color ramp that you like so that it is either linear or radial. You can then re-create the gradient's color ramp inside Illustrator. Here's how.

Fill a rectangle with your chosen gradient by using Kai's Power Tools from within Photoshop. Save the document that contains the original gradient-filled rectangle. Make another copy of the image and change it to Indexed Color mode in Photoshop. I used 20 colors as my cutoff. Save this image, too. It's the "work plan" for the gradient. The bands of discrete color make it easier for you to find the defining colors in the gradient.

Open the Indexed Color image in Illustrator. Place the original gradient in the same file. Draw a rectangle between the two bitmapped images that spans the width of the document. Use the Selection tool to stretch the bitmaps until they are the same size as your vector rectangle. You can see this layout if you open KAIGRAD.AI in Illustrator.

Select the rectangle. Next, choose the Eyedropper tool. Click on the first color band in the Indexed Color image to set the rectangle to that color. Then, drag the Fill swatch from the Color palette onto the left edge of the Gradient Color slider in the Gradient palette. You now have a ramp from the new color to whatever was already in the Color slider. You can remove the other Color Stops from the Color slider. Click at the end of the Color slider to create an ending Color Stop. Use the Eyedropper tool with Shift pressed to pick up the last color in the gradient from the Indexed Color image.

Keep adding colors to the Gradient palette by selecting them from either the Indexed Color image or the original bitmapped gradient (with Shift pressed). When you add a new stop to the Color Bar, leave room between the last and the new Color Stops. You can move the Color Stop into position as soon as you're sure it's colored properly. Use the original gradient as your guide for spacing (which is why you made all three rectangles the same size). You can add colors from the original gradient that didn't make it into the Indexed Color version (like the orange in the KAI GRADIENT). When you have a group of colors defined in the Color slider, you can press Option/Alt and drag the color to create a duplicate Color Stop (if you need to use the color more than once). Make sure that you release the mouse button before you release the modifier key.

A word about color modes: If you try to import an image that isn't in the same color mode as your existing image, Illustrator will warn you of the problem.

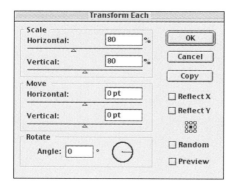

Figure 8.54

You can use the Transform Each command to scale the entire group of letters and copy them in one command.

5. Create a new layer. Move the selected object rectangle from Layer 1 to Layer 2 in the Layers palette (moving the scaled text to Layer 2).

6. With the letters in Layer 2 still selected, enter "31" into the Angle box on the Gradient palette and deselect. Figure 8.55 shows the result.

Figure 8.55
"Metal" now looks metallic.

The metallic gradient technique works well on Web objects, such as buttons, and it need not be confined to use on text. The secret of the technique is to apply the same gradient to the inner and outer copies of the object but at different angles.

Of course, the gradient that you apply needs to look metallic before it is applied to anything. A metallic gradient is a color ramp that moves unevenly from the base color (silver, gold, bronze, or whatever) to a highlight of white or near white and then cycles back and forth to the base color.

Sometimes, the realism of a metallic gradient is improved by adding a few stranger colors into it. A *stranger* color is my name for a color close to the primary color in value but slightly different in hue. It's a color that you would tend to say "clashes" with the base color if you were to try to wear both colors together. You can also form an additional color by adding black to the base color. This method doesn't clash as much and isn't of the same value as the base color. It's also an effective way to add tone to the gradient.

I used two copies of the text for a very basic reason: Illustrator doesn't allow you to add a gradient to a stroke. Therefore, to create a wider lip for the rim of the letters, you need to use the text and create a copy to serve as the inner form. You must deal with two filled objects. You could also create a single object with two fills and use the Offset Path effect to create the larger outline for the lip of the text.

You can also apply the metallic effect by using the Gradient tool and stretching the gradient across the entire word. However, because the character of metal is to be reflective, I felt that it looked better to apply the gradient so that each letter contained the full range of colors. Of course, you're free to try it the other way. Nothing is sacred about the gradient angles that I used. They can be anything that you want, as long as they are different for both the inner and the outer shapes. Don't forget to try the technique using the transferred KPT gradient from Project 8.8.

David Xenakis, artist and technical reviewer for this book, contributed MOLDED.AI for the companion CD-ROM. The file shows three stunning examples of achieving dimensionality by using gradients. In the self-teaching example, David shows the amazing elevation changes you can achieve simply by rotating one of the shapes. Check it out.

Can You Really Not Apply a Gradient to a Stroke?

You can't choose a gradient as a stroke color. If you try, Illustrator simply uses the clicked-on gradient as the fill. However, you can create a gradient-on-a-path by making a pattern out of the desired gradient and using that pattern to stroke the path. You can also create the same effect as you just produced by using the Transform Each command at 80 percent on the solid selected text outlines and not copying them. Then, stroke the text with an 8-point stroke in a different solid color. Expand the stroke and fill. Fill all the expanded strokes with the gradient fill going in one direction and the solid shapes going in the opposite direction. Fill each outline and shape individually.

Gradients for Realism

Of course, one of the major reasons to use gradients is to add realism to your image. In the hands of a master illustrator, the image would appear to be a photograph. Creating such an image takes a special talent (of which I possess a limited amount). Perhaps the most critical skill needed—in addition to an ability to draw—is the ability to organize and segment. You need to analyze every inch of your subject to see how it reacts to light. You need to know the front-to-back layering needed to make the object look real.

The Pen

In a departure from the norm in this book, I invite you to take apart the image PEN.AI in the Chapter08 Ends folder on this book's companion CD-ROM. The pen is the creation of David Xenakis (also my coauthor on *Photoshop 5 In Depth,* by The Coriolis Group). David is a tremendously skilled illustrator. The pen is a marvel of realism. By clicking on each object, you can see exactly how it was constructed. The shadow is a rasterized copy of the image on which the Unite filter was run. Figure 8.56 shows the pen in grayscale; see the Illustrator 9 Studio to view it in color.

Figure 8.56
Pen, by David Xenakis, shows how realistic an object can look when created using gradients.

Spray Those Germs Away

The spray can that you'll re-create in the "Realistic Metallic Gradients" project is another attempt at realism. Although it's simple drawing (simpler than you would probably want if this were a "real" project), the image still has quite enough shapes to keep you occupied. Therefore, I've given you all of the starting shapes so that you don't need to create your own.

When I started this chapter, I knew that I wanted one project that showed how to apply a metallic-looking gradient to a real object. I wanted to demonstrate how to look at the light and try to capture the reflections of metal. While at the dentist's office, I became so fascinated by the play of light on a spray can that the dental assistant finally insisted that I take the can home. You'll re-create most of this spray can in Project 8.10. You'll apply gradients to a number of shapes to simulate the play of light.

Realistic Metallic Gradients

The following steps provide a simplified version of how many of the realistic shading effects are done:

1. Open the document CAN.AI from the companion CD-ROM. Figure 8.57 shows the starting image. It's flat and lifeless.

Another Realistic Approach

In Chapter 3, you created a coffee cup using the new blend modes and transparency settings. Because you created a new-style realistic object there, I wanted to use the more traditional methods appropriate to the metallic spray can here. However, your Illustrator 9 program CD-ROM includes an image created by Adobe called ROSE.AI. It's located in the Sample Art folder in the Sample Files folder. Open the file and look carefully at each layer in turn. The folks at Adobe did an incredible job of creating a semitransparent glass bottle. You'll learn all the necessary techniques for creating glass looks just by deconstructing that image. Experiment as well with using the Adjust Colors filter on the background of the ROSE.AI image. Change the Magenta to -30 and see what it does to the bottle in the image.

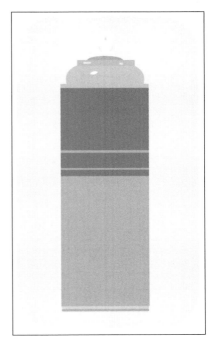

Figure 8.57
This is the starting point for a spray can that is about to gain depth and dimension.

2. Poke around the image before you actually start editing. Figure 8.58 shows the image in pseudo-line mode. I filled most of the shapes with None and stroked them in black so that you can see the actual objects. You can easily match the very long Layers palette (shown in Figure 8.59) to the objects on each layer (by using Command+Option+click on the Mac or Alt+Ctrl+click in Windows) to select the object(s) on that layer. You can also unlock the layer and click on the button next to the layer to select it. My naming isn't scientific (or accurate), so you might need to look at the layer names to find what I mean when I say, "Select the Squirt Stand." Lock all the layers after you finish exploring.

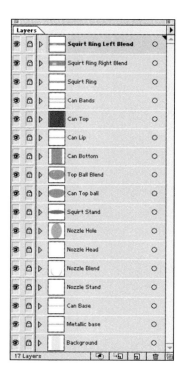

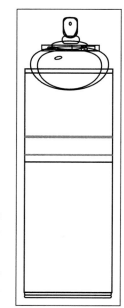

Figure 8.58

(Left) Here, the can looks much
as it would in Artwork mode.

Figure 8.59

(Right) This is the Layers palette
for the image.

3. Let's create the main body of the can first—the areas where the pink bottom of the can meets the blue top of the can. My premise is that if you want the spray can to look realistic, you need to match the gradients as they change color. The play of light needs to be identical even if the hue set changes. To start, remove the lock on the Can Bottom layer. Select the entire image (Command/Ctrl+A). Only the pink bottom of the can is selected because all the other layers are locked (or should be).

4. Click on the New Pink Gradient swatch in the Swatches palette to apply it to the object (make certain that the fill is the active Color palette component) to apply a soft, satiny pink metallic gradient to the object. Figure 8.60 shows the Gradient palette so that you can see the gradient Color Stops. Lock the layer again.

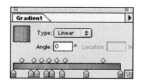

Figure 8.60

The New Pink Gradient swatch as
defined in the Gradient palette.

5. Unlock the Can Top layer; this layer is the blue top of the can. Remember that you can click on the circle next to any layer name in the Layers palette to select the object(s) on that layer. If you're experienced at designing gradients, you can simply click on the New Gradient Swatch 6 in the Swatches palette and go to Step 7. If you want to practice turning pink into blue, go to Step 6.

6. Select the blue can top object on the Can Top layer. Click on the New Pink Gradient to apply it. Hmmmm…. This object is supposed to be

blue (but it has to match). Click on the first Color Stop on the left of the Color slider in the Gradient palette. Set the Color to CMYK: 97, 88, 0, 0. Click on the second Color Stop. The following list indicates values for the Color Stops in the gradient:

- *Color Stop 1*—CMYK: 97, 88, 0, 0

- *Color Stop 2*—CMYK: 96, 54, 0, 0

- *Color Stop 3*—CMYK: 97, 77, 0, 0

- *Color Stop 4*—CMYK: 96, 54, 0, 0

- *Color Stop 5*—CMYK: 97, 78, 0, 0

- *Color Stop 6*—CMYK: 96, 54, 0, 0

- *Color Stop 7*—CMYK: 97, 88, 0, 0

- *Color Stop 8*—CMYK: 97, 88, 0, 27

Figure 8.61 shows the Gradient palette for the blue gradient. Notice that its stops are in the identical locations as the pink gradient.

7. Unlock the Metallic Base layer. Select the metallic base (the gray shape at the very bottom of the can). Click on the Gray Gradient in the Layers palette to apply it. Lock the layer again. As you apply my preset gradients, look to see how each one is defined. The Can Base layer remains a solid pink, so you don't need to touch that layer. Lock all the layers.

8. Unlock the Can Lip layer. Click on the Gray Gradient to apply it. Change the Angle to 90 degrees. That's better, but the shading isn't quite right. Choose the Gradient tool. Drag the Gradient tool line from the bottom of the Can Lip object vertically up until it is out of the object by a distance equal to the height of the object. Figure 8.62 shows a close-up of the Can Lip object with the gradient correctly applied. Lock the layer.

9. The only other layer that gets a "simple" gradient is the Squirt Stand layer (the gray, rounded shape beneath the nozzle assembly). Unlock the layer and select the object. Apply the Squirt Stand gradient to it (this is actually the same as the Gray Gradient applied at an angle of 1.64 degrees). Lock the layer again.

10. The Can Top Ball, Squirt Ring, Nozzle Hole, Nozzle Stand, and Nozzle Head layers are solid and already correctly colored. You don't need to touch them. Five more layers remain to color, and each of them contains a blend rather than a gradient. Let's start with the easiest one. Unlock the Can Band layer and fill both bands with the New Pink Gradient.

Figure 8.61
The blue version of the metallic gradient uses the same Color Stops as the pink gradient in Figure 8.60 shown previously.

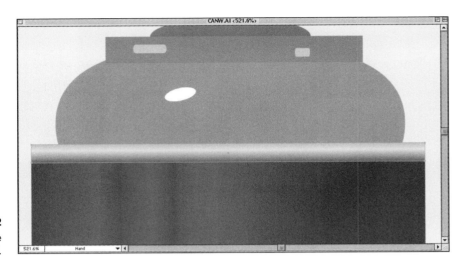

Figure 8.62

The lip of the can needs to be delicately shaded.

Choose Object|Blends|Blend Options and change the Specified Steps number to 2. Choose the Blend tool and click on the top-left corner of both shapes to create the blend. You can blend shapes that contain gradients, and when both the starting and ending shapes use the same gradient, Illustrator can easily calculate the correct result. Because the bands use the same gradient as the bottom shape, the lighting is automatically in the correct location. Lock the layer.

11. Unlock the Top Ball Blend layer. Figure 8.63 shows the layer before the blend is applied. The objects on the layer are a gray shape (the same color gray as the Can Top Ball layer that is the background for this blend) and a small highlight shape. Select the entire image (Command/Ctrl+A), which selects just the gray and the highlight shapes. Choose Object|Blends|Blend Options and set the Spacing to Smooth Color. Choose the Blend tool. Click on the center point inside the highlight shape to set your first point. Then, click on the center point of the gray shape to finish the blend. Figure 8.64 shows the finished blend. Because the figure is from a screen capture, you can also see the spine of the blend. Lock the layer.

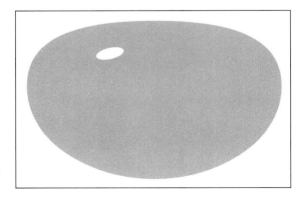

Figure 8.63

The Top Ball Blend layer before being blended. It has just two shapes.

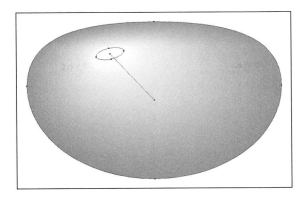

Figure 8.64
The Top Ball Blend layer after the blend has been applied shows the two shapes and the spine of the blend.

12. Unlock the Nozzle Blend layer. The two shapes on this layer are a white front piece and a gray back piece. Select both shapes. With the Blend tool, click on the control points (see Figure 8.65) to establish the smooth blend. Lock the layer.

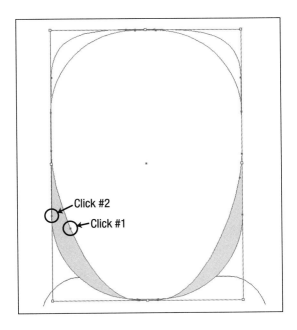

Figure 8.65
Click on the control points as marked to create this blend.

13. The remaining two blends form the dual highlights on the rim of the can (which I have called the "squirt ring" because I was running low on part names). They are the shapes on the Squirt Ring Left Blend and Squirt Ring Right Blend layers. Unlock the Squirt Ring Right Blend layer. Again, I have used the trick of making a smaller "stop blend" shape that is the same color as its base object. This smaller shape keeps the highlight from spreading farther than it logically should. Select both shapes on the layer. With the Blend tool, click on the center marker inside the highlight shape, and then click on the center marker inside the gray shape. Lock the layer again.

14. Unlock the Squirt Ring Left Blend layer, select the objects, and blend from the center point of the highlight to the center point of the gray stop-blend shape as you did in Step 13. If you have hidden any layers or changed them to Artwork mode, make everything visible now and admire your handiwork. Figure 8.66 shows the finished spray can in grayscale.

Figure 8.66
The finished spray can is more realistic looking than the flat object you first opened.

The most difficult part of creating this project was creating the metallic blend. The Swatches palette still contains some of my early attempts. In the light of my studio, the metallic surface of the can gleamed with many more light-to-dark vertical lines than I put in the blend. I discovered that you need to be very cautious about balanced blends (A-B-C-D-C-B-A) that are used to simulate metallics. The eye sees depth so easily that all too often my blend made it look as if the object itself was rolling in and out. Because I wasn't trying to make the spray can look like a theater curtain, I needed to carefully edit the gradient and watch that the colors didn't vary too much along the Color slider. The worst dimensionality occurred when there were sharp differences between the light and the dark tones. I had to work at the gradients until I saw a round can rather than a tin ribbon.

Gradient Mesh Objects

Adobe introduced the gradient mesh object in Illustrator 8. This object gives the artist a marvelous tool for capturing light and dark and subtleties of shading. Along with exciting possibilities, however, comes a fairly steep learning curve. The creation process is complex. The mechanics of it, as you'll discover in this section, are not too difficult. The challenge comes from trying to make it do what you want it to do. Let me say this bluntly: You can train an ape to sit at the typewriter and make letters appear on a piece of paper, but only Shakespeare can write *Romeo and Juliet*. An elephant can brush paint onto canvas, but it will never be a Picasso. Although I'm neither Shakespeare nor Picasso, I can give you guidance in the basics of using this tool. You can then take it as far as your own capabilities allow (the more experience you have in painting and in creating chiaroscuro, the easier you'll find it to be).

A gradient mesh is a class of gradient that you can use to create a shaded object by filling points or patches on a grid with color that blends softly into the surrounding color. You can control the mesh by adding or deleting points along its surface, editing the points as if they were control points on an object, and selecting the colors and locations at which to place the colors.

Mesh Basics

The Gradient Mesh tool is complex enough that I don't want to take the time or space to do an in-depth review of the tool. Please take the time to read the manual or to review the online Help for the Gradient Mesh tool. The "nutshell" review of the tool is as follows:

- *To create a gradient mesh*—Click on an object with the Gradient Mesh tool or choose Object|Create Gradient Mesh.

- *To remove the entire gradient mesh*—Sorry, you lose! You cannot remove the gradient mesh except by deleting the entire object.

- *To color a gradient mesh point*—Click on the point with the Gradient Mesh tool to select it, drag and drop a color swatch onto the point, or use the Paint Bucket tool. The real trick is making the point contain the color that you want. Dragging and dropping a swatch works well. The Paint Bucket tool also works well if you click exactly on the point with the tip of the tool. The problem with using the Paint Bucket is that, unless the color you want is already in the Fill color well in the toolbox, you'll change any selected area in your Gradient Mesh object when you click to select a new fill color. Perhaps the easiest way to change a point is to click on it with the Gradient Mesh tool to select it and *then* adjust the color of the point by dragging the sliders in the Color palette.

- *To color a gradient mesh patch*—Drag and drop a color swatch onto the patch, or use the Paint Bucket tool. If you click inside the patch with the Gradient Mesh tool, you'll create a new Mesh point (and its associated lines).

- *To edit the shape of the gradient mesh*—Use the Gradient Mesh tool or the Direct Selection tool and move the anchor points and direction lines as if there were regular Path anchor points and direction lines.

- *To slide a point along a mesh line*—Press Shift as you move it.

- *To add a new mesh line*—Click on the object with the Gradient Mesh tool where no mesh line currently exists (the cursor arrow will show a plus sign).

- *To add a mesh without a color change*—Press Shift and click on the object with the Gradient Mesh tool where no mesh line currently exists (the cursor arrow will show a plus sign).

- *To delete a mesh line*—Press Option/Alt and click on a mesh line (the cursor arrow will show a minus sign).

In the next several projects, you'll get plenty of practice using these techniques. Figure 8.67 shows the anatomy of a gradient mesh object.

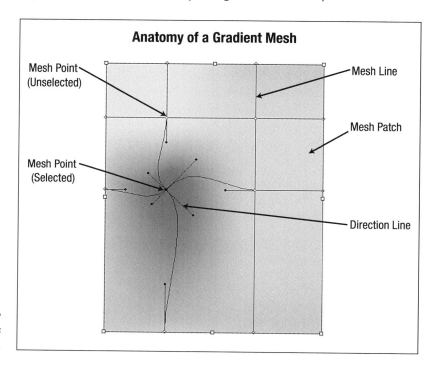

Anatomy of a Gradient Mesh

Mesh Point
(Unselected)

Mesh Line

Mesh Patch

Mesh Point
(Selected)

Direction Line

Figure 8.67
This image shows the anatomy of
a gradient mesh object.

Gradient Mesh Objects: Inside and Out

This section provides a hands-on introduction to gradient meshes through two simple projects. In the first, you'll see how you can use a gradient mesh object as the background for scratch-it-off artwork, and in the second, you'll see how you can adapt a popular style of Illustrator art to use gradient mesh objects.

Scratch Art

These days, you can buy scratchboard and easily create scratch art, though I remember doing this in grammar school with crayons and poster paint. If you keep your scratch design simple, you can even use Illustrator to simulate scratch art. You can do so in many ways, and the way that I've selected is not necessarily the most efficient, but I'll explain my choices as we go along. I have chosen to create a compound path on the top shape so that a unified gradient mesh shows up beneath it.

PROJECT 8.11 Scratch-It-Off (or Make a Compound Path of It)

Here's how to create one form of scratchboard art in Illustrator:

1. Open the image SWIRL.AI. It is a piece of clip art from Ultimate Symbol's Design Elements collection (and one of the demo images). Figure 8.68 shows the original image.

Figure 8.68
SWIRL.AI: clip art from the Ultimate Symbol Design Elements collection.

2. Choose Object|Compound Paths|Release. You'll see what looks like black flower petals on a black shape.

3. Deselect and then click in the center of the image to select the largest black object. Delete to leave just the petal shapes.

4. Lock the layer. Create a new layer by clicking on the New Layer icon at the bottom of the Layers palette. Drag the new layer below Layer 1.

5. With nothing selected, change the Stroke to None and the Fill to yellow.

6. Choose the Rectangle tool. Press Option/Alt and click once in the center of the petal form to open the Rectangle Tool Options dialog box. Enter 4 inches for the width and 3.2 inches for the height.

7. Move the rectangle to the left so that the flower form is closer to the right edge. Figure 8.69 shows this positioning.

8. Deselect everything. Change your Fill color to green. Select the Gradient Mesh tool. As you drag the cursor over the rectangle, the cursor changes to show a plus sign (+), signifying that you can add a gradient mesh there. Click on one of the petals (remember, the petal layer is locked and you're actually painting *underneath* it). You've created one gradient mesh line.

Figure 8.69
Move the rectangle to the left so that the flower is closer to the edge.

9. Deselect and then change your Fill to hot pink. Click on another petal to leave a second gradient mesh line.

10. Continue to deselect. Change the Fill color and create another two or three points. They don't all have to be on the petals (though only those will show when you are done).

11. Use the Gradient Mesh tool or the Direct Selection tool to move mesh points around. Figure 8.70 shows my gradient mesh.

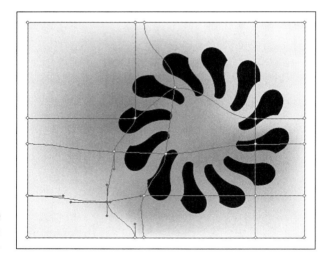

Figure 8.70
Gradient mesh showing mesh points that have been moved.

12. Lock Layer 2. Create a new layer directly above Layer 2.

13. Change your Fill color to black with no Stroke. Choose the Rectangle tool and draw a rectangle just a tiny bit larger than the gradient mesh object.

14. Unlock Layer 1. Select the entire image (Command/Ctrl+A). Click on Exclude in the Pathfinder palette. Figure 8.71 shows the result.

Figure 8.71
By excluding the petal shapes from a solid rectangle, you create holes through which the gradient mesh object can show.

15. Lock all the layers and create a new layer that is at the top of the layer stack.

16. Set the Fill to None and the Stroke to white. Choose the Paintbrush tool with the second Calligraphic brush in the Brushes palette (the 10-point oval).

17. Draw approximately five lines with the Paintbrush. Keep the lines short and simple and make all of them start outside the left edge of the rectangle. They need to be similar to those shown in Figure 8.72.

Figure 8.72
Add some simple calligraphic strokes to the left edge of the image.

18. Select the entire image (Command/Ctrl+A). Choose Object|Expand. Expand the object and deselect the Stroke and Fill options. Ungroup (Shift+Command, Mac; Ctrl+G, Windows) and then deselect.

19. Use the Selection tool (and Shift) to select each of the lines individually until they are all selected. Choose Object|Hide Selection. Select the entire image (Command/Ctrl+A). Now, you should see a bunch of paths that have no stroke or fill. Choose Object|Show All, and then deselect.

20. Unlock Layer 1. Select one white line and the black rectangle. Click on Minus Front on the Pathfinder palette. Press Shift and click on the next white line. Click on Minus Front on the Pathfinder palette. Continue to press Shift, select the next line, and then use the Minus Front command until you either run out of lines or Illustrator tells you that the path is too complex. (For now, because you're probably not going to print this project, you can ignore the warning.) Figure 8.73 shows the finished effect in grayscale.

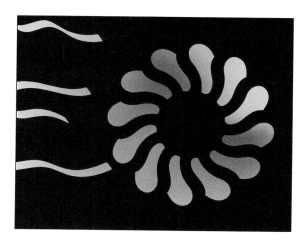

Figure 8.73
Scratch art, done.

What can you do if you want to create a complicated scratch art image? You can choose from several possibilities. You could create a large number of small gradient mesh objects and fill each one with a different set of colors. However, this approach would lose the continuity of the supposed underlying art board.

Another possibility is to segment the black rectangle. Instead of drawing it all in one piece, you can create it out of a large number of smaller rectangles so that you reduce the complexity of the paths.

You can find a much easier way to complete the entire project by creating all your scratchboard shapes inside an opacity mask. Simply create a black-and-white image of what you want your scratchboard to look like and then paste it inside the mask. You could also draw freehand on the mask. You just need to remember that white in the mask reveals the black rectangle and black in the mask hides it and shows the rainbow gradient mesh object underneath.

Stroke Pictures

If you flip through the pages of almost any clip art collection, you'll see images that use a delightfully breezy style of a simple outline over a quick calligraphic stroke. Figure 8.74 shows an example of this style of artwork using an image from volume 1 of Ultimate Symbol's Design Elements collection.

Figure 8.74

Coloring not quite within the lines is a very good way to personalize clip art. This outline is from the Ultimate Symbol Design Elements collection.

Using gradient mesh objects adds a new dimension to this style. You can use a gradient mesh as the scribble—though not quite as easily as it would seem. Let's try it in Project 8.12. You'll work two short versions of this exercise. In the first part, you'll use the gradient mesh as a soft background. In the second part, you'll use the gradient mesh as the sketch stroke itself.

PROJECT 8.12 Sketch Art

You can change the starfish from plain to fancy. Here's how:

1. Open the image STARFISH.AI. Again, I have to thank the folks at Ultimate Symbol for allowing me to use their demo images. This one is from the Nature Icons collection. I have already modified it a bit here to make the project easier (and faster) to work with. Figure 8.75 shows the starting image.

2. Lock the Starfish and Brush Stroke layers. Select the dark gold rectangle on the Background layer.

3. Select the Eyedropper tool and click inside the starfish. The rectangle changes to the same color as the starfish.

4. Choose Object|Create Gradient Mesh. Figure 8.76 shows the dialog box. Enter 4 rows and 4 columns and set the Appearance: To Edge with a Highlight of 100%. Setting the Appearance: To Edge places a highlight at the outer edges of the object. You can control the amount of the highlight by entering a number lower than 100%. Click on OK.

Can You Make the Background Less Plain?

After you set your color for the gradient mesh and use the To Edge option, you have a solid-color ramp that gets lighter on its edges. I then selected intersection points along the grid with the Gradient Mesh tool and added touches of stronger color just under the stroke. I then moved the control points around to move some of the color under the starfish and leave softer tones visible. In addition, I moved some of the control handles at the edges of the gradient mesh object so that the soft, almost white color came closer to the stroke. I also changed the opacity of the Stroke layer and set its Blend mode to Multiply. You can see this version of the image in the color Illustrator Studio.

Figure 8.75
Starfish, from Ultimate Symbol's Nature Icons collection (brush stroke and background by the author).

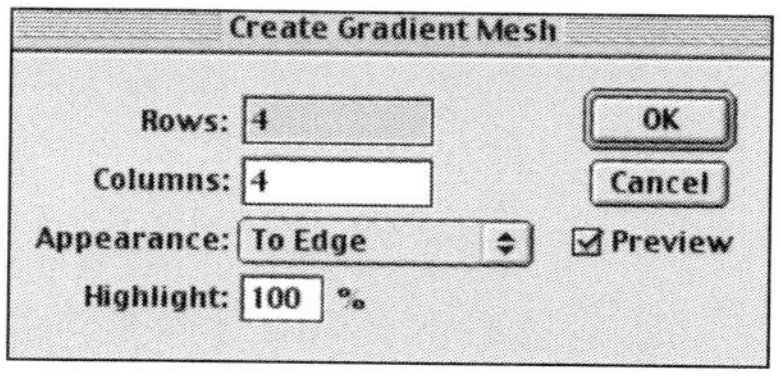

Figure 8.76
The Create Gradient Mesh dialog box.

5. Unlock the Starfish layer and drag its entry in the Layers palette to the New Layer icon at the bottom of the Layers palette to create a copy of the layer. Drag the copy below the original in the Layers palette.

6. Change the Stroke color to black or 75% gray. Drag the object just slightly to the right and down to act as a shadow. Figure 8.77 shows the finished example.

Figure 8.77
You can finish a sketched object by using a soft gradient mesh background.

7. Save a *copy* of the image under a different name and revert the
    STARFISH.AI image back to its original.

8. Hide the Background layer and the Starfish layer. You can change the
    Brush Stroke layer into a gradient mesh object. To do so, select the Gra-
    dient Mesh tool (don't select any objects yet). Set your Stroke to None
    and the Fill to white. With the Gradient Mesh tool, click on the Brush
    Stroke object to set a white highlight somewhere in the brush stroke.
    Figure 8.78 shows the rather messy result of the selected object. When
    you create a gradient mesh by clicking on the object with the Gradient
    Mesh tool (or even when you use the Create Gradient Mesh dialog box
    on a nonrectangular shape), the mesh lines follow the shape of the
    object. This result could be very good, but here it's just confusing and
    leaves a jumbled highlight as well.

Figure 8.78
A less-than-successful attempt
to create a gradient mesh.

9. Undo the gradient mesh. You'll tackle this task in a different way.

10. Drag the Background layer entry to the New layer icon at the bottom of
    the Layers palette. Drag the copy below the original and rename the
    layer "Gradient Mesh". Lock the layer.

11. Make sure that both the Starfish and the Gradient Mesh layers are
    locked. Select the entire image (Command/Ctrl+A). Create a compound
    path (Command/Ctrl+8). Set the Fill for the compound path to white.
    Now, only the stroke and the starfish seem visible.

12. The Background layer no longer contains anything. You can toss it into
    the Layers palette trashcan.

13. Lock the Brush Stroke layer and unlock the Gradient Mesh layer.

14. Change the Fill color on the Gradient Mesh layer object to something a
    bit lighter.

15. Deselect the object, choose a color, select the Gradient Mesh tool, and add a mesh point. Keep adding mesh points and editing them as you wish. Make a shadow as you did in Steps 5 and 6. Figure 8.79 shows my version in grayscale.

Figure 8.79
The gradient mesh object becomes the background behind a compound path made from the original brush stroke.

At the start of this topic, I stated that creating a stroke sketch would not be as easy as it seemed it should be. As you've seen, a complex shape is not the easiest to control when it's used as a gradient mesh object. The simpler the shape with a gradient mesh, the better time you'll have adding colors to it.

Another problem with this technique (that I kept from happening in this project) is that your stroke can become so complex that you cannot fuse it together to make a single shape. How did I get the stroke? Exactly the same way you used previously in this chapter to add lines to the swirl image. I used a calligraphic brush stroke and then expanded it. I needed to find the skeleton no-fill-no-stroke strokes and delete them, and then I used the Unite command on the Pathfinder palette to glue the strokes together into a single object. I discovered that it is much easier to unite the expanded strokes if you create only single strokes that go in one direction and don't double back on themselves. Scribbling a stroke is a recipe for hours of extra work. You need to lay down each stroke carefully.

What If the Make Compound Command Doesn't Work?

Sometimes, if your path is complex, the Object|Compound Paths|Make command either does nothing or gives you an error message. If that happens, try the Exclude command in the Pathfinder palette. It also creates a compound path but doesn't seem to be as fussy about it.

If the compound doesn't work, it's usually because some inner shapes have paths going in the wrong direction. To solve this mystery, use the Direct Select tool to select the shapes and click on one of the two buttons almost in the center of the Attributes palette. Click on the one that isn't slightly darkened. That trick should fix the problem.

Painted Gradient Mesh

You can, of course, use gradient mesh objects to achieve subtle and not-so-subtle shading effects. Figure 8.80 shows a fantasy flower that I created from a rectangle filled with a gradient mesh object. In Project 8.13, I'll show you how I constructed the flower.

Figure 8.80
A fantasy flower constructed from a variety of gradient mesh objects.

PROJECT 8.13 How Does Your Garden Grow?

You can create a simple rectangular gradient mesh object and manipulate it to become a flower that never graced a garden by following these steps:

1. Open a new file in Illustrator.

2. Select the Rectangle tool and choose a light blue for the Fill and None for the Stroke.

3. Draw a rectangle that is about twice as high as it is wide.

4. Choose Object|Create Gradient Mesh. Make the mesh 4 rows by 4 columns.

5. Choose the Gradient Mesh tool. Select an intersection and change the color by clicking on another color in the Swatches or the Color palette. Fill a number of the control point intersections with a different color. Fill some of the points along the outer edge of the rectangle as well.

6. Using the Gradient Mesh tool, move some of the points to mix the colors better. Figure 8.81 shows the gradient mesh object with the control points moved around.

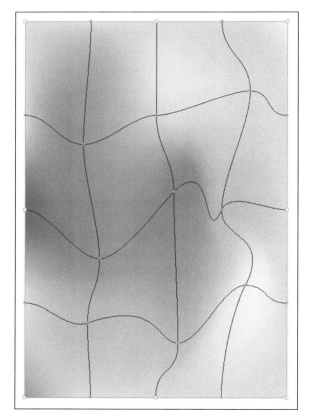

Figure 8.81

Move the points in the gradient mesh object to blend the colors together irregularly.

7. Choose the Direct Selection tool. Distort the boundaries of the object perimeter until you have a shape that is similar to a petal. Figure 8.82 shows the shape in my petal.

8. You can create the flower by rotating the petal. To start, select the petal and choose the Rotate tool. Click on the bottom point where you want the rotation point to be while pressing Option/Alt. Enter -60 in the dialog box. Click on Copy. Then, Transform Again (Command/Ctrl+D) four more times. Instant flower!

9. Select all the petals and group them (Command/Ctrl+G).

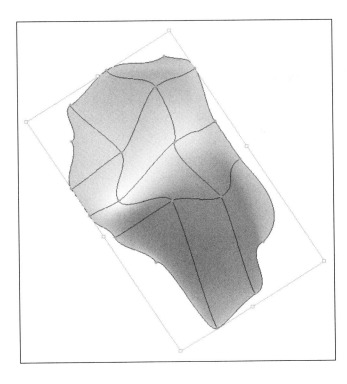

Figure 8.82
Make a petal shape from the rectangle by adding, subtracting, or changing points on the rectangle with the Direct Selection tool.

10. With the layer active but with no objects selected, choose Duplicate Layer 1 from the side menu in the Layers palette.

11. Click on the button next to Layer 1 to select the objects on the layer. Use the arrow tool with Option/Alt pressed to resize the flower from the center. You can judge the size relationship by looking at the finished image that was shown in Figure 8.80.

12. Select the Layer 1 copy layer objects and change the Blending mode to Multiply. Yes—you can apply Blending modes and opacity settings to gradient mesh objects.

I created the stem by drawing a rectangle. Then, I changed it into a two-column, eight-row gradient mesh object. To control the color, I clicked on the top point and selected a green. For each point down the stem, I added a bit more black to the green in the Color palette. To make the stem bend, I selected a group of points by using the Direct Selection tool and then moved them to the right.

To create the leaf, I first drew a leaf shape with the Pen tool. I filled the leaf with a custom gradient that went from a light green to almost black and then back to light green again. I used the Gradient tool to set the angle. I then used the Object|Expand|To Gradient Mesh command to turn the object into a gradient mesh object. I adjusted the coloring in the leaf by altering the Color palette sliders to create subtle variations after I clicked on a point with the Gradient Mesh tool. I made the leaf edges by choosing Object|Path|Add Anchor Points several times and then adding a Roughen effect with corner points and 5 percent size. I painted the spine onto the leaf on a separate layer using the Paintbrush tool with a calligraphic brush.

Finally, I created a drop shadow for the flower and leaf. Although I had a number of possibilities, I opted for what I considered a "safe" way of doing it. I could have attached a drop shadow effect to the flower, the leaf, and the stem. However, the gradient mesh objects are complex enough that I didn't want to risk it. I couldn't simply copy the objects and fill them with a shadow color because a gradient mesh object cannot be changed back into a regular object. Again, I didn't want the overhead and complexity of using a gradient mesh object to hold a solid color. Therefore, I used the Pen tool on a low layer in the Layers palette to create a loose approximation of the entire flower-stem-leaf shape. I filled it with black and lowered its opacity to 80 percent. I change the mode to Multiply and applied a Feather effect of 15 points. To get more separation between some of the points on the leaf and the shadow, I lassoed the tip of the leaf's shadow and dragged it to the right. Moving it gives the effect that the center of the leaf is closer to the background plane than the tip of the leaf. Being able to create this type of depth is one of the benefits of using an independent drop shadow object.

Gradient Mesh Object from a Bitmap

One of my "gee whiz" discoveries with the Gradient Mesh feature is that it's possible to turn a bitmapped image into a gradient mesh object. Of course, processing slows almost to a crawl if the image is large and the gradient mesh object that you create is complex, but what fun is it if you don't push the edge sometimes?

This final project is a perfect finish for the chapter on gradients, blends, and meshes. It brings together elements of everything that you've done so far. It also gives you the freedom to spend five minutes seeing the basic effect possible or several hours to reconstruct all my work and take it further than I did for this book. If you are not familiar with the commands used to place Photoshop images into Illustrator, you might want to read some of the projects in Chapters 10 and 11.

I've constructed an abstract image of a photograph that I took several years ago on Halloween at a local schoolyard. Work through the project just to see what a bitmap looks like when converted to a gradient mesh object, and then I'll share with you the steps I used to create the starting image.

PROJECT 8.14 Halloween Horror

Follow these steps to convert a photograph into a gradient mesh object:

1. Open the image HALLOWEEN.AI on the companion CD-ROM. When you open the image, you'll notice that almost all the layers are locked and that two of them are hidden, as you can see in Figure 8.83.

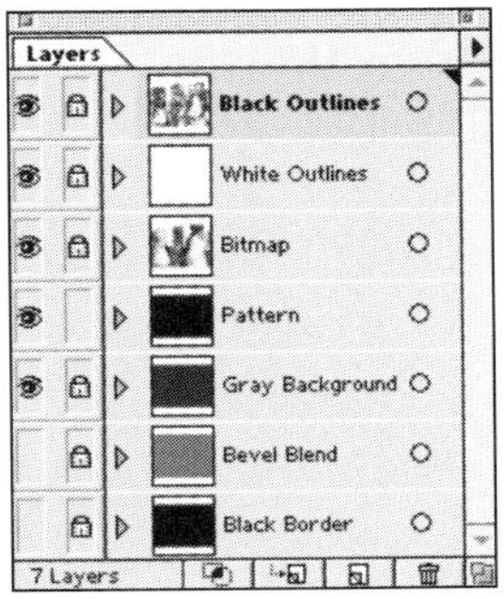

Figure 8.83
The Layers palette from HALLOWEEN.AI shows that two layers are hidden, and all but one layer are locked.

2. Select the entire image (Command/Ctrl+A). Because all but the Bitmap layer are locked, only the bitmapped object embedded in the image is selected. This image is a cropped version of the original with a clipping path on it. The original image is shown in grayscale in Figure 8.84.

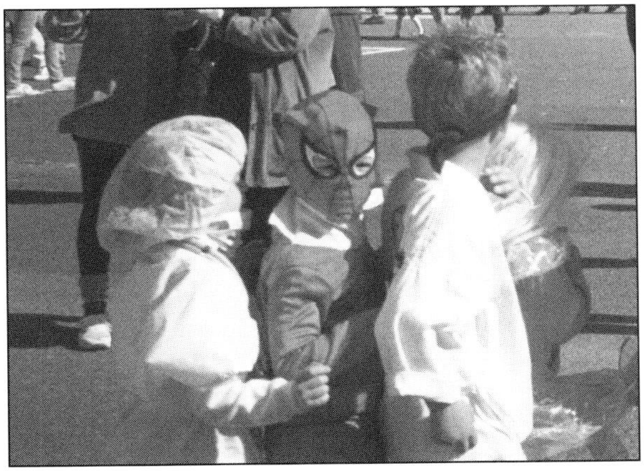

Figure 8.84
The original image of children dressed in Halloween costumes at school.

3. Zoom in to the image so that it fills the screen. Choose Object|Create Gradient Mesh. Try a variety of values for rows and columns from four rows, four columns to as high as you can go without killing your machine or your patience. See what each setting does to the image and select the one that you like best (remember to select the Preview checkbox so that you don't need to click on OK until you are actually ready to perform the conversion). Figure 8.85 shows the settings that I eventually used. Click on OK when you're finished experimenting.

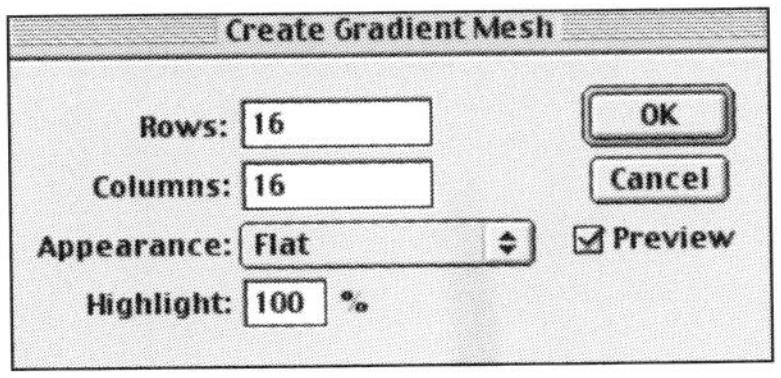

Figure 8.85
I used these settings to change the photograph into a gradient mesh object.

4. Make the bottom two layers visible.
5. Change your page layout so that it is in Landscape mode.

6. Unlock all the layers. Select the entire image (Command/Ctrl+A). Move the image to the upper-left corner. Press Shift and drag the lower-right corner of the bounding box as far down and to the right as it will go while still remaining inside the page boundaries. Save your work. Figure 8.86 shows the finished example.

Figure 8.86
The bitmap layer has become a gradient mesh object, and a wide border with a bevel gives the finishing touch to the image.

This very short project required quite a lot of work to produce the starting image—and you're not necessarily finished with the final image, either. In brief, here's what I did.

In Photoshop, these were the steps:

- I opened the KIDS.PSD image (you have it on the companion CD-ROM).

- I loaded the Cropping Channel alpha and chose Image|Crop.

- I used the Shape channel to select just the children and move them to a new layer.

- I used the process described in the "David" example in Chapter 11 to develop a set of black lines for the image (your shortcut would be to use the Black Outlines channel in the KIDS.PSD image to re-create the layer or the selection). I used the selection to save a path named "Black Outlines". (Another shortcut: In the Assemble folder on this book's CD-ROM is BLACKPATH.AI, all ready for you to use.)

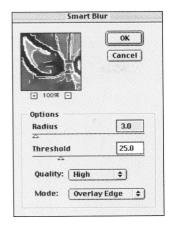

Figure 8.87
I used these Smart Blur settings to create white outlines on the image.

- I made a duplicate copy of the layer containing the children and applied the Smart Blur filter to it in Photoshop. Figure 8.87 shows the settings I used.

- With the Magic Wand Tolerance set to 0 and the Anti-Alias checkbox deselected, I clicked on a white outline in the image. I then chose Select|Similar. I saved the selection to a channel, blurred the channel, and used the tricks shown in Chapter 10 to thicken the line. (The Filter|Other|Maximum filter can also help thicken the line.) If you're feeling lazy, you can use the White Outlines channel to make the selection to create the White Outlines path. (If you're feeling even lazier, you can use the WHITEPATH.AI image in the Assemble folder.)

- I used the Shape channel—or the selection of the nontransparent Layer pixels (Command/Ctrl+click on the Layer name in the Layers palette)— to create a Shape path, which I then turned into a clipping path. I tossed out all the layers except for the image of the children that used the Shape channel and saved the image as an EPS file so that the clipping path was saved.

- I exported the Black Outline path and White Outline path, each in its own file, as paths to Illustrator. (You need to export them individually; otherwise, the paths become intertwined, and you can't get them colored or untangled.)

These steps worked in Illustrator:

- I assembled the whole thing in Illustrator. I opened the EPS file first. Then, I opened the BLACKPATH.AI file and filled the shapes with black and opened the WHITEPATH.AI file and filled the shapes with white (if you use mine, they are already filled for you). I grouped each of the path images. I dragged both images (each on a separate layer) into the EPS file, selected everything, and used the Align palette to align them.

- I created the Background layer, made a small pattern with a transparent background to place over it, created the large black border, and made the shapes for the bevel blend. You can see how I completed each of these steps by pulling apart the starting image.

Where can you go from here? I gave you the "simple" route to creating the gradient mesh object. You can go back into the object and edit it to add colors left out from the original or to change the coloring completely. You can make it as realistic or abstract as you wish. You could also revert to the original starting point and, instead of converting the bitmap layer into a gradient mesh object, use it as a basis for creating your own gradient mesh object. This gradient mesh could be as large as the bitmapped image or could be done as several smaller gradient mesh objects. The choice is yours. Enjoy!

Moving On

Although I could say much more about any topic in this chapter, it is regretfully time to move on. You have learned how to create blends and to use them either to mimic shaded objects or to create linear blends, which can be opened or closed.

You've discovered many ways to create and edit gradients and ways to use them, in conjunction with blends, to simulate reality. I had neither time nor room to show you how to create an entire image made up of blends and to segment the image into sections that could be adjusted with the Filter|Colors|Adjust Colors filter. However, if you remember this suggestion, you'll have all the knowledge that you need to create this effect after you have finished the book.

Finally, you had the chance to create gradient mesh objects and to learn how they react. They are wonderful tools when you learn how to deal with them.

In Chapter 9, David Xenakis shows you how to create some incredible effects using type.

Chapter 9

Textures with Type

By David Xenakis

*Contemporary graphic design places an incredible
message burden on type. More than almost any era in
Western history since the era of illuminated manuscripts,
type is used simultaneously as decorative element, image
container, and literal information conveyer.*

Entire books have been devoted to spectacular effects using software such as Adobe's two superb programs, Illustrator and Photoshop. Designers have learned to make letters appear to be metallic, transparent as glass, surrounded by fire, or made visible with otherworldly light. They have also created many other effects of unprecedented complexity.

The shapes of type characters have proliferated as well. Letters have become distorted in subtle or blatant ways. Coexisting in this complex world of letterforms are fonts of great subtlety and elegance and fonts of unbelievable grotesquerie. In short, many sophisticated tools have been placed in the hands of graphic designers.

In this chapter, the goal is to deliver two more techniques to add to the contemporary array. These two are not the sorts that produce the visual splendor of gleaming and embossed metal. They are quieter and, frankly, require a good deal of meticulous work for them to work successfully. However, I hope you will enjoy the intricate beauty of letters used as textures, as well as the rigors of accomplishing these two techniques with precision. In the process, you will learn a number of useful Illustrator techniques that you will be able to apply to many other situations.

Black Ink and White Paper Produce the Illusion of Gray

It's likely that no one working in the printing industry is immune from the wonder of being able to reproduce continuous-tone grayscale images using a single, opaque ink. Tiny dots of ink represent the relative darkness or lightness in an area of an image. Each dot is placed in the center of an area that is identical in size to every other area. Some of these dots fill a small percentage of the area; others fill most or all of the area. Between this array of ink dots, you'll find only the white of the paper on which the dots are printed. When the dots are tiny, as they are in most printing situations, your eyes cannot see them individually. Instead, your brain averages the darkness of the dots and lightness of the paper, causing you to see tones of gray.

It surprises many people that gray values can be accomplished using shapes other than round dots. Dots can be ovals, diamond-shaped, cross-shaped, or any number of small, regular shapes that can be scaled with a minimum of computation. One fascinating shape is the linear dot function. The linear dot is not often used as a substitute for the conventional round dot, especially at high screen frequencies. However, at quite low frequencies, it produces a decorative effect that is arresting. To begin this chapter, let's look at this interesting photo effect. By understanding it, you'll understand the principle behind both of the type textures that you will learn in this chapter.

Try the linear dot for yourself if you have a copy of Adobe Photoshop. Use any photograph; the procedure is simple. Begin with a grayscale image such as the one shown in Figure 9.1. For best results, it's wise to make the image quite a bit lighter than normal, but take care that the highlights do not become washed out or that the shadows do not become too dark.

Figure 9.1
This photo was prepared by lightening it overall and by carefully managing the very dark and very light tones. It's ready to be converted to a halftone using a linear dot function.

In Photoshop, take the following steps:

1. From the Image menu, select Mode|Bitmap. The dialog box shown in Figure 9.2 then appears. In this dialog box, you can make the resolution of your image much higher. In this case, the resolution doubles. This situation is one of the few times when using Photoshop that it is not harmful to increase the resolution.

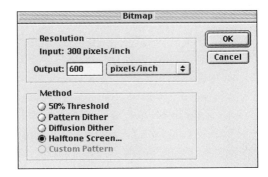

Figure 9.2
This dialog box appears when a Grayscale image in Photoshop is switched to Bitmap mode.

2. Choose also the Halftone Screen option in the lower part of the box. When you click on OK, another dialog box appears, as shown in Figure 9.3. Here, you enter the Frequency of the screen, or how many lines you want to see in one inch. You also enter the angle and the shape of the dot. In this case, I have chosen Line and an Angle of 0 degrees. These choices will make the resulting lines horizontal.

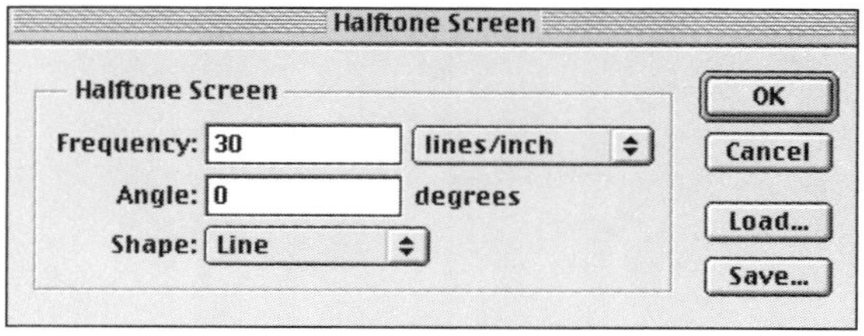

Figure 9.3

Another dialog box appears if the Halftone Screen option is chosen from the choices shown in Figure 9.2.

3. Click on OK. The image then changes to that shown slightly magnified in Figure 9.4. You can see the lines even more clearly in Figure 9.5.

Figure 9.4

(Left) This stylized effect is the result of choosing a linear screen at 0 degrees. Notice the way the lines indicate the tone values by widening or narrowing.

Figure 9.5

(Right) This magnification of Figure 9.4 shows how the lines do not change abruptly but blend smoothly as they become more or less wide.

Notice how the lines express the dark and light tones by becoming wider or narrower as the values dictate. Notice also that the lines do not abruptly jump from one width to another but smoothly change from wide to narrow and back. You will be putting your new knowledge of how this all works to good use.

Making Type Work as a Halftone Effect

For Macintosh users there is a fascinating shareware program called Pict2Ascii. The program is by the French programmer Pascal Lamboley. Pict2Ascii reads PICT format files and generates text, using a monospaced font, to represent the picture. The author of this program has cleverly assigned the letters of whatever font is used an arbitrary grayscale value. The program then places the letters where they are equivalent to the gray values of the original. A copy of this program is included on this book's companion CD-ROM.

Note: Programs equivalent to Pict2Ascii may be available for Windows users, but I have not been able to locate them on the Internet.

Using this program is simple:

1. Begin with a grayscale image. Adjust it in Photoshop, as I suggested previously.

2. Make the contrast of the image as strong as possible without making the highlights too light or the shadows too dark.

3. Save the file in the PICT format.

   For purposes of illustration, I'm using the photo in Figure 9.6, one of three photos used in this chapter taken from the modeling portfolio of South Dakota model and fitness expert David Hardick. An enlarged detail of this photo is shown in Figure 9.7.

4. After you start the program, use the Open command to choose the file on which to operate. Figure 9.8 shows with what success the image is reinterpreted using letters of the Andale Mono font.

Figure 9.6
(Left) Photo of David Hardick, used as a trial image for some of the texture effects in this chapter.

Figure 9.7
(Right) Enlarged detail from the image in Figure 9.6.

One value of this program is that a photograph can be reduced to a text file. The resulting file is many times smaller than the original photo. However, this size difference comes at the expense of file resolution. As interesting as this program is, it doesn't allow much interactivity. The assignment of the letters is automatic, and the program doesn't have built-in editing capabilities. To work on this image, you need to place it in a text editor and hope for the best. What if (rather than automatic assignment of values) you could perform this task in Illustrator, using letter shapes of your choice and could interpret the brightness values of the image far more successfully?

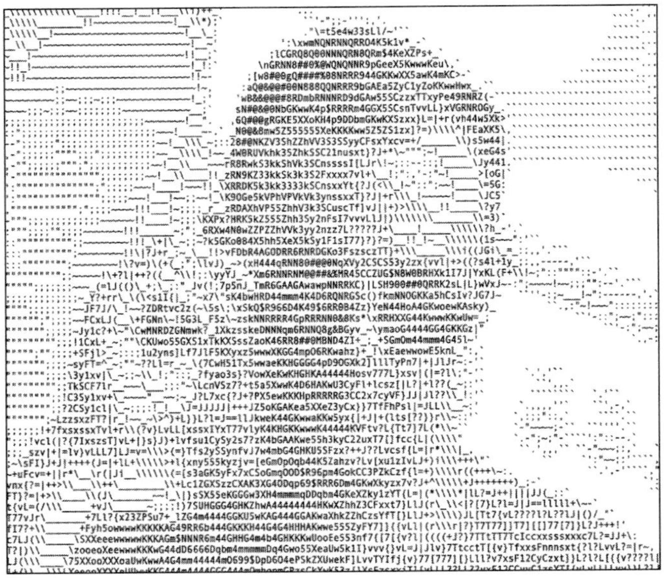

Figure 9.8

Detail of the image in Figure 9.6 after it was converted to text by the program Pict2Ascii. For a close look at the results of applying this program to this photo, see the file fxCD_09_01.eps on this book's companion CD-ROM.

PROJECT 9.1 Making the Photo Image-Ready

You can, in fact, perform the same task in Illustrator! The results probably will surprise you and give you many ideas for other treatments. In this project, you will work magic using the same photo. The file you'll use is located on this book's companion CD-ROM. The file is titled fxCD_09_02.eps.

1. Open the image in Photoshop and convert it to Grayscale mode.

2. Choose Image|Adjust|Posterize. Enter the value "16". The slightly unattractive results of the posterization are shown in Figure 9.9.

Figure 9.9

This figure shows the photo after it is subjected to Photoshop's Posterize command. The total number of gray values has been reduced to 16.

Before you can operate directly on this file in Illustrator 9, you need to convert the photograph to a set of filled paths. I used Adobe's Streamline program, software that traces around areas of color and converts those

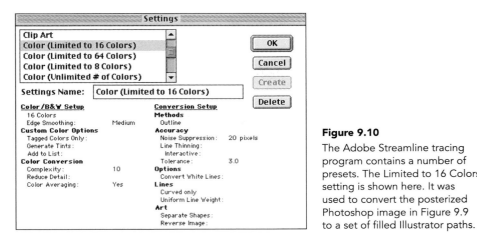

Figure 9.10

The Adobe Streamline tracing program contains a number of presets. The Limited to 16 Colors setting is shown here. It was used to convert the posterized Photoshop image in Figure 9.9 to a set of filled Illustrator paths.

shapes to paths. Streamline furnishes a number of presets. This example uses the one shown in Figure 9.10, a setting that ensures that the number of colors stays at 16. If you don't have access to Streamline, you can still follow along by using the file fxCD_09_02.eps located on this book's companion CD-ROM. If you don't own Streamline and intend to use the effects shown in this chapter, I recommend that you purchase a copy. (Internet vendors at the time of this writing offer Streamline at an average price of $130. Among the sources for this program are **www.adobe.com**, and a number of other software resellers, including **www.eyewire.com** and **www.macconnection.com** or **www.pcconnection.com**.) Streamline fills a specialized need, but it's invaluable when that need arises. If you want, you can construct your Paths in Photoshop and then transfer them to Illustrator. However, this process is so tedious, cumbersome, and time-consuming that it really isn't worth your while to do so.

After Streamline finishes converting the Photoshop file, the image will look much like the original. The converted file is shown in Figure 9.11. Here, it's shown in Preview mode from within Illustrator. However, if you look at the image in Outline view, you can see the set of paths drawn by Streamline (see Figure 9.12).

You'll perform one more series of operations on this file before you leave it to prepare the type that will substitute for the 16 colors. You will select all the shapes of the same color, one at a time, and move similarly colored objects to layers of their own.

3. Click within a shape that is filled with the lightest color.

4. Choose Edit|Select|Same Fill Color.

5. Click on the New Layer icon at the bottom of the Layers palette. Double-click on the new layer on the palette. When the Layer Options dialog box opens, rename this layer "01" and click on OK.

Figure 9.11

(Left) After Streamline converts the photo to a set of filled paths, the file opens in Illustrator. In Preview mode, the image looks much the way it did before.

Figure 9.12

(Right) The same file, viewed in Outline mode, shows the paths drawn by Streamline.

6. On the far right of each item on the palette list, you'll see a small, colored rectangle—usually blue for the beginning layer. This rectangle indicates that some or all of the objects on the layer are selected. Drag this small rectangle up to the next layer to transfer the objects from the original layer to the new layer. Click on the eye icon of Layer 01 to hide it.

7. Select the original layer again. Click on an object filled with the lightest remaining color. Use the Edit|Select|Same Fill Color command to select all the other objects that are the same.

8. Create a new layer and name it "02". Transfer the selected objects to this layer and click on the eye icon to hide the layer's contents.

Note that because you created this layer while the lowest layer on the palette was selected, the new layer is now beneath the first. As you create succeeding layers, you will be building a list from 01 to 16, reading from the top down, one layer for each color. After you finish, your monitor will show an arrangement similar to Figure 9.13. Although this set of steps may seem needlessly fussy, you will find that it prevents many possible mistakes later.

Creating the Components of the Type Texture

The type specimens in Figure 9.14 are parts of an amazing species of font called Multiple Master. This Multiple Master, named Myriad, is published by Adobe. Myriad is a font of subtle elegance. When put into the Multiple Master format, it very nearly supplies all the fonts you will ever need.

Multiple Masters are built, usually, on axes of dimension. Other axes such as optical scaling can be added. As you can see in the figure, Myriad has two axes, one for weight and one for width. The labeled slider on the MM Design palette controls each axis. Note that you can summon the MM Design palette by selecting the fifth command down in the Type menu.

Figure 9.13
All the shapes containing similar colors have been moved to independent layers. The lightest shapes are on the uppermost layer, and the darkest are on the lowest layer. The layers are named with numbers, 1 through 16.

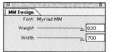

Figure 9.14
The type texture will be created from the Adobe Multiple Master font named Myriad. As you can see from these samples, Myriad is tremendously flexible.

The weight axis runs in a range of the lightest weight at value 215 to a black weight at value 830. Between these extremes are 615 separate, independent weights. You can almost think of the two samples in the upper part of Figure 9.14 as the endpoints of a font blend. The other axis is for width with a range between 300 and 700. They are shown in the two lower samples of the figure. Imagine that you can read from the upper row to the bottom row and have your choice of 400 individual font widths in a range between Condensed and Extended. Note that these width instances are not examples of the horizontal scaling allowed by most page-layout programs, but they are scaled in both directions. Each change in width is a separate and beautifully proportioned face. Horizontal scaling, by contrast, distorts the type so that vertical strokes become wider, while the horizontal strokes remain the same. Overall, horizontal scaling is a dismal thing to do to any font.

As you can see, the difference between a Multiple Master font and a traditional font is substantial. Traditional fonts can contain from four to eight or more variations of the named face. They might include Roman, Oblique, Bold, and Bold Oblique. The Myriad Multiple Master, by contrast, has 246,000 separate faces! An equal number of faces is available from the companion font Myriad Multiple Master Italic. Between the two, then, you have 492,000 separate faces. If this font cost $1,000, it would still be a bargain! (Fortunately, it doesn't!) Within Illustrator, you can pick any face you need by using the sliders on the MM Design palette.

In Project 9.2, you will use the great variety of Myriad MM fonts to create some of the color effects for the type texture you are creating.

PROJECT 9.2 Creating the Elements for Type Texture

1. Open a new document and type the name "DAVID" (the name of the model in the photograph), in uppercase and at a point size of about 30.

2. If you have the Myriad MM font installed, select the word with the Selection tool (press V) and set both of the MM Design sliders to the far left.

   If you do not have Myriad MM, you can open the file fxCD_09_03.eps on this book's companion CD-ROM. It contains embedded versions of the characters shown in Figures 9.15 through 9.18.

3. Hold down Option/Alt and drag a copy of this word directly below the first word (shown in Figure 9.15). Be sure to press Shift after you begin to drag to ensure that the second word is exactly beneath the first.

4. Hold down Command/Ctrl and press D 14 more times. By doing so, you have used the Transform Again command to create a total of 16 versions of the word, all precisely spaced vertically and exactly aligned along the left edges. You have one set of letters for each of the colors used in the Streamline file.

5. The easiest way to assign a light to dark range of tones to these sets of letters is to change the weight values. If you subtract 216 from 830, you have a range of 615 to assign in equal increments. Beginning at 215, each weight value is incremented by 41 (615/15=41). That makes the series of weights assigned as 215, 256, 297, 338, 379, and so on.

6. As you can see from the first column of words in Figure 9.16, changing the weights also changes the width of the words. Fortunately, you have the width slider on the MM Design palette to fix this problem. Zoom in to very close magnification of the lowest word. If your window rulers are not visible, press Command/Ctrl+R.

7. Then, drag a guide out of the vertical ruler and position it precisely on the left edge of the lowest word. Still working at high magnification, drag another guide and place it so that it lines up with the farthest-right curve of the last letter, *D*. Begin at the top of the column of words.

8. Go to the highest magnification with the right edge of the top word and the right-hand guide visible. Select the word. Now, carefully move the width slider on the MM Design palette to the right.

   Your goal is to widen the word so that it exactly touches the right guide. Repeat this same procedure for all the upper 15 words. You should now have a column of words that resemble those on the right in Figure 9.16.

Original (weight only)	Weights
DAVID	215
DAVID	256
DAVID	297
DAVID	338
DAVID	379
DAVID	420
DAVID	461
DAVID	502
DAVID	543
DAVID	584
DAVID	625
DAVID	666
DAVID	707
DAVID	748
DAVID	789
DAVID	830

Figure 9.15
The 16 versions of the name *DAVID* have been assigned true tonal differences by changing the weights evenly across the entire range.

Original (weight only)	Weights	Width Adjusted	Widths
DAVID	215	DAVID	482
DAVID	256	DAVID	470
DAVID	297	DAVID	458
DAVID	338	DAVID	446
DAVID	379	DAVID	434
DAVID	420	DAVID	422
DAVID	461	DAVID	410
DAVID	502	DAVID	398
DAVID	543	DAVID	386
DAVID	584	DAVID	374
DAVID	625	DAVID	362
DAVID	666	DAVID	350
DAVID	707	DAVID	338
DAVID	748	DAVID	326
DAVID	789	DAVID	314
DAVID	830	DAVID	300

Figure 9.16
Changing the weights of each word also changes the widths of the words (right). By using the width slider on the MM Design palette, you can make all the words exactly the same length.

9. To make the dark to light differences between each of the 16 versions of the name even more pronounced, you will also assign tints of black to each. Beginning with the lightest weight, assign a fill of 15 percent black. The next word is filled with 20 percent black. Each descending item becomes 5 percent darker until the bottom value, 90 percent, is reached. Your column of letters should now resemble the right-hand column in Figure 9.17.

Original (weight only)	Weights	Width Adjusted	Widths	Black Tints	Percent
DAVID	215	DAVID	482	DAVID	15
DAVID	256	DAVID	470	DAVID	20
DAVID	297	DAVID	458	DAVID	25
DAVID	338	DAVID	446	DAVID	30
DAVID	379	DAVID	434	DAVID	35
DAVID	420	DAVID	422	DAVID	40
DAVID	461	DAVID	410	DAVID	45
DAVID	502	DAVID	398	DAVID	50
DAVID	543	DAVID	386	DAVID	55
DAVID	584	DAVID	374	DAVID	60
DAVID	625	DAVID	362	DAVID	65
DAVID	666	DAVID	350	DAVID	70
DAVID	707	DAVID	338	DAVID	75
DAVID	748	DAVID	326	DAVID	80
DAVID	789	DAVID	314	DAVID	85
DAVID	830	DAVID	300	DAVID	90

Figure 9.17
Beginning with a light tint of black at the top and increasing by 5% on each item down (right-hand column), the range of tones contained in the 16 items is even more pronounced.

10. Select the entire set of words and change the point size to the final size, 7 points. The right column in Figure 9.18 shows this last transformation.

11. Zoom up very close to the word at the top of the column. Change to Outline mode. Draw a rectangle around the top word, centering it as accurately as you can. If, when you are finished drawing the rectangle, it is not centered as well as it could be, adjust the position of the rect-angle and not the position of the type. Make the fill of this rectangle white. Choose Object|Arrange|Send to Back.

Original (weight only)	Weights	Width Adjusted	Widths	Black Tints	Percent	Reduced to 7 pts
DAVID	215	DAVID	482	DAVID	15	DAVID
DAVID	256	DAVID	470	DAVID	20	DAVID
DAVID	297	DAVID	458	DAVID	25	DAVID
DAVID	338	DAVID	446	DAVID	30	DAVID
DAVID	379	DAVID	434	DAVID	35	DAVID
DAVID	420	DAVID	422	DAVID	40	DAVID
DAVID	461	DAVID	410	DAVID	45	DAVID
DAVID	502	DAVID	398	DAVID	50	DAVID
DAVID	543	DAVID	386	DAVID	55	DAVID
DAVID	584	DAVID	374	DAVID	60	DAVID
DAVID	625	DAVID	362	DAVID	65	DAVID
DAVID	666	DAVID	350	DAVID	70	DAVID
DAVID	707	DAVID	338	DAVID	75	DAVID
DAVID	748	DAVID	326	DAVID	80	DAVID
DAVID	789	DAVID	314	DAVID	85	DAVID
DAVID	830	DAVID	300	DAVID	90	DAVID

Figure 9.18
The final transformation, right column, reduces the point size of all the words to 7.

12. Press V to choose the Select tool. Hold down Option/Alt to drag a copy of this rectangle down the column to frame the second word (see Figure 9.19). Make sure that you hold down Shift as you start to drag. You have already spent time ensuring that the 16 iterations of the word are exactly lined up and exactly the same width. Now, you must ensure that each word is precisely centered within the rectangle and that all the rectangles are precisely aligned. Note that if you are working with the words magnified as large as they are in Figure 9.19, aligning the rectangles by eye is sufficient precision.

13. Press Command/Ctrl+0 (zero) to zoom out to Fit In Window view. Sweep-select all 16 of the rectangles and copy. Reopen the fxCD_09_02.eps file from this book's CD-ROM. Paste the 16 words onto this file. Move the words so that they are positioned along the right-hand edge of the image, as shown in Figure 9.20. It may be helpful also to arrange your Layers palette and your Swatches palette next to each other, as shown in the figure. In a little while, you'll see why this placement is very convenient.

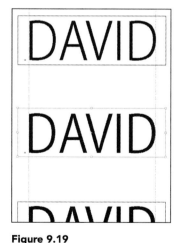

Figure 9.19
After the versions of the word DAVID have been modified, a rectangle filled with white is placed behind each.

Figure 9.20

After pasting the 16 words into the image document, arrange the Layers and Swatches palettes so that they are next to each other.

14. If you have any pattern swatches showing in your palette, getting rid of them might be a good idea. You will be working with 16 crucial swatches, and it is easy to make a mistake. Eliminating the other swatches eliminates one place where you may choose incorrectly. Don't worry; deleting them affects this document only. Next, click on the Pattern icon at the bottom of the Swatches palette. From the triangular pop-up menu in the upper-right corner, choose Select Unused. After the patterns have been selected, click on the Trash icon to delete them. The pattern portion of your palette should now be empty.

15. Sweep-select the top word, the one with the lightest color and the lightest type weight. From the Edit menu, choose Define Pattern. In the dialog box that appears, name this pattern "David 01". Do the same for each of the words, from the top down. Name each in the same way with the name and a number.

After you finish making all 16 patterns, your two palettes will line up perfectly. The lightest pattern, David 01, coincides with the layer containing the lightest-colored objects.

Note: I typically begin numbering files or figures with a zero preceding the single-digit integers. Computer operating systems are notoriously clumsy when arranging numbered files in List View, often placing a number such as 10 before the number 1.

Assembling the Final Image

The next step is to lock all the layers except the top. From here until the completion of the image, you need to click back and forth only on the two palettes. This is the fun part!

16. In Figure 9.21, notice that a small circle appears on the right side of every layer. According to those most familiar with Illustrator 9's latest refinements, this small circle is called—with all the elegance you have come to associate with Adobe products—a *meatball*. This circle has a number of important functions; one of the handiest: When you click on it, everything on that layer becomes selected. Click on the circle for Layer 01.

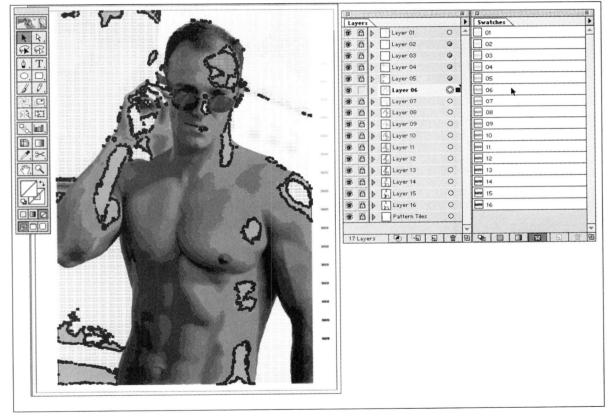

Figure 9.21

As you unlock each layer, one at a time, you select everything on that layer and fill it with the pattern swatch that has the same number.

17. Click on the David 01 pattern on the Swatch palette to immediately change the lightest fill color on the image to the lightest of the letter patterns.

18. Lock Layer 01, unlock Layer 02, and click on pattern David 02.

From here, you need only follow this same procedure for all 16 layers, and your work is done! Figure 9.22 shows the way the image will look after you have filled the first six layers with their patterns.

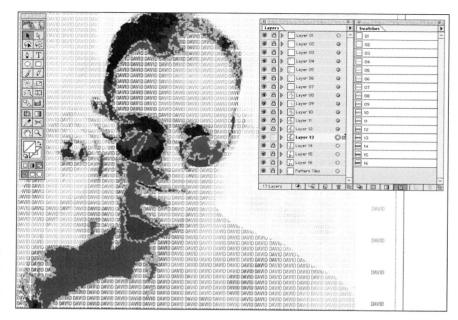

Figure 9.22
This figure shows the assembly process after the first 12 of the layers have been filled with their equivalent pattern swatches.

Note: The file fxCD_09_04.eps on this book's companion CD-ROM contains the finished image. You can open it to look closely at the details.

You've spent quite a bit of time getting ready. Now the final assembly of the image with your type texture is absurdly fast. Take a few moments to study your image or the detail shown in Figure 9.23. Notice how effectively the 16 weights of type, combined with the 16 tints of black, provide an amazing amount of detail. This detail occurs despite the fact that the objects you are using as your screen function are quite large. Pay particular attention to the way all the words are readable and are not disrupted as they cross color boundaries. You could have made this image without this particular bit of wizardry, but it wouldn't have been nearly as cool! All the time you spent ensuring that the words were perfectly aligned and perfectly uniform in width pays off when you see what result it brings.

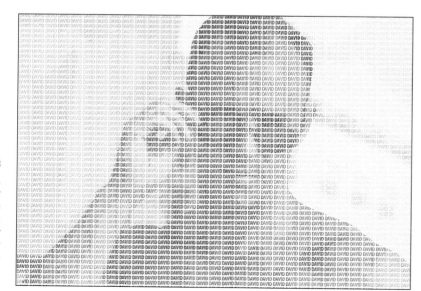

Figure 9.23
In this detail of the final image, notice that the 16 words easily express the gray tones of the original. The image suffers a detail loss, but you have other visual interest to replace it. For example, note how the words can cross tonal boundaries with no interruption of the words.

As you work with this technique, you might want to experiment with some variations. The first look at this technique resulted in a uniform grid within which was the word *DAVID*. Though the effect is quite successful, the rivers of white may seem somewhat intrusive. These white streaks could be made less noticeable in several ways. You could have made the rectangle around each word a closer fit when you constructed the original patterns, for example, you could have made the words smaller. However, this would mean that the cleverness of the technique would be visible only from very close to the image. Another way, shown in progress in Figure 9.24, is to turn the patterns 45 degrees off horizontal.

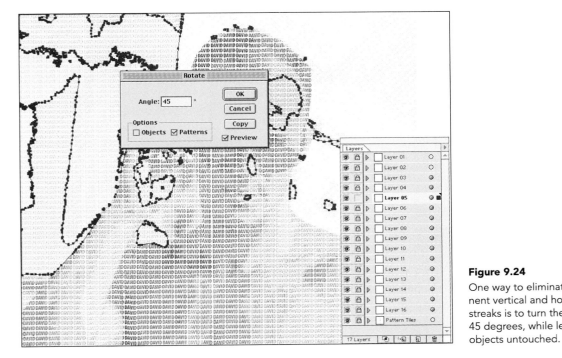

Figure 9.24
One way to eliminate the prominent vertical and horizontal white streaks is to turn the patterns 45 degrees, while leaving the objects untouched.

This procedure is, if anything, even easier than the previous. If you like, you can apply this effect to the work you just finished. Alternatively, you can open the file fxCD_09_05.eps from the CD-ROM. This file has all the patterns turned so that you can look at the finished effect on your monitor.

1. Hold down Command/Ctrl and press 0 (zero). This action fits your image into the window. It also allows you to see the upper-left corner of your artboard. This step is important, as you'll soon see.

2. Lock all your layers except the top. Click on the layer's Target circle, the same one you clicked before to select everything on the layer.

3. Press R to select the Rotate tool. Place your cursor as precisely as you can on the upper-left corner of the page. Hold down Option/Alt and click once. The Rotate dialog box shown in Figure 9.24 then appears. Type "45" in the data entry field.

4. For Options, the Objects checkbox should be off (unchecked), but the Patterns checkbox should be on. These settings rotate the patterns within the selected objects without moving the objects. You can repeat this procedure for each layer.

The effect is also shown in Figure 9.25.

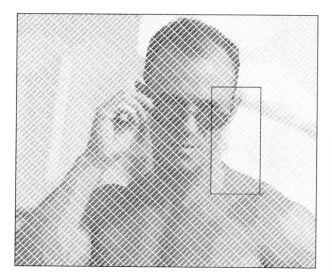 

Figure 9.25
This image is an enlargement of the effect of rotating the patterns after they have been applied as horizontal.

It is important to note that you must click precisely on the upper-left corner of the page as you rotate the patterns. You need to click here because patterns are calculated beginning at the upper-left corner, or the *origin* of the page. Were you to select the Rotate tool and simply click on the target that appears at the center of the selection, the patterns would rotate around that center instead of around the origin of the page. If each pattern rotates around its own center, the patterns will not align as they cross color boundaries. You will still have the halftone effect, but without the bonus of coherent words everywhere in the image.

A More Complex Variation of the Pattern Effect

You can disturb the white streaking in the image in a third way. Instead of stacking the words so that they align vertically and horizontally, you could stack them as staggered shapes to produce an all-over brick-like texture. To do so, you will have to do some work on the original patterns. This work is not difficult, but as before, it demands precision if the final image is to be as effective as the first two have been:

1. From the book's CD, open the file fxCD_09_07.eps. This file contains the original tiles used for this project. You will modify them to learn how to make a set of words that will combine into the brick configuration.

2. Change to outline mode and zoom in to the top word of the column. Press V to choose the Selection tool. Sweep-select both the word and the rectangle and select Group from the Object menu.

3. Zoom in to maximum magnification. Drag a guide from the vertical ruler and position it exactly atop the two center live points of the bounding box.

4. Hold down Option/Alt and drag a copy of this rectangle up and to the left, as shown in Figure 9.26. Take care that you make the rectangle of the new shape align precisely with the top of the original rectangle and with the guide (see Figure 9.27).

Figure 9.26
Copy and move the rectangle copy.

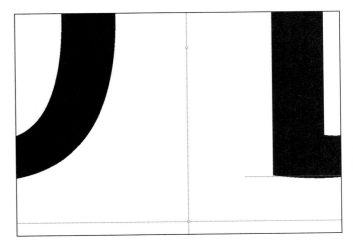

Figure 9.27
Make sure the work is done at maximum magnification to ensure that the boundary lines of all three words are perfectly aligned.

5. Hold down the same key and drag another copy to the right. Hold down Shift as you begin to drag to ensure that the copy will be perfectly aligned with its neighbor.

6. Select all three words and select the Ungroup command from the Object menu.

7. Sweep-select the top two words and lock them by holding down Command/Ctrl and pressing the number 2. Select the word in the tile below and lock it as well.

8. Press A to change to the Direct Select tool. Hold down Shift after you begin to drag the top of the lower rectangle up toward the top of the upper rectangles (see Figure 9.28). As before, zoom in to make sure that the two paths are perfectly aligned.

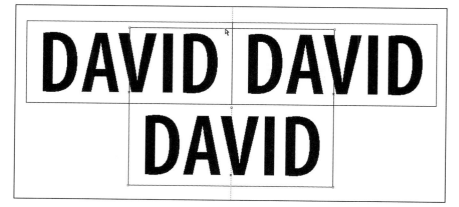

Figure 9.28
Drag the lower rectangle up so that it perfectly matches the top lines of the other two rectangles.

9. Hold down Command+Option/Ctrl+Alt and press 2 to unlock the locked objects. Press V to switch to the Selection cursor. Delete the two upper rectangles. You have nearly finished the tile, and your work should look similar to Figure 9.29.

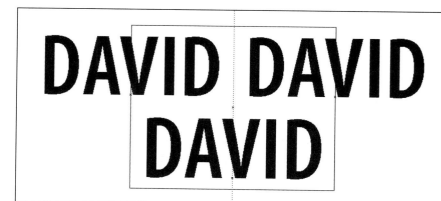

Figure 9.29
After you delete the two upper rectangles, the tile is nearly finished.

10. You now have the boundary of the new tile. What you want of the new tile is to trim off the portions that extend beyond the boundaries so that it will appear as in Figure 9.30 and join side to side the way you see it in Figure 9.31. To make this happen, Illustrator has an odd requirement: the lowest object in the stacking order must be a rectangle the same size as the boundary rectangle but must have no fill and stroke. In this case, select the boundary rectangle and copy it. Now, use the

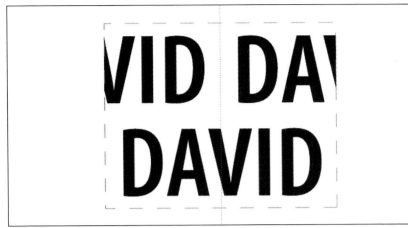

Figure 9.30
The final tile will appear like this. The parts of the words extending past the rectangle will be cut off when the Pattern is defined.

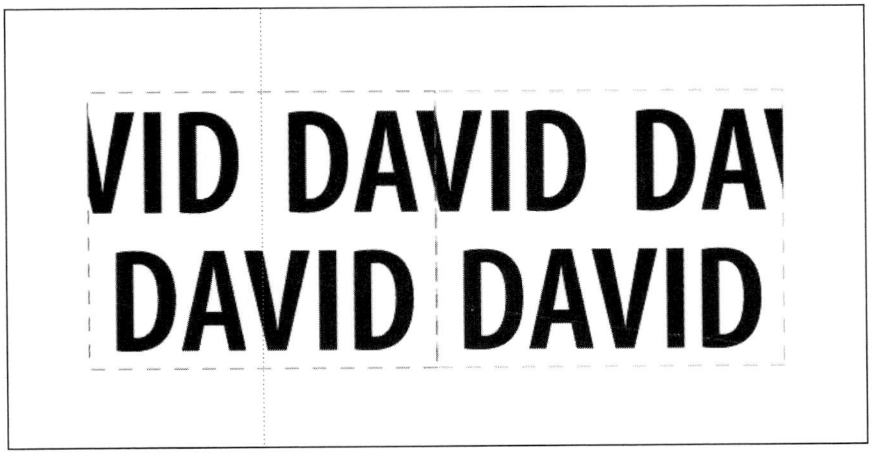

Figure 9.31
Because of the way the tile was constructed, the pattern tiles join with no visible seam.

Paste in Back command (Command/Ctrl+B). This special paste puts a copy of the object exactly behind itself. While this rectangle is still selected, change its fill from white to none. You are now finished with the first brick pattern. Now you perform exactly this sequence of manipulations on each of the other 15 words.

11. Select all your modified tiles and copy them.

12. Open, again, the original file from this book's companion CD-ROM, fxCD_09_02.eps. The file is just as it was before you applied the original tiles to it. Paste your modified tiles into the document and drag them over to the edge of the pasteboard (see Figure 9.32). Sweep-select each of the tiles and use the Define Pattern command (Edit menu). After you have defined all 16 patterns, line up the Swatches and Layers palettes as before.

Figure 9.32
Paste the newly constructed word groups onto the original layered file. Define the patterns as before.

13. Unlock the top layer and change its fill to the top pattern. Repeat this procedure for each of the 15 remaining layers. After you have finished, your image will look similar to that shown in Figure 9.33. The magnified detail in Figure 9.34 shows how the care used during the construction of the tiles pays off with perfect transitions between the tiles and across the fill boundaries. You can find the final file on this book's companion CD-ROM as file fxCD_09_06.eps.

Type Textures Using the Pen & Ink Filter

The previous texture and the one explored in the second half of this chapter have many similarities. In both cases, you use type as a texture to replace solid colors. Both techniques make use of seamless pattern tiles. Both apply the tiles in the same manner. The difference is in how the tiles are constructed. In this exercise, you will be making use of the Illustrator Pen & Ink filter to generate the type tiles.

Figure 9.33

After the new patterns are substituted for the simple fill colors, the result is this brick-like arrangement of the pattern tiles.

Figure 9.34

This close-up shows how care in making the tiles ensures excellent transitions between the words and across color boundaries.

PROJECT 9.3 Expressing Halftone Values with Jumbled-Letter Tiles

You will begin, as before, with a photograph. The image in Figure 9.35 is another shot from the portfolio of South Dakota model and fitness expert David Hardick. After I adjusted and posterized the photo, I saved it and then converted to paths by using Adobe Streamline (see Figure 9.36).

If you don't have access to Streamline, you can follow along with this exercise by opening the file fxCD_09_08.eps from this book's companion CD-ROM.

Figure 9.35

(Left) For the second type texture, you will use another portfolio shot of the model used in the first example.

Figure 9.36

(Right) The photo was prepared in the same way as the first. It was then converted to paths by Adobe Streamline. This image has also been reduced to 16 colors.

This file is the same as shown in the Figure 9.36. Also, you can open the file fxCD_09_06.eps, on which you'll find the Myriad MM tiles used in the first exercise. Because the work has already been done, you may as well use these letter sets again—but for a very different purpose.

1. To start, make the file fxCD_09_06.eps your active window. Select all the rectangles that defined the original tiles and delete them.

2. Select All and set the fill of the letters to solid black, no tints.

3. While all the letters are selected, choose Create Outlines from the Type menu.

4. Change your view mode to Outline.

You are going to be using these sets of letters as hatches with the Pen & Ink filter, objects that the filter will use to create an all-over texture made up of the letters. The hatch will show the five letters sprinkled over an area. All the letters will occur in a variety of sizes, and all will be shown in a variety of orientations. If you like, take a quick look forward to Figure 9.58 to get an idea of how a hatch looks.

You could put the letters into the filter as they now stand. However, the filter does not understand compound paths. Because of that, it will treat the inner paths of the *D* and the *A* as separate objects. These two letters, then, won't have the counter holes in them. To make them appear to be real letters, you need to do some surgery. You will need to take any letters like the *D* and the *A* and make them into something that resembles a compound path but is not.

1. Press A to choose the Direct Select tool. Sweep-select across the two path segments marked by the arrows in Figure 9.37.

2. Cut these segments (see Figure 9.38).

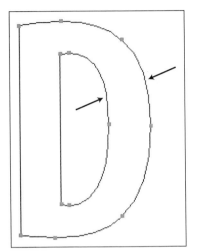 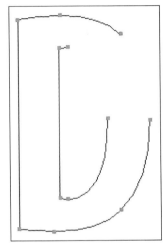

Figure 9.37
(Left) Sweep-select across the path segments marked by the arrows.

Figure 9.38
(Right) Cut the two segments from the shape.

3. Sweep-select across the two points at the lower part of the missing paths. Hold down Command/Ctrl+J (Join). A line then stretches between these points to join them. The result is shown in Figure 9.39.

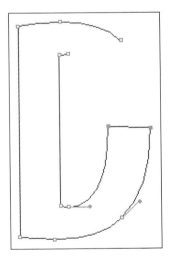

Figure 9.39
Use the Join command to place a path across two of the endpoints.

4. Hold down Command/Ctrl and press the number 3. This command temporarily hides the paths.

5. Your clipboard still holds the two paths you cut from the letter. Use the Paste in Front command from the Edit menu to put a copy of the two paths precisely where they were before you cut them (see Figure 9.40).

6. Sweep-select across the two lower points and use the Join command again, as shown in Figure 9.41. Hold down Command+Option/Ctrl+Alt and press 3.

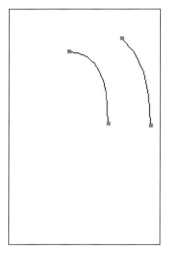 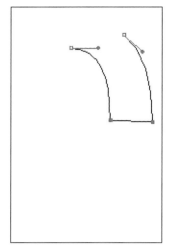

Figure 9.40

(Left) Hide the cut letter shape, and use the Paste in Front command to put the two cut paths back into position.

Figure 9.41

(Right) Join the two lower path endpoints.

7. This command is the opposite of the Hide command; it shows whatever was previously hidden.

8. Now, sweep-select across the two nodes marked by the upper arrow in Figure 9.42. You need to select in this way because you have two points, one sitting exactly atop the other. Use the Join command. When the resulting dialog box appears, you can decide whether you want the new join to be a Smooth point or a Corner point. In this case, the correct choice is Smooth.

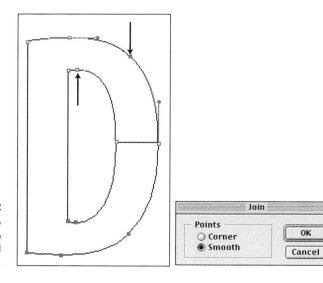

Figure 9.42

Show the hidden part of the shape. Sweep-select the two sets of overlapping points and join each.

9. Sweep-select the other pair of points (marked by the lower arrow in Figure 9.42) and join them as well.

What you have accomplished with this series of moves is the slicing of the letter but with the sliced ends so close to each other that the letter appears to be a true compound path. You could, if you wanted, move the slice lines apart. Figure 9.43 shows how the altered *D* would look if you did.

Some Tips on Making Letters into Non-Compound Shapes

The method of slicing letters you just learned was calculated to teach you exactly what is involved with the process. However, a much easier way to do the job is shown in the following steps:

1. Choose the Pen tool. Click outside the letter shape. Click again on the other, inner, side of the letter shape. (You have just drawn a path that crosses the letter.)

2. From the Object menu, choose Path|Slice. That's it—very simple and quick.

If you attempt to alter a letter such as the uppercase *B* shown at the left of Figure 9.44, the temptation is to slice across the center horizontal because it requires only one cut. As you can see from the center of Figure 9.44, moving the two edges apart reveals that you have changed only one compound path to another. The letter shape needs to be sliced in two places (see Figure 9.44, right).

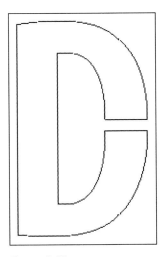

Figure 9.43
Moving the two slice lines away from each other reveals that the letter is no longer a compound.

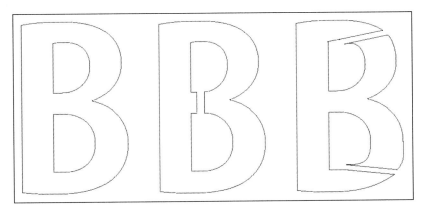

Figure 9.44
When you're slicing a shape such as the *B* on the right, the temptation is to slice across the middle horizontal section because it is less work. The center shape reveals that this technique slices the letter shape, but it is still a compound path. The right-hand shape shows that the *B* must be sliced twice to change it so that it is no longer a compound.

Sometimes, you might want to use letterforms that are composed of two or three separate pieces. The lowercase *i* shown in Figure 9.45 is one example. Using this shape with the Pen & Ink filter separates these detached shapes and treats them as separate objects. For the letter to seem to stay intact, a different kind of treatment is required.

Figure 9.45

(Left) Letter shapes that are composed of detached pieces present a special case because the Pen & Ink filter treats the two shapes as separate.

Figure 9.46

(Right) Two guides have been placed very close together. The Scissors tool was used to cut two small segments where the guides crossed the shapes. These segments have been deleted.

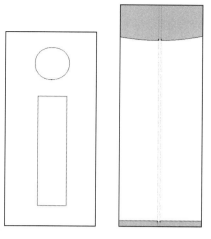

You need to work in Outline mode and, though you need to have the shapes magnified as much as possible, you need to be able to see both the bottom of the circle and the top of the rectangle. These parts are shown in Figure 9.46. The figure also shows that a pair of guides has been placed closely together near the centers of both shapes.

1. Use the Scissors tool to cut on each guide where they cross both shapes.

2. Select the small segments between the cuts and delete them. Figure 9.46 showed that the segments have been eliminated.

3. With the Direct Select tool and the Shift key held down, click on the left-hand endpoint of both shapes to select them at the same time. Apply the Join command.

4. Do the same to the other two endpoints. When you finish, you will have a narrow band that joins the two pieces into a single closed shape. The result is shown in Figure 9.47.

Figure 9.47

The endpoints of the upper and lower paths have been joined so that you no longer have two shapes but one. The two are now connected with the narrow connector caused by joining the endpoints.

5. Still using the Direct Selection tool, sweep-select all four of the points at the top and bottom of this narrow piece. Hold down Command+Option/ Ctrl+Alt and press J. The Average dialog box then appears (see Figure 9.48). Choose the Vertical option, and click on OK.

All four points are now forced into vertical alignment. That step closes the narrow corridor between the upper and lower shapes into a connection of no width (see Figure 9.49). You will always be able to see this line when you work in Outline mode. It will also be faintly visible even in Preview mode. If you try to use a shape such as this in an Illustrator file, you will find that the connecting line will be faintly visible on a printout. The connecting line is so faint, however, that you may have trouble seeing it. If you rasterize the letter, you may see the connector on the screen, but it is unlikely that it will print, even at very large sizes. The appearance of the line—vector reproduction on the left and raster reproduction on the right—is shown in Figure 9.50.

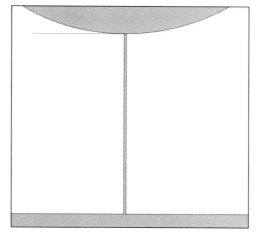

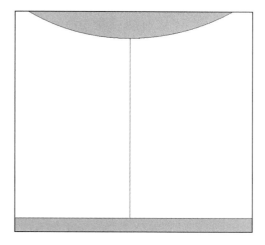

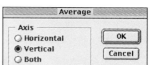

Figure 9.48

Use the Average command to force all four of the connector points into vertical alignment.

Figure 9.49

(Left) After aligning the points, the shape is still closed. The connector is now 0 points wide.

Figure 9.50

(Right) In Preview mode, the connector is still visible as a faint line on the left. Under some circumstances, this line will be visible when printed. In other cases, it will not be visible.

To save you some time when you want to experiment later, you can use the file titled fxCD_09_09.eps on this book's companion CD-ROM. A reduced view of the contents of this file is shown in Figure 9.51. As you can see, I included the uppercase, lowercase, and special characters of that ubiquitous font Times. I also included the uppercase sets for Goudy OldStyle, Huxley Vertical, and Cotillion. The file also contains four other sets of letters. One is a mixed font group containing all the upper- and lowercase letters. The other three are mixed-font groups of the uppercase letters *A*, *B*, and *C*. All these letters have been changed to outlines, all the compound paths have been sliced, and all the noncontiguous letters have been joined the way the preceding example was joined.

Making Hatches with Your Altered Letter Shapes

To begin the next part of this exercise, you must slice all occurrences of the letters *D* and *A* in the 16 type samples contained in file fxCD_09_06, the file you now have open. After you finish, you will be ready to create hatches with your letter shapes.

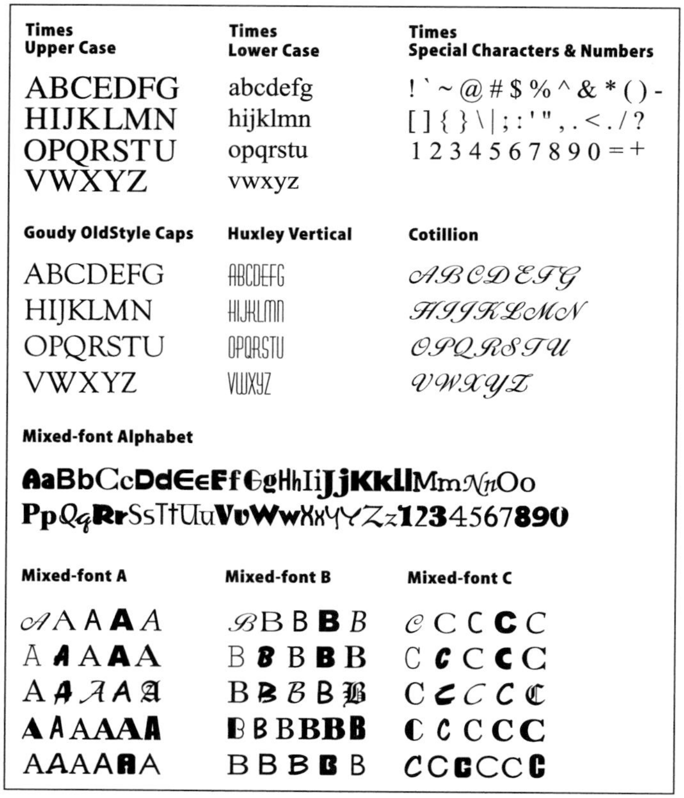

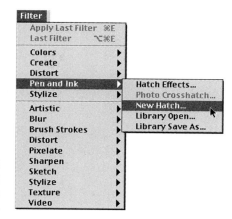

Figure 9.51

So that you can experiment with letter shapes as hatches, I included the file fxCD_09_09.eps on the book's companion CD-ROM. This figure shows the file's contents.

1. To get started, first select the top group of letters—those of the lightest weight of Myriad MM. Choose Filter|Pen And Ink|New Hatch (see Figure 9.52).

Figure 9.52

With one group of your altered letter shapes selected, choose the New Hatch command.

2. When the New Hatch dialog box opens, click on the New button. Another dialog box then appears; here, you type the name of your new hatch. Continue the convention you have been using and name the new hatch "David 01". These two dialog boxes are shown in the top dialog box in Figure 9.53. Click on OK and then OK again to close them.

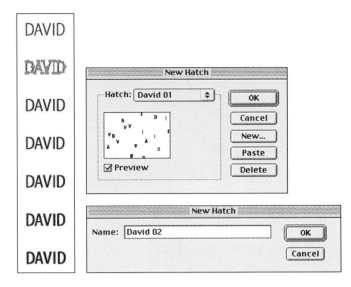

Figure 9.53

The top dialog box appears when you choose Filter| Pen And Ink|New Hatch.

3. Select the next set of letters and repeat the process. This time, name the hatch "David 02" (see the bottom dialog box, Figure 9.53).

4. Repeat this procedure 14 more times. When you finish, the pop-up menu in the New Hatch dialog box will look similar to Figure 9.54.

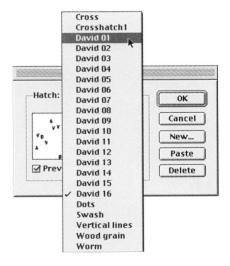

Figure 9.54

One at a time, each of the letter sets is defined as a hatch. The naming convention used throughout this chapter has been maintained.

5. After you have entered all 16 of the letter sets, open the CD-ROM file named fxCD_09_10.eps. On this file, you will see 16 small rectangles. All are filled with tints of black, the same tints used for the letters in the first example in this chapter.

6. Click on the square marked 15 (% of black). Under the Filter menu, choose Pen And Ink|Hatch Effects. A complex dialog box (see Figure 9.55) that seems to contain far too many choices then appears! You'll tame those choices shortly.

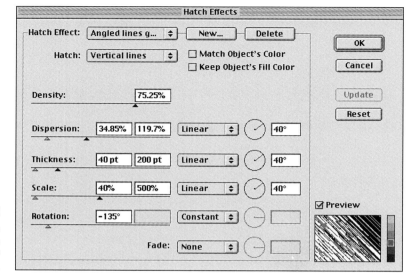

Figure 9.55

When you first meet the Hatch Effects dialog box, it seems to contain a bewildering number of choices.

Figure 9.56

The Hatch Effect pop-up menu contains 25 presets. This texture effect will use Stipple Medium.

7. The Pen & Ink filter has a number of built-in settings. You can, if you like, experiment with the choices that appear when you click and hold open the Hatch Effect pop-up menu (see Figure 9.56), but when you have finished looking, select Stipple Medium.

8. Click on the Hatch pop-up menu Hatch Effect area. Then, select the hatch David 01. You need to change some of the settings that appeared when you selected Stipple Medium. Make your settings agree with the dialog box shown in Figure 9.57.

9. Click on the New button at the top of the Hatch Effect area. A new dialog box appears. It is shown at the top of Figure 9.57. Type a name such as the one shown at the top of the figure and click on OK. Note that it is important that you click on the checkbox labeled Match Object's Color.

Let's quickly run through the meaning of some of the settings here. Within the parameters of the former Stipple setting, the Density is set to its maximum. The other settings—Dispersion, Scale, and Rotation—are all set to function at random. The two numbers for each serve as the minimum and maximum values for that option.

10. Click on OK in the Hatch Effects dialog box.

The 15% box is suddenly filled with a variety of objects. You need to deselect these objects to see what the Hatch filter has produced. The square is transformed and now appears as shown in Figure 9.58. Notice the random rotation of the letters, the differences in size, and the random dispersal of the letter shape. When you change to Outline mode, the square appears as shown in Figure 9.59. The Pen & Ink filter changed the original square to a mask and applied the square's original color to the letters.

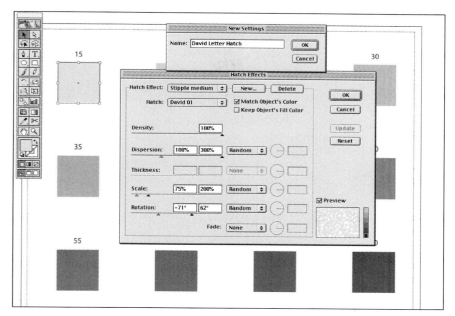

Figure 9.57

Most of the settings to be used in this exercise use a Hatch Effects setup very close to this one.

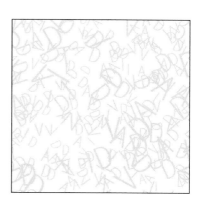

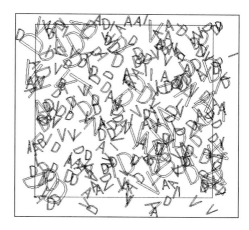

Figure 9.58

(Left) The 15% square looks like this after the filter has operated on it. The square has been changed to a mask, and the square color has been applied to the letters.

Figure 9.59

(Right) In Outline mode, the mixture of letters is even more clear.

11. Make each of the squares into a hatch-filled object. As you move from one square to another, be sure to change the hatch to the next number of the 16 you defined. The squares become filled with ever darker and heavier letter shapes.

Modifying the Hatch-Filled Squares

The Pen & Ink filter works beautifully—but with one small flaw for the use you will find for it here. To fill the area more completely, you need to change the scale option. The upper limit must be closer to 400 percent instead of the 200 percent used in the setting. However, a setting of 400 percent produces a cluttered hatch effect that loses the individual letters. To remedy this problem, you will do some work on this square.

1. If you are not in Outline view mode, switch to it. Click on the square to select it.

2. You need to eliminate the mask. Choose Object|Clipping Mask|Release.

3. From the same menu, choose Ungroup.

4. Click away from the objects to deselect them. Click on the rectangle, change its fill to white, send it to the back, and lock it.

5. Sweep-select all the hatch letters. Hold down Option/Alt and drag the letter group to the right. Make sure that you press Shift after you begin to drag. You have now cloned all the letter shapes and have moved the copies so that they overlap the right half of the original set (see Figure 9.60).

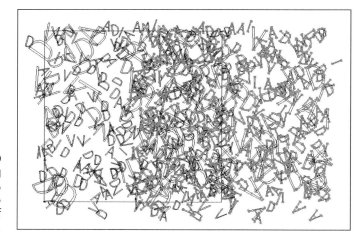

Figure 9.60

Select all the letter shapes and drag a clone of the group to the right. Position the new group so that it overlaps the right half of the originals.

6. Press the same modifier key and drag another group to the left so that this group overlaps the left half of the originals (see Figure 9.61). You have now doubled the density of the letter shapes within the rectangle's boundaries.

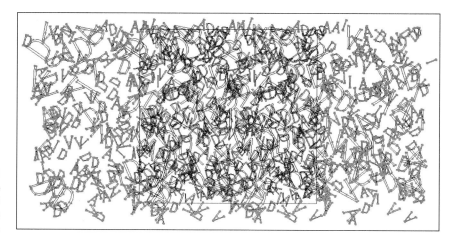

Figure 9.61

Without deselecting, drag a clone of the group to the left. Position this group so that it overlaps the left half of the originals.

7. Sweep-select the letters outside the square and delete them. When you select, make sure that you do not get too close to the edges of the square; just eliminate most of the shapes outside the boundaries. You'll eliminate the rest later.

The next task is to make the square, and the letters enclosed by it, into a seamless tile. This means that you want to be able to put many iterations of this square next to each other and not be able to detect the edge of the square. You can achieve this effect in a number of ways, but the following method is probably the easiest.

1. Unlock the rectangle. Select all the objects and temporarily group them (Edit menu).

2. Hold down the clone modifier keys and drag a copy of the rectangle straight up. Make the lines of the two squares exactly match. Use maximum magnification to ensure that they do.

3. Drag another copy to the left, another straight down, and another to the right. Figure 9.62 shows the last square being dragged into position.

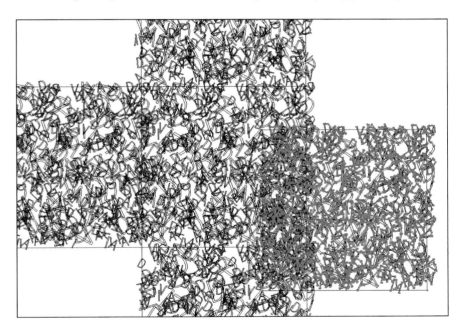

Figure 9.62
Drag copies of the letter-filled square so that you have perfect matches along all four sides.

4. Select all and ungroup (Edit menu).

5. Sweep-select across the top two-thirds of the upper rectangle. Delete these shapes.

6. Do the same for the outer two-thirds of each of the others. You can actually get very close to the inner rectangle (see Figure 9.63). Just be sure that you don't delete any of the characters that extend from the outside of the square to the inside.

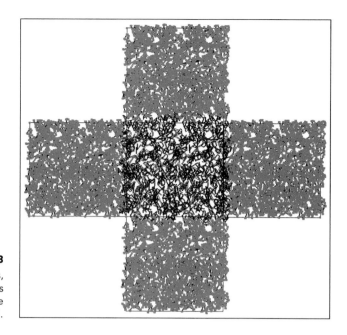

Figure 9.63
After you ungroup the objects, delete all the extra rectangles and letter shapes except those closest to the original.

Next, you need to change this hatch object into a pattern tile.

1. Select the rectangle and make certain that it is behind the letters. Because you have shapes extending past the boundary of the rectangle, you must copy it and then use the Paste Behind command.

2. While the pasted object is selected, change its Stroke and Fill to None.

3. After you've altered all the squares, copy them. Make the file fxCD_09_08.eps your active window and paste the squares to the right of the pasteboard.

4. One by one, lightest to darkest, select each group, select Define Pattern from the Edit menu, and name each tile as shown in Figure 9.64.

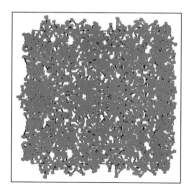

Figure 9.64
Select each of the letter-filled rectangles and define each as a pattern swatch.

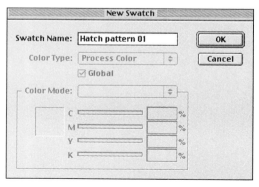

An Illustrator Problem and a Photoshop Fix

I wish I could say that, from this point, everything will proceed just as it did when you filled the shapes of the other image with patterns to replace the fill colors. You can try it if you want. This technique may work. In theory, it should. If this works for you, congratulations! You might be wondering in what way this procedure wouldn't work. It has to do, I suspect, with the fact that this kind of pattern contains an enormous number of small objects.

As pattern tiles, the ones you have just defined are about the most complex tiles possible. As you begin with the 01 layer and fill it with the 01 tile, everything will seem normal. By the time you reach the 04 layer, however, I predict your computer will slow to a crawl. Unlocking a layer may take half a minute, clicking on the targeting circle of the layer may require another half minute for the layer to become selected, and applying the pattern tile to the selected shapes may take a couple of minutes. With each layer completed, the wait will become longer. By layer 08, you will be sure that your machine is frozen.

Fortunately, you can complete this task by moving the pieces over to Photoshop. Inside Photoshop, you can use the pattern tiles you just created and assign them to substitute for the fill colors on each layer. First, you need to change your Illustrator files to Photoshop format by taking the following steps:

1. Begin with the layered file containing the image of David. From the Illustrator File menu, choose Export. The Export dialog box then appears. From the Format pop-up menu at the bottom, choose Photoshop 5. Another dialog box appears. For Mode, choose Grayscale instead of RGB. Select the resolution you think appropriate. Note that if you want to print this file on an inkjet printer with 1440×720 resolution, 360 ppi is a good resolution to use. A grayscale file of this size at this resolution is only about 9MB.

2. After you have exported the file, close your Illustrator file and open the exported file in Photoshop, where you will see that all 16 layers have been preserved. If you want to bypass this step, you can find a high-resolution layered file containing this image on the book's CD-ROM. The file name is fxCD_09_12.psd.

3. Return to Illustrator, where you will make some quick modifications to the hatch rectangles. The file in which you constructed the hatch effects requires simple changes. One by one—working in Outline mode—select the boundary rectangle.

4. Bring the rectangle to the front (Edit menu).

5. Sweep-select the entire group of objects, letters, and rectangle.

6. Hold down Command/Ctrl and press the number 7. The latter command converts the rectangle to a mask.

7. Before deselecting, group the set of objects.

8. Follow this procedure for each of the remaining 15 groups.

9. Select the first hatch group and copy it.

10. Switch to Photoshop. From the File menu, select New. When the New dialog box opens, give it a preliminary name such as "Pattern 01", change the color mode to grayscale, and be sure that the resolution matches the layered file already open.

11. Continue this procedure until you have moved all the Illustrator tiles into separate windows in Photoshop. If you want to save some time after you're sure that you understand this procedure, you can find all the rasterized hatch tiles on this book's companion CD-ROM.

Assembling the Hatch Pattern Image in Photoshop

The rest of the exercise is very simple:

1. Select each of the 16 layers in the image of David. Click on the Preserve Transparency checkbox at the top of the Layers palette. The quick way to do this is to click on each layer and press the / (forward slash) key.

2. Bring the window containing the tile designated as 01 to the front and Select All. From the Edit menu, select Define Pattern (see Figure 9.65).

3. Switch back to the image file and select the top—01—layer.

4. Hold down the Shift key and press the Delete or Backspace key. The dialog box that appears is shown in Figure 9.66. Change the top pop-up menu so that it reads Pattern. Leave the rest of the options as they are in the figure. Click on OK, and the layer fills with the 01 pattern tile. Notice that this operation is nearly identical to the procedure used to apply the type textures to the Illustrator files.

5. For the next layer, bring the second pattern's window to the front.

6. Select All, and use the Define Pattern command again.

As the patterns continue to be applied to the layers, the photo becomes the stylized image shown partially completed in Figure 9.67.

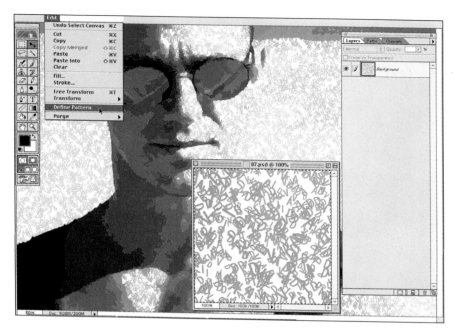

Figure 9.65
With the first tile window active, Select All. Then, choose Define Pattern from the Edit menu.

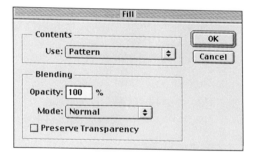

Figure 9.66
Press Shift+Del or Shift+backspace. The Fill dialog box that appears allows a layer or selection to be filled with a pattern.

Notice that this figure shows another way of applying the pattern. With this method, the original layers are preserved while the pattern is applied to new layers above each. The method is simple:

1. As you select a layer, click on the New Layer icon at the bottom of the palette to create a new layer just above the layer you just selected.

2. It's helpful if you take the time to name this layer so that it corresponds to the layer just below it.

3. Hold down Option/Alt and click on the palette on the boundary line between the two associated layers. This action changes the two into a clipping group.

4. Apply the fill to the upper layer. Because of the clipping group, the pattern is visible only where pixels are present on the layer below.

This procedure makes the file a bit larger, but it does allow you to change your mind later. You can also hide the layers containing the patterns to look at the original layered file.

Figure 9.67

This screen capture shows the image with the hatch patterns applied down through Layer 10.

After you've reached the bottom layer and filled all the areas with the hatch patterns (see Figure 9.68), your image has a brand new look, one very different from the words used as patterns. This texture appears to be much more freeform than those that you tried earlier in the chapter. From a little distance, the textures have a rough stucco quality. If you view the image closer (see Figure 9.69), you can see that the texture is composed of thousands of scattered letter shapes. An even closer look shows that only the letters *D-A-V-I-D* have been used.

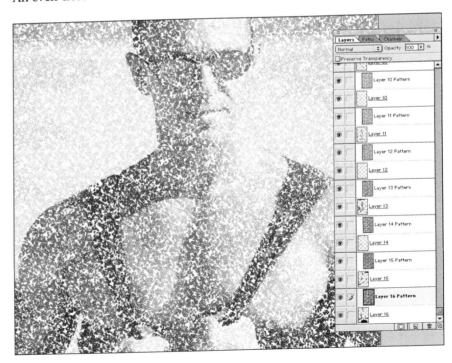

Figure 9.68

When the last layer is filled, the posterized image is changed to this highly stylized version.

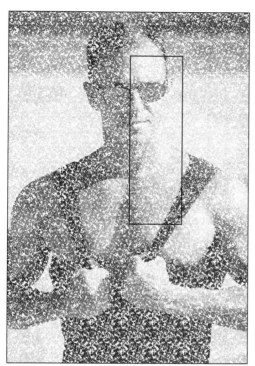 

Figure 9.69
From a distance, the texture appears to be a rough, stucco-like surface. Closer up, you can see that the texture is composed of the letters of the model's name.

As you may have noticed, creating all the type textures in this chapter has required many repetitive tasks but none were difficult. You can, if you want, decrease the work by choosing to posterize the photos with which you work to fewer than 16 colors. The image you choose may be entirely suitable for some number such as 8. If that is the case, then you will have half as much work as for any of the projects discussed here. These photos were chosen deliberately because they were difficult. The idea was to show you how much you could accomplish.

Moving On

You learned a good deal about type in this chapter, including a detailed examination of the tremendously flexible Multiple Master fonts. You used fonts in an unaccustomed way as a personalized texture, able to provide shading and texture in defining a photographic image. Most of what you learned can be adjusted and changed to make the methods exactly suitable for any purpose you might choose.

In Chapter 10, you learn to handle raster techniques expertly. You will also use two wonderful new Illustrator 9 features—blend modes and Transparency.

Chapter 10

Raster Rag

Adobe Illustrator is one-half of a perfect graphics program—Photoshop provides the other half.

By Sherry London

Using Illustrator without Photoshop (or other pixel-based editing programs) is like buying basic cable without premium channels, buying a fast sports car to drive only in city traffic, or buying the introductory Lego construction kit without the Lego people. Illustrator alone can do wonderful things; so can Photoshop alone. Together, they exponentially expand your possibilities. You can place Illustrator images in Photoshop and Photoshop images in Illustrator and finally place both image types in PageMaker, InDesign, or QuarkXPress. In this chapter, you look at a variety of techniques used to complete projects that require both raster and vector components.

What's This Raster Stuff?

Because this is an intermediate-level book, you should already know the difference between *raster* and *vector* images, but let's start here anyway. Adobe Illustrator is a *vector-editing* program. Therefore, the paths and shapes that you create are actually mathematical constructs. Rather than store every point along a rectangle, for example, Illustrator stores only the coordinates of the upper-left and lower-right corners, along with the notation that the shape is a rectangle. Each path that you create is an individual object, and you can manipulate each path independently of the other. You can select any individual object from the place on screen where it lurks and know that Illustrator has retrieved every piece of it.

A *raster* program, however, doesn't know the difference between a drawing of the Mona Lisa and a picture of a garbage dump. A raster program understands only *pixels*—the little dots that are formed by the firing of the three electron guns in the computer monitor. Adobe Photoshop, MetaCreations Painter, and Corel PhotoPaint are examples of raster image-editing programs. Although you can certainly make and move selections in a raster program, you need to identify to the program the group of pixels that it needs to move. The selection operation—far from being the point-and-click breeze it is in Illustrator—can represent hours of work and require an extraordinary amount of facility with the program.

You'll sometimes hear Illustrator—and its relatives, Freehand and CorelDRAW— referred to as *object-oriented* programs. This is the same as saying that they are vector programs. Photoshop is a *raster*, or bitmapped, program and uses pixels. Because Photoshop stores the color and location of every pixel in the image, it has no way of calculating which pixels belong together. In recent years, Adobe tried to overcome this Photoshop limitation by allowing you to create layered images, where all the pixels on a layer can be treated as a group. Now, you can place objects on their own layers and, as long as they stay there, Photoshop knows how to select and change them for you.

All images are changed to raster images when they are printed. If you send images to a service bureau, you probably are familiar with the term *rip* (no, it doesn't mean "rest in peace"). This acronym stands for *raster image processor*— the machine that produces the film that is used to make film for printing plates. This machine reads the image files on your disk and changes any vector images to bitmapped (raster) images so that they can be printed. This process is similar to taking letter shapes and forcing them to fit into a regular grid. The rip decides where on the page to print each point from the processed shape. Because graphics professionals also have their jargon (why should they differ from academicians or government bureaucrats?), *rip* is also a verb (as in "I need to rip the file" or "There was an error when this image was ripped"). As a verb, rip is the process of sending an image to a raster image processor. This process is also known as *rasterizing*. It's what ATM (Adobe Type Manager) does continuously as it changes font outlines to smooth type on screen or allows you to print smooth type from a non-PostScript printer.

You can tell Illustrator to rasterize any vector shape that you have created and turn it into a pixel-based object. Illustrator then stores this collection of pixels as part of the file, along with the vector information. You can also rasterize entire Illustrator images to save them in Photoshop or another pixel-based format. The difference in printing a raster versus a vector image is that the vector image can be resized almost indefinitely without losing its sharp edges. The raster image has already specified a fixed resolution and will degrade if you substantially resize it.

One major reason for using a vector format is to create images that can be resized to any size (within reason—obviously, if you reduce an image to a small enough size, you lose the detail regardless of the file format). Vector images will also print at the resolution of the printer; raster files must specify the resolution in advance. Therefore, you get sharp print quality without needing to worry about the printing process itself. However, you lose the ability to work with continuous-tone (photographic) images. Although you can put a photograph into an Illustrator file, it still handles like a resolution-dependent pixel-based image.

By using Illustrator and Photoshop together, you can mix the best of both types of graphics and use the best format for the task.

Illustrator-to-Photoshop Dynamics

Many Illustrator projects eventually move into Photoshop documents. You can move your Illustrator files into Photoshop in a number of ways. Before you consider why you might want to move files to Photoshop, let's spend some time exploring the various options.

Vector In: How?

You can get Illustrator images into Photoshop in five basic ways:

- You can use Photoshop's File|Open command.

- You can use Photoshop's File|Place command.

- You can use the Copy and Paste commands.

- You can drag images from Illustrator directly into a Photoshop file.

- You can save the image in Illustrator as a layered Photoshop file.

Open Sesame

Photoshop allows you to use either the File|Open or the File|Place command to import an Illustrator file. Opening the file (File|Open) brings in the Illustrator image just as if it were a normal Photoshop file. It is the most straightforward way to use an Illustrator file, and it does not require that any file be already open in Photoshop. When you open an Illustrator file, you can specify the size of the image, the resolution, and whether it is to be anti-aliased. However, you cannot rotate the image or change its placement when you use the Open command.

In Project 10.1, you open a Chinese robe image from the Racine's Costume Historique collection from Direct Imagination (DIMAGE). You'll then use this Japanese kimono print to fill a kimono shape.

10.1 Manipulating an Illustrator Image

1. In Photoshop, select File|Open. Choose the image J-03.AI on this book's companion CD-ROM. Make sure that the Constrain Proportions checkbox is marked. Set the Resolution to 300 ppi and the Mode to CMYK Color. Set the Height to 900 pixels. Photoshop automatically calculates the width, as shown in Figure 10.1.

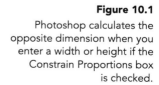

Figure 10.1

Photoshop calculates the opposite dimension when you enter a width or height if the Constrain Proportions box is checked.

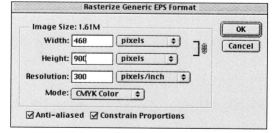

2. Click on OK to close the dialog box. Figure 10.2 shows the image that has been imported.

3. Open the image KIMONOMASK.PSD. Choose the Move tool (V) and drag the kimono shape into the J-03.AI file. Center it as well as you can; it's too large to fit into the image.

4. Select the Free Transform command (Command/Ctrl+T). Press and hold Shift+Option/Shift+Alt and drag the upper-left bounding box corner toward the center. Coax the kimono to fit into the image (it might take a few tries). Figure 10.3 shows the kimono shape on top of the original image.

Figure 10.2
(Left) J-03.AI is a lovely kimono pattern from DIMAGE's Racine's Costume Historique.

Figure 10.3
(Right) The kimono shape can be resized to fit on top of the rasterized fabric.

5. In the Layers palette, drag the kimono layer below that of the original image. Make the top layer (now Layer 1) active by clicking on it in the Layers palette. Group the layers (Command/Ctrl+G). Figure 10.4 shows the Layers palette.

6. Choose the Rectangular Marquee tool. Drag a marquee around the kimono so that it encloses the entire image and leaves a bit of extra room. Crop the image (Image|Crop). Figure 10.5 shows the final effect.

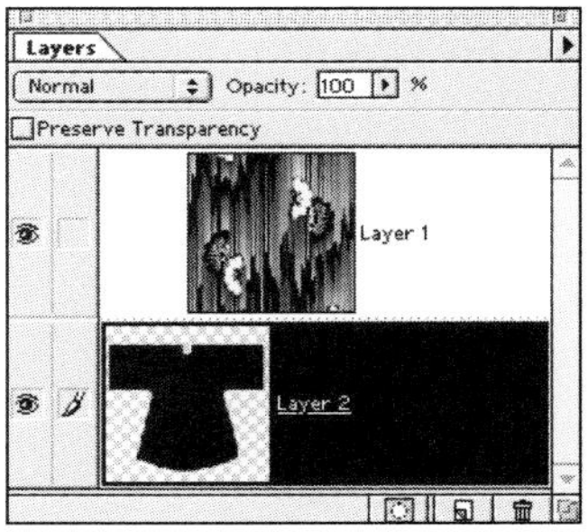

Figure 10.4
The Layers palette shows that the fabric (Layer 1) is on top and that it is grouped with the kimono shape (Layer 2).

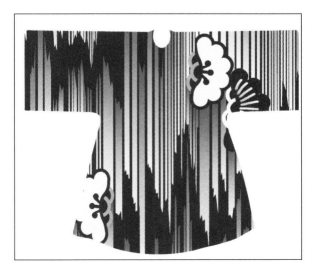

Figure 10.5
The kimono fabric fills the shape when the images are grouped properly.

Because you used the Open command to bring the Illustrator image into Photoshop, you had no flexibility to move the fabric around. Because the fabric was rectangular, that is probably not a major flaw. However, let's continue the project and build a much more interesting kimono (maneuvering room lets you try so many more things). You'll again use the Open command, but this time you'll composite the kimono inside a second image. This part of the project shows you another way to use an imported Illustrator image.

7. Close all the open files. Open the Preferences (Command+K, Command+5/Ctrl+K, Ctrl+5) and change the Units to Pixels.

8. Open the file KIMONO.PSD. It looks as if it is empty—the image is totally blank. The image has three channels, however, that enable you to reconstruct a kimono.

9. Click on the Body channel to make it active (Command/Ctrl+6).

10. Using the new Measure tool in Photoshop 5, drag it across the widest part of the kimono body to read the measurement in pixels (look at the Info palette to see the amount). Now you know the needed width for the fabric file (approximately 580 pixels).

11. Load the Body channel (Command+click on the channel name or press Command+Option+6/Ctrl+click on the channel name or press Ctrl+Alt+6). Make the Composite channel active (Command/Ctrl+~).

12. Make a new layer (click on the New Layer icon at the bottom of the Layers palette). Press D to set the colors back to the default of black and white. Fill the selection (Option/Alt+Delete) and then deselect (Command/Ctrl+D).

13. Open the file J-03.AI. In the dialog box, enter your measurement amount (580 pixels) for the width. Make sure that the Constrain Proportions checkbox is marked.

14. Select the Move tool (or press Command/Ctrl). Drag the fabric from the J-03.AI file into the KIMONO.PSD file. Place it over the body of the kimono. (Let it stay in its own layer.) Group the two layers (Command/Ctrl+G). Move the fabric so that it covers the entire body shape and so that flowers appear near the top right of the form. Figure 10.6 shows the result.

The fabric for the right arm needs to make a perfect 90-degree miter. This part of the project is a bit tricky to accomplish. Here's how:

15. Make a base for the clipping group. Make a new layer (click on the New Layer icon at the bottom of the Layers palette). Load the Right Sleeve channel (Command/Ctrl+click on the channel name or press Command+Option+7/Ctrl+Alt+7). Fill the selection with black (Option+Delete/Alt+Delete) and then deselect (Command/Ctrl+D).

Figure 10.6
The fabric easily covers the kimono body.

16. Drag the kimono fabric layer (Layer 2) to the New Layer icon at the bottom of the Layers palette to copy it. Move the thumbnail for the copy to the top of the Layers palette. Figure 10.7 shows the Layers palette at this point.

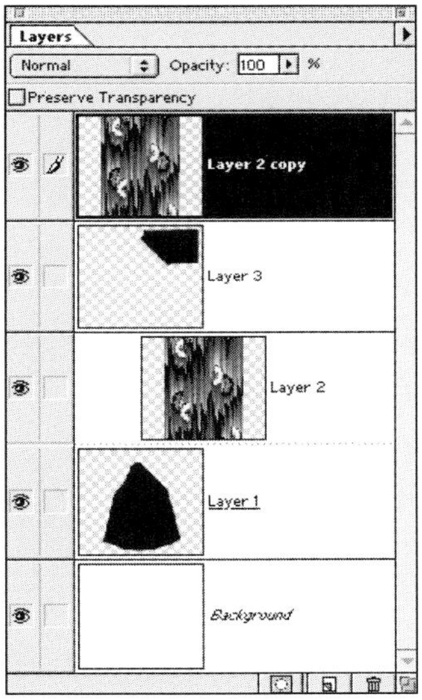

17. To miter something, you need to flip and then rotate it. To start, choose Edit|Transform|Flip Horizontal. Using the Move tool with Shift pressed to constrain movement to the horizontal, move the fabric in the Layer 2 copy to the right. Press the numeric 5 key to set the transparency to 50% so that you can see the fabric on the kimono body. Keep Shift pressed and move the fabric so that the flower on the sleeve layer is just to the right of the matching flower on the kimono body. Figure 10.8 shows this view of the image.

Figure 10.7
The Layers palette shows the grouped kimono body and the right sleeve ready to be mitered and grouped.

Figure 10.8
You can line up the flipped flower if you change the layer opacity to 50 percent.

18. Choose the Free Transform command (Edit|Free Transform; Command/ Ctrl+T). Drag the center of the rotation marker to the underarm seam (where the body and right sleeve meet). Figure 10.9 shows the repositioned center of the rotation marker (but all the layers have been made lighter for the screen capture so that you can see the marker more clearly).

Figure 10.9
You can change the center of the rotation or transformation by dragging its marker to a new location.

19. Place your cursor outside the bounding box. You'll see a double-headed curved arrow cursor; it is the Rotation cursor. Press Shift and drag downward to rotate the image counterclockwise. Rotating the sleeve 90 degrees should take six "tugs" on the image. (Shift constrains the rotation to 15-degree increments). When the fabric is in the right spot, press Return/Enter to set the transformation.

20. Group the two layers (Command/Ctrl+G). Press the numeric 0 key to return full opacity to the fabric. Move the fabric as needed (with the Move tool) so that you create a perfect matching miter. Figure 10.10 shows the kimono with the miter completed.

21. Make a new layer (click on the New Layer icon at the bottom of the Layers palette). Load the Left Sleeve channel (Command+click/Ctrl+click on the channel name or press Command+Option+5/Ctrl+Alt+5). Fill the selection with black (Option/Alt+Delete) and then deselect (Command/ Ctrl+D).

Figure 10.10
The kimono with a perfectly mitered sleeve.

22. Drag the fabric from the J-03.AI image into the KIMONO.PSD image again. Flip it horizontally (Edit|Transform|Flip Horizontal). Rotate the fabric -45 degrees (Edit|Transform|Numeric; don't forget to enter the minus sign in front of the 45 degrees). Group the two layers (Command/Ctrl+G). Move the fabric until the double flower pattern sits near the wrist on the left sleeve, as shown in Figure 10.11.

Figure 10.11
The completed basic kimono shows both sleeves with a slightly different fabric treatment.

We could consider the kimono image complete (after all, you have now seen one reason that you might want to be able to move an Illustrator image around—which was the purpose of this section). However, you can make the effect more artistic, so let's play with this project a bit more.

23. Let's add a trim for the garment. Click on the Foreground Color Swatch in the Toolbox and choose a true red (CMYK: 0, 100, 100, 0). Make a new layer (click on the New Layer icon at the bottom of the Layers

palette). Load the Left Sleeve channel (Command+Option+5/ Ctrl+Alt+5). Stroke the selection (Edit|Stroke|8 pixels, Center) and then deselect (Command/Ctrl+D).

24. Make the Channels palette active. Load the Body channel (Command+Option+6/Ctrl+Alt+6). Add the Right Sleeve channel to the selection (Shift+Command+click on channel 7/Shift+Ctrl+click on channel 7). The Shift key adds the channel to the current selection. Because the two selections overlap, no line indicates where the right sleeve and the body meet—which is precisely what we want. Stroke the selection (Edit|Stroke|8 pixels, Center) and then deselect (Command/Ctrl+D). Figure 10.12 shows the stroked trim on the kimono (I have hidden the kimono itself for this screen shot).

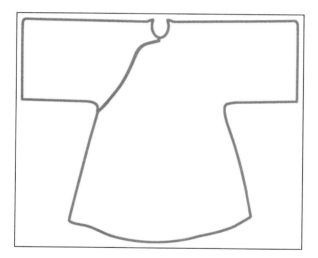

Figure 10.12
You can create trim by stroking the edges of the kimono components.

25. Let's add a bit of pattern to the trim; choose the Magic Wand tool (W). Press Return/Enter to show the Magic Wand options. Set the Tolerance to 15 and Anti-aliased to On. Do not mark the Use All Layers checkbox.

26. Make the Layer 2 copy layer (the fabric from the right sleeve) active. Click inside the upside-down yellow flower to select it. Press Shift and click inside the blue triple arches above it (to add the blue thing to the selection). Copy it to the clipboard (Command/Ctrl+C).

27. Create a new document (File|New). Accept the defaults; they will be the size of the copied selection. Paste in the selection from the clipboard (Command/Ctrl+V). Turn off the Eye on the Background layer. Turning off the Background layer allows the final pattern to contain transparency so that it doesn't obliterate all the red outline trim.

28. Reduce the flower image to 35 percent of its original size (Image|Image Size, 35 Percent, Bicubic Interpolation). Select the entire image (Command/Ctrl+A). Define it as a pattern (Edit|Define Pattern).

29. Fill the trim layer with the pattern (Shift+Delete|Use: Pattern, 100 Percent Opacity, Normal, Preserve Transparency: On). When you fill with the Preserve Transparency checkbox marked, only the outline of the trim will "catch" any of the pattern. Figure 10.13 shows the trim that has had the pattern added to it.

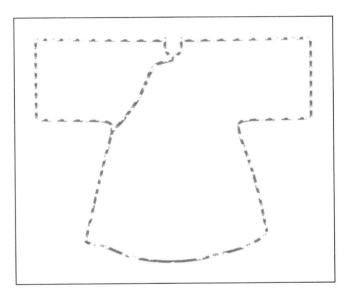

Figure 10.13
You can apply a pattern to only the trim by checking the Preserve Transparency box in the Fill dialog box.

We can do much more to dress up this image, but we have much more to cover in this chapter, and it is time to move on. Figure 10.14 shows the final version (look at the color version as well). You can find the completed image on this book's companion CD-ROM.

Here is a brief description of what I did. I added a drop shadow for both the garment and the upper-right neck edge. Next, I created a mosaic (four-way) pattern from the double flower in the fabric and filled a layer with it. Then, I used a Hue/Saturation Adjustment layer to turn it a light blue (and reduced the opacity of the layer as well). Finally, I increased the Canvas size to give room to stroke the edge of the background pattern (on a new layer) and apply the same pattern to the stroke that I used as the garment trim.

To Anti-Alias or Not to Anti-Alias

When you open an Illustrator image in Photoshop, you also risk cutting off some of the image detail if you anti-alias the image. Unfortunately, this problem exists whether you open or place the file, so you need to be aware of the consequences of your decisions. You can easily resolve this problem when you recognize what is happening. Project 10.2 will make this solution clear.

Figure 10.14
The finished Kimono image has a background pattern and a final border added to it.

PROJECT 10.2 Rasterizing Illustrator Images in Photoshop

Just follow these steps to see what happens when you choose to anti-alias or alias an image:

1. In Photoshop, open the image BUTTERFLY.AI (File|Open). This image is from the Ultimate Symbol's Nature Icons series that I have colored. Open the file at 600 pixels wide. Make sure that the Constrain Proportions checkbox is selected. Do not mark the Anti-aliased checkbox.

2. Use the Canvas Size command (Image|Image Size) to add 100 pixels to each dimension, as shown in Figure 10.15.

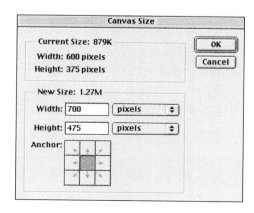

Figure 10.15
You can use the Canvas Size command to add more working space to your image.

3. Magnify the image until you can see the edge of the butterfly's right wing, where the arrow appears in Figure 10.16. Notice that this portion of the wing is quite straight and almost looks cut off. Because the image is not anti-aliased, it does not look out of place. This portion was the area where the wing touched the edge of the original image.

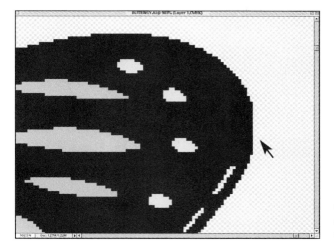

Figure 10.16
The arrow shows a flat area where the butterfly's wing butted the original image border.

4. Close the BUTTERFLY.AI image and then open it again (File|Open). This time, open the image with the Anti-aliased checkbox marked. Use the same dimensions as before. Repeat Steps 2 and 3. Figure 10.17 shows a close-up of the butterfly's wing. Notice that the same area on the wing is still straight, but that the rest of the image is anti-aliased.

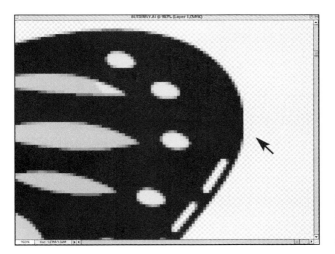

Figure 10.17
Close-up of butterfly wing with anti-alias turned on; the same area of the wing is straight.

5. Repeat Steps 1 through 4, using the image BUTTERFLY2.AI. Figure 10.18 shows the jagged version, and Figure 10.19 shows the anti-aliased version. The jagged version still contains the same straight edge, but the anti-aliased version has a smooth edge on the wing.

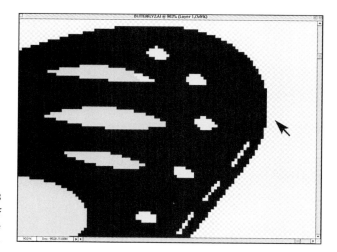

Figure 10.18
The aliased version of
BUTTERFLY2.AI shows the same
straight edge as BUTTERFLY.AI.

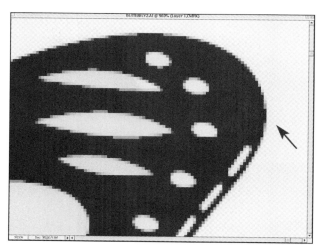

Figure 10.19
The anti-aliased version of
BUTTERFLY2.AI sports a
smooth wing.

BUTTERFLY.AI and BUTTERFLY2.AI seem to be the same image. What has changed? You might have noticed that the two images do not contain the same number of suggested pixels, even though you rasterized both at a width of 600 pixels. Switch to Adobe Illustrator, and we'll look at the two images.

6. In Illustrator, open the file BUTTERFLY.AI. Choose the Selection tool (V) and then click on the butterfly. Notice that the box that surrounds the grouped objects hugs the boundary of the butterfly. Figure 10.20 shows BUTTERFLY.AI with all objects selected.

Raster Rag**395**

Figure 10.20
BUTTERFLY.AI's bounding box is directly up against the butterfly.

7. Still in Illustrator, open the file BUTTERFLY2.AI. Click on the butterfly with the Selection tool. As you can see in Figure 10.21, the rectangular, outside box is well away from the image itself.

Figure 10.21
The bounding box of BUTTERFLY2.AI does not touch the butterfly itself.

The Case of the Bounding Box

The box that defines the perimeter of a shape is known as the *bounding box*. This PostScript notation defines the height and width of the object. The bounding box of an object is the smallest rectangle that can contain the shape. A problem occurs when you either move the object into Photoshop or you rasterize it in Illustrator. If you rasterize and anti-alias an object with a bounding box that touches it, the object parts that touch the bounding box cannot be anti-aliased because no room is left to do so—the bounding box is in the way. It's like trying to produce a Gaussian Blur in Photoshop with a selection marquee in the way—the selection cuts off part of the blurred edge.

If you group objects, the bounding box is the one that is furthest out. When the image is placed into Photoshop, it is given the dimensions of the smallest rectangle that can hold all the objects in the file.

To restate the problem, if you bring an Illustrator file into Photoshop, and the bounding box of the image touches one or more of the objects, those objects won't be anti-aliased where they touch the bounding box. The obvious solution is to make sure that the bounding box of the file itself doesn't touch any of the objects. But how?

You only need to draw a new rectangular object that is the size of the area that you want to import. Give this object the attributes of no stroke and no fill; therefore, it is a transparent object. However, because PostScript images all objects without regard to their fill or stroke, this "dummy" rectangle is used as the real bounding box of the image and gives the image its new border. Try it with the simple example shown in Project 10.3.

 A New Bounding Box

You can create a bounding box as follows so that no detail is lost when you open the image in Photoshop:

1. Create a new file in Illustrator (File|New).

2. Select the Ellipse tool (L). Draw a circle with the tool anywhere in the image.

3. Click on the Fill icon in the Toolbox to make it active. With the circle selected, choose a Fill color from the Swatches palette.

4. Save the file in Illustrator format (File|Save).

5. Open the file in Photoshop as an anti-aliased image using the Open command. Using the Move tool, move the circle and zoom in until you verify that the edges of the circle that touched the image borders are not anti-aliased. Close the image and do not save it.

6. Back in Illustrator, open the circle file (if you closed it). Click on the Rectangle tool (M). Draw a rectangle on top of the circle so that it more than covers the circle. Set the Stroke and Fill for the rectangle to None. Save the file again.

7. Open the file in Photoshop as you did before. This time, you should see an anti-aliased edge all the way around.

Placing Illustrator Images

The Place command in Photoshop is similar to the Open command in that it displays the Illustrator image for you to edit. However, it has two significant differences: You must already have a file open when you invoke the Place command, and you can interactively resize, rotate, skew, or distort the image to be rasterized. The disadvantage is that you cannot specify on the spot whether to anti-alias the Illustrator artwork, nor can you specify the precise measurements to use. Project 10.4 shows an example of placing Illustrator images.

So, which command should you use? Your choice really depends on what you want to accomplish—which is why you are given the option to either open or place the file.

PROJECT 10.4 Placing Images (The War Room)

In this project, you'll have the opportunity to place a number of images (both text and graphics) and resize and rotate them as you place them into the main image. I took the base picture in London, in Churchill's underground World War II headquarters. This place was the command center where Churchill coordinated Britain's efforts to fight the Germans. The image shown here is the map room. Figure 10.22 shows the final image, with all the Illustrator graphics in place. You may use that as a guide or do your own thing.

Figure 10.22
The War Room contains a variety of placed, resized, and rotated graphics added to a photograph.

All the images that you need are in the War folder inside the Chapter 10 Starting graphics folder on this book's companion CD-ROM for this book. Most of the Illustrator elements are converted to outlines from three FontFont fonts: Apocalypso (a picture font), Bastard Even Fatter, and NixonScript Regular. They are from the Virus Font series (so named because they are so sick!).

1. In Photoshop, open the Preferences file (Command/Ctrl+K). Select the Anti-alias PostScript checkbox. Close the Preferences dialog box. You can always change your mind and decide to not anti-alias the placed files. However, you need to make your decision *before* you place the Illustrator images. The General Preferences dialog box is the place where you decide the default behavior for anti-aliasing. You cannot change your mind as you are importing the images.

2. In Photoshop, open the image MAPROOM.PSD.

3. Choose File|Place. Select the ENGLAND.AI file. Figure 10.23 shows the image as it is being placed.

Figure 10.23

Placing the map of England image into the map room file.

Photoshop automatically shows the placed image at the largest size that will fit into the host image. You see a bounding box with an X through it. The box has eight control handles—one at each corner and one at the center of each side. You use these handles to resize the image, just as you would in any other graphics program. If you move a corner handle, you can resize in both directions. Pressing Shift as you drag a corner handle maintains the original aspect ratio of the image. Dragging a center handle resizes either horizontally or vertically. If you place the cursor outside the bounding box, it changes to a double-pointed curved arrow—the Rotate cursor. You can modify this behavior with several different keystrokes.

During a normal Photoshop transformation, you could also press Shift, Command/Ctrl, or Option/Alt together to distort your image. However, neither the Distort nor the Perspective commands are available while you are placing an image.

4. Place your cursor on the lower-right handle of the bounding box. Keep Shift pressed and drag the cursor up and to the left to make the map smaller. (I kept the rulers on and sized the image so that the height went from pixel 200 to pixel 475 along the vertical ruler. I started the left corner at pixel 20 on the horizontal ruler.) When you are satisfied with the size of the image, place your cursor inside the map (although not on the center point marker) and drag the map into the approximate place where you want it to go. Press Return/Enter. Figure 10.24 shows the map just before the transformation is accepted.

5. Place the map of Germany (GERMANY.AI) the same way that you did the map of England. I sized this map so that the top of the map went

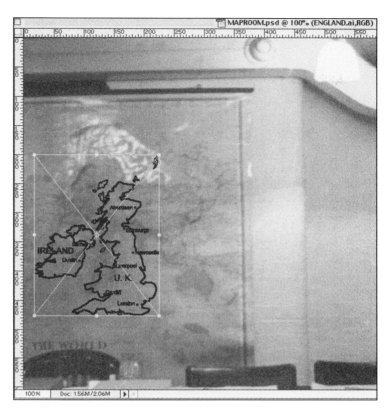

Figure 10.24
The map of the UK is in position and ready to be rasterized into the image.

off the image a tiny bit, the bottom of the map was at the level of the town of Aberdeen on the map of the UK, and the town of Hamburg appeared inside the light slightly to the right of the center top of the map room image.

6. Place the NAZIPLANE.AI file (File|Place). When it fills the entire window, place your cursor on the bottom-right corner of the image. Press and hold Shift and drag the corner handle up and to the left until the right edge of the image no longer is on top of the outlines of the map of Germany.

7. Drag the plane (still with its bounding box around it) until the back fin on the plane is just in front of the label for the city of Hannover. Click on the center point marker and drag it so that it sits on top of the dot that identifies Hannover on the map of Germany. Place your cursor outside the bounding box and rotate the plane to the desired angle. I rotated it so that the propeller of the plane just touched the outline of the map of England. I needed to make the plane a bit smaller as well. Figure 10.25 shows the plane before it is rendered. I lightened the background in the hope that you will be able to see the altered center point near the city of Hannover. Table 2.1 shows you some useful key commands for controlling transformations.

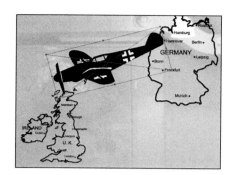

Figure 10.25

You can change the center point of an image and rotate it when placing it into Photoshop.

Table 2.1   Some helpful keystrokes that you can use in transformations.

Keystroke	Result
Shift	Constrains the angle of rotations and skews; keeps resizing proportional
Command, Ctrl	Allows you to skew images
Option, Alt	Makes transformation happen from the center point

8. You can place the BOMBS.AI file multiple times and rotate each one differently.

9. Place the file DEATHS.AI. Drag it by its lower-left corner so that it fits into the upper-right corner of the image. You might want to skew this text a bit. If you put your cursor on the center handle at the bottom of the image and press Command/Ctrl, you can skew the text. I didn't skew it in my final image, but Figure 10.26 shows how it might look.

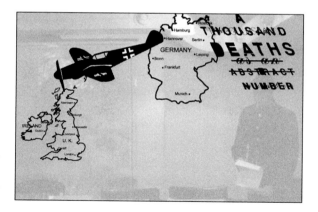

Figure 10.26

You might want to skew the text object to make it look more dramatic.

You can look at the finished image in this book's Illustrator Studio section to get an idea of how I used red and yellow for emphasis. When I placed the word *War*, I used a copy of the placed layer colored red and another copy, colored yellow, as a primitive embossing. I placed both layers beneath the original text and moved one layer up a bit and the other layer down.

I left the BANG.AI image large. I set its Apply mode to Multiply with an opacity setting of 57 percent. You can see the way the other layers were set up in

WARROOM.PSD in the CH10Ends folder on the book's companion CD-ROM. I encourage you to use the provided text and create your own statement using the various features of the Place command.

In the instructions, I asked you to place the bomb image multiple times. Why should you bother to correctly size and position the placed image when you could do it after you have placed the image? The simple answer is that doing it first gives you the best possible results. Every time you resize, rotate, or otherwise mangle a raster image, you lose data, and the anti-aliasing that occurs causes your image to lose sharpness. If you know the size and location that you want, you are much better off fiddling *before* you finalize the Place command. Try the brief (I promise) example in Project 10.5.

PROJECT 10.5 A Rotation and Quality Loss Primer

In this short project, you'll see why it is so important to render an Illustrator image at the angle that you want rather than rotate the image after it is placed in Photoshop.

1. Launch Photoshop. In Photoshop, create a new document (File|New, Width: 500 pixels, Height: 500 pixels, Resolution: 300, Mode: CMYK Color, Contents: White).

2. Place the image LADYBUG.AI (File|Place). Do not finalize the placement yet.

3. Pull down the Edit menu (one of the few menus not grayed during this operation). Choose Transform|Numeric Transform. Deselect the Position and Skew checkboxes. Mark the Constrain Proportions checkbox under the Scale section and scale the image to 25%. Change the Angle of rotation to 62 degrees. Click on OK. Figure 10.27 shows you this dialog box. Figure 10.28 shows a close-up of one of the ladybugs.

> **How to Say "I Accept"**
>
> You can finalize the Place command in several ways. Adobe prefers that you use the "newer" version of just pressing Return/Enter, but you can also double-click inside the bounding box as you did in early (pre-version 4) incarnations of the program. In addition, if you press Control on the Mac or the right mouse button in Windows, you bring up a context-sensitive Help menu. One of the options on this menu is Place, which also will rasterize the placed image into your file.

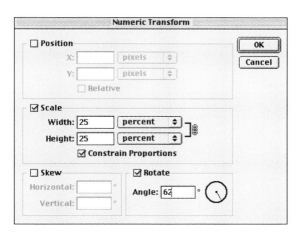

Figure 10.27

You can use the Numeric Transform dialog box when you place an image into Photoshop.

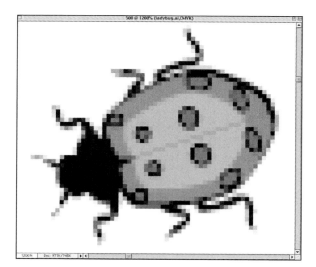

Figure 10.28
Notice that the ladybug is crisp
and clear (note "full circle" spots).

4. Create a new document the same size and resolution as the one you created in Step 1.

5. Place the file LADYBUG.AI. This time, when you see the bounding box, simply press Return/Enter to set the Place command.

6. Choose Edit|Transform|Numeric Transform. It should contain the last transformation that you did. Change the Scale percentage to 74 (don't ask me why this setting gets you approximately the same number of pixels as you have in the first image—I had to ask my husband for this calculation—I just know that it works). Leave the Rotate angle at 62%. Press Return/Enter to execute the transformation. Figure 10.29 shows a close-up of the same ladybug, which looks a bit worse for wear. Check the line across her back if you want to find one of the most clearly defined areas of damage.

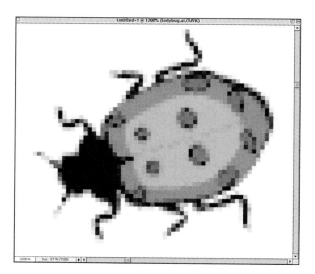

Figure 10.29
A too-blurry ladybug shows that it
was placed first and rotated later.

The moral of this tale? Rotate your image to its final resting place when you first place it. Should you not discover what this number is until later, delete the layer and place the image again at the correct angle.

Be a Copy-and-Paste Cat

You can also copy and paste images between Illustrator and Photoshop. This process is fairly simple, although it uses clipboard memory and overwrites whatever was previously on the clipboard. One advantage that this method has over Open or Place is that you can copy a single path or element without having to bring over the entire file. You are given the option to paste the path itself into Photoshop or to rasterize the object that the path defines. You may also decide whether to anti-alias the pasted path if you opt to rasterize it. The object pastes at the resolution of the Photoshop file that you have created but at the size that was defined in Illustrator. You have no chance to scale or transform it.

If you want to try this method, follow along with Project 10.6.

PROJECT 10.6 Copy and Paste (Paths and Pixels)

In this project, you'll create a simple shape, copy it from Illustrator, and paste it into a Photoshop document:

1. In Illustrator, create a new document.

2. Use the Polygon tool to create a filled hexagon (or any other shape that you prefer). Make it fairly small. Fill the polygon with a solid color.

3. Select the polygon with the Selection tool and copy it to the clipboard (Command/Ctrl+C).

4. In Photoshop, create a new document (File|New, Width: 500 pixels, Height: 500 pixels, Resolution: 300, Mode: CMYK Color, Contents: White).

5. Paste in the selection from the clipboard (Command/Ctrl+V). The dialog box shown in Figure 10.30 appears. Choose Paste As Pixels and Anti-Alias. Click on OK.

6. Select the Paste command again. This time, paste the object as Paths. We'll finish off this project by stroking the path with the Paintbrush.

7. In the Paths palette, double-click the work path and save it (just accept the suggested name).

8. Choose a bright color as your foreground color. Click on the Paintbrush tool in the Toolbox and select a 65-pixel brush in the Brushes palette.

9. Click on the Stroke path icon at the bottom of the Paths palette (the second icon from the left). You'll see a bright, soft line around your image.

Figure 10.30
You are given the choice of pasting pixels or paths when you transfer an object from Illustrator to Photoshop via the clipboard.

10. Try this exercise again after creating a 500-pixel square file at 72 ppi. The Illustrator shape is much smaller now.

It's a Drag

You can drag a selection from Illustrator into Photoshop as long as you have a file open in Photoshop and you can see both the Illustrator and the Photoshop files at the same time. The drag-and-drop operation does not use clipboard memory and does not replace the image on the clipboard. Figure 10.31 shows an object being dragged from Illustrator to Photoshop. Notice how a black line forms along the border of the Photoshop image when the image is ready to receive the object.

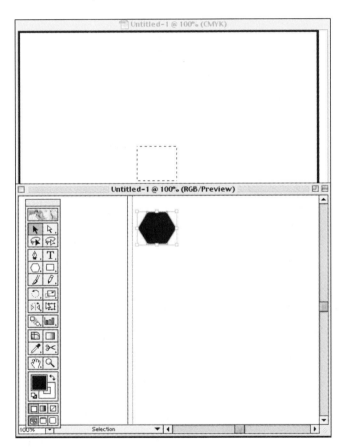

Figure 10.31
You can drag an object from Illustrator into Photoshop.

When you drag and drop, the dropped object will always be anti-aliased, regardless of the status of the Anti-alias PostScript toggle in the Preferences. If you want to paste paths, press Command/Ctrl as you drag and drop.

The Layered Look

You can also save Illustrator layers as separate layers in a Photoshop document. Being able to do so is an incredible time-saver and convenience, especially if you take the time to organize your Illustrator document into layers. By saving layered images, you can move things around in Photoshop or apply filters and effects on an object-by-object basis. One of the best things about saving a Photoshop file as layers is that if you save live text (that is, text that you haven't converted to outlines), Photoshop creates a text layer when it opens the image. Because Photoshop text layers can be edited, you can then change the text in Photoshop if you want.

Vector In: Why?

We've spent a lot of time just getting to the point of discussing why you might want to take Illustrator images into Photoshop. One advantage of Illustrator (or other vector) images is that they are sharp and crisp. They also have the advantage of small file sizes. Both of these advantages are lost when you move the vector images into Photoshop. However, Illustrator is very good at doing some things that are difficult or impossible in Photoshop:

- Illustrator has many more options for creating and designing text.

- You can much more easily manipulate paths in Illustrator than in Photoshop.

- If you need to create an image with several pieces engineered from basic shapes, it's much faster to do so in Illustrator.

Many artists create all their basic shapes in Illustrator and then move the composition into Photoshop. Because we know that they lose the resolution independence and small file size when they bring images into Photoshop, what benefits are gained from the transfer? This question is even more relevant in Illustrator 9, which has added transparency, blend modes, and Live Effects to its bag of tricks:

- You can create beveled edges and embossed surfaces with greater ease.

- You can more efficiently apply filters to the imported images.

- You can actually change the pixels in the underlying image—something that you cannot do while working with a raster graphic from inside Illustrator.

Ultimately, you need to decide on a case-by-case basis which program is best for the job at hand. You might want to take the image back into Illustrator when you are done to either link or embed it, or you might want to leave some vector shapes in Illustrator and composite the pieces from the two programs in PageMaker or QuarkXPress.

Illustrator allows you to have text on a path, which you cannot do in Photoshop (without a third-party plug-in), and in general, you'll probably find the experience of creating text to be more pleasant in Illustrator. If you need decorative type or are going to fill the type with a photo (which you can also do in Illustrator), it's reasonable to move the text into Photoshop. For most other needs, it's a toss up if you are up-to-date on your Photoshop upgrades.

Project 10.7, which is fairly long, shows how to create a piece of advertising art that shows many of the uses of Photoshop for images begun in Illustrator. Although you are not starting this image from the beginning (as I did when I created it), you'll get a chance to field-test a number of reasons to exploit the Photoshop/Illustrator combination.

PROJECT 10.7 The Hard Wrap Candy Case

Creating the Basic Image

Just follow these steps to prepare the layers in Illustrator so that you can export them to Photoshop:

1. In Illustrator, open the image CANDY.AI. Figure 10.32 shows the image in Illustrator format.

Figure 10.32
This is the original CANDY.AI image.

2. Your first task is to prepare this file to be saved in a layered Photoshop format. If you look at the Layers palette in Illustrator, you'll see that, currently, the file contains only one layer. Each group or element—and there are nine of them—needs to be on its own layer. With the Selection tool, click on the solid text. Both the solid and the open text are selected (that's because I already created the appropriate groups for you).

3. Click on the New Layer icon at the bottom of the Layers palette. Figure 10.33 shows the Layers palette after the new layer is created. You need to move your selection from the bottom layer to the top layer. Notice the tiny dot to the right of the layer entry on the bottom layer; it indicates an active selection. Drag the dot to the top layer. The bounding box around the selection changes color to match the color swatch shown on the left of the text entry of the top layer. (It was originally blue and then turns red, at least on my Mac. On a PC, it may appear slightly different.) Notice that the highlighting on the top layer shows that this layer is currently active.

4. Double-click on the layer name and change it by entering the word "TEXT".

5. You can also click on the right-pointing arrow next to Layer 1 and drop down all the objects on that layer. By clicking on the circle icon next to the object that you want, you can easily select the object. Try that to select one of the pink candies.

6. Repeat Steps 2 through 4 to place each piece of candy and the scribble on its own layer (you can either click on the object or select it via the Layers palette). When you have finished, double-click on Layer 1 and change its name to "White Rectangle" (yes, another shape is there, and it will show up in Photoshop eventually). A bounding box "control" object (unfilled and unstroked) also lurks on that layer. Figure 10.34 shows my Layers palette with all the layers named.

7. Choose File|Export and locate the directory into which you want to save the new file. Name it CANDY.PSD and select the Photoshop 5 file format from the drop-down list.

8. When you click on OK, you'll see another dialog box, as shown in Figure 10.35. In the Photoshop Options dialog box, you can select the resolution and color mode (choose CMYK). You can also determine whether you want to save the layers (you do) and whether to anti-alias (set Anti-alias to On). Because you copied all the objects into their own layers, you don't need to save nested layer objects (an option new to Illustrator 9). Select the Other resolution and enter "125" ppi into the box as shown. The image is quite large. When I designed it at 300 ppi, I ended up with a 128MB file in Photoshop (28MB on disk) after all the effects were completed. If you are low on RAM, you might want to export the image at 72 ppi.

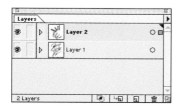

Figure 10.33
The Layers palette shows the status of the layers that are present in your document.

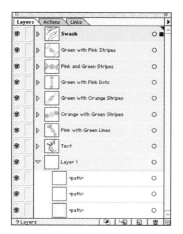

Figure 10.34
CANDY.AI now contains nine layers.

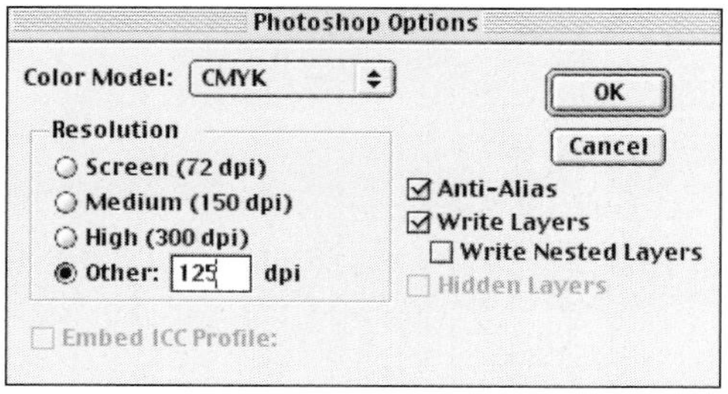

Figure 10.35

In the Photoshop Options dialog box, you can select the characteristics of the Photoshop file to be saved.

9. Close Illustrator now if you want. You won't need it for a while. It's time to see how you use Photoshop's special features to enhance this design (and if you decide later that you prefer "before" to "after," that's all right, too).

10. Open Photoshop. In Photoshop, open the CANDY.PSD file that you just created.

11. To begin, let's get the TEXT and Swash layers out of our faces. Click on the Eye icons next to the layers TEXT and Swash to hide them from view. We'll deal with them later.

12. Press D to set the colors back to the default of black and white. Choose the Eyedropper tool and change the Foreground color to the same orange as the bottom candy (the Orange with Green Stripes layer). Make the Background layer active. Fill the layer (Option/Alt+Delete). Surprise! Only the border area turns orange because of the practically invisible rectangle on the White Rectangle layer.

13. Some of the candies look a bit too close together. Double-click on the Move tool to open the Move Options palette. Mark the Auto-Select Layer checkbox. This toggle, when turned on, sets the active layer to the layer that has the highest opacity percentage in the spot where you clicked. (If more than one layer exists with 100 percent opacity, Auto-Select chooses the one closest to the top of the layer stack.) Usually, I like to keep it off because it puts me in the wrong place if I'm not paying attention, but for rearranging objects, it's wonderfully convenient. Move the candies as you want them to be. You can rearrange the stacking order of the candies by dragging their thumbnails in the Layers palette. Figure 10.36 shows the spacing that I chose.

14. Let's add some layer effects to the candy. Make one of the candies active (it doesn't matter which one). Choose Layer|Effects|Drop Shadow. The Drop Shadow defaults to black in Multiply mode. Change the Opacity to 67% and the Angle to 120 degrees and mark the Use Global Angle checkbox. Set the Distance to 24 pixels and the Blur to 19 pixels. Leave the Intensity set to 0. Don't click on OK yet. Figure 10.37 shows these settings.

Why Work in CMYK?

You don't have to export your Illustrator image in CMYK mode. However, if you have worked in CMYK color space inside Illustrator and you don't need to apply any RGB-only filters to the CMYK image, there's no reason to convert to RGB only to convert back to CMYK for printing. In this project, you aren't using any photographic images (another reason that you might want to stay in RGB color space during the creation process). If you have an ICC profile that you usually use with CMYK images, you can choose to embed it by choosing that option in the Color Settings dialog box. (If you don't know what I'm talking about, you might want to invest in either, or both, of the following books: *Photoshop 5 In Depth*, by David Xenakis and Sherry London, The Coriolis Group, or *Real World Photoshop 5*, by Bruce Fraser and David Blatner, Peachpit Press.)

Figure 10.36
You can move each candy within Photoshop to change the spacing between them.

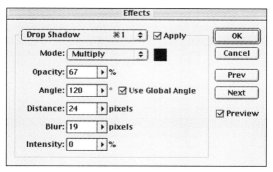

Figure 10.37
Setting the options for a layer effect drop shadow.

An Alternative to Auto-Select

If choosing Auto-Select makes you crazy every time that you land in the "wrong" place, but you like the convenience of not having to use the Layers palette to choose a layer, try this tip. When the Move tool is selected, hold down the Command key and click to select a layer on the Mac, or right-click to select the layer in Windows.

15. Let's also add an inner shadow. This effect is one of my favorites. I like the play of shadow that it creates. From the Effects drop-down menu on the Layer Effects dialog box, select Inner Shadow. Place a checkmark next to the name of the effect to turn it on. Set the Opacity to 20%, the Angle to 120 degrees (leave Global Angle selected), the Distance to 53 pixels, the Blur to 12 pixels, and the Intensity to 0. Figure 10.38 shows this dialog box. Click on OK.

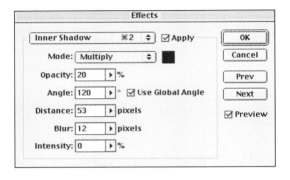

Figure 10.38

You can also set up additional effects, such as an inner shadow, at the same time you create a drop shadow.

16. You can easily give these same effects to the other pieces of candy. With your current candy layer still active, click on the empty column next to the Eye column in the Layers palette for all the candy layers (except the active one—it already has a Paintbrush icon in that column). This action links the layers together so that they move and transform as one. Figure 10.39 shows the Layers palette with all the candy layers linked.

Figure 10.39

Linking layers in Photoshop allows them to move and transform together.

17. Now that the layers are linked, they can all be given the same Layer Effects. To do so, choose Layer|Effects|Copy Effects. Then select Layer|Effects|Paste Effects To Linked. Figure 10.40 shows the image in progress with the Layer Effects applied.

Figure 10.40
CANDY.PSD now sports some layer effects and a border.

Pattern Work

In this section of the project, you'll create two types of background tiles for the image—one from Photoshop and one in Illustrator. This part of the project gives you a good opportunity to evaluate the ways and whys of using one program versus the other for creating patterns.

Photoshop Patterns

You'll now create a pattern for the background. When you select the Edit|Define Pattern command, Photoshop takes a picture of whatever is present in the image that falls within the selection and makes it into a pattern tile. It captures the image from every visible layer. Therefore, you'll pick up the shadows and layer effects in the area as well as the objects themselves. (If you want to see where you are going with this example before you choose your pattern, look in the Illustrator Studio section of the book or open the finished example on this book's companion CD-ROM.)

1. Figure 10.41 shows the area of the image that I marqueed. I used a rectangular marquee that was 42×576 pixels. Just drag the marquee over any area that looks interesting. It doesn't matter which layer is active. Choose Edit|Define Pattern.

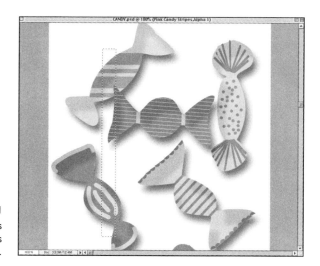

Figure 10.41

The rectangular marquee shows the area that I selected to use as a background pattern.

2. Deselect (Command/Ctrl+D) the pattern tile. Make the White Rectangle layer (Layer 1) active. Drag the layer to the New Layer icon at the bottom of the Layers palette to copy it. Double-click on the thumbnail for the copied layer (which is above the original) and change its name to "Pattern". Click on OK to close the dialog box. Fill the image with the pattern (Shift+Del, Using: Pattern, 100% Opacity, Mode: Normal, Preserve Transparency: On). Figure 10.42 shows the Fill dialog box, and Figure 10.43 shows the result.

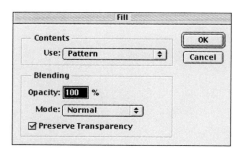

Figure 10.42

(Left) You can preserve the transparency of the layer as you fill it with a pattern.

Figure 10.43

(Right) You can create a pattern fill based on a slice of the image.

3. The result is a bit garish (to my eye, at least). Let's tame it down. Reduce the Opacity of the layer to 90%. You have many different possibilities, but you can just add an Adjustment layer for now—to make a monotone of the pattern. Changing the pattern to a monotone helps it fade into the background and not fight with the candies. Select the nontransparent Layer pixels of the Pattern layer (Command/Ctrl+click on the Layer name in the Layers palette). Create a new Adjustment layer (Command/Ctrl+click on the New Layer icon in the Layers palette). Select a Hue/Saturation Adjustment layer. Click on Colorize *before* you start to adjust the settings. I set the Hue to 131 (a green), the Saturation to 50, and the Lightness to +69. Figure 10.44 shows the Hue/Saturation dialog box and the settings that I used.

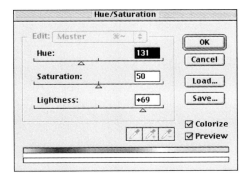

Figure 10.44
By colorizing the pattern, you can make it less of a distraction in the image.

4. Save your work as "CANDY.PSD".

Illustrator Patterns

You're now going to create a layer of patterns that uses three of the candies in a repeat that runs down a 45-degree angle. Figure 10.45 shows what the pattern layer looks like when it's done; however, the background of the pattern layer will be transparent (not white), and you'll be able to blend it into the Hard Wrap candy image using an Apply mode.

You'll make this pattern in Illustrator for the following reasons:

- If you create a straight pattern in Illustrator, you can render the entire image on an angle in Photoshop more easily than you could create and rotate it in Photoshop.

- Rotating a layer of this size in Photoshop can be very slow—even on a machine with a fast chip and a lot of RAM. To produce a rotated pattern, you would need to expand your image canvas in Photoshop to much too large a size for comfortable working speed.

Transparency and the Pattern

I left the White Rectangle layer in the image so that I could reduce the opacity of the pattern as low as I wanted it to go without revealing the orange Background layer underneath. If you are low on memory, you can merge the White Rectangle layer into the Background layer if you want. The white will still be there as needed behind the pattern layer.

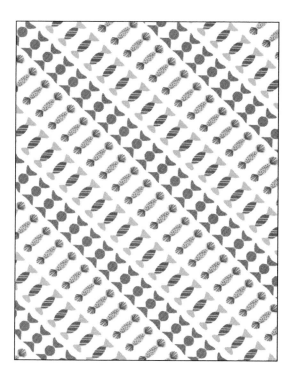

Figure 10.45
This is the pattern layer that
you will create.

By the way, if you want to skip over the entire pattern-making process, PATLAYER.AI is on this book's companion CD-ROM.

1. Launch Illustrator (you can close Photoshop if you do not have enough RAM for both of them to remain open).

2. Open the file CANDY.AI (this is the original on this book's companion CD-ROM). Use the Selection tool (V) to select the pink candy with the thin green stripes, the green candy with the pink polka dots, and the yellow-green candy with the thick and thin orange lines.

3. Create a new document (File|New). Drag the selected candies from the CANDY.AI file into the new image. You can close CANDY.AI if you want.

4. Deselect (Command/Ctrl+Shift+A). Select the orange and yellow-green candy. Choose the Rotate tool (R). Press Shift and drag to constrain rotation to 45 degrees.

5. Select the polka dot candy. With the Rotate tool, keep Shift pressed and rotate the candy 90 degrees clockwise.

6. Select the thin-striped candy. Double-click on the Rotate tool. In the dialog box, change the angle of rotation to 4.2 degrees (yes, it took some experimentation to figure out that this exact amount would make the stripes lie straight, horizontally across the candy). Figure 10.46 shows the three candies properly rotated.

Figure 10.46
The pattern-to-be candies are rotated to make them look horizontal.

7. Select the entire image (Command/Ctrl+A). Double-click on the Scale tool. In the dialog box, change the Uniform Scale amount to 27%, as shown in Figure 10.47.

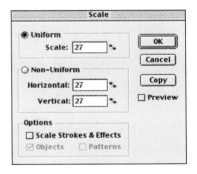

Figure 10.47
You need to scale the candies to 27 percent.

8. Drag the candies into a straight line so that the pink candy is on the middle and the polka dot candy on the left. Select the orange and yellow-green candy, as shown in Figure 10.48. Notice that its bounding box is the only one that really looks angled. Choose Object|Transform|Reset Bounding Box to make the bounding box hug the new orientation of the object and help avoid problems. (It isn't strictly necessary to reset the bounding box. However, because Adobe included the feature, it seems safer to use it.)

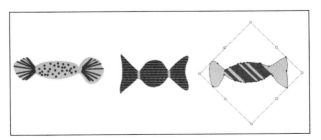

Figure 10.48
You need to reset the bounding box around the candy on the right.

9. Select the Rectangle tool (M). Click once in the image to open the Rectangle Options dialog box. Change the width to 2.556 inches and the height to 0.403 inches. Click on OK. Change the color of the box to gray (or any color that isn't in the candies—you are using this box only as a temporary spacer). Send the box to the back (Command/Ctrl+Shift+[). Drag the candies (in their current order) into the box.

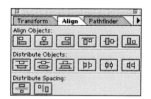

Figure 10.49

You can use the Align palette to easily space your objects.

10. Deselect (Command/Ctrl+Shift+A). Select just the gray box and the polka dot candy on the left. Click on the Align Left icon on the Align palette. It is the leftmost icon on the top row shown in Figure 10.49. This action ensures that the box and the leftmost candy share the same left edge.

11. Drag the candy on the right so that it is inside the box. Select it and the box. Click on the Align Right icon in the Align palette (the third icon on the top row).

12. Now that the left and right objects are in the correct place, deselect the gray box and select all three candies. Click on the Vertical Align Center icon (next-to-the-last one of the top row). If you do not see three rows of icons on the Align palette, choose Show Options from the sidebar menu on the palette to reveal the Distribute Spacing commands. Click on the Horizontal Distribute Spacing icon to evenly space the three candies. Figure 10.50 shows the candies now correctly lined up inside the gray box.

Figure 10.50

The candies are evenly spaced and are horizontally aligned with one another.

13. Click on the gray box and delete it because it's no longer needed. Select the three objects (Command/Ctrl+A) and then group them (Command/Ctrl+G).

14. Select the Rectangle tool (R). Click in the image to open the Rectangle Options dialog box. This time, create a filled, unstroked rectangle that is 2.681 inches wide and 0.458 inches high. This is the final size of the pattern.

15. Send the candies to the front (Command/Ctrl+Shift+]). Drag the candies on top of the new box. It is not critical that they be centered (although I centered them by eye) as long as they are entirely within the box. Change the Fill and Stroke for the box to None. Group the candies and the box and drag the group to the Swatches palette. Your pattern is now complete. (For more details on creating patterns, see Chapter 7.)

16. Let's actually create the pattern layer now. For safety's sake, choose File|Save A Copy and save the image in the Swatches Library folder of your Illustrator installation. That way, you can either edit the original pattern again if you want or import the Swatch containing the pattern into another document.

17. Select the entire image (Command/Ctrl+A) and then delete. This action leaves the pattern still in the Swatches palette.

18. You need to create a new box that is exactly the same size (in inches or points) as your Photoshop file. I'll save you the trouble of looking. Choose the Rectangle tool (R) and click in the image to open the Rectangle Options dialog box. The box needs to be 6.672 inches high by 8.864 inches wide.

19. The box should have no stroke. Click on the new candy pattern to make the pattern into the box fill. Figure 10.51 shows the filled box.

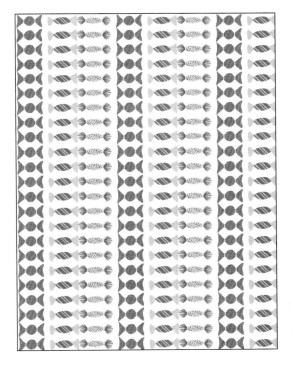

Figure 10.51
The candy pattern is used to fill a box that is the same size in inches as the original image.

20. You need to rotate the pattern fill. Click on the sidebar menu in the Transform palette, as shown in Figure 10.52, and select the Transform Fill option. Then click on the Rotation drop-down menu at the bottom left of the Transform palette and select 45 degrees as the angle of rotation. The pattern rotates to look almost as it did in Figure 10.45.

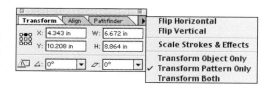

Figure 10.52
You can elect to transform only the pattern fill from the Transform palette.

21. You may, if you want to, be obsessive (as I am) and force the pink candy to appear in the top-left corner of the box. I can't give you an exact setting here because it depends on where in the box you placed the candies and where on the page the box is located. Turn on the Rulers (Command/Ctrl+R). If you centered the candies as I did, drag the ruler origin from the upper-left corner of the document window so that the horizontal line is parallel to (and touches) the top of the box, and the vertical line is at about the –1/2" mark on the vertical ruler. Undo (Command/Ctrl+Z) the original change if you do not get it right and try again. It may take several tries. Figure 10.53 attempts to show the correct location for centering the candy pattern.

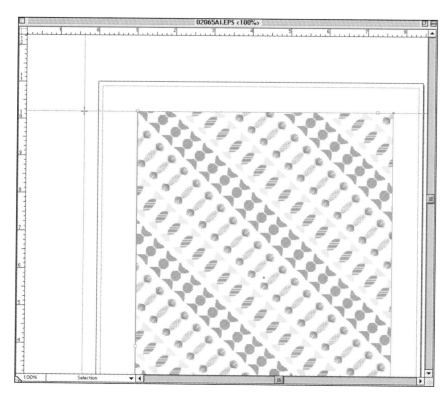

Figure 10.53
In my image, dragging the origin point as shown centered the pink candy in the upper-left corner of the object.

22. Save the document as "PATLAYER.AI". You can quit Illustrator now if you cannot run both Illustrator and Photoshop at the same time. The image that you created looks exactly like Figure 10.45.

Was All This Measuring Really Necessary?

No, it wasn't really necessary to fool around with the gray spacer box. If you had been designing this image, you could have made the pattern any size that you wanted. Because you are reproducing my results, I needed to find a way for you to exactly duplicate my measurements. This approach was the easiest (short of my just giving you the pattern).

The second box was needed. The precise measurements are mine, but you do need an invisible box to set the boundary of your pattern, or else the candies would touch one another when the pattern is repeated. The purpose of the outer box is to define the amount of white space around the repeat.

Finishing Up: Returning to Photoshop

How do you get the pattern layer back into Photoshop? You have just tried a number of different methods. The easiest method is simply to place the file into the Hard Wrap image. You can also drag and drop. The drag-and-drop feature works perfectly in this instance.

Using Copy and Paste is not a wonderful idea because the image is really too large for the clipboard. You could, instead, export the pattern layer within Illustrator as a Photoshop file and open it in Photoshop, but this approach is much trickier than you might expect. Because you rotated the pattern, the rasterizer in Illustrator cannot properly anti-alias it. If you leave the pattern fill alone and export the image, the candies are distressingly jagged, although some anti-aliasing is done. Should you need to export a rotated or skewed pattern fill, you need to expand (Object|Expand) it first. This technique works, although it produces a Photoshop file with white space around the edges that needs to be cropped to size before placing it into the image. You learned about the Expand command in Chapter 7.

To wrap up this project, take the following steps:

1. Launch Photoshop. Open your saved copy of CANDY.PSD.

2. Let's add a bit of texture to some of the candy. Click on the Orange Stripe candy to select it. Press D to set the colors back to the default of black and white. Use the Eyedropper tool (I) to set your Foreground color to the orange of the candy wrapper end. Press X to exchange the Foreground and Background colors. (Or you could press Option/Alt as you click to set the Background color to begin with.) When you apply a Pointillize filter, the color of your Background swatch determines the background color behind the color dots that the filter produces.

3. Choose Filter|Pixelate|Pointillize. Set the Cell Size to 5. Figure 10.54 shows the filter dialog box.

Moving a Pattern within an Object

You can move the starting location of a pattern in an object by changing the 0,0 ruler origin point of the document. Just drag the ruler origin from the upper-left corner until you like the new location of the pattern in the selected object. This is not one of Illustrator's most shining moments. You cannot preview the result, and getting the pattern exactly where you want it takes a frustratingly long time. Worse, you also can't depend on other patterns staying put if you fiddle around with the origin point on a new patterned object.

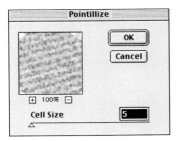

Figure 10.54
The Pointillize filter adds wonderful dots of color to the object.

4. Change your Background color (Option/Alt+click with the Eyedropper tool) to the green used in the bands on the Pink Candy Stripe layer. Make that layer active. Choose Filter|Pixelate|Pointillize again or Option+Command/Alt+Ctrl+F to reopen the Filter dialog box. Set the Cell Size to 3. Click on OK. Now choose Filter|Fade Pointillize. Change the Opacity to 60%. Click on OK. Figure 10.55 shows the Fade Filter dialog box.

Figure 10.55
You can reduce the effect of any filter after you have applied it by selecting the Filter|Fade Filter command.

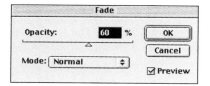

5. Make the TEXT layer active. Choose File|Place and locate the PATLAYER.AI image. Choose it and click on OK. The preview box should fit exactly and doesn't need to be adjusted. Press Return/Enter to execute the Place command.

6. Change the Apply mode to Multiply and the Opacity for the pattern layer to 40 percent. Figure 10.56 shows the Hard Wrap image at this point.

Figure 10.56
By changing the pattern layer Apply mode to Multiply and lowering its opacity, you can softly mix it with the rest of the image.

7. Change the Foreground color to CMYK: 69, 39, 64, 77 (a dark charcoal) and the Background color to CMYK: 31, 0, 31, 0 (a light green). Make the TEXT layer active. Fill the text with the Foreground color with Preserve Transparency On (Shift+Option+Delete or Shift+Alt+Backspace). Change the Apply mode to Color Burn at 100 percent opacity. The effect needs more punch.

8. Drag the TEXT layer to the New Layer icon at the bottom of the Layers palette to duplicate it. Repeat this step so that you have a third identical layer.

9. Make another copy of the TEXT layer the same way (it is called TEXT copy 3).

10. Make the TEXT layer active (yes, the original one at the bottom of the collection). Fill the layer with the Background color with Preserve Transparency On (Shift+Command+Delete or Shift+Ctrl+Backspace). Change the Apply mode for this layer back to Normal and lower the Opacity to 60%. The text is now nicely shaded and stands out quite well. It just needs a little more dimensionality.

11. Let's create a white drop shadow for the text. Although Photoshop has Layer Effects drop shadows, we will create this drop shadow the old way because we need to mask it.

12. Drag the TEXT layer to the New Layer icon at the bottom of the Layers palette to duplicate it (again). Move this copy below the TEXT layer in the Layers palette. Double-click on the layer thumbnail and change the layer name to "Text Glow". Change the layer opacity to 100 percent (now you know why we need to mask it—the wonderful text shading disappears).

13. Press D to set the colors back to the default of black and white. Fill the layer with the Background color with Preserve Transparency On (Shift+Command+Delete or Shift+Ctrl+Backspace).

14. Select the Move tool (V). Press the right-arrow key three times and the up-arrow key three times to offset the white drop shadow.

15. With the white Glow layer still active, select the nontransparent Layer pixels on the TEXT layer (Command/Ctrl+click on the TEXT Layer thumbnail in the Layers palette). You do not need to have the layer active to be able to load the layer transparency.

16. Choose Layer|Add Layer Mask|Hide Selection (or Option/Alt+click on the Add Layer Mask icon at the bottom of the Layers palette). Figure 10.57 shows the Hard Wrap image after all the text has been styled.

Figure 10.57

The text is finally in place for the Hard Wrap image.

17. At this point in the creation process, I began to feel as if the candy was fighting a little bit with the text. Therefore, your next step is to lighten just the candies in the image (but in such a way that you can easily change your mind). Make the Pink Striped Candy layer active (the highest of the candy layers). Select the nontransparent Layer pixels (Command/Ctrl+click on the Layer name in the Layers palette). Press and hold Shift and load the nontransparent pixels on all the other candy layers (Shift allows you to add to the selection). When you are done, only the six candies should be selected.

18. Create a new Adjustment layer (Command/Ctrl+click on the New Layer icon). The selection is automatically changed into a mask for the Adjustment layer. Choose Hue/Saturation as the type of layer to create. Increase the Saturation to +23 and the Lightness to +25, as shown in Figure 10.58. Click on OK.

You need to create only one more effect, and you still need to fix the Swash layer. The design seems to need a celebration, so I added a ribbon swirl (that's the layer that's still hidden). I feel that the original black is much too strong for the packaging, although you are certainly free to disagree. Let's decorate this layer and soften it.

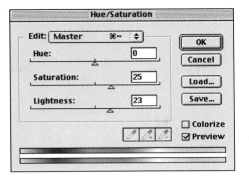

Figure 10.58
You can change the Saturation and Lightness of just the candies in the image.

19. Make the Swash layer active. Change your Foreground color to CMYK: 31, 0, 31, 0. This color is the same light green as the base TEXT layer. Fill the text with the Foreground color with Preserve Transparency On (Shift+Option+Delete or Shift+Alt+Backspace).

20. Use the Eyedropper tool with Option/Alt pressed to make the orange in the border the Background color. Apply the Pointillize filter (Filter|Pixelate|Pointillize) with a Cell Size of 11.

21. Choose Filter|Distort|Wave and use the settings shown in Figure 10.59.

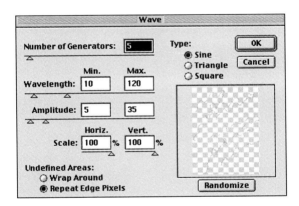

Figure 10.59
Use these Wave filter settings to make the Swash layer flow.

22. Your Foreground color should still be the light green. Fill the Swash with the Foreground color with Preserve Transparency On (Shift+Option+Delete or Shift+Alt+Backspace). This color, of course, covers the result of the Pixellate filter, so choose Filter|Fade Fill and change the Opacity to 40%. Save your work and take a rest. You've earned it! Figure 10.60 shows the final image in grayscale, but it looks much better in color.

What have you done in this image that you could not do in Illustrator? You can create the inner shadows more easily and more automatically in Photoshop. You also created Adjustment layers that allow you to easily change your mind about the specifics.

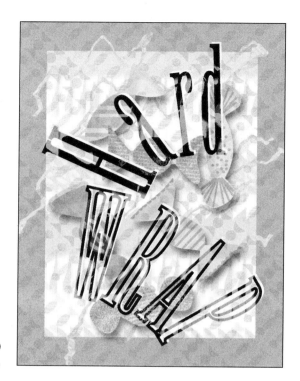

Figure 10.60
The Hard Wrap candy box is done.

Could you have built the entire image in Photoshop? Probably, except that the candy would not have been as crisp, the candy pattern would have seriously anti-aliased as you reduced and rotated it, and you could not have set type on a path at all.

The final call of which program to use is yours. With the newest releases of both Illustrator and Photoshop, the line between these programs is seriously blurred. You still can't do pixel-level editing in Illustrator. You algorithmically create pixels in Illustrator as the result of effects you apply, but you cannot individually change so much as a single pixel. Illustrator adds sharp, resolution-independent shapes and superior type handling to complement Photoshop's strengths. Together, the combination is unbeatable.

Moving On

In this chapter, I described how Photoshop treats Illustrator images. You learned how to open, place, cut and paste, and drag and drop images that are in Illustrator format. Most of these techniques also work with Freehand images.

You also learned how to export layered images from Illustrator. I discussed the advantages and disadvantages of each method of rasterizing an Illustrator file. I briefly touched on resolution and some of the Illustrator-to-Photoshop "gotchas" that exist.

In Chapter 11, you'll look at the same raster-vector issue from the other perspective: How do you bring Photoshop images into Illustrator, and why would you want to?

Chapter 11

Raster Images
in Illustrator

*Photoshop can serve as a wonderful source for Illustrator
imagery. You can easily get scanned line art from Photoshop
and change it to vector format. You can also place raster
images directly into Illustrator and have them interact with
Illustrator objects.*

By Sherry London

Photoshop to Illustrator: Going My Way

In the old days—oh, about 10 years ago—the only way to get an Illustrator drawing started was to draw it yourself. Yes, you could get a primitive scan of a document—I remember that I had a tiny hand scanner for the PC by 1990. Illustrator 88 (Mac version—the first Windows incarnation of the program was terrible) did have an autotrace tool. If you clicked near a line on the imported bitmapped image (your template art), you sometimes ended up with a usable shape.

In the 12 years since Illustrator 88, so much has changed in the world of digital graphics that it's like moving from the Middle Ages into the Space Age in about three months. One of the nicer changes is the ability to place raster and vector images in the same program and to leave them where they make the most sense to output. In Chapter 10, you learned how you can take Illustrator images and "finish them off" in Photoshop. In this chapter, you take the voyage the other way and explore ways in which you can use Photoshop-originated imagery in Illustrator. As before, you'll look first at how you can move the images back and forth and then consider why you would want to do so. Finally, you'll look at some examples of images that wander from program to program before coming to their ultimate resting place.

Illustrator 9 has many more reasons for being "Photoshop-friendly." Because of the addition of transparency, blend modes, opacity masks, and live effects, you can get even more mileage out of your Photoshop imagery now. Illustrator 9 can import Photoshop images as layered files and make separate objects out of each layer, while still preserving the transparency and blend modes. It can also use Photoshop images as opacity masks.

Photo In: How?

Just as you have a number of ways to get a Photoshop image into Illustrator, you have an equally extensive list of options for bringing raster or originally raster images into Illustrator:

- You can open a Photoshop file directly into Illustrator.

- You can place a Photoshop image into an open document.

- You can copy and paste Photoshop images into Illustrator.

- You can use the drag-and-drop method to move images from Photoshop into Illustrator.

- You can pass Photoshop paths to Illustrator by using any of the first three methods listed here.

Because you practiced using the Open, Place, drag-and-drop, and copy-and-paste features from Illustrator to Photoshop in Chapter 10, I can't think of a reason to make you do it in reverse. The process is the same. However, a few gotchas exist for the Photoshop-to-Illustrator route that make it either different or more complex than the Illustrator-to-Photoshop route.

It's a Real Drag

Image resolution seems to be a tricky and complex topic for most people. I usually urge folks to work in pixels inside Photoshop because pixels are fixed: A 900-pixel-wide image contains 900 pixels, regardless of its ppi. However, if the ppi is set to 300, the 900-pixel image prints at 3 inches wide; if the ppi is set to 100, the 900-pixel image prints at 9 inches wide—but it still contains only 900 pixels across. Therefore, I find it much easier to think in pixels.

The scenario becomes more complex when you move your image into Illustrator. Three of the transfer methods are no problem; however, when you drag and drop an image, the image resolution changes to the next lowest multiple of 72 ppi. Unlike the previous Photoshop example (the unchanging 900-pixel image), when you drag a 900-pixel-wide image from Photoshop to Illustrator and the Photoshop resolution is 300 ppi (a 3-inch width), the resulting Illustrator image is slightly larger than 3 inches wide but it prints at 288 ppi (the nearest multiple of 72) rather than 300 ppi. This result is actually a welcome change from earlier versions of Illustrator in which the resolution dropped to 72 ppi when an image was dragged and dropped (except that at 72 ppi, Illustrator at least got the physical size right). You're not likely to notice much deterioration of image quality in the most common drag-and-drop situation (a 300 ppi image dragged and dropped into Illustrator will print at 288 ppi, which is probably enough resolution on an imagesetter, and is more resolution than a desktop printer can use anyway). However, if you want your image to be 3 inches wide, no other size is likely to satisfy you.

You can see the resolution of an embedded image by selecting it and then looking at the File|Document Info palette. When the Document Info palette is visible, choose Embedded Images from the side drop-down menu. As you can see in Figure 11.1, you can easily find the effective resolution of your embedded object.

You can raise the resolution of an embedded image by making it smaller in Illustrator. Because Illustrator is not a pixel-editor, it can't change the number of pixels in an image. Therefore, making the image smaller packs the same number of pixels into a smaller area, thus increasing the image resolution. One way to get both the size and resolution correct is to first use the Image|Image Size command in Photoshop to set the resolution to a multiple of 72 ppi. Make sure that the Resample Image checkbox is not selected; you don't want to change the number of pixels in the image. Then, drag and drop the image into Illustrator. Go back into Photoshop and change the image resolution back to 300 ppi (or the desired resolution); then make note of the actual image dimensions (you can use the Image|Image Size dialog box for this, but you

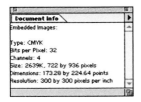

Figure 11.1
The Document Info palette shows the resolution of the embedded image.

Another Way to Set Resolution

If you know the size before you drag, you'll find the image bigger after you drag it into Illustrator. You can then enter the original dimensions in the Transform palette in Illustrator, and the physical size changes back to the original value at the desired resolution.

need to click on Cancel when you're finished). In Illustrator once again, select the raster object and type in the correct width and height in the Transform palette. You can check the Document Info|Embedded Images palette to see the change in both size and image resolution.

The only issue remaining with drag-and-drop is that the dragged image is embedded inside Illustrator rather than linked. We'll tackle this topic next.

To Place or Parse (or to Link or Embed)

When you embed a raster file, you actually include the image in the Illustrator file. All its data is converted to PostScript format (although you still get a single raster object rather than editable paths), and no external files are needed when you go to print. If you embed a large file, the file size increases dramatically. However, if you want to apply filters to a raster image in Illustrator, you must embed the file. Images that are either dragged and dropped or pasted into Illustrator are automatically embedded.

When you link a file (using the Place command), you don't store the image inside the Illustrator file. Rather, you store only an indication of the place where the original is located. The file size doesn't increase by much, but you lose the capability to apply filters to the image. You need to remember to include the originals when you take the image to a service bureau. However, you gain flexibility. If you decide to change the original image, you need to do so in only one place (the original image), and Illustrator can follow the link to retrieve the updated image. If you use the Place command, Link is the default method of placing the file.

The other problem with an embedded file is that it is not an automatic process to edit the original. If you edit the image that you dragged and dropped, Illustrator has no way of knowing that it has anything in common with the open image in Illustrator. If you copy the object from Illustrator and place it into Photoshop for editing, your object in Illustrator is not automatically updated when you make changes to it in Photoshop. If the image had been linked, the updates would be automatic. However, you can get around this a bit by using the Replace option in the Place command. You can select the file that has been placed, use the Place command again and select the Replace option. This puts the new file in and applies the same set of filters, and so on.

You can tell whether a file is linked or embedded in either of the following two ways:

1. A linked file is shown with an X through it when the object is selected, as shown in Figure 11.2.

2. The file name shows in the Links palette. If the file is embedded, an object icon appears after it in the Links palette, as you can see in the bottom two entries in Figure 11.3.

Figure 11.2
Linked files are shown with an X across the box.

You can take other actions with the Links palette to help manage the images that you place into Illustrator. You can see information about the scale, size, and orientation of the placed images. You can also quickly embed a linked image from the Links palette.

The Passing of the Path

Photoshop allows you to create vector paths by using the Pen tool. Chapter 10 showed ways to take an object from Illustrator and use its path in Photoshop. You can also take a path created in Photoshop and send it to Illustrator. Paths can be sent individually (through copy and paste) or exported by using the Paths To Illustrator option in the File|Export menu. Additionally, paths are saved with any file that you store in Photoshop format and are available for use if you open the file in Illustrator.

Although the Illustrator manual seems to hint that you can drag and drop paths from Photoshop to Illustrator, you can't. However, enough other ways exist to accomplish the same goal. You'll try some of these ways a bit later in this chapter.

Figure 11.3
The Links palette also helps you to spot the linked and embedded files.

Photo In: Why?

Although it used to be more common to move Illustrator images into Photoshop, you might take them in the other direction for many reasons. You can scan a drawing or photograph in Photoshop and then move it to Illustrator to prepare it further. You can use Adobe Illustrator to create a clipping path that you want to later use in Photoshop (the Illustrator Bézier tool is much better than Photoshop's). You might need to place a Photoshop image into Illustrator so that you can use it as a template for type to be composited in a page-layout program. You might also want to create a texture in Photoshop and use the texture in Illustrator to add surface interest.

Illustrator 9 adds even more reasons to use Photoshop imagery in Illustrator. You can place Photoshop images and lower their opacity. You can make Photoshop images and vector objects interact by changing Blend modes. You can even use Photoshop images as opacity masks for vector (or for raster) objects in Illustrator 9. In the sections that follow, you'll explore these reasons a bit more.

The Best AutoTrace Tool in Town

I find it very frustrating to scan an image and then have to spend hours getting the image into a usable vector format. If *I* can see the "edges" of the shapes that I want, why can't the computer? Of course, the computer can't "see" anything—and that is just the problem. Adobe provides a variety of ways for you to tell the computer how to create outlines from line art or continuous-tone images.

You can use the Illustrator AutoTrace tool—although normally using this tool is a bad idea. It doesn't work well, and it gives you only one line at a time. You can use Adobe Streamline. This slick autotrace program can work with line art or full-color images and can be tweaked to decently automate the entire process. A number of folks have had a lot of success with this method, although I'm not one of them. I lack the patience to sufficiently tweak my images. Actually, if I were only to scan, Streamline, and print, I too would probably be satisfied. However, I usually manipulate an image much more than that, and I'm typically not happy with the individual shapes that come out of Streamline (although, again, this is a personal preference).

You can get editable shapes from a raster image in yet another way. Place the image in Illustrator into a new layer in the Layers palette and choose Template from the Layers palette side drop-down menu. Use the Pencil or Pen tool to trace over the shapes by hand. This method gives the maximum possible control over your result. I rarely have enough time, however, to use this approach.

My favorite method of getting usable shapes is to select the areas inside Photoshop, create paths from the selections, and send the paths into Illustrator. This approach gives you a marvelously easy autotrace facility that can handle multiple shapes at one time. The result can be either simple or complex, depending on your starting image. Let's work though two examples—one easy and the other one more intricate.

PROJECT 11.1 | Candy Raster to Candy Vector

For the first project, we'll revisit the candy that we used in Chapter 10. The candy shapes came from a scan of some glass candies that I have displayed on a knick-knack shelf at home. I simply placed each piece of glass on my scanner and acquired the scan. The image that you'll use as a starting place was colored for a long-ago project. All that you want from it are the shapes of the candy.

1. Open the image RAWCANDY.PSD in Photoshop.

2. Press Command/Ctrl and click on the thumbnail of Layer 1 in the Layers palette to load the nontransparent pixels on the layer as a selection. (In practical terms, this selects the entire object in the layer.)

3. Press and hold Shift, then press Command/Ctrl and click on the thumbnail of Layer 2 in the Layers palette to add Layer 2 to the current selection.

4. Repeat Step 3 to add Layers 3 through 6 to the selection. Figure 11.4 shows the final selection.

Figure 11.4
All six layers of candy are selected.

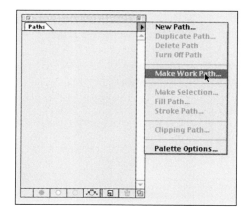

Figure 11.5
Make Work Path changes the
selection into a path.

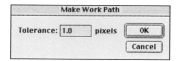

Figure 11.6
Using the Make Work Path
dialog box, you can determine
how faithfully the path should
reproduce the original selection.

You Can Split Long Paths

If you are afraid that your
artwork may be too complex
to print, you can choose the
Printing & Export panel in the
Document Setup dialog box
and select the Split Long Paths
checkbox. This makes several
smaller and less complex paths
from the one long one. However, you should finish the
editing of your image before
you select this option.

5. Select Make Work Path from the side menu in the Paths palette, as
   shown in Figure 11.5.

6. Accept the default Tolerance of 1.0 in the dialog box that appears (see
   Figure 11.6). *Tolerance* refers to the fidelity with which the path hugs the
   original. A tolerance of 1.0 is quite faithful to the original (0.5 is the
   tightest tolerance). A lower tolerance also means that more points are
   created to define the shape. Although using a small tolerance has the
   potential to cause printing problems, the candy shapes are not complex
   enough to cause difficulties.

7. Double-click on the work path in the Paths palette. Accept the default
   path name to save your paths.

8. Choose File|Export|Paths to Illustrator. Figure 11.7 shows the dialog
   box. Save the document as RAWCANDY.AI. Notice that a box allows
   you to select which path to save. If you have multiple paths, you can
   save them all at one time. It was just as easy here to create all the
   paths at once. If the paths were more complex, creating them all at one
   time might not have been a good idea.

   What have you created? Open Illustrator and find out.

Figure 11.7
Saving the paths as an Illustrator
document is as easy as saving
any other file.

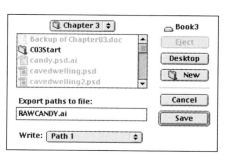

About Imported Crop Marks

When you export paths from Photoshop, Photoshop writes the boundaries of the document into the file. These boundaries show up as crop marks. If you want to keep them—so that you can export the same-size document back to Photoshop—just make sure that your drawing falls completely inside of them. Should you prefer to delete them, choose Object|Crop Marks|Release, and they will turn into an unstroked, unfilled rectangle around the candies. You can then delete this rectangle.

David Xenakis also reminds me that you might find it beneficial to leave the rectangle. If you group it with the other paths and then import the original image, you could use the Align command to place the paths precisely atop the placed photo.

---

9. In Adobe Illustrator, open the RAWCANDY.AI file that you just saved. Figure 11.8 shows a screen capture of the result that you will see. *Don't panic!* I know that it looks empty.

Figure 11.8
When you open an exported paths file from Photoshop in Illustrator, only the boundary of the document is visible.

10. Why *does* the image look empty? Photoshop creates paths that have no stroke and no fill. Therefore, when you open the image in Illustrator, everything is invisible. The easiest way to make things show up is to select the entire image (Command/Ctrl+A). As you can see in Figure 11.9, everything is still there.

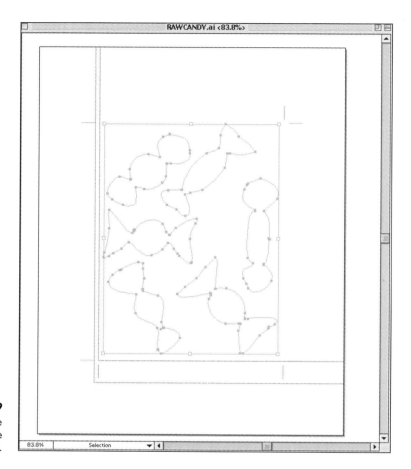

Figure 11.9
When you select the entire
document, you can see the
unstroked, unfilled paths.

11. Make the Stroke Color selector active and choose black as the Stroke color. In this way, you can find the paths more easily. With the paths stroked in black, you can edit them as you desire and change the colors when you finish. I used this method to prepare the candy images you used in Chapter 10.

12. When you import paths from Photoshop, you'll often want to adjust them to make them smoother or to remove extra points. Now that you have the shapes in Illustrator, you can easily edit them as you want. Figure 11.10 shows one candy in a "before" (on the left) and "after" (on the right) view. I changed "before" into "after" by removing all the points on the right side of the candy body and by using the Pencil tool to draw a new top wrapper for the candy.

You can play with the shapes if you want, or you can close this file and go on to the next exercise. You now know how I started Project 10.7 so that you can design your own version or work on a similar project. One interesting exercise would be to see how much of Project 10.7 you can now do completely in Illustrator.

Figure 11.10
The candy shape (left) as placed into Illustrator. The edited candy shape (right).

I used the candy project to show how to use the layer transparency of an object as a basis for a selection and how to make exportable paths from that selection. Creating the candies was easy because they were solid objects. They would have been fairly easy to create even if they had been flat, scanned objects against the Background layer. If you had scanned the glass candies, you would have needed to make a selection around each candy and place it into its own layer (or color each candy a solid black and use the Magic Wand to select all the candies).

PROJECT 11.2 Exporting Complex Paths

This project is more complex. It's an extension of my Photoshop woodcut technique that I tend to overuse because I like it so well. Although this project starts with a photographic scan, you won't need to create your own paths. I've already created the selection paths and channels that you'll need, so you can concentrate on the most instructive part of the exercise.

Creating Complex Paths in Photoshop

Meet my nephew David (who was growing new teeth when this photo was taken several years ago). He's now a very talented teenager who dresses all in black and sports bleached blonde, spiked hair. Luckily, I needed only my sister's permission to use the image—not David's—who might not forgive me for publishing it!

1. Open the image DAVID.PSD in Photoshop. Figure 11.11 shows the original image.

Figure 11.11
This is David, in the original Photoshop version.

2. Load the Alpha 1 channel (Option+Command/Alt+Ctrl+4). This step selects David's shirt.

3. Create a New Layer via Copy from the selection (Command/Ctrl+J).

4. Choose Filter|Other|High Pass, Amount: 1.6. This step creates an image that looks as though it has lost all detail and all contrast. It has lost contrast and isn't usable as is, but the High Pass filter has left highly detailed edges embedded in the image, and the next step will bring them out.

5. Select Image|Adjust|Threshold. Set the slider to 129, as shown in Figure 11.12. Figure 11.13 shows the result. Notice how much detail appears in the stripes of the shirt.

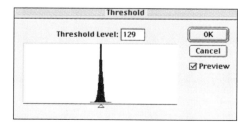

Figure 11.12
You can force an image to black and white by adjusting the image threshold.

DAVID.PSD is a large file that will use over 29MB of RAM inside Photoshop. If you're working on a low-RAM machine, you should reduce the image by 50 to 66 percent before you continue with the instructions.

Figure 11.13
After you apply the threshold command to David's shirt, the stripe detail appears crisp and sharp.

Next, you need to smooth the lines that were created to get a more solid look to the black and white.

6. Choose Filter|Blur|Gaussian Blur, Amount: 3. This step adds a large number of gray tones to the image. Usually, you should not blur the image this much, but I wanted to create more grays than needed to force this detail to a fairly solid black and white.

7. Choose Image|Adjust|Levels (Command/Ctrl+L). Figure 11.14 shows the Levels setting that I used. I brought the Black Input slider to 118 and the White Input slider to 152. Click on OK to exit the Levels dialog box. Figure 11.15 shows the result.

8. Make the Background layer active. Load the Alpha 2 channel (Option+Command+5/Alt+Ctrl+5).

9. Create a New Layer via Copy from the selection (Command/Ctrl+J). Now, David's head is on its own layer.

10. Choose Filter|Other|High Pass, Amount: 1.6.

11. Select Image|Adjust|Threshold. This time, use a setting of 128. (The head was processed separately from the body because you needed to be able to select a different Threshold setting. Also, if you had used all of David's face instead of just the features that I selected, he would have looked diseased.)

Smoothing Out Line Art

The Blur-and-Levels technique shown in Steps 6 and 7 comes from a tip posted by Kai Krause (formerly of MetaCreations) on AOL many years ago. It's a marvelous technique for making scanned line art smooth. The basic premise is that you take your starting black-and-white (bitmap) scan and slightly blur it (1 or 2 pixels), which creates gray tones that you can then force to white or black again by using the Levels command. You can manipulate these gray tones by moving the White and Black Input sliders in the Levels dialog box closer together. If you move the group of three sliders to the left, the image becomes lighter; as you move the sliders to the right, it becomes darker.

Figure 11.14
The Levels command is used to smooth the edges of a blurred selection.

Figure 11.15
David's shirt now has more solid areas of black and white, but the edges are quite smooth.

12. Apply a Gaussian Blur of 2 (Filter|Blur|Gaussian Blur, Amount: 2.0).

13. Choose Image|Adjust|Levels, as shown in Figure 11.16. I used a Black Input level of 131 and a White Input level of 168. Figure 11.17 shows the result.

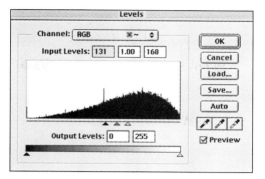

Figure 11.16
The Levels command settings used for David's head.

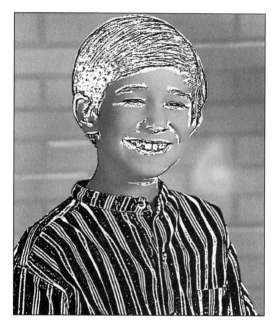

Figure 11.17
David's head and body are now ready to convert to paths.

14. Now, you need to prepare the line art for tracing. Make the Background layer active. Create a new layer (click on the New Layer icon at the bottom of the Layers palette). Fill the layer with white. You now have a choice: to preserve the body and head layers for some future purpose or to make the image smaller. If you don't care whether the image grows to 29MB of RAM, go to Step 15. If you want a smaller working file, follow Step 16. In either case, continue to Step 17.

15. Make the top layer active. Make a new layer (click on the New Layer icon at the bottom of the Layers palette). Create a merged image in the new layer (Shift+Option+Command+E/Shift+Alt+Ctrl+E). Figure 11.18 shows the completed line art.

16. Make the top layer active. Merge Down (Command/Ctrl+E). Merge Down again. Now, you have only two layers. Figure 11.18 shows the completed line art.

Figure 11.18
David has now become all
line art.

17. Make sure that the line art layer is the active layer in the Layers palette. Load the Composite channel of the image (Command+Option/ Alt+Ctrl+~), which selects all the white pixels in the image. You need the *black* pixels to be selected, so reverse the selection (Select|Inverse, Shift+Command/Ctrl+I).

18. In the Paths palette, choose Make Work Path from the side menu. Leave the Tolerance at 1.0. Save the path (double-click on the pathname in the Paths palette and accept the default name offered). This process can take awhile. Figure 11.19 shows the paths "posed" against a white background (for the purpose of this screen shot).

19. Choose File|Export|Paths to Illustrator. The default name of DAVID.PSD.AI is fine. Write only the line art path (it should be named Path 1). Export, too, is a bit slow, so don't be concerned if it seems to take a long time to write the new file.

20. Save your work in Photoshop, as you are not yet done with the Photoshop part of this image. If RAM limitations require it, close Photoshop.

21. In Illustrator, open the DAVID.PSD.AI file that you just saved. (Remember, it will open and look empty.)

22. Select the entire image (Command/Ctrl+A). Set the Fill to black. Figure 11.20 shows this image. Notice that it seems as if you have lost some shirt detail and that David's teeth are black. We'll fix this problem next.

Figure 11.19
The line art version of David has been selected and converted to paths.

Figure 11.20
The paths that you saved in Photoshop are filled with black in Illustrator.

23. Let's fix David's mouth first because this part of the image is the most distracting. Open the Preferences dialog box (Command/Ctrl+K) and choose the Area Select checkbox. Close the General Preferences dialog box. Magnify David's mouth area and select the outside shape of his lips (click near the outside border of his lips to select them). You should have one large shape, as shown in Figure 11.21.

Figure 11.21
David's mouth is selected.

24. Choose Object|Hide Selection. The mouth temporarily disappears, making it much easier to find the teeth. Figure 11.22 shows three separate tooth shapes selected. Change their Fill to white. Choose Object|Show All. Figure 11.23 shows David with his teeth filled with white. You can fix David's smile more by poking around to find more black shapes that look better filled with white. The area between the two left teeth can be filled with white.

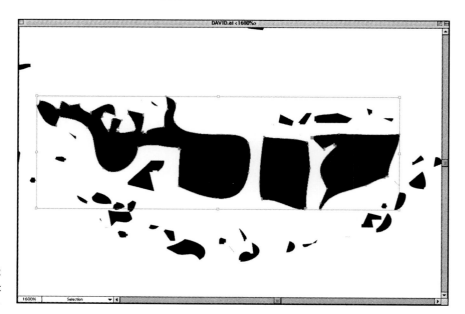

Figure 11.22
David's teeth are selected so that they can be filled with white.

Figure 11.23
When you show all the objects, David's mouth now looks much better.

25. Some black shapes can still be seen on top of David's teeth. They add a woodcut feel to the image. If you don't like them, select these spots and delete them. If you want to make up your mind later, create a new layer and move the "tooth spots" onto it. This way, you can view the image "with" and "without" as many times as you want until you decide.

Notice how much less detail shows in the stripes in David's shirt when compared to the image that you saved in Photoshop. The reason you get this result is the same as the reason you got the black teeth. Photoshop creates what actually are compound paths but doesn't write compound paths to the exported file. Therefore, when you import the Photoshop paths and fill them with black, every path is filled with black, and nothing is subtracted, as it would be in a true compound path. If you like the way the stripes look, you can leave them. You can recover either all the lost detail (a bit tedious) or most of the lost detail (much easier).

26. If you want to recover most of the woodcut-like detail, drag a marquee with the Selection tool across the bottom half of the image so that you select all of David's shirt but don't select the short line that defines his chin. Choose Object|Compound Paths|Make (Command/Ctrl+8). Figure 11.24 shows the image with the compound path.

How to Get the Maximum Detail from the Image

To get as much detail as possible in the shirt stripes, you need to do more work—and *not* create a compound path. First, select the large black shapes in the shirt (it has only three or four). As you find each major piece, hide it from view. Finally, select the entire shirt area (with the large pieces hidden) and move the remaining pieces to a new layer. Set the fill for these objects to white. Show the entire image. The major pieces are on the bottom layer, and you can protect them from change by locking the layer (click in the Lock Layer column on the Layers palette). Some of the shapes that you just filled with white should really be filled with black. You need to find and fill them individually—basically, by clicking where you think they might be. No shortcut exists that I can recommend for this job. Don't use this method if you want to work the rest of this project. You'll need the compound path created in Step 26.

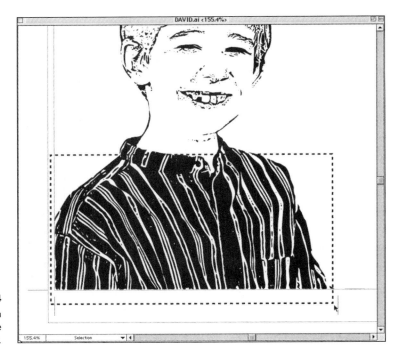

Figure 11.24

Creating a compound path is an easy way to restore detail to the stripes in David's shirt.

PROJECT 11.3 To Take a Photo beyond Where Photoshop Can Go Alone

After the line art is prepared in Illustrator, you can turn your attention to making the image into a stylized finished project. Because this image is to be a vector drawing, let's place a background and create an only-possible-in-Illustrator effect on it. The project continues, but we'll start the numbering back to Step 1 because this is a new phase to the example. You can peek at the final image in color in the Illustrator 9 Studio section of this book, if you want to see where we're heading with this image.

1. In Photoshop, open the original DAVID.PSD image (the one from the CD-ROM that you didn't edit). Choose Filter|Blur|Gaussian Blur, 30 to apply a significant blur to the image. Change the mode to CMYK (Image|Mode|CMYK). Save the file as DAVIDBLUR.PSD. If necessary, close Photoshop. Figure 11.25 shows the blurred image.

2. In Illustrator, first create a new layer and drag it to the bottom of the layer stack. Leave it as the active layer and choose File|Place. Select the DAVIDBLUR.PSD image that you just saved (yes, it's also in the folder on the CD-ROM, just in case you're feeling lazy). Drag the image into position behind the line art layer.

Figure 11.25
A 30-pixel blur applied to the entire image makes it into a suitable background.

3. It looks good—except for the glaringly white teeth! You need to do something about that. I warned you that a compound path was needed rather than white paths so that David's shirt would look right. Figure 11.26 shows an enlargement of David's teeth with all the objects inside his mouth selected. You need to do the same thing on your image (select all the pieces of his mouth). Now, choose Object|Compound Paths|Make. Like magic, the white areas of the teeth drop out, and the problem disappears (as you can see in Figure 11.27).

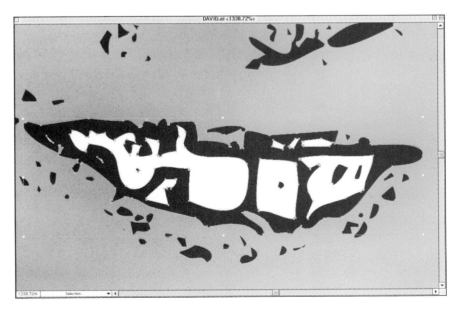

Figure 11.26
All the objects in David's mouth area are selected so that a compound path can be created.

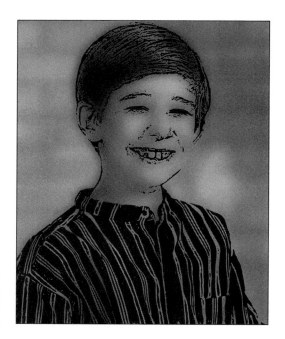

Figure 11.27
Once you have made a compound path, the white areas of David's teeth become transparent.

4. Lock all the layers in the Layers palette so that nothing in the image can be changed. Then, create a new layer (click on the New Layer icon at the bottom of the Layers palette). Drag the empty layer so that it rests just above the bottom layer of the image.

5. Create a rectangle that's the same size and in the same location as the imported background image. You can create it by eye because the exact measurements are not critical.

6. Change the fill for the rectangle to a black-to-white gradient with the black area on the right, as shown in Figure 11.28.

7. Use the Hatch Effects feature in Illustrator to change the gradient rectangle into a series of gradated objects that form a texture over the background of the image. Choose Filter|Pen and Ink|Hatch Effects. A complex dialog box, shown in Figure 11.29, appears. For now, just enter the settings I request. Choose these settings:

- Hatch Effect: Angled Lines Gradient

- Hatch: Swash

- Match Object's Color: Off

- Keep Object's Fill Color: Off

- Density: 40%

Figure 11.28
A gradient fill has been placed over the background in preparation for the next step.

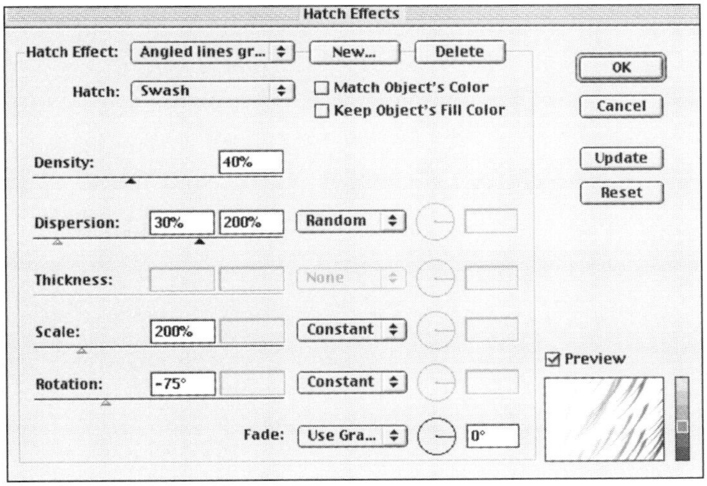

Figure 11.29
The Hatch Effects settings for the gradation that cover the background image imported from Photoshop.

- Dispersion: 30% to 200%, Random

- Thickness: N/A

- Scale: 200%, Constant

- Rotation: –75%, Constant

- Fade: Use Gradient, 0%

Figure 11.30 shows the result—just what's needed to perk up the background image, except that it also covers David's face, hair, and shirt. We'll fix this problem next.

Figure 11.30

The hatch pattern adds an interesting texture, but it's out of place on David's hair, face, and shirt.

You need to create a mask so that the hatch effects show up only in the background of the image—not inside David, where it looks odd. The mask that you need already exists in Photoshop, so let's retrieve it.

8. In Photoshop, open the original DAVID.PSD image (or, if you already have it open, you can use one of the other copies). The David Outline path is the first path in the Paths palette. Press Command/Ctrl and click on the David Outline Path palette entry to load it as a selection. This selection is the *opposite* of what we need. An Illustrator mask shows only what is inside the masked area (which is the exact opposite of how a Photoshop layer mask works). Reverse the selection (Select|Inverse, Shift+Command/Ctrl+I). In the Paths palette, choose Make Work Path from the side menu. Use a Tolerance of 1. Double-click on the path name to save it.

9. Select the Arrow tool from the Pen tool pop-out menu in the Toolbox. Position your image so that the window that contains it is larger than the image itself. With the Arrow tool, drag a marquee around the entire image to select all the points on the path. Copy the path to the clipboard (Command/Ctrl+C). Close Photoshop, if necessary.

10. In Illustrator, add a new layer (click on the New Layer icon at the bottom of the Layers palette). This layer should be directly above the Hatch Effects layer. All the layers (except the new one) should be locked. With the new layer active, paste in the path from the clipboard (Command/Ctrl+V). Press D to set the colors back to the default of black stroke and white fill. Drag the path into place so that it lines up with the background and the hatch effects.

11. Remove the lock on the Hatch Effects layer. Select the entire unlocked image (Command/Ctrl+A). Choose Object|Masks|Make (Command/ Ctrl+7). Although the hatched objects are already masked by the rectangle that originally contained the gradient, they accept the new mask. Finally, the vision of a woodcut image with texture and some color is realized, and it took both Photoshop and Illustrator to do the job. Figure 11.31 shows the finished image.

Figure 11.31
David—a stylized version of a photograph.

12. If you feel that the hatch effects are too sharp or strong, you can reduce their opacity, or you can see whether you prefer one of the Blend modes to make them react to the underlying image.

If you check the Links palette, it shows that you need DAVIDBLUR.PSD available when you print.

This example was long, but it shows a good use of features from both Photoshop and Illustrator and, because of the Hatch Effects, also shows a technique that couldn't be done in Photoshop alone. The other benefit of placing the line art layer in Illustrator rather than leaving it in Photoshop is that you have gained the ability to print the image at varying sizes, with no loss of resolution. Because of the blur in the background image DAVIDBLUR.PSD, you can scale up the image much more than would be possible with a finely detailed photographic image, and the vector objects are infinitely scalable.

About Clipping Paths

You can save Photoshop images that have clipping paths in them and place them into Illustrator. Actually, this topic had trouble finding a home for itself.

Clipping paths or masks can be used and created in so many ways that I had trouble trying to decide whether it was an Illustrator-to-Photoshop thing or a Photoshop-to-Illustrator thing. In reality, it is both or either.

You can do the following:

- Create a shape in Illustrator, pass the path to Photoshop, and create a clipping path in Photoshop.

- Create the entire clipping path and image in Photoshop and send it to Illustrator.

- Place a Photoshop image into Illustrator and create a shape in Illustrator to use as a mask.

What's the difference between a *clipping path* and an Illustrator *mask*? Only the name and the way in which it's used differ. A clipping path is a vector object you use to cut away part of a raster image. It gives a smooth, hard edge to a raster image when the EPS file that holds the clipping path is printed from a PostScript program. A masked object in Illustrator is one in which a vector shape is used to reveal only part of another vector or raster shape in the program.

You might have a number of reasons to mask out part of a raster image. Typically, you do so if you need to change the background of the image—for example, if you have a female model and want to place her against a solid background. You can also use a clipping path to trim a texture and make it conform to a shape. The most successful clipping path is one in which the image is a bit larger than the path that contains it. Because a clipping path is a PostScript vector object, it prints at the resolution of the printer. Therefore, the exact borders of the path are not set until the image goes through the rip. At that time, the outline is matched to the printing grid. The clipping path then permits any part of the raster image that falls inside of it to print. Until that moment, it isn't clear exactly which pixels near the edge of the clipping path will actually print. If the path has extra raster image area to cut off, the edge will always be smooth and crisp, with no accidental white space or background peeking through.

The other important point to remember about a clipping path is that you should have the boundary of the rectangular image as close to the borders of the clipping path as possible. When the file is imaged by the rip, the rip must draw the entire raster image in memory before it decides what to clip off. Therefore, to have a small clipping path on a large image is a waste of valuable and expensive rip time.

In the "Out, Around, and About" section later in this chapter, you'll have a chance to work on a greeting card that contains clipping paths and masks.

That Touchable Texture

You can use Photoshop to create bitmap textures that add interest to an Illustrator image. In this section and in Project 11.4, you'll play with the combination of Photoshop and Illustrator. You'll also see how Illustrator can make good use of raster images in combination with vector graphics.

PROJECT 11.4 Rhino Texture

In this project, you develop a texture from a photograph that I took of a rhinoceros in the zoo and use this texture to enhance the image in Illustrator. You then use the new Blend mode features to make the white drop out of the images.

Developing the Texture

In the first part of this project, you'll create a texture based on a photograph and apply it to a vector image in Illustrator.

1. In Illustrator, create a new document.

2. Choose File|Place and then select the image RHINOTEMP.PSD. In the dialog box, select the Template checkbox, as shown in Figure 11.32. Make sure that the Link checkbox is *not* selected. The next dialog box, shown in Figure 11.33, enables you to place an image as separate objects or as a flattened, single object. Because the RHINOTEMP.PSD image is only a single-layer image anyway, you have only one option. Figure 11.34 shows the Layers palette with the placed image as a write-protected template.

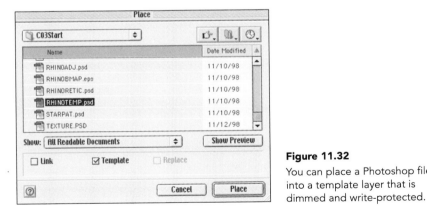

Figure 11.32
You can place a Photoshop file into a template layer that is dimmed and write-protected.

Figure 11.33
You can place a Photoshop image as an individual object or as a single, flattened object.

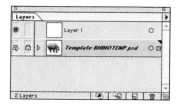

Figure 11.34
The Layers palette shows the write-protected template layer.

3. Using the Paintbrush tool and the 6-point flat Calligraphic brush (the first one in the default Brushes palette), stroke over the most significant lines in the image in a manner similar to the one shown in Figure 11.35. Figure 11.36 shows just the lines (without the template).

Figure 11.35
You can create a sketch of the rhino by stroking the most significant lines based on the template.

Figure 11.36
When you remove the template, the strokes should be able to stand up on their own.

4. In Photoshop, open RHINO.PSD. This file contains the original image, and I added a path so that you can easily create a rhino shape. In the Paths palette, click on the Rhino Outline path. Choose the Arrow tool from the Pen tool flyaway in the Toolbox. Drag a marquee with the Arrow tool around the entire path to select it and copy it to the clipboard (Command/Ctrl+C).

5. In Illustrator, paste in the path from the clipboard (Command/Ctrl+V). Create a new layer and transfer the selected path to the new layer. Drag the layer in the Layers palette into position above the template layer. Drag the path on top of the rhino so that it falls into place.

6. With the Eyedropper tool, pick up a rhino color from the template layer. Use this color as the fill for the rhino path. The stroke should be set to None.

7. Now that the path is colored, offset it a bit from the calligraphic strokes in a manner similar to Figure 11.37.

Figure 11.37
The stroked and colored rhino.

8. Save the image as RHINO.AI. You now need to develop a texture for the rhino in Photoshop.

9. Back in Photoshop, open the RHINO.PSD image (if it isn't already open).

You can develop a texture in many ways. The result needs to be a bitmap (black and white) EPS file, with transparent whites. To get to that point, you could convert your image to grayscale and then into a bitmap by using the 50% Threshold, Diffusion Dither, Pattern Dither, or Halftone conversions built into the grayscale-to-bitmap conversion process. Based on your original image, you might (or you might not) like what happens. The trick is to exert some control over the resulting bitmap. You can do so by controlling the values in your image and by controlling the way in which the bitmap pattern is created. As a first try, use the Reticulation filter to create an interesting pattern that lends itself to being bitmapped.

10. Choose Image|Duplicate and click on OK to make another copy of the edited RHINO.PSD image. Drag the Background layer to the Layers palette trashcan. This action leaves only the rhino itself. Select the nontransparent layer pixels (Command/Ctrl+click on the layer name in

Gamma Vs. Output Correction

You could correct the rhino by moving the gamma input slider to the area on the left where you notice a huge increase in the number of dark levels in the Histogram. Although moving the slider this way would create a more pleasing image with better contrast, the somewhat flat-toned image that you created in Step 12 by removing all dark values works better for this technique. Changing the gamma slider would still leave true black in the image—which would "plug up" the texture that you are about to create.

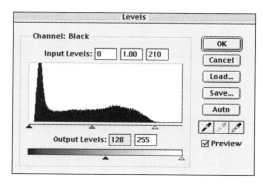

Figure 11.38
The Levels command is used to remove all the dark values from the image.

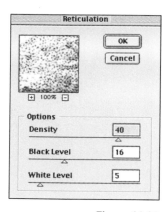

Figure 11.39
The Reticulation filter brings out image detail as texture.

Figure 11.40
The rhino has been filtered with the Reticulation filter.

the Layers palette). Select Layer|Flatten. The rhino stays selected but gains a white background.

11. Choose Image|Mode|Grayscale and then click on OK to discard color. The rhino is still selected.

12. Open the Levels dialog box (Command/Ctrl+L). Drag the White Input slider to the left until it reaches the start of the data in the image. Drag the Black Output slider to the right until it reads 128, as shown in Figure 11.38. Dragging the sliders cuts out half the values in the image and significantly lightens it, which makes a small but critical difference to the filter that you'll apply next.

13. Choose Filter|Sketch|Reticulation and use the settings shown in Figure 11.39. Use a Density of 40, a Black Level of 16, and a White Level of 5. Figure 11.40 shows the filtered rhino.

14. Invoke the Levels command again, but this time press Option+Command+L/Alt+Ctrl+L to reuse the last settings (the ones that you used in Step 12). Click on OK.

15. Choose Image|Mode|Bitmap and use the Diffusion Dither, as shown in Figure 11.41. Figure 11.42 shows the result. Because you used the Levels command to remove the dark values, the result is fairly light and unobtrusive.

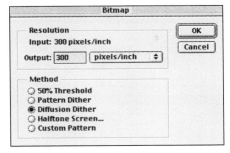

Figure 11.41

You can convert an image to Bitmap mode in a variety of ways. Here, we use the Diffusion Dither.

Try the Sketch Filters

The Sketch filters were part of the original Adobe Gallery Effects series of filters. These filters generally create two-color versions of the image that look similar to sketches. They range from mezzotint-type effects to posterization effects. Try them all when you have the time to experiment.

Figure 11.42

The rhino is now in bitmap form.

16. Save the image as RHINOBMAP.PSD.

17. In Illustrator, open the RHINO.AI image if it's closed. Create a new layer (click on the New Layer icon at the bottom of the Layers palette). Lock the original layers.

18. Choose File|Place and select the RHINOBMAP.PSD file. You need to embed the EPS image, or the image preview is truly rotten. The file is placed on the top layer. You'll see more of the pixels in the image if you zoom in to about 400 percent.

19. Drag the layer to the middle of the layer stack (between the fill and the outlines).

20. Drag Layer 3 into position. Figure 11.43 shows the finished image.

You can force a bit more contrast into the final bitmap by using the Threshold command to separately process the darkest areas of the image. RHINOADJ.PSD

New in Illustrator 9

In previous versions of Illustrator, you would have had to save this bitmapped image as an EPS file with transparent whites. That step is no longer necessary. Saving the image in Photoshop format does just as well. When the image is a bitmap, the whites automatically drop out. If you were to change the image back to grayscale in Photoshop before saving it as a PSD file, the whites would not drop out. However, you could then change the Blend mode to Multiply and get the identical effect.

Figure 11.43
The Diffusion-Dithered PSD image adds an interesting texture to the rhino.

shows how I achieved this effect. I copied the reticulation-filtered image to a new file and duplicated the starting image (the top layer in the RHINOADJ.PSD image, and it has the Eye turned off). I used the Threshold command on this layer to make a solid area of black. I then touched up the black area to make it even more solid and painted on the layer in white to separate the black areas so that I could easily select them with the Magic Wand. I used the resulting image to build a selection mask.

I duplicated the Background layer again and, with the selection still active, created a Threshold Adjustment layer with a Threshold of 69. This procedure confined the Threshold operation to only the area that had been selected. I then used black with a soft Paintbrush to create a blend area between the area that was thresholded and the area that was not. At that point, I saved RHINOADJ.PSD. Finally, I duplicated the image as merged layers to a new file and converted it to a bitmap. Figure 11.44 shows this version (which has more detail but required more effort).

Figure 11.44
A more detailed texture can be created with a bit more work.

Seeing Stars

Before we leave this topic, let's see what happens to the bitmap if it's created by using a custom pattern.

1. In Photoshop, if you cannot use the History palette to get back to the last Levels command from Step 15 of the last project, open the image RHINORETIC.PSD. It is my image from that step.

2. Open the image STARPAT.PSD. Select the entire image (Command/Ctrl+A). Define it as a pattern (Edit|Define Pattern).

3. Make the RHINORETIC.PSD image active. Choose Image|Mode|Bitmap and use the Custom Pattern option at 300 ppi. Save the image as RHINOSTAR.PSD.

4. Hide Layer 3 in the RHINO.AI image. Create a new layer and place the PSD file as an embedded file.

Repeat Steps 19 and 20 from the preceding Project 11.4 exercise. Figure 11.45 shows the result.

Do You Want a Larger and Less Dense Texture?

If you look at the bitmapped image and decide you would prefer a texture that has larger dots that are not as closely packed, you can create that effect in two ways. The first method is to create the bitmap at 72 ppi and the same physical size in inches. The second method is to reduce the image before it is bitmapped to about 33 percent of its size, change it to a bitmap, and enlarge it by 300 percent (keep track of the number of pixels so that the file goes back to its original size). Either way, you get a texture that is much more coarse.

Figure 11.45
Starry, starry rhino is complete.

Rasterizing

You don't always need Photoshop to change vector images into raster images. Using Illustrator, you can rasterize images within Illustrator and then use them as embedded objects. This approach cuts out a step if you only want to create some objects, manipulate them as pixels, and then leave them in Illustrator.

Filtered Pixels

The main reason that you might want to rasterize areas of an Illustrator image is so that you can apply Photoshop filters to them. You can apply filters to RGB raster objects and sometimes to CMYK or grayscale raster objects. You

Not Cutting It Off

What do you do when you need to apply a filter, such as a Gaussian Blur, and you really do not or cannot use Photoshop? If you add an unstroked, unfilled rectangle around the object that you want to blur and select it as well as the object when you choose the Rasterize command, the rectangle (rather than the smaller object) will define the raster object's bounding box. Using this technique is an easy way to give yourself room for a filter when you rasterize.

might also rasterize an object when you want to use the Create Object Mosaic or the Photo Crosshatch filters, which work only on raster objects.

Be aware, however, that Photoshop still gives you more control because you can fade filter effects and change their Apply modes. Also, because you cannot enlarge the size of the bounding box that surrounds the raster object, any filter that visually seems to increase the number of pixels in the image (such as the Gaussian Blur filter) might look as if it is cutting off part of the filter effect. Therefore, use the Rasterize command for a fast filter, but depend on Photoshop for the rest.

Rasterize for the Nice RIP

The "nice rip" has a nasty habit of both taking a long time to rasterize a complex Illustrator image and then, on occasion, ending up with a PostScript limit-check error for its efforts. A limit-check error occurs when too many points exist on an object for the rip to handle. Too many points occur when a clipping path or mask contains an overabundance of points or when the object has simply become too complex. Although you can take steps in Illustrator to help avoid the problem (by increasing Flatness settings, breaking up long paths, or keeping compound paths to the minimum), you also can rasterize the problem. After it is changed to a raster image, the rip no longer needs to do anything other than write it out—all the processing is already done.

I once had a service bureau tell me that it was taking a long time to rip my files because I had used gradient. I pointed out to them that the gradient happened to be located in a Photoshop file, but they couldn't see why that mattered (I used their services only once). Believe me, it matters! A gradient in a Photoshop file has no need to be rasterized—it already is. It cannot possibly choke the rip. If you find that an *Illustrator* gradient is too complex, rasterize it. If you find that the gradient is banding, rasterize it and place it in Photoshop, where you can add a small but different amount of noise to three of the four channels. The banding will disappear.

Out, Around, and About

Many images spend a lot of time in transit between Photoshop and Illustrator. They start out in one, visit the other, and end up back where they started (or go through the cycle again). All my images end their journey in a page-layout program (usually QuarkXPress—although I'm not endorsing it over PageMaker or InDesign). I don't need to place an image into a page-layout program if it's a single page. However, I know that most service bureaus are more comfortable producing output from a Quark file, so I send them one. Process-color output is too expensive for me to experiment with (I would rather spend my extra income on clothes, books, software, yarn, and Broadway shows). Therefore, even though you don't have to use a page-layout program, you'll probably do so anyway.

Before we discuss compositing in page-layout programs, let's look at a project that uses opacity masks and Photoshop raster images.

Paths and Masks

As we discussed previously, the shapes for clipping paths or masks can easily be created in either Illustrator or Photoshop. They can then be placed where they will do the most good. A fine line exists between a clipping path and an opacity mask—especially if the opacity mask is solid. However, the newfound capability of Illustrator 9 to use raster or vector objects as opacity masks opens up a new way of working with the program. In this project, you'll try out a variety of different methods as you create a holiday greeting card. I like the technique so well that, for the moment, I'm going to dodge the issue of "Will it print?" Let's just look at it on screen!

 Season's Greetings

This project shows a number of ways to work on a single project in both Photoshop and Illustrator. Because it is fairly long and complex, I've divided it into pieces.

Building the Tree

In this section of the project, you'll construct the two main "text trees."

1. In Illustrator, open the image XMASTEXT.AI. Figure 11.46 shows the two small snippets of text that the file contains.

2. Using the Selection tool, select the Merry Christmas object. This text was turned into outlines. The original font is ErikRightHand (from the very talented type designers at FontFont). The object also contains a diamond from the Zapf Dingbats font. Copy the selection to the clipboard (Command/Ctrl+C).

3. Create a new document (Command/Ctrl+N). Make sure that the new document is in RGB mode for now. Paste in the selection from the clipboard (Command/Ctrl+V).

4. Drag the selection to the Brushes palette. The dialog box shown in Figure 11.47 appears. Click on Pattern Brush.

Figure 11.46

"Merry Christmas" and "To You" will be used in the Season's Greetings project to construct a greeting card.

Making a Pattern Brush from Text

When you create a Pattern brush from text, you no longer need to create outlines from the text before you can create the pattern. However, because I can't give you the font, I made outlines for this example.

Figure 11.47

In the New Brush dialog box, you can specify the type of brush that you want to create.

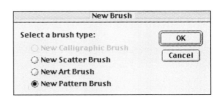

5. After you decide to create a new Pattern brush, the dialog box asks for more details. Name the brush and give it a 20% Scale with 5% Spacing. Let it approximate the path. You don't need to flip it or colorize it in any way.

6. Delete the text that you used to create the Pattern brush. Because the text is saved as a brush, you won't need it again.

7. Select the Paintbrush tool and draw a curvy path that goes back and forth to create a stylized version of a Christmas tree, as shown in Figure 11.48 (this image was altered to show you the path). As soon as you draw your path, it should look like Figure 11.49 (unless you have accidentally set a fill). If your fill is not set to None, change it now.

Figure 11.48
(Left) Draw this path with the Paintbrush tool.

Figure 11.49
(Right) Your brush pattern should look like this.

8. To change the shape of the path, you can use the Direct Selection tool to edit it as you would any other Illustrator path. Press Shift and click on a point along the path to let the tool know where to begin. If you want to make changes in the scale of the pattern or in its spacing, double-click on the Brush entry in the Brushes palette. If you cannot produce the shape that you want and get frustrated (although it isn't difficult to draw or edit the path), you can open my ready-made TREEPATH.AI image, select the path, and choose the Christmas Tree brush with the Paintbrush tool.

9. Select the tree-text-on-a-path object. Copy it to the clipboard (Command/Ctrl+C). Lock the layer.

10. Create a new layer. Drag the new layer to the bottom of the layer stack.

11. Place the image TEXTURE.PSD (File|Place). This image is a mixed Noise and Pixellate texture in a basic Christmas green. Although you could have done most of the filtering on this image in Illustrator, I've already prepared it for you as a Photoshop image.

12. Use the Selection tool to resize the raster image so that it is as large as the text-pattern-on-a-path.

13. From the side drop-down menu in the Transparency palette, choose Make Opacity Mask. Click on the thumbnail of the opacity mask to select it.

14. Paste in the selection from the clipboard (Command/Ctrl+V). Select the Invert Mask checkbox. Click on the object thumbnail to select it. Figure 11.50 shows a close-up of the tree path masking the texture image.

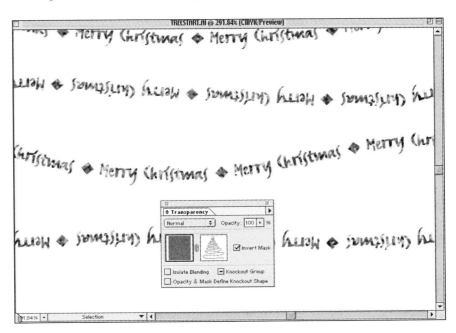

Figure 11.50
The Pattern brush is used to mask the raster texture placed in Illustrator.

15. If you had prepared the tree in Photoshop, you could have easily used a Hue/Saturation Adjustment layer to tint the TEXTURE.PSD image red (see the following tip for the method). However, I prefer that you try it a different way. With the first masked tree layer selected, choose Duplicate Layer from the side drop-down menu in the Layers palette.

16. Lock the original tree layer.

17. Choose Release Opacity Mask from the side drop-down menu of the Transparency palette. Now, the texture object and the text that had been used as the mask are both on the layer.

How to Tint TEXTURE.PSD in Photoshop

You tint the texture red by opening the TEXTURE.PSD image in Photoshop and creating a new Hue/Saturation Adjustment Layer (Command/Ctrl+click on New Layer icon). Drag the Hue slider to –121, which turns the texture into a nice Christmas red (at least it does on my monitor—fiddle with the suggested setting if your monitor doesn't match mine). Merge Down (Command/Ctrl+E).

18. Twirl down the arrow on the layer in the Layers palette until you can see each object on that layer. Use the radio button to select the text pattern object and cut it (Command/Ctrl+X).

19. Use the Rectangle tool to create a rectangle the same size as the TEXTURE.PSD object. Color it red. Make sure that it is on the same layer and above the raster object. Change the Blend mode of the rectangle to Color. Select both the rectangle and the vector object and group them (Command/Ctrl+G).

20. Now, you should see the grouped object in the Transparency palette. Mask the group with the cut text Pattern brush object as you did in Steps 13 and 14.

21. Move the red masked image so that it is to the right and down and fits inside the empty spaces in the green image. (This approach shows you another method of working with the paths.) Figure 11.51 shows both portions of the tree.

Figure 11.51
The red and green layers are offset from one another and, in color, look quite festive.

The Trunk

It's time to make sure that the tree can stand up. You'll create the trunk next.

1. Make a new layer (click on the New Layer icon at the bottom of the Layers palette). Open the file XMASTEXT.AI if it isn't already open. From the file, copy the words "TO YOU" and paste them into your working image of the tree. This text extract uses Copal Solid from the Adobe Type Library. Copal has the advantage of being an extremely heavy typeface, which makes it useful when you want to place a design inside the letters.

2. Paste "TO YOU" in position under the tree so that it looks like a short tree trunk. With the object selected, press Option/Alt and then drag a copy below the first one. Press Shift after you begin to drag-copy the image so that it constrains the direction of the copy. Make another two copies (which gives you four copies of "TO YOU"). Select all four copies and click on Vertical Distribute Top in the Align palette. Group the selection (Command/Ctrl+G). Figure 11.52 shows the image with the tree trunk in place.

> ### Color Modes and the Image
>
> When you first created the new file for this image, you selected an RGB color space. The Cross-hatch filter doesn't work in CMYK color. When the image is finished, you can convert the image to CMYK color space if you want. To do so, choose File|Document Color Space|CMYK. However, you need to flatten the appearance of the Live Effects layer before you convert modes.

Figure 11.52

Multiple copies of the words "TO YOU" form the trunk of the tree.

3. Choose Object|Rasterize. In the dialog box that appears, select a high-resolution image (unless you are running short on RAM), anti-alias and make a mask, and make an RGB object. Figure 11.53 shows these settings selected in the dialog box.

4. Choose Effects|Pixelate|Pointillize with a size of 30. Then, choose Effects|Brush Strokes|Crosshatch with Stroke Length: 50, Sharpness: 10, and Strength: 3. The large Pointillize values give the Crosshatch filter a good start. Figure 11.54 shows the Crosshatch dialog box, and Figure 11.55 shows a close-up of the filtered raster object. Because you created a mask when you rasterized, only the text shows the effects of the filter.

Figure 11.53

Using this dialog box, you can change a vector object into a raster object.

The Angel

Every Christmas tree needs an angel. This time, you'll build an object to rasterize that you can mask with a piece of clip art (the angel from Ultimate Symbol's Design Elements collection).

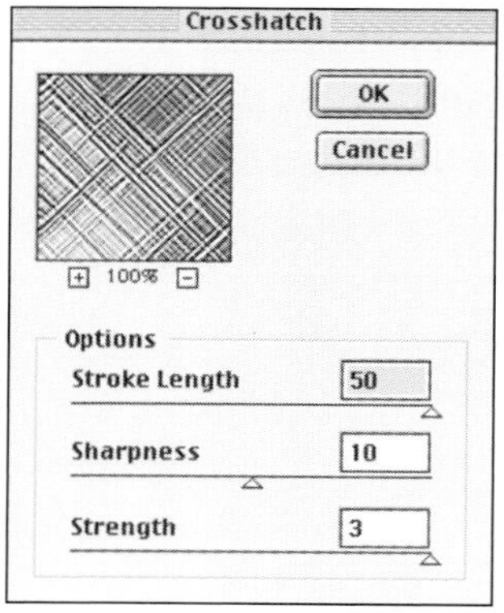

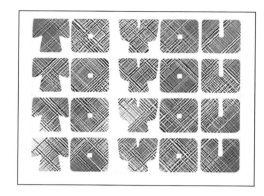

Figure 11.54
(Left) The Crosshatch filter
dialog box.

Figure 11.55
(Right) A close-up of the tree
trunk after the Crosshatch filter
has been applied.

Placing Illustrator Files

I ask you to place the Cupid
file instead of opening, copying, and pasting because if you
placed and linked the file, you
couldn't use it as a mask. If you
embedded it in the image, it
contains an invisible mask
around it that needs to be
released, located, and deleted
to be able to use the angel as
a mask.

1. Select the Rectangle tool. Click near the top-left corner of the image to
    create a rectangle 1.5 inches wide by 1.2 inches high. Choose
    Window|Swatch Libraries|Other, and select the GOLDGRAD.AI image
    from the start folder for this chapter on the CD-ROM. The gold metallic
    gradient is now available. Drag the swatch into the rectangle that you
    created. Also, drag it into the Swatches palette for this image.

2. Chose Object|Rasterize. Make it a high-resolution RGB object. Anti-alias,
    but *do not create a mask*. Click on OK. Choose Filter|Distort|Ocean Ripple,
    with a Ripple Size of 5 and a Ripple Magnitude of 20. Figure 11.56 shows
    a close-up of the result of this filter. (You could also use the Effect version
    if you prefer.)

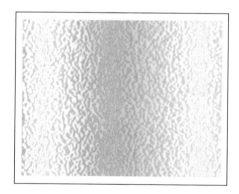

Figure 11.56
The Ocean Ripple filter is applied
to a rectangle with a gold
metallic gradient.

3. Open the image ANGEL.AI. Copy it to the clipboard (Command/Ctrl+C).
    Return to your working tree image. Paste in the selection from the clip-
    board (Command/Ctrl+V). You could also drag and drop the angel into
    the working image. Drag the angel on top of the filtered rectangle and
    scale the angel proportionally until it fits. (Yes, it's a cupid angel, but
    that's okay.) Position the angel inside the rectangle until you like the
    place in the gradient that it covers (it's easier to see, although harder to

move, if you remove the fill). When you're satisfied, select both the angel and the rectangle and create a mask (Object|Masks|Make, Command/Ctrl+7). Figure 11.57 shows a close-up of the angel.

4. Drag the angel into position on the top of the tree. Figure 11.58 shows the result.

Figure 11.57
The angel creates a mask so that the ocean ripples texture you created now takes the form of Cupid.

Figure 11.58
The angel now sits atop the tree.

Ornamentation

Let's try one more task—create an ornament shape using a filter that's not available in Illustrator. You'll then make a path from the ornament and copy it into Illustrator to use it as a mask for an Illustrator gradient.

1. Save your work in Illustrator. Close the program if you need to and open Photoshop. In Photoshop, create a new document (Command/Ctrl+N). Make the document 491×550 pixels, 300 ppi, Grayscale.

2. Select the Elliptical Marquee tool. Press Return/Enter to bring up the Options palette. Select Anti-Aliased with a Feather of 0. Choose Fixed Size for the Style and enter a size of 450×450 pixels. Click near the center of the image to place the circle. Press D to set the colors back to the default of black and white. Fill the area (Option/Alt+Delete/Backspace) and then deselect (Command/Ctrl+D).

Figure 11.59
The Polar Coordinates filter creates an unusual shape when used multiple times on an object.

3. Choose Filter|Distort|Polar Coordinates, Rectangular to Polar. Repeat this filter (Option/Alt+Command/Ctrl+F) seven more times. Figure 11.59 shows the unusual shape that appears.

4. Select the Move tool (V) and drag the shape up toward the top of the image. This step automatically changes the Background layer into Layer 0. Choose Layer|Flatten Image to get it back to the Background layer.

5. Apply a Gaussian Blur of 2.0 to the image (Filter|Blur|Gaussian Blur, 2.0). Open the Levels dialog box (Command/Ctrl+L). Drag the Black Input slider to the right until all three sliders touch. The Black Input level will be 230. Click on OK. The object is now much smoother and a bit thicker.

6. Load the values of the layer (Command/Ctrl+Option/Alt+~). Reverse the selection (Select|Inverse, Shift+ Command/ Ctrl+I). Now, the black areas are selected.

7. From the Paths palette side menu, choose Make Work Path. Give it a Tolerance of 2 (you don't need to make it hug this shape exactly). Double-click on the Work Path entry in the Paths palette to save the path as Path 1.

8. Use the Arrow tool from the Pen palette pop-out menu to select the entire path. Copy it to the clipboard (Command/Ctrl+C). Save your shape and close Photoshop.

9. Back in Illustrator, open the tree image if it isn't still open.

10. Make a new layer (click on the New Layer icon at the bottom of the Layers palette). Drag the layer to the bottom of the Layers palette. Select the Rectangle tool. Click in an unused spot in the image to create a rectangle .79 inches wide by .74 inches wide. Click on the Rainbow gradient in the Swatches palette to use this as the fill.

11. In the Gradient palette, change the Angle to 90°.

12. Make a new layer (click on the New Layer icon at the bottom of the Layers palette). Paste in the selection from the clipboard (Command/Ctrl+V). Change its Fill to black so that you can clearly see it. Drag it on top of the rainbow gradient. Use the bounding box control handles on the ornament shape to scale it so that it fits inside the rainbow gradient rectangle. Double-check to ensure that the ornament is *on top* of the gradient.

13. Select both the rainbow gradient and the ornament and make a mask (Object|Masks|Make, Command/Ctrl+7). Select both objects and group them (Command/Ctrl+G). Figure 11.60 shows the completed ornament (which is an all-vector shape).

Figure 11.60
The masked ornament is composed totally of vector shapes.

14. Lock the layers that contain the two trees, the tree trunk, and the angel. Drag the ornament over to the tree and "hang" it. Because it's on a bottom layer, it should appear behind the other layers so that you can see it through the tree. Use Option/Alt to duplicate the ornament as you drag it. Place about five ornaments. Figure 11.61 shows the finished greeting card.

Figure 11.61
The greeting card design is now complete.

This project was somewhat long, but you've learned how to use a variety of clipping path types:

• An Illustrator path is used as an opacity mask.

• A vector object in Illustrator is rasterized so that its outlines become its mask. The filter is visible only in the unmasked areas.

• A vector object is rasterized and filtered and then masked with a piece of vector clip art.

• Photoshop is used to create a path, and the path (when pasted into Illustrator) becomes the mask for another vector shape.

You should now be able to mix and match techniques to get the best use of the clipping path strengths of each program.

Page Layout Composites

One reasonable question that you might have at this point is, "Where do I do my image compositing?" Is it better to place Photoshop TIF or EPS files into a page-layout program or to place raster images into Illustrator, or do you get the best results by using the programs individually and then layering the resulting images in QuarkXPress or PageMaker?

I spoke to the folks at Adobe tech support, and their "official" response was that it should make no difference. This response, of course, is somewhat simplistic. It probably doesn't make enough of a difference that you need to avoid placing Photoshop images into Illustrator. However, you should use common sense if "official" wisdom is lacking. If all I need from Illustrator is to add some text to a Photoshop image, I'll create the text in Illustrator and place it over the Photoshop image in QuarkXPress. I see no reason to burden my Illustrator file with a large raster object (or even a linked raster object).

However, the "gotcha" for the text-over-a-photo example is trapping. If my text is black, I can select the Overprint checkbox in Illustrator, and (assuming that I don't exceed my ink limit) all is well. However, when you place an EPS file into a page-layout program, it cannot be trapped by the application. The PostScript commands in it are "encapsulated" (which is what EPS means), and nothing else can touch the instructions that the file carries. QuarkXPress will report the EPS file as "knocking out" its background, and you cannot change this result. In brief, any trapping you need must be done in Illustrator or by your service bureau by using a high-end trapping application (if you are lucky enough to deal with a service bureau that can afford this kind of equipment).

Check the Appendix in this book for a brief discussion of Illustrator and trapping, written by my technical reviewer—and dear friend—David Xenakis, one of the most knowledgeable folks on this earth about all things prepress.

You should have no problems placing an EPS or TIF file into an Illustrator document and printing it from QuarkXPress. You also should have no problems if you place an Illustrator file with an embedded raster object into QuarkXPress. However, if you saved the raster image as a DCS file (DCS 1.0 or 2.0), beware. You won't see an accurate rendering of the image if you print from a composite printer (such as an Epson 3000 or 5000—or almost any other composite printer), and if you try to rip the image, you are likely to get no film. This isn't an Illustrator problem, however. It's a problem with the other components of the prepress mix. David Xenakis adds that a catch exists that you might not know. If RIP software is older—Level 2 or lower—there may be problems with files with embedded bitmaps. Level 3 RIPs handle them with ease—as they do the truly large number of points on a path.

As long as you confine yourself to EPS or TIF files, you can let convenience and comfort be your guide as to where you want to do your image compositing.

Moving On

You should now be an expert in moving images into and out of Photoshop and Illustrator. In this chapter, you learned how to adjust the resolution of placed raster images, create a woodcut image in Illustrator from a black-and-white Photoshop image, use Photoshop to create a texture bitmap to use on top of an Illustrator image, and use clipping paths to move any which way.

In Chapter 12, you'll learn about the new features that Illustrator has added for Web support.

Chapter 12

Web Graphics

By Eric Floch and
Karen Tanner

With the staggering growth of the Web over the past few years, graphics tools like Illustrator that have always been oriented toward a traditional print workflow have had to adapt to new challenges.

In Illustrator 9, users have a number of new and powerful Web tools at their disposal. In this chapter, you learn about Save For Web and its cohort, Pixel Preview mode; learn how to quickly create eye-catching Web buttons with Styles; see how to easily generate imagemaps using the Attributes palette; and use Release To Layers and Export To Flash (SWF) to create a typewriter animation. At the end of the chapter, you'll assemble all these projects together into a Web site mockup so that you can see how they might be utilized in the real world.

The Save For Web Feature

Save For Web is a brand new feature in Illustrator 9 (see Figure 12.1), but one that should be familiar to users of Photoshop 5.5 or ImageReady 2. Whereas the standard Save As dialog box lets you save your illustrations in native AI, EPS, and PDF formats, and the Export dialog box allows you to save files in more esoteric formats, the Save For Web dialog box is, as its name implies, all about the Web. It allows you to preview, optimize, and save your illustrations to four of the most common raster image formats associated with the Web: GIF, JPEG, PNG-8, and PNG-24.

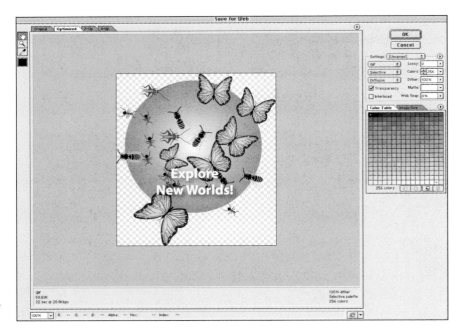

Figure 12.1
You can do a lot with the Save For Web dialog box.

The key point here is the preview and optimize part. Using the Save For Web dialog box, you can see exactly what your optimized file will look like and how big it will be *before* you actually save the file. Gone are the days when you had to fiddle with different settings and save out multiple versions of a single file to achieve the desired result. With Save For Web, you can see the effects of various settings previewed in realtime so that you can be sure you're getting exactly the file you want.

Web Formats

First, let's cover the four *Save For Web* formats. Here, you get a quick overview of each and then learn how to choose which format is best for you in any given situation.

GIF

GIF files use only 8-bit color and *lossless* compression (no data is discarded when you save the file). However, because these files support only 8-bit color, saving 24-bit images as GIFs means a significant loss in image quality. You can also create what is called a *lossy GIF*. This type of file is appreciably smaller but has artifacts similar to a JPEG file. GIF supports *background transparency* (placing a file so that the object's background doesn't shop up in the browser) and *matting* (changing the partially transparent pixels in an image to a specific opaque color).

JPEG

JPEG, which supports 24-bit color, is a lossy format; its compression schemes discard data. Depending on the Quality setting you specify, you might see patterns or blocky areas of banding in your JPEG. A higher Quality setting means fewer of these artifacts, but also bigger file size. You can create a progressive JPEG, in which a low-resolution version of the final image appears in your browser while the full image is downloading. JPEG does *not* support background transparency. All transparent pixels in your artwork are converted to the selected matte color when you write JPEG-format file from the Save For Web dialog box.

PNG-8

Similar in most respects to GIF, PNG-8 is another 8-bit lossless format. The difference between the two lies in the compression scheme used. PNG-8 files can be a fair bit (10 to 30 percent) smaller than GIF files.

PNG-24

Another 24-bit format, PNG-24 uses the same lossless compression method used by PNG-8. Thus, PNG-24 files are usually larger than their JPEG counterparts are. PNG-24 supports background transparency and matting, just like GIF and PNG-8, but it goes those formats one step better. It supports 8-bit transparency (256 levels) rather than simple 1-bit transparency (on or off).

Which Should You Choose?

The format you should use (there are four to choose from) varies from situation to situation. One factor to consider is that, right now, GIF and JPEG are by far the two most common image formats used on the Web. Many browsers do not yet support PNG-8 or PNG-24. Therefore, you should use only GIF or JPEG if you want your images to be accessible to the greatest number of eyes.

However, the main factor to consider is file size. When it comes to the Web, smaller is better. Every Web surfer out there has suffered through that interminable wait while too-large graphics download like molasses through the modem. Many times, that wait is enough to push people away from a site. The smaller you can make your images, the faster they will download and the more viewers you will retain.

Now, consider these general guidelines:

- GIF files compress solid areas of color while still preserving hard edges well. You should use GIF for logos, line art, and illustrations with type.

- JPEG, on the other hand, is much more effective for 24-bit images, whether they are photographs or other continuous-tone images (for example, images containing gradients or gradient meshes). In photographs, the artifacts common to JPEG files are less noticeable.

- PNG-8 files are slightly smaller than equivalent GIF files (10 to 30 percent). This difference is reason alone to consider using the format. Again, though, it *is* a newer format, and some older browsers might not support it.

If your main concern is transparency, you might want to look at PNG-24. Because this format supports 256 levels of transparency, it can handle a feathered drop shadow on a transparent background, for example (see Figure 12.2). The disadvantages are bigger file size and the fact that many older browsers out there might not be able to read PNG-24 files.

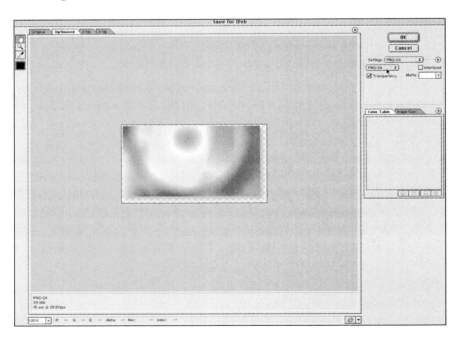

Figure 12.2
PNG-24 can handle a drop shadow that fades to transparency.

Pixel Preview

Save For Web is intended for use with another of the new features of Illustrator 9: Pixel Preview. Pixel Preview is a viewing mode just like Preview or Artwork (see Figures 12.3 and 12.4). Simply put, it allows you to see your artwork as pixels, the same 72 pixels per inch that are generated when you save for the Web (or even Export to some raster formats). In other words, in Pixel Preview mode, your artwork looks just as it would in a Web browser.

Figure 12.3
A butterfly in Preview mode at 800 percent magnification might look like this.

Figure 12.4
The same butterfly at 800 percent in Pixel Preview mode looks very different.

The main advantage to using this feature is that you can preview the anti-aliased edges of different objects and make sure that they are properly aligned (or not aligned if you so desire) to the pixel grid.

You must follow three basic rules when using Pixel Preview:

1. Always turn on Pixel Preview *before* you create your artwork.

2. Always turn on Pixel Preview *before* you create your artwork.

3. Always turn on Pixel Preview *before* you create your artwork.

If you turn on Pixel Preview *after* creating your artwork, all bets are off. Nothing is aligned to the pixel grid, and all the edges of your objects are anti-aliased randomly (see Figure 12.5).

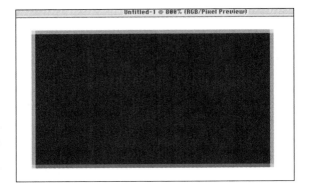

Figure 12.5

Turn on Pixel Preview after creating your art and you could be sorry. Look closely at the anti-aliasing on the edges of the rectangle.

Snap To Pixel

When you turn on Pixel Preview, the option Snap To Pixel—also located in the View menu—is automatically turned on. Any object you draw snaps to the pixel grid. Its edges do not anti-alias.

If you actually want the edges of an object to anti-alias, simply turn off Snap to Pixel and draw your object. The color of an anti-aliased edge depends on how much of the object falls into that particular row or column of pixels. If an object barely spills into a row or column, the anti-aliasing is faint; if the object takes up most of a row or column, the anti-aliasing is darker.

PROJECT 12.1 Explore New Worlds

Now, you can put all this theory to work. In Pixel Preview mode, you will create an illustration to be used on a Web page mockup and then save an optimized image using Save For Web. Along the way, you'll learn about repopulating views in Save For Web, choosing predefined versus custom settings, manipulating color tables, using transparency versus background matting, resizing the image, and finally saving your settings for future use.

1. Create a new RGB document. All images used on the Web are RGB, and it pays to start the right way.

2. Go to the Color palette menu, and select Web Safe RGB. Choosing this option ensures that all the colors you specify in this file will fall within the standard 216-color Web palette.

3. Select View|Pixel Preview. As you learned previously, Snap to Pixel is automatically turned on, and any objects you draw are precisely aligned with the pixel grid.

4. Start by creating a background object. Select the Ellipse tool and click on the artboard. In the Ellipse dialog box, give it a width and height of 350 pixels.

5. Create a new gradient that will look good with your sample Web site. Choose Window|Show Gradient. In the Gradient palette menu, select Show Options to see a default grayscale gradient. Set the Type to Radial. Click at the right edge of the gradient bar at the bottom of the palette. Two gradient sliders then appear. Click on the right slider. Now, go to the Color palette menu and select Web Safe RGB. Enter these values: R=F8, G=31, B=0E. That end of the gradient should go red (see Figure 12.6). Leave the left end white. Now, drag the Gradient Fill swatch onto the circle you created in Step 4. Finally, set the stroke of the circle to None.

Note: To save the gradient for later use, drag the Gradient Fill swatch onto the Swatches palette.

Figure 12.6
The red radial gradient is the background for this illustration.

6. Now that you have a background object, draw some insects. Choose Window|Brush Libraries|Animal Sample. The Animal Sample palette appears. In the Appearance palette, click on the Clear Appearance button for a fresh start here. Click on the Bee scatter brush in the Animal Sample palette. Now, click on the Brush tool. Draw a sweeping curve over the red radial gradient, and you should see a number of bees appear scattered along the curve (see Figure 12.7). It's okay if some of the bees spill over the edges of the circle; in fact, you want that to happen.

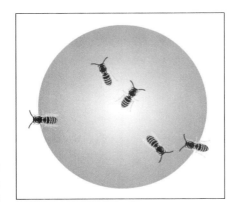

Figure 12.7
If you draw a wiggly line, the
bees scatter naturally.

7. Do the same thing with some of the other insect brushes: Butterfly 1, Grasshopper, and Red Ant. When you're finished, you should end up with an image that looks like Figure 12.8.

8. Now, it's time to add a caption. Choose Type|Character. Set your font to Myriad Bold 36 pt. Select the Type tool and click inside the circle. Type "Explore", press Return/Enter, and then type "new worlds!". Set the Fill color to white. With the text object selected, go to the Paragraph palette and click on Align Center. The last thing is to apply a drop shadow. Choose Effect|Stylize|Drop Shadow and accept the default values. At this point, you might want to save the file to AI (see Figure 12.9).

 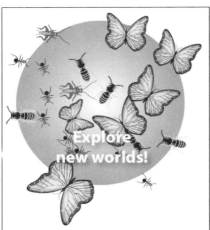

Figure 12.8
(Left) One of the advantages of
scatter brushes is their inherent
randomness.

Figure 12.9
(Right) Your final illustration
should look something like this.

9. Now, you're ready for the fun part. Choose File|Save For Web. Four tabs appear at the top of the resulting dialog box: Original, Optimized, 2-Up, and 4-Up. The Optimized tab comes up with GIF as the default format. You can change your output format by using the Format menu, but you should leave it on GIF for now.

10. Apply one of the predefined sets of optimization settings (see Figure 12.10). Using these sets is a quick way to get started optimizing your images. In the Settings menu, select GIF 128 Dithered to reduce the color palette of the image to 128 colors (from 256) with 88 percent Dither. You'll see some subtle banding in the gradient, but that's okay. The information beneath the image tells you that you've reduced the file size to 47.58K. Save For Web also tells you the approximate download time. In this case, it should take about 18 seconds to download at 28.8Kbps.

11. Now, you can start customizing. First, look at how to repopulate views. Click on the 4-Up tab. You should see four windows, each with a different version of your illustration. As you can see from its caption, the upper-left window shows the original file, with a size of 722K—very big and very slow to download. The upper-right window shows the GIF with the predefined settings you just applied. The lower two windows contain variations on that GIF. You should be able to see subtle differences between the four images. Click on the GIF in the lower right, open the Optimize menu (the circled triangle next to the Settings menu), and choose Repopulate Views. The selected image moves to the upper-right window, and Save For Web generates new images in the lower two windows using new settings. At any point in 2-Up and 4-Up view mode, you can select an optimized version of the file and repopulate views; Save For Web creates new variations on your image.

12. You can mix and match formats in 2-Up and 4-Up views (see Figure 12.11). Select the lower-right window. Then, go to the Format menu and select JPEG. Note that only *that* window changes to JPEG; the others are still GIF. Being able to examine multiple formats at once like this can be an invaluable tool.

13. Go back and select the GIF in the upper-right window. Click on the Optimized tab so that you can see the entire image. Look at the Color Table tab in the right half of the dialog box (see Figure 12.12). With GIF and PNG-8 images, you can manipulate the color table in a number of different ways (with JPEG and PNG-24, you can't). You can change the basic color table used, add or delete colors, lock them so they don't get dropped if you subsequently reduce the overall number of colors, and even shift them so that they are all Web Safe. All this functionality is aimed at reducing the overall number of colors in the file, which makes the file smaller and quicker to download. Unfortunately, all the different permutations of the color table are beyond the scope of this project. You should consult the Illustrator 9 manual to find out more. For now, you can keep it simple. Selective is the default color table selected, and it's probably a good choice here because it produces images with the greatest color integrity.

Figure 12.10
In the Settings menu, you can choose from many predefined sets.

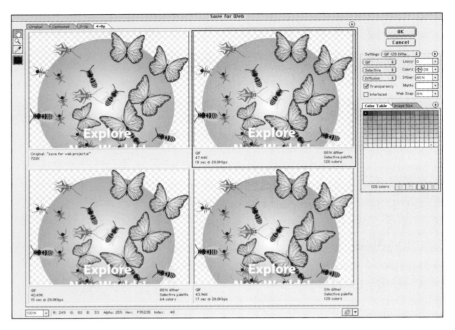

Figure 12.11

(Left) You can preview multiple formats at once in the 2-Up and 4-Up views.

Figure 12.12

(Right) The Color Table menu offers numerous options.

Figure 12.13

You've just applied a background matte to match your Web page background.

14. Let's talk about transparency versus background matting. The Transparency box is checked by default when you open the Save For Web dialog box. Uncheck it now. You should see the gray and white transparency grid surrounding the image turn to white. When Transparency is checked, all transparent pixels in the image are preserved. When Transparency is unchecked, all transparent pixels in the image are filled with the specified matte color, which for now is white. Both of these techniques allow you to place a nonrectangular graphic (like the one you're working with in this project) against a Web page background. So, when should you use transparency, and when should you use background matting? If the Web page background is a solid color that you know ahead of time, you can use background matting. If it's a pattern, background matting doesn't match, and you should most certainly use transparency. As far as the different formats go, as you learned earlier in the chapter, GIF, PNG-8, and PNG-24 all support transparency to varying degrees. With them, you can use either transparency or matting. Because JPEG does not support transparency, you always have to use background matting with this format. Right now, apply background matting to your GIF. Transparency should still be unchecked, so go directly to the Matte pull-down menu and select Other to call up the Color Picker. Check Only Web Colors and enter "123466" in the # field. Click on OK, and the background matte is applied (see Figure 12.13).

15. Much as you can with the predefined optimization settings, you can automate the creation process with Optimize to File Size. Choose this option from the Optimize menu. Set the Desired File Size to 32K and Start With to Current Settings. Save For Web repopulates views using settings that make the image 32K or less. At this point, you can simply pick the best of the lot.

16. So, what can you do if the artwork as drawn is the wrong size for your Web page? You can easily fix this problem. Click on the Image Size tab. The image is currently 407×454 pixels. You can resize the image by entering new pixel values or entering a number in the Percent field. For now, type "75" and click on Apply (see Figure 12.14). Constrain Proportions is automatically checked, so the image doesn't warp.

17. Before you finish, save your new settings. In the Optimize menu, select Save Settings. In the Save Optimization Settings dialog box, name the new settings "Children's Museum GIF" and click on OK. Go back to the Settings menu, and you should see "Children's Museum GIF" at the top of the menu. You can now apply that same group of settings whenever you like.

18. Click on OK to open the Save Optimized As dialog box. Give your file a name and save it. You're now ready to place it into a Web page.

Figure 12.14
Save For Web lets you resize your image on the fly.

You can play with a lot of different settings in the Save For Web dialog box, but we simply don't have the room to go into depth on all of them. Remember that the whole feature is for one purpose: making your files as small as they can be while still maintaining the integrity of the image. You have to walk a fine line here, and you should play around with Save For Web to develop a feel for the process. Read the manual, try things out, and soon you'll be an old hand at using this exciting technology.

Building Buttons Using Styles

Styles make it easier than ever to create a consistent look for buttons or other frequently used Web site graphics. After you build a style you like, you can save it as a new style in the Styles palette and apply it to other artwork. One of my favorite things is to create a style that I like for buttons, and then modify the style slightly and create a second or even third style based on the original. Then, I can select all my buttons and apply each style in turn, which allows me to compare them visually and pick the best one for the Web site design I am working on.

Buttoned Up in Style

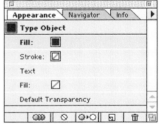

12.2 This project shows you how to create a graphic style that can be applied to type objects to create fast, consistent buttons. Pay close attention to your selection in the Appearance palette at each step, or you may get unexpected results!

1. Create a new RGB document in Illustrator.

2. Choose the Type tool and click in a new document. Type "Cool New Style". Click on the Selection tool to select the type object.

3. In the Appearance palette menu, choose Add New Fill. Note that this option adds a new black fill at the top of the list in the Appearance palette (see Figure 12.15). Click on the white swatch to change the type object fill from black to white.

Figure 12.15
The Appearance palette shows a new black fill.

4. Click on the bottom None fill listed in the Appearance palette to target it (see Figure 12.16). Click on a gradient swatch to apply it. I like to use the Steel Bar II gradient swatch.

5. Choose Effect|Convert to Shape|Rounded Rectangle (see Figure 12.17). Make sure the Relative radio button is selected. Enter "8 pt" in the Extra Width field and "3 pt" in the Extra Height field. Click on OK.

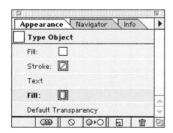

Figure 12.16
(Left) The bottom fill is targeted in the Appearance palette.

Figure 12.17
(Right) In the Shape dialog box, you can see the Rounded Rectangle options.

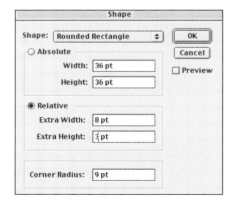

6. Choose Effect|Stylize|Drop Shadow to add a drop shadow to the gradient fill. Click on OK to accept the default settings.

7. In the Appearance palette menu, choose Add New Fill again. Note that this step adds a gradient fill to the Appearance palette right above the gradient fill you just created. Make sure this new fill is targeted in the palette (see Figure 12.18).

8. Choose Effect|Convert To Shape|Rounded Rectangle. Make sure the Relative radio button is selected. Enter "4 pt" in the Extra Width field and "1 pt" in the Extra Height field. Click on OK.

9. Running the effect on the fill deselects it in the Appearance palette, so you need to target the fill in the palette again. Click on the color swatch that you want to use as the immediate background for your type (I like to use the Gray swatch). Your type is now transformed into a button (see Figure 12.19). If you select the type object and choose Type|Size|24 pt, the type size increases, and the style is reapplied to match the new dimensions of the object.

Figure 12.18
The Appearance palette shows that the new fill is targeted.

Figure 12.19
The button is complete.

10. Now, for the exciting part—with your type object selected, click on the Styles palette menu and choose New Style. Name your style and click on OK. Now, you can apply your custom style to any object to quickly create a consistent appearance for your buttons.

Creating an Imagemap

You've probably seen at least a couple of imagemaps in your travels around the Web. An imagemap is a piece of photography or art (whether a single image, group of icons, or cluster of buttons) saved as a single file with any number of different *hotspots*, each linked to a URL (Uniform Resource Locator). As one of the most attractive and interesting ways to set up the links on a Web site (artistically speaking), an imagemap can be as complex or as simple as you want. The image or set of images you use doesn't matter; anything you can create in Illustrator 9 can be turned into an imagemap.

Creating an imagemap used to be a painstaking process. You had to figure out and manually code into Hypertext Markup Language (HTML) all the boundary coordinates of your various objects. Illustrator 9 makes this procedure automatic, as you'll see in Project 12.3.

Bugs in the Program

PROJECT 12.3 Creating an imagemap in Illustrator 9 is fast and easy. For this project, you'll create an imagemap that you can use on your sample Web page. First, you'll quickly draw a simple image to use. Then, you'll set up the various links by using the Attributes palette.

1. Create a new RGB document.

2. Go to the Color palette menu and select Web Safe RGB.

3. Select View|Pixel Preview.

4. Select the Rectangle tool and click in the document. In the Rectangle dialog box, enter "325 pts" for the Width and "90 pts" for the Height.

5. With the rectangle selected, go to the Color palette and set the Fill color to R=12, G=34, B=66. This color exactly matches the blue background of the sample Web site. Make sure that the rectangle has no stroke.

6. Choose Window|Brush Libraries|Animal Sample.

7. In the Brushes palette, click on the Bee scatter brush and drag it to the artboard to create a single instance of that brush. Do the same with the Butterfly 1, Red Ant, and Dragonfly 1 brushes. You should now have four objects on the artboard.

8. Add drop shadows to your insects. Go to the Layers palette and expand Layer 1 so that you can see the four different insects. For the bee, click on the circle just to the right of "<group>" to target that group. Now, choose Effects|Stylize|Drop Shadow and accept the default settings. This step should apply a simple drop shadow to the whole group (rather than the individual objects that comprise the bee). Do the same for the other three objects.

9. Position all four insects on top of the blue rectangle. You can use the Align palette to arrange them. Choose Window|Show Align. Then, select all four objects. In the Align palette, click on Vertical Align Center and then Horizontal Distribute Center. Now, the objects should be evenly aligned and spaced.

10. Create some captions by creating four text objects: "Hive", "Chrysalis", "Catacomb", and "Bizarre". Set them in Myriad Bold 12 pt and set the fill color to white. Arrange them under the bee, butterfly, ant, and drag-onfly, respectively (see Figure 12.20).

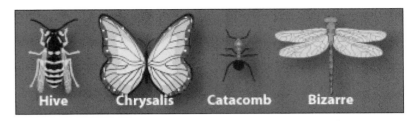

Figure 12.20

In the finished artwork, the insects and type are properly aligned.

11. Now, it's time to set up your links. Select the bee. Choose Window|Show Attributes to open the Attributes palette, where you'll see a pull-down menu called Image Map. Set it to Polygon, as shown in Figure 12.21 (of course, if you have a rectangular object, Rectangle would be the better option).

Figure 12.21

Select Polygon in the Image Map pull-down menu in the Attributes palette.

12. Because you don't have a multiple-page Web site for which to set up links, set up a link to an existing Web site. With the bee still selected, in the URL field in the Attributes palette, type "http://www.adobe.com". The "http://" is necessary (see Figure 12.22). Entering "www.adobe.com" doesn't work.

13. Select the butterfly and make it a Polygon imagemap. Give it a URL of "http://www.apple.com". Do the same with the dragonfly. Make the URL "http://www.microsoft.com".

Figure 12.22

Don't forget the "http://" when you're entering a link in the URL field.

14. Save the file by choosing File|Save For Web. Select GIF as your output format and click on OK to accept the default options. For now, you don't need to worry about optimizing the file; just make sure the imagemap works. You can optimize an imagemap just like any other image. In the Save Optimized As dialog box, click on the checkbox for Save HTML File (see Figure 12.23). When you check this option, Illustrator 9 saves two separate files: a GIF file and an HTML file.

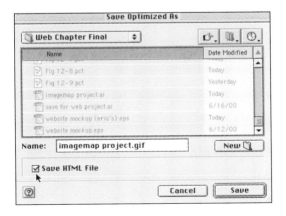

Figure 12.23

Make sure that you click on the checkbox for Save HTML File.

15. Launch your Web browser, choose File|Open, and open the HTML file you just created. Note: If you want to look at the actual HTML code, simply open this HTML file in a text editor.

16. Move your mouse cursor over the bee. The cursor should change into a pointer, indicating a link. Now, click on the bee. You should end up at the Adobe Web site. Clicking on the butterfly and dragonfly should take you to the Apple and Microsoft Web sites, respectively.

You've just created a very simple imagemap. In practice, you can add text for captions, transparency, and opacity masks, whatever you want. Anything Illustrator 9 can do is fair game.

Before you move on, check out this quick tip for creating imagemaps that are a little more graphically complex. You can easily import complicated raster files from applications such as Photoshop (using the Place dialog box) and use them to create stunning imagemaps.

1. Choose File|Place and place your image file.

2. Draw some objects on top of your image in whatever shapes you want your hotspots to take (rectangles, ellipses, freeform shapes, and so on). Set these objects to no stroke and no fill (see Figure 12.24).

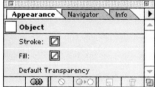

Figure 12.24
Your hotspots should have no stroke or fill.

3. Make these objects imagemaps by using the Attributes palette and enter the appropriate URLs.

4. Save the file through Save For Web. Don't forget to check Save HTML File.

Using Release To Layers and Export To Flash (SWF) to Create a Typewriter Animation

The Macromedia Flash (SWF) format is a vector-based graphics format designed for use on the Web, and it is the final output format for both Macromedia's Flash application and Adobe's LiveMotion. Because it is a vector-based format, graphics in SWF files are resolution independent and may be scaled in a Web browser without degradation. In Illustrator 8, if you wanted to export artwork to the SWF format, you had to use Macromedia's free Flash Writer plug-in. In Illustrator 9, the capability to export SWF is an integrated feature of the application, and you can use Illustrator to quickly and easily create animations for the Web or basic animations that you want to edit further in the Flash application or place into LiveMotion. Illustrator 9 offers SWF export options that are similar to Flash Writer's options and a few options that are unique.

What's with the Auto-Create Symbols Option?

The Flash (SWF) Format Options dialog box contains a checkbox called Auto-Create Symbols, but this feature isn't quite what it seems. Illustrator tags the SWF file it creates with a symbol generation hook that tricks Flash into thinking that each object in the file exists for more than one frame—which means that all objects in the file are treated as symbols when imported into Flash. Note that we say *all objects*—and we mean exactly that! If you have five identical ellipses in your Illustrator file, and you export to SWF with Auto-Create Symbols turned on, you might expect to get one symbol and five instances of that symbol when you import the SWF file into Flash. Instead, you get five identical symbols in your document library. Therefore, you have to delete four of them and repopulate your file with instances of the remaining symbol if you want to minimize your file size. Also, don't forget to delete the blank frames that are created when this checkbox is turned on! The symbol generation hook adds a blank frame for every frame in the file, which can range from one to... well, a lot more! Each extra frame costs only two bytes, but if you have a long animation or are keen on minimizing your file size, don't forget to remove these additional frames when you're editing the SWF in Flash. The only time you will find the Auto-Create Symbols checkbox useful is when you have numerous unique objects in your Illustrator document that you want to automatically turn into symbols when you import into Flash.

You can choose to export an Illustrator document so that the whole document maps to a single SWF document or export so that Illustrator layers map to individual SWF files, or even have Illustrator layers map to SWF frames. The last feature is very handy for quickie animations, and it is covered in detail in Project 12.4. A feature that dovetails nicely with Illustrator's SWF

Exporting to LiveMotion

LiveMotion cannot open an SWF file. However, you can save an Illustrator file in Illustrator 8 format and place it into LiveMotion. If you have saved layers in your original file, you can then place them as separate objects or as a sequential animation in LiveMotion.

Note: A short disclaimer: The material presented in this section makes sense only if you are already a Flash user. Flash is a complex application, and Flash users should easily understand this discussion. Rather than explaining Flash to those of you who don't use it, skip the section. If you don't use Flash, this information just doesn't apply to your situation.

layers-to-frames capability is Release To Layers, which you can use to expand individual graphical elements of a brush stroke or characters in a text string onto layers that can be mapped to frames when you're exporting to SWF. As the animation plays, the brush stroke or text string draws on screen.

PROJECT 12.4 Typewriter Animation

This project shows how to use the Release To Layers feature to build content that can be quickly animated by exporting to SWF using the Layers to Frames option. In this example, you outline type and then release it to layers in a way that creates a "typewriter effect" when exported to SWF, where each successive frame in the animation displays another character. The visual result is like watching someone type a sentence on screen.

1. Create a new RGB document in Illustrator.

2. Choose the Type tool and click in the document. Type "Find the hidden Phasmida (walking stick) insect!". Click on the Selection tool to select the type object.

3. Choose Type|Create Outlines.

4. Click on the drop-down triangle in the Layers palette to expand Layer 1. Outlining the type creates a group that is listed in the Layers palette; click on this group in the Layers palette to target it (see Figure 12.25).

5. Holding down the Shift key, choose Release To Layers from the side drop-down menu in the Layers palette. Choosing this option creates the layers so that successive layers "build" on each other; for instance, your bottom-most layer will contain only the first character of the sentence, while the next layer up will contain the first and second characters, and so on (see Figure 12.26). If you choose Release To Layers without holding down the Shift key, each layer will contain just a single character (see Figure 12.27).

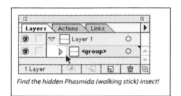

Figure 12.25

The group of outlined type is targeted in the Layers palette.

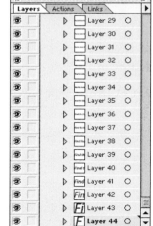

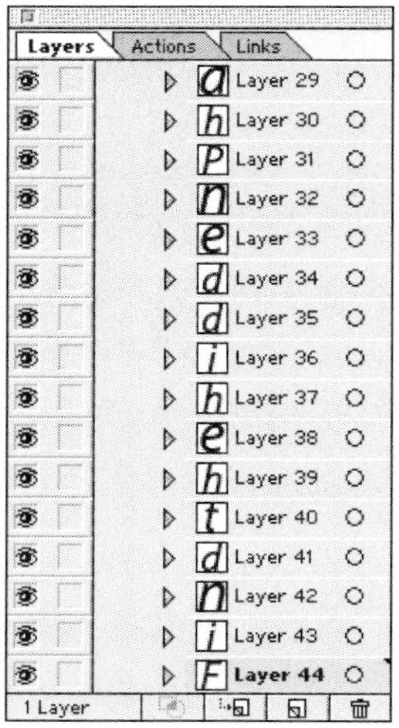

Figure 12.26

(Left) You get this result in the Layers palette when you choose Release To Layers while holding down the Shift key.

Figure 12.27

(Right) The Layers palette looks like this if you choose Release To Layers *without* using the Shift key.

6. Choose File|Export and pick Flash (SWF) from the Format pop-up. Click on Export.

7. In the Flash (SWF) Format Options dialog box (see Figure 12.28), click on the Export As drop-down menu and choose AI Layers to SWF Frames to map your layers to frames in the exported SWF file.

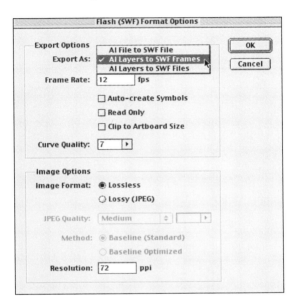

Figure 12.28
Here's a look at the Flash (SWF) Format Options dialog box.

8. You can also modify the Frame Rate if you want the animation to play faster or slower than the default of 12 frames per second. Click on OK to export the SWF file, and an animated SWF is created. Illustrator 9 cannot open SWF files, so to view the SWF animation, you need to open it in Macromedia's free Flash Player (available at **www.macromedia.com**) or import it into a document in the Flash application, where you can do further editing. If you choose File|Import in Flash, the layers are automatically mapped to frames when the SWF is imported.

Why Is My Artwork Different in SWF?

When you're creating artwork that is intended for export to SWF, you need to keep in mind a few points. SWF supports round caps and joins only; beveled and square caps or joins need not apply. Gradient meshes and gradients with more than eight stops are also unsupported by the SWF format, so these objects are rasterized when exported to SWF. Transparency attributes are limited to basic opacity values (from 0 to 100 percent opacity); complex transparency features such as blend modes and opacity masks are ignored when exporting to SWF. If you want to keep the appearance of complex transparent areas, select your artwork and choose Object|Flatten Transparency before exporting to SWF. Beware, flattening your artwork will likely rasterize portions of it and greatly increase the size of what should be a nice, small vector SWF file. Type and fonts are another area where unexpected changes can occur. You may want to consider creating type outlines if you absolutely want to retain the appearance as it looks in Illustrator.

Moving On

You've now concluded your exploration of the new Web features of Illustrator 9. Figure 12.29 shows what the finished product might look like if all these projects were assembled into a Web page.

Figure 12.29
The finished Children's Museum Web page might look like this if all the projects were assembled.

In this chapter, you learned how to save images for the Web, and you learned a bit about the file formats that you can use to display images on the Web. You should be able to decide between GIF and JPEG—or possibly even PNG. You learned how to preview images as pixels and design with pixel-precision by snapping images to a pixel. You learned to use create styles to make buttons. You learned how to create an image and how to use the Release To Layers feature to produce an easy Flash animation.

By David Xenakis

Appendix

Trapping in Illustrator 9

Trapping is one of the most misunderstood and confusing topics in the world of digital prepress. This confusion has nothing to do with the difficulty of the subject. Instead, it has to do with the color printing process—where the trapping is crucial—taking place at some remove in time and space from the construction of the digital files that require trapping.

General Trapping Information

Many users of graphics software are brilliant in the execution of their software but have no clear idea how a press actually transforms the digital files into ink on paper. Illustrator is one of the few programs in which trapping is almost completely a manual process, and it is one—with Adobe Photoshop—that allows you to see how your trapping will look after printing. These two factors make it a good program for learning to grasp what trapping is and how it works.

A color press isn't really a single press. A color press is actually a set of presses, hooked together with rollers, that draw a sheet of paper from one to the next. Each press puts down a single ink color. The completed piece is ejected from the press with all inks present. Figure A.1 shows the process graphically in four steps.

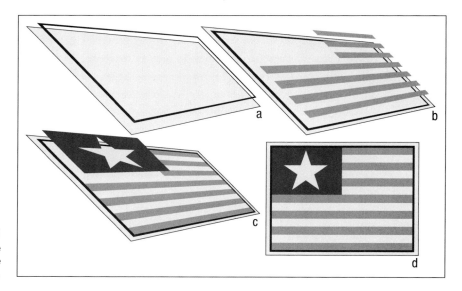

Figure A.1

Three inks are printed, one at a time, to make the completed figure.

Imagine that the press is to print this graphic using three colors: red, blue, and black. First, the dark border is placed on the blank sheet (a). The red horizontal bars are added next (b). Finally, the dark blue area surrounding the star is added (c) to complete the flag (d). Note that the light stripes and the star are simply places where there is an absence of ink.

If all goes well and the press keeps the sheet in perfect registration as it moves through the inking stations, the printed figure will look perfect. However, the world—and most presses—are a bit less than perfect: As the sheet emerges from the other end of the press, you are likely to find that instead of the color boundaries matching one another perfectly, you have a sheet that has printed as shown in Figure A.2.

The red ink of the horizontal bands has slightly shifted so that it doesn't line up with the black rule. The blue rectangle containing the star has also shifted so that it doesn't line up with anything. What should have been simple now appears to be embarrassing and amateurish.

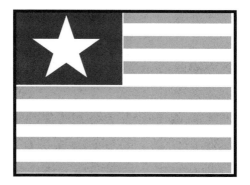

What happened? As the sheet of paper was drawn through each station of the press, it moved slightly off track. As a result, the inks did not go onto the sheet in the proper places. Was the press or the pressperson at fault? Neither; misregistration is a fact of life. Presses are typically engineered with incredible precision. However, it's a mechanical impossibility that a sheet of paper—which is not without imperfections and small variations in its thickness—can move through the press, sometimes at a speed of 3,000 feet per minute, without some misregistration.

Trapping is the means of fixing the visual problem presented by misregistration. Trapping does not prevent the problem; it simply disguises it. When a graphic document containing multiple inks is trapped, the color boundaries are moved so that the colors overlap one another. The amount of the overlap, or trap, is the amount of misregistration predicted for a given press. For an accurate trapping measurement, you should consult the print house where your job is being done.

Don't be intimidated by the idea of trapping. The principles involved are straightforward.

Overprint Preview

Among the new features of Illustrator 9 is a viewing option that has been absent from nearly all graphics software except Adobe Photoshop. This feature is the Overprint Preview (in the View menu). With this option selected, you can, in theory, see the effects of the manipulations you perform to trap your artwork. Considering that prepress work was one of the principal motivations for the development of programs such as Adobe Illustrator, the fact that users were required to wait for years and for the ninth iteration of this program is surprising.

That Adobe should be forced to override the display systems of the two main GUI computers to achieve this result reflects poorly on the software engineers who have produced the operating systems for those two computers. This statement is made in light of the fact that it was the prepress world that made the Macintosh—and later Windows—such a commercial success. Still, Illustrator users now are able to see trapping, if conditions are right, and new users are better able to visualize what trapping is and how it will look when printed. This is a situation that is better late than never. Unfortunately, the Overprint Preview feature is flawed. If the two trapping colors share so much as 1% of a common color, the Preview doesn't operate. For example, if you want to trap a color such as 100% cyan plus 1% black to a color composed of 100% magenta plus 1% black, Overprint Preview will not function. This may be considered as one step forward, three-quarters of a step back.

Simple Trapping: Principle 1

Principle 1: If two adjoining color areas employ significant percentages of the same ink, no trap is required. For example, the object in Figure A.3 shows a yellow oval atop a red rectangle. Working on the computer, you are likely to think of red and yellow as separate colors. However, remember when you're working with process colors that red is a *built color,* that is, a color made up of two or more inks printing atop one another—*overprinting*—and is composed of 100 percent magenta and 100 percent yellow. Yellow is, then, a common color, used both in the oval and in the darker area surrounding the oval. No trapping is required.

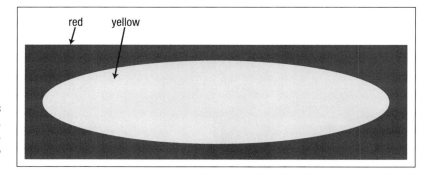

Figure A.3
When two adjoining colors share a substantial percentage of the same ink (yellow in this case), no trapping is needed.

Take a moment to make sure that you understand this point completely. It will save you a lot of work! Think through the process as you look at Figure A.4. Remember that red is not, in process color work, a single ink color. In this case, a magenta area is put down on top of an all-over yellow area. Any misregistration of the two inks is visible only along the outer edges of the figure, where it isn't as noticeable.

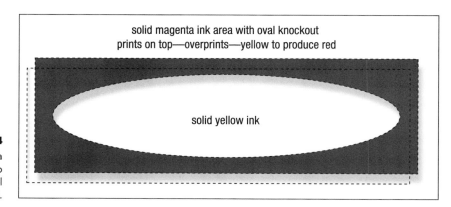

Figure A.4
Yellow (upper) and magenta (lower) inks printing one atop the other give the yellow oval surrounded by red.

Simple Trapping: Principle 2

Principle 2: When any two colors meet each other, you need to determine which is the lighter of the two colors. The lighter of the colors should overlap into the area of the darker color. Get this one straight: You'll see why later.

Because the lighter color must extend into the area of the darker color, it's fortuitous that Illustrator furnishes a perfect way to extend the color of an object past its path boundaries—the stroke. It also furnishes a way to ensure that the two colors in the overlapping area mix with each other rather than butt up against each other—overprint.

Imagine that the three star shapes in Figure A.5 are 100 percent yellow on a 100 percent cyan background. The dotted lines in the figure represent the paths. The star on the left has no stroke. The middle star is stroked with yellow. The one on the right is stroked with cyan. Both strokes are set to overprint. Yellow is the lighter color. Following the previously stated rule, the middle star is correctly trapped. The right-hand shape is included to illustrate one of the reasons for the rule: If you use cyan as the trapping color, the darker color enters into the boundaries of the light-colored object and shrinks it.

The inverse color arrangement is shown in Figure A.6: yellow background and cyan stars. The original is on the left. The center star is stroked with yellow (the lighter color extends into the darker color), whereas the right-hand star is stroked with cyan. As in the previous figure, the dotted line represents the original path. Notice that the left-hand star appears larger than the other two.

Which Color Is Lighter?

Sometimes it's difficult to tell which of two colors is the lighter; for example, 100 percent cyan and 100 percent magenta are both vibrant colors, but it isn't easily apparent which of the two is darker. If you are unsure, here's a quick way to tell. First, select objects filled with the colors in question and then choose Filter|Colors|Convert To Grayscale. After you see the colors in grayscale, you'll have no doubt about the relative darkness and lightness of the two. Use the Undo command to restore the objects to their former colors.

Figure A.5

Three yellow stars on a cyan background. The center star is correctly trapped because it extends the yellow color into the darker surrounding color. The star on the right is incorrectly trapped: The darker color spreads into the boundaries of the lighter object and visually shrinks it.

Figure A.6

Three cyan stars on a yellow background. The center star is correctly trapped because it extends the yellow (lighter) background color into the darker object color. The star on the right is incorrectly trapped: The darker object color spreads into the boundaries of the lighter background and visually enlarges the star shape.

Although these two cases might not seem serious, imagine the consequence of incorrect color movement when it comes to type. Imagine, for example, cyan text on a yellow background, as shown in Figure A.7. Note that the dotted lines indicate the original letter shapes. The word on the right is stroked with yellow; the one on the left is stroked with cyan. The right-hand letters have apparently been bolded. Although the bold might not cause serious problems

Figure A.7
The importance of correct color movement in trapping. The left word has been correctly trapped. Incorrect trapping on the right has resulted in bolded letters, which, in the case of smaller letterforms, might result in filled counters.

Overprint and Knockout

These two terms—*overprint* and *knockout*—mean precisely what they seem to mean. If an object is set to overprint, the colored inks that compose it print on top of any other object beneath it in the Illustrator stacking order. If an object is not set to overprint, it knocks out its own shape from any objects beneath it. Illustrator allows you to set the overprint status for both the stroke and the fill of an object. You set these attributes by clicking on the appropriate checkboxes on the Attributes palette (choose Window|Show Attributes).

with large-scale display type, the consequences are more serious when smaller letters are used. Book text seems to become bold text, and in some cases, the counters will begin to fill in.

Simple Trapping: Principle 3

Principle 3: Where colors overlap, it is usually a good idea to cut back on the amount of ink of the spreading color *in the zone of the trap so that it is as inconspicuous as possible.* This process is best illustrated in Figure A.8, by showing the familiar stars as cyan shapes on a magenta background. Cyan and magenta are strong colors. When they are used together, they form a deep, rich blue that is noticeably darker than either of the others. If the stroke is set to the same 100 percent value as the fill, the star is shown with a dark outline. This is the case, whether the color of the overprinted stroke is cyan or magenta.

If you change the ink percentages (see Figure A.9) to 100 percent magenta and 40 percent cyan, the object is still correctly trapped, but the visually intrusive dark line has been made relatively inconspicuous.

Figure A.8
Two strong colors can blend in the zone of trap to form a dark outline around the shape. This outline might not be objectionable, but it can be visually intrusive.

Figure A.9
If the ink percentages are changed—in this case, the trapping color has been reduced by 60 percent—the trap is much less visible.

How Much Trap Is Enough?

The amount of trap is a figure that can be furnished by your print house. The figure varies widely, but a good general figure is about .004 inch. Expressed in points, this number is .288. Remember that because the stroke width is on both the inside and the outside of the object, the stroke weight needed for a trap of .004 inch is .576 points (2x.288).

Common Trapping Situations: Closed Shapes Placed on other Closed Shapes

The two possibilities for this situation are illustrated by the drawing in Figure A.10. The examples in the upper part of the figure are easy to figure out. A simple stroke (with overprint) in the lighter color will handle the job. Using the stroke will increase the size of the protruding light object on the right, but not by any amount that is visually significant. (Note that the stroke for the upper-right object must be identical to the color of the object: If the ink percentages are reduced, they will show as lighter-colored lines wherever the shape extends past the darker background.) The trap for the right-hand object in the lower set is also straightforward: Add an overprinting stroke in the lighter color. With this color, the ink percentage can safely be reduced.

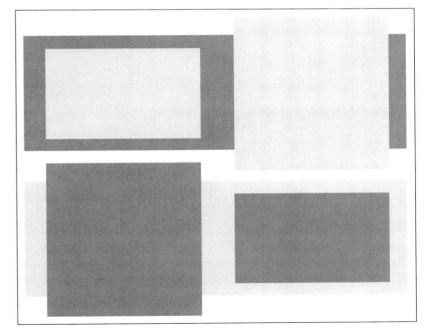

Figure A.10
The most common trapping situation involves closed shapes that sit atop other closed shapes.

The left-hand shape in the lower part of Figure A.10 provides a more challenging problem. The obvious solution, a stroke in the lighter color, will not work because the stroke will be visible when it is outside the light-colored back rectangle. The easiest way to deal with this problem is to use the *oh, what the heck* solution: Stroke (with overprint) the dark object in its own color.

A few other solutions might work better in critical situations. The following is one possibility:

1. Click on the dark rectangle to select it. Press Command/Ctrl+C to copy it.

2. With the object still selected, choose Object|Path|Slice. The drawing then changes from the way it is shown in Figure A.10 to a solid-colored background object that has been carved into three pieces (see example a in Figure A.11).

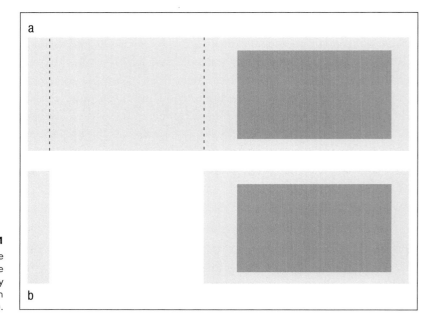

Figure A.11
The Slice command carves the background rectangle into three pieces (a). The area originally behind the dark rectangle can now be deleted (b).

3. Click on the shape that was behind the original dark rectangle and delete it (see example b in Figure A.11). Use the Paste In Back command (Command/Ctrl+B). This command places the dark rectangle back into the drawing and in a new place in the stacking order, *behind* the two light-colored rectangles.

4. Select the two light-colored rectangles and apply an overprinted stroke in the light color (see image a in Figure A.12). This stroke overlaps the large dark rectangle (because the two light rectangles are now in front of it in the stacking order) only where the two smaller light-colored rectangles touch it. Note that this procedure slightly enlarges the two light-colored rectangles.

5. A more elegant way to construct the trap for the dark rectangle, and one that doesn't enlarge the background shapes except in the trap zone, is to click (with the Direct Select cursor and Shift held down) on the two boundary lines next to the dark rectangle. The arrows in image

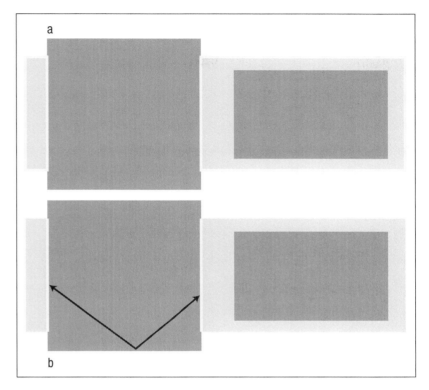

Figure A.12
After you use Paste In Back, the dark rectangle is restored to the drawing. The light rectangles, now in front of the dark shape, can be stroked—with overprint—to make the upper trap (a). A better trap (b) is made by copying the two line segments of the light rectangles, pasting them in front, and stroking them—with overprint—with the light color.

b in Figure A.12 show these lines. Copy and use the Paste In Front command (Command/Ctrl+F). These two line segments should be set to no fill and with a stroke—overprinting—of the same color as the light background shape. This solution is a much more satisfactory way to construct the trap.

Common Trapping Situations: Shapes Where the Stroke Requires Trapping to an Adjacent Color

In the example shown in Figure A.13, the lighter object is a single stroked line (no fill) sitting atop a darker background. The stroke cannot be spread along its edges, and overprinting will simply merge the entire object with the background color. To solve this problem, you can follow either of two procedures. Both work perfectly, and the method you use depends on circumstances and your own preferences.

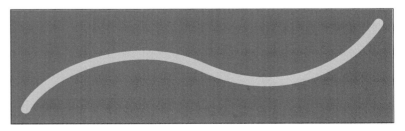

Figure A.13
Here is a special trapping problem: The light object is simply a stroked path. Setting the path to overprint simply merges the color with that of the background.

For the first method, follow these steps:

1. Select the stroke and copy it (be sure that overprint is not turned on). Use the Paste In Back command.

2. Change the width of the pasted path to .576 points wider than the original stroke, and set it to overprint. The example in Figure A.14 shows the new stroke as slightly lighter than the original for the sake of clarifying the process. After you're finished, only the light-colored edge area overprints, making the edge of the upper stroked path trap perfectly to the background.

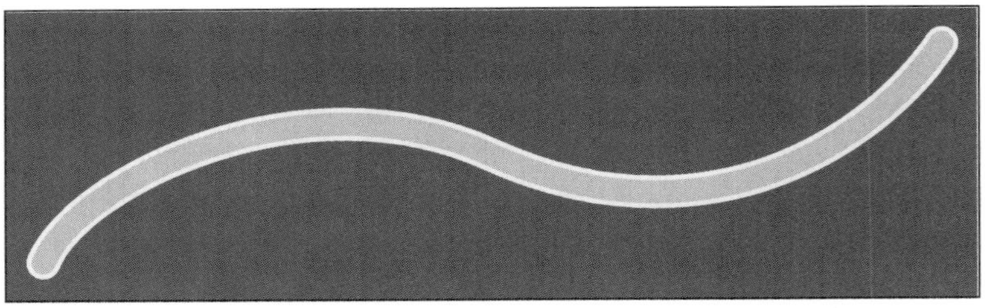

Figure A.14

Using Paste In Back, a slightly heavier stroke can be set to overprint. The upper path doesn't overprint, leaving the zone of trap as just the narrow, light area surrounding it. Alternatively, the path can be outlined (Object|Path|Outline Stroke) and an overprinting stroke applied to the resulting filled object.

For the second method, follow these steps:

1. Click on the stroke to select it.

2. From the Object menu, select Path|Outline Path. This operation converts the stroked path to a filled object of the same shape. Assign an appropriately colored overprinting stroke to the new object.

Another trapping problem involving strokes is shown in Figure A.15. Assume that this figure shows a worst-case configuration in which all three of the tones are separate inks and the dark borders around the uppermost rectangles are strokes. As you can see, a number of trap problems exist here because the edge of each stroke must trap (or be trapped by) the colors on the inside and the outside of the path.

You can satisfactorily handle these problems by using the Outline Path command. To do so, select each of the four shapes and run the filter. Before deselecting, press Command+Shift/Ctrl+Shift+G to ungroup the objects, as the filter groups all the objects. This filter outlines the edges of the stroke and converts it to a narrow compound object perfectly positioned where the stroke originally existed. This compound shape is now filled with the original stroke color.

Begin with the two upper rectangles. Use the Direct Select cursor with Option/Alt held down. Carefully click the inner edge of the two compound frames. Copy and use the Paste In Front command. An exact copy of the inner edge of the frame is now sitting atop the inner edge of the frame. Change its paint attributes to no fill and an overprinted stroke of the light color (see Figure A.16). Perform the same operations with the outer frame of the upper-left rectangle and use the medium color (overprinting) for its stroke. Treat the lower-right rectangle in the same way.

As you can see from the examples in Figures A.15 and A.16, trapping is sometimes very complex. As you work in Illustrator, you usually focus your attention on only one or two objects at a time. This way, you can easily think about trapping relationships and take care of them as you go. After a bit of practice, you'll find that you do your trapping by second nature. Remember that you *must* do your trapping correctly if you don't want your printed piece to look as if an amateur constructed it.

If you really can't stand the idea of trapping as you go, open your finished artwork and start trapping the objects at the top of the stacking order. As you take care of various objects, use the Hide command (Command/Ctrl+3) so that you know which elements you have trapped and which you have not. When you're finished, use the Show All command (Command+Option/Ctrl+Alt+3) to restore your artwork to visibility.

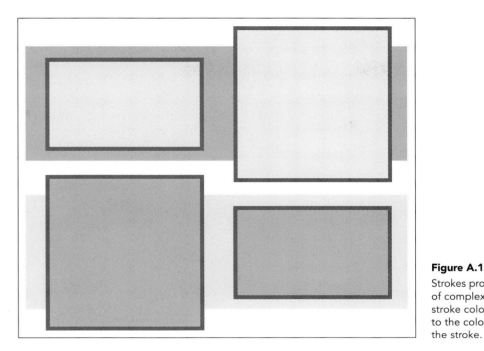

Figure A.15
Strokes provide a further element of complexity in this figure. The stroke colors must be trapped to the colors on each side of the stroke.

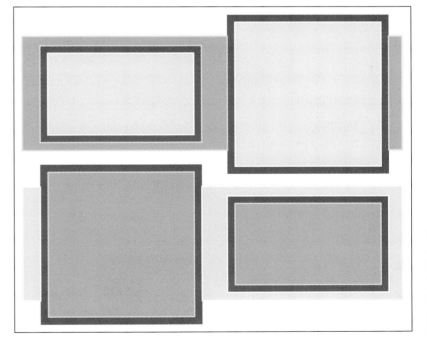

Figure A.16
After using the Outline Path command on all the strokes, the individual paths of the compound shapes—inside and outside—can be used for trapping by assigning them overprinting strokes.

For the larger rectangles, click on and copy the outer paths. Use these paths with the Slice command to create separate shapes of the backmost objects as described previously. Apply the strokes to these objects. The diagram shows the strokes applied (in lighter colors to make the trap relationships clear).

Common Trapping Situations: Trapping Gradients

The example in Figure A.17 shows a gradient sitting on top of a solid color. The background could also be another gradient. This configuration could be handled in several ways. Because the background is a solid color and is generally lighter than the gradient object, it should be possible to place an overprinting stroke of the background color on the gradient object.

Figure A.17
Trapping a gradient is simple if the gradient sits atop a solid-colored background. Just stroke the gradient object—overprinting—with the background color.

If the background object is filled with a different gradient, you can still make a satisfactory trap. First, assign an overprinting stroke of some color (the color doesn't matter because it will change) to the oval object (see Figure A.18). With the oval shape selected, use the Outline Path command. The shape created by this filter, as mentioned previously, is a narrow compound path that can now be filled with the same gradient as the oval (or with the gradient of the background) and with the fill set to overprint. If the two gradients aren't aligned (see Figure A.19), select the narrow compound shape and the large oval gradient shape and use the Gradient Vector tool on both (see Figure A.20).

If the background of the shape contains a gradient, you might need to trap the inner with the background gradient attribute. Assign the compound shape (overprinting fill) the background gradient. If needed, select the narrow shape and the background and re-vector the gradients to cause them to align.

Figure A.18
First, assign an overprinting stroke to the gradient-filled object. It makes no difference what color you use because it will change later.

Figure A.19
After using the Outline Path command, fill the narrow compound shape with the same gradient and set the fill to overprint.

Choke and Spread

Choke and *spread* are traditional trapping terms. If the surrounding color is brought inside the object to be trapped, the object is described as choked. If the color of the object is brought outside into the background, that color is described as spreading. Two other more colloquial trapping terms in general use are *skinny* (meaning the same as choke) and *fatty* (meaning the same as spread).

Figure A.20
If the two gradients don't align (as they do not in Figure A.19), select both shapes and use the Gradient Vector tool to make them match.

Common Trapping Situations: Trapping with Patterns and Brushes

When you're using patterns and brushes, options for choke and spread are limited. However, patterns and brushes must be trapped in the same way any other Illustrator objects are trapped. The fundamental rule for pattern tiles and brushes that trap is that the trapping must be done on the original artwork before the pattern or brush is created. Otherwise, you have to use the Expand command and individually trap each of the hundreds of objects laid down by your use of pattern fills and brushes. The drawing in Figure A.21 shows four patterns and illustrates what is required for the patterns to trap correctly.

Reducing the Size of the Circles

A quick and precise way to reduce the size of circles—and other objects that will be enlarged by a trapping stroke—is to assign the stroke and then to use the Outline Path command. After you use the command, look at the shape in Artwork mode. You'll see three concentric paths. Use the Direct Select cursor to select and delete the outer two paths, retaining the inner path. This inner path, the one you didn't delete, is now filled with the original color, and the overprinting stroke is added to it. With the stroke added to it, it is exactly the same size as the original circle.

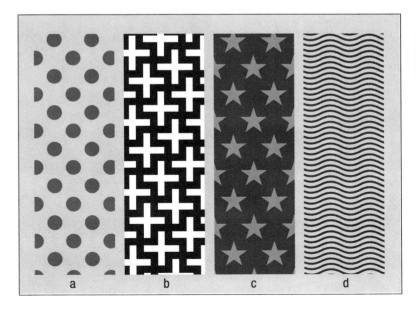

Figure A.21
This drawing illustrates four possible problems that confront an Illustrator user whenever tiled patterns or brushes are used in the artwork.

The pattern fill shown in image a of Figure A.21 is a tile that contains colored circular shapes and a bounding rectangle of no stroke or fill. If the pattern-filled shape always sits on an area of the background color—in this case, the color is lighter—it's simple to define a new pattern based on this one. In the new pattern, each of the small circles is stroked (with overprint) in the background color. If the background is darker than the circles, the stroke is the same color as the circles.

This solution does not solve the problem of using the pattern when it might be placed on several different background colors and sometimes several colors at the same time. In such a case, the only solution is to give the small circles in the tile an overprinting stroke in the same color as the circles. Note that in this case, color reduction is not a good idea because the scaled-back color would show up as a lighter stroke if the pattern were used on areas where no background color exists.

Trapping this pattern in this way is not a very satisfactory solution because it makes the small circles larger than they were in the original pattern. To compensate for this problem, you can make the original circles slightly smaller so that the addition of the stroke spreads them to the desired size (see the tip "Reducing the Size of the Circles" above).

The pattern shown in image b in Figure A.21 is a set of black shapes on a lighter color. If the color is white, the black shapes need no modification. If the lighter color is not white, the black shapes should be stroked (with overprint) with the lighter color.

Trapping the objects of the pattern tile does not solve the trapping of the pattern-filled object to the color behind it. In the example shown, stroking (with overprint) the patterned object with the color of the large background rectangle could solve the problem. If the rectangle extends beyond the boundary of the background rectangle, it must be treated as shown in Figures A.12 and A.22, with the resulting background pieces stroked with their own color. When the procedure has gotten to this point, use the Direct Select cursor to click on the ends of the light rectangular background shapes (dotted line). Copy these lines and use the Paste In Front command. Change the paint style of these lines to overprinted stroke in the color of the light rectangles (shown lighter in Figure A.23 for clarity).

The pattern in image c in Figure A.21 has the same trapping challenges, except that the star shapes are light on a darker background. You would trap the stars to the background before defining the pattern or brush and then trap the edge of the pattern-filled rectangle separately.

The pattern in image d in Figure A.21 presents the most challenging of the samples. The pattern is made up of simple stroked paths, and the solution is really not very complex. The pattern tile used is shown in Figure A.24 with the

Figure A.22
Although the rectangle on the left has been filled with a pattern, it can still be used to slice a segment out of the background shape.

Figure A.23
Select the line segments at the inner ends of the background rectangles. Copy and Paste In Front. These two segments can be assigned an overprinting stroke.

bounding rectangle—no stroke or fill—delineated as a dotted line. When you're using a pattern of this sort, the only practical way to trap is to spread the strokes used for the tiles. The reasons are the same as for the example shown in Figures A.13 and A.14. You spread the strokes by using the previously described procedure. The trapped tile would appear as shown in Figure A.25: Wider, overprinting strokes underlie narrower, non-overprinting strokes in position on top.

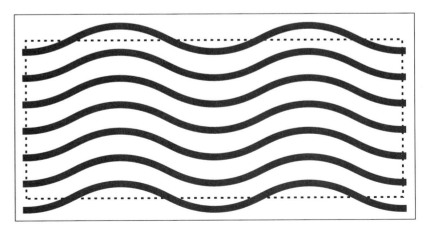

Figure A.24
This pattern is composed of stroked lines.

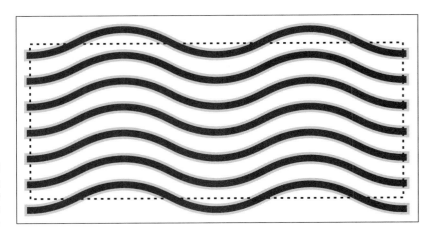

Common Trapping Situations: Anti-Trapping When Using Rich Black

Often, when large areas of black are used in a design, it is common practice to mix percentages of other process colors with the black to increase its density. For example, the reversed letters in image a in Figure A.26 might be surrounded by an ink area composed of 100 percent black and 100 percent cyan. This area would give the black a density and richness that it would otherwise lack. The problem is that misregistration on press can cause the identical areas of cyan and black to print slightly out of alignment (see image b in Figure A.26). If this happens, you see the edges of the black area and edges of the letters fringed with cyan dots. This aspect of trapping requires some thought because, to prevent the fringing effect, you need to add black strokes that *do not overprint*.

Figure A.26
When using a black composed of more than one ink, it's a good idea to surround all reversed areas and the edges of the rich black shapes with zones of pure black set not to overprint (image c). This prevents the extra ink colors from fringing the white areas.

To add these strokes, begin with the white letters. Select, copy, and hide them. Use the Paste In Back command to place new copies of the letters in the identical position. Stroke these letters with a width appropriate for a trap. Make the stroke solid black (only black) and be sure to *not* set the stroke to overprint.

Use the Show All command to bring the original letter back. You cannot see any difference to your artwork, but you have accomplished a minor piece of magic. Surrounding the white letters is a narrow zone of just black ink that knocks out the cyan component of the surrounding color and drives the cyan away from the edges of the letters. (The effect is shown in image c in Figure A.26 with the edges of the letters lightened to make them easy to see.)

Next, select and copy the black background rectangle. Use the Paste In Front command to place a new rectangle precisely over the first. Set the new rectangle's fill to be None and use the same stroke of black as you used for the letters. Be sure this stroke doesn't overprint.

If you want to get really fussy about the whole thing, use the Paste In Front command once more, sweep-select all the rectangles and letters, and use the Objects|Masks|Make command. This procedure eliminates the outer edge of the stroke around the background rectangle and leaves the artwork exactly the same size it was when you began.

The Illustrator Trap Command

Sometimes, Illustrator objects can be subjected to Illustrator's own Pathfinder Trap command (see Figure A.27). The cases in which this command works are limited, but it does perform superbly in those cases.

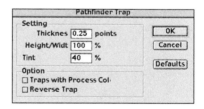

Figure A.27
The Illustrator Trap dialog box.

You can use the Trap command only with color-filled objects atop (completely or partially) other color-filled objects. The items to be trapped cannot have strokes, nor can they be filled with patterns or gradients. Notice that this dialog box allows you to reduce the color in the trap zone. It can also convert the traps of spot colors to process colors as well as make the trapping color spread the wrong direction (Reverse Trap). With respect to the former, I cannot imagine a case in which this solution might prove necessary or even desirable. However, the option has been present as long as the Trap command has been a part of Illustrator.

When you use the Trap command (click on the right-hand icon in the bottom section of the Pathfinder palette) on a set of shapes such as those shown in Figure A.28, a small, filled object that perfectly extends the light color into the darker color is created. This shape is created without the necessity of slicing the background object, preserving the original artwork's editability and illustrating a valuable feature of the Trap command. When you need to use the Trap

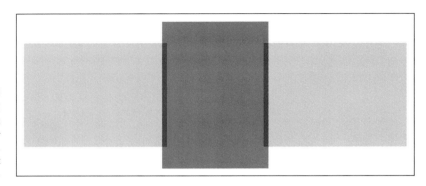

Figure A.28
The Pathfinder's Trap command
constructs small overlaid shapes
filled with the appropriate color
needed to trap the two objects.
The Trap command does not
work with strokes.

command, it is a good idea to convert any strokes to filled compound objects by using the Outline Path command. The Trap command will then function very well indeed.

Index

What's on the CD-ROM

The *Illustrator FX and Design's* companion CD-ROM contains elements specifically selected to enhance the usefulness of this book, including:

- *The tutorial images in the book, arranged by chapter*—In each chapter folder is a START and an END folder. The START folders contain all images needed to work through the projects. The ENDS folders contain the finished projects for you to deconstruct.
- *VirtualMirror's Vector Studio*—Full working demo version (will not save or print).
- *Adobe Illustrator 9 demo*—for Mac and Windows
- *Adobe LiveMotion demo*—for Mac and Windows

System Requirements

Mac

Software

- OS 8.5 or higher.
- Acrobat Reader 4.
- Illustrator 9 (to save and/or print—needed to complete the tutorials).
- Adobe Photoshop 5.5 or 6 is recommended (and needed for several tutorials).

Hardware:

- Any PowerPC processor.
- 64 MB of RAM is the minimum requirement.
- Illustrator 9 requires approximately 105MB of disk storage space.
- A CD-ROM drive and a graphics card with at least 800×600 monitor resolution.

Windows

Software

- Windows 98, NT, or 2000 minumum.
- Acrobat Reader 4.
- Illustrator 9 (to save and/or print—needed to complete the tutorials).
- Adobe Photoshop 5.5 or 6 is recommended (and needed for several tutorials).

Hardware:

- A Pentium-class processor or faster.
- 64 MB of RAM is the minimum requirement.
- Illustrator 9 requires approximately 105MB of disk storage space.
- A CD-ROM drive and a graphics card with at least 800×600 monitor resolution.